WORLD'S TRANSITION TOWARD A GREEN ECONOMY

Achieving the United Nations' Sustainable Development Goals and Promoting the Role of Green Finance

WORLD'S TRANSITION TOWARD A GREEN ECONOMY

Achieving the United Nations' Sustainable Development Goals and Promoting the Role of Green Finance

Xugang Yu
Dentons-Dacheng Law Office, China

Mario Tettamanti
Link to China Consulting Partnership, China

Cristiano Rizzi
Link to China Consulting Partnership, China

World Scientific

NEW JERSEY • LONDON • SINGAPORE • BEIJING • SHANGHAI • HONG KONG • TAIPEI • CHENNAI • TOKYO

Published by

World Scientific Publishing Co. Pte. Ltd.
5 Toh Tuck Link, Singapore 596224
USA office: 27 Warren Street, Suite 401-402, Hackensack, NJ 07601
UK office: 57 Shelton Street, Covent Garden, London WC2H 9HE

Library of Congress Control Number: 2023027634

British Library Cataloguing-in-Publication Data
A catalogue record for this book is available from the British Library.

WORLD'S TRANSITION TOWARD A GREEN ECONOMY
Achieving the United Nations' Sustainable Development Goals and Promoting the Role of Green Finance

ISBN 978-981-126-874-8 (hardcover)
ISBN 978-981-126-875-5 (ebook for institutions)
ISBN 978-981-126-876-2 (ebook for individuals)

For any available supplementary material, please visit
https://www.worldscientific.com/worldscibooks/10.1142/13212#t=suppl

Desk Editors: Aanand Jayaraman/Yulin Jiang

Typeset by Stallion Press
Email: enquiries@stallionpress.com

Preface

This book presents the *World's Transition Toward a Green Economy* as the title states, and the necessity to shape a sustainable and sharable future in line with the UN's Sustainable Development Goals, with a particular focus on the role of *Green Finance* which is of fundamental importance to sustain this transition. The themes treated in this book and their many facets are of extreme interest for the entire global community which needs to act quickly and in a coordinated manner to avoid the catastrophic consequences of climate change and global warming. If this issue is not tackled properly by adopting specific measures to reduce carbon emissions, then global warming will continue threatening life as we know it. It is therefore necessary to transition the entire global economy toward a more green and sustainable modality. This necessary transformation involves many aspects of our society and it implies a shift of our priorities, putting at the center of our concern the preservation of our environment and ecosystems. These elements are intrinsically connected, and only with concerted action and dedicated policies focused on green development will it be possible to grant humanity the achievement of the goals indicated by the United Nations and a shared future. When discussing the 'green transition,' there are many aspects that need to be considered and dealt with in an orderly manner, such as the shaping of sustainable development and a more nature-friendly economy that favored the conceptualization of the so-called *dual circulation strategy* by incorporating important political and economic implications and representing a sort of revolution with respect to our development mode.

The book evidences the commitments of the major economies to advance and shape a nature-positive or 'green economy,' putting at the center of the analysis the directions indicated by the United Nations (refer to the 2030 Agenda for a sustainable development) and of course the measures and policies adopted by the major economies to reach the goals indicated by the Paris Convention. The initiatives adopted by the leading economies not only serve their own interests by reinventing or redirecting their development modality, and of course propel those countries to a net-zero-emissions path to be reached in 2050 (this objective for China is fixed for 2060), but also serve as examples for the rest of the global community. Because the energy sector plays a fundamental role in the so-called 'green transition,' this book offers a precise and exhaustive picture of the initiatives the major players are now implementing to favor the use of alternative, renewable, and cleaner sources of energy, explaining the opportunities to be gained from this green transition.

Each of the six chapters treats the concerned topic in an exhaustive manner, presenting the connections with the subsequent chapter. Chapter 1 stresses the importance of the continued reforms process adopted by China illustrating not only the achievement of the first centenary goal, i.e., the eradication of extreme poverty, but also the advancements toward the second centenary goal, i.e., the realization of a modern and socialist country that is prosperous, strong, democratic, culturally advanced, and harmonious by 2049 (the time the PRC celebrates its 100th anniversary). It also demonstrates the necessity to transition China toward a green economy through new reforms, in particular reinforcing its 'Green Finance' market which will be of paramount importance to finance the green transition and reach the two targets of peaking carbon emissions before 2030 and becoming a carbon-neutral economy by 2060.

This book also stresses the necessity for coordinated efforts to tackle climate change and shape a new multilateralism conducive to the achievements of global goods where the environment comes first. Only with a more functional multilateralism will it be possible to face and find the solutions for the many challenges (and conflicts) the world is experiencing (the crisis in Ukraine is one of them). Chapter 2 introduces the concept of the *Dual Circulation Strategy* and links it to the measures which need to be implemented to achieve sustainable development. This new paradigm was also adopted by the EU where the so-called *Green Deal* was introduced in order to reach a nature-positive economy, or carbon-free economy, to achieve the goals of the Paris Convention. Chapter 3 then focuses on the green partnership between China and the EU and the necessity to reinforce international cooperation to tackle climate change and thus avoid disastrous consequences, adopting measures which can mitigate changes in climate patterns. Chapter 4 focuses on the development of green and low-carbon energy sources, explaining the central role of renewables in green transition, and introduces the policies the major economies are adopting in order to favor the widespread use of clean and renewable sources of energy.

One aspect which deserves particular attention is *green finance*, treated in Chapter 5, because this element is intrinsically connected with the green transition which can be achieved only with the development of new green financial instruments to finance it. This chapter in fact offers a complete panorama concerning green or sustainable finance, illustrating the principles of these new instruments and how they can be used to sustain green projects, adding an interesting analysis on the promising development of this green market, especially for investors willing to support this transition toward a green, sustainable, carbon-free global economy.

The importance of alternative, renewable, and clean sources of energy, which is a fundamental part of the transition toward the green economy, is well presented together with the measures adopted by the major economies in order to favor their development and the investment opportunities they offer when it comes to further developing these sources of energy. Chapter 6 offers a detailed analysis of the investment opportunities derived from the further development of renewable such as solar and wind energy which will play a major role in the near future to respond to our needs. Advancements in technology will also allow the exploitation of new forms of clean energy. Thus, the last chapter is of particular importance in guiding investors to select the best opportunities for the development of renewables.

About the Authors

Xugang Yu is Senior Partner at 'Dentons' (Beijing), heading the Chinese Capital Market Committee. Mr. Yu specializes in foreign investments, securities transactions, mergers and acquisitions, private equity, and general corporate practice, with comprehensive experience domestically and internationally. Mr. Yu holds a Ph.D. in International Law and a Master's degree in International Economic Law from Peking University Law School (2001). Mr. Yu is a member of the Central Economic Committee of China Democratic League, a member of the Fixed Income Committee of Securities Association of China, and a part-time professor at Peking University Law School. Currently, Mr. Yu is also the Independent Director of Polaris Bay Group Co. Ltd. (Shanghai Stock Exchange, Securities code 600155), Shanghai Kinlita Chemical Co. Ltd. (the Shenzhen Stock Exchange, Securities code 300255), Dafeng Port Heshun Technology Company Limited (the Stock Exchange of Hong Kong, Securities code 08310), Xi'an Geely Electronic New Materials Co. Ltd., and Shengang Securities Co. Ltd. Mr. Yu is the sole author of Chapter 1.

Mario Tettamanti is Partner at and CEO of 'Link to Beijing Consulting Partnership' and he holds a Ph.D. in Economics and Finance from University of Neuchâtel (Switzerland). He has worked in Mainland China for 8 consecutive years. Mr. Tettamanti is Editorialist and Chief Redactor of the Economic Section at '*Corriere del Ticino*' (Switzerland). Mr. Tettamanti is also Professor at the '*Centro di Studi Bancari*' (Lugano — Switzerland). Mr. Tettamanti has vast experience in the financial field and he has worked as Deputy Head of the Financial Department and as Head of the Investment

Advisory Committee at 'Banco di Lugano' (UBS Group). During the period from 1985 to 1987, Mr. Tettamanti was responsible for Italian, French, and German clients at UBS New York, in the position of Vice President. Mr. Mario Tettamanti is the sole author of Chapter 5.

Cristiano Rizzi is a foreign professional who has been working on the ground in Mainland China for the past 12 years and is now collaborating with Mr. Xugang Yu and Mr. Mario Tettamanti to find investment opportunities in the European Union (EU) for Chinese investors. Mr. Rizzi holds the twofold qualifications of *Abogado* (incorporated at the '*Ilustre Colegio de Abogados de Salamanca — Spain*') and 'Established Lawyer,' according to EU Directive 98/5/EC (*Milan Bar*). Mr. Rizzi holds an L.L.M. in Chinese Law from Peking University, an L.L.M. in Spanish Law from the University of Valladolid (Spain), and an L.L.M. in International Law from Exeter University (U.K.). Mr. Rizzi is a scholar and expert in Chinese Law and is frequently an invited speaker at Peking University (School of Law) for lectures on business relations between China and the EU based on his numerous publications. Mr. Cristiano Rizzi is the sole author of Chapters 2, 3, 4, 6, and Conclusions.

Acknowledgments

This book titled *World's Transition Toward a Green Economy: Achieving the United Nations' Sustainable Development Goals and Promoting the Role of Green Finance* is the result of the joint efforts by three professionals who decided to put together their expertise in different areas and examine in the most comprehensible manner the political initiatives of the major economies to transition the world toward a green economy. These initiatives together with the input of the United Nations are pushing the entire global community toward more sustainable development. It seems that the entire world is experiencing an epochal change, advancing toward carbon-neutral development which offers opportunities but also challenges. In order to better understand the 'initiatives' the major players are adopting and putting in place to reach this goal, the authors have analyzed the frameworks favoring this green transition. This was possible thanks to the expertise and help of two professionals, namely, Mr. Xugang Yu, a Chinese professional with vast experience in securities transactions including IPOs, mergers and acquisitions, and venture capital, and Mr. Mario Tettamanti, a Swiss economist who worked as a top executive at UBS group with vast expertise in international finance. The result of this work is an analytical explanation of the policies and measures adopted at the international level by the major economies to tackle climate change.

Putting together all the meaningful parts which make up this book was not an easy task, but with the help of these two top professionals, the result is a unique guide concerning the measures and policies the major economies are implementing to not only reach the goals of the United Nations and shape a carbon-neutral economy free of fossil fuels but also reinforce international cooperation for global good. In order to reach these goals, it is necessary to sustain green projects with adequate resources, and green finance is emerging as the solution to respond to the needs of this green transition. This theme is also at the center of this manuscript, given its importance in reaching green and sustainable development. Thus, I would like to express my gratitude to my two friends for their views and interesting analyses on the particular aspects they treated in this book and for their encouragement in pursuing this new project.

With the help and guidance of Mr. Xugang Yu and Mr. Mario Tettamanti, I have tried to explain the reasons why it is not possible to delay the green transition any further, highlighting the policies adopted by China, the EU, and the US while also emphasizing their common interest in collaborating and encouraging the entire global community in shaping a sustainable, green, and shared future.

Cristiano Rizzi

Contents

Abbreviations and Acronyms

ADB	Asia Development Bank
AEEP	Africa Europe (EU) Energy Partnership
AI	Artificial Intelligence
AMAC	Asset Management Association of China
ASEAN	Association of Southeast Asian Nations
BITs	Bilateral investment treaties
BoC	Bank of China
BRI	Belt and Road Initiative
BRICS	Brazil, the Russian Federation, India, China, and South Africa
BRIGC	Belt and Road Initiative International Green Development Coalition
CAI	Comprehensive Agreement on Investment
CBAM	Carbon Border Adjustment Mechanism
CBD	Convention on Biological Diversity
CBI	Climate Bond Initiative
CBT	Carbon Border Tax
CEAP	Circular Economy Action Plan
CINEA	European Climate, Infrastructure, and Environment Executive Agency
COP	UN Climate Change Conference of the Parties
CORSIA	Carbon Offsetting and Reduction Scheme for International Aviation
CPTPP	Comprehensive and Progressive Agreement on Trans-Pacific Partnership
CPC	Communist Party of China
CPCC	Communist Party Central Committee

CSR	Corporate Social Responsibility
CSRC	China Securities Regulatory Commission
DCS	Dual Circulation Strategy
DOE	Department of Energy (USA)
DOI	Department of Interior (USA)
EC	European Commission
ECECP	EU–China Energy Cooperation Platform
ECL	European Climate Law
EGD	European Green Deal
EGDIP	European Green Deal Investment Plan (same as SEIP)
EIB	European Investment Bank
EU	European Union
ESG	Environmental, Social, and Governance
ESMA	European Securities and Market Authority
ETFs	Exchange Trade Funds
ETS	Emission Trading System
EUR	Euro (unit of currency used in the EU)
EVs	Electric Vehicles
FTA	Free Trade Agreement
FYP (or 5YP)	Five-Year Plan
GBP	Green Bond Principles
GBS	Green Bond Standards
GDP	Gross Domestic Product
GGA	Global Geothermal Alliance
GHG	Greenhouse Gas
GNP	Gross National Product
GPGs	Global Public Goods
GSS	Green, Social and Sustainability
HSR	Health Silk Road
IATA	International Air Transport Association
ICAO	International Civil Aviation Organization
ICAP	International Carbon Action Partnership
ICMA	International Capital Markets Association
IEA	International Energy Agency
IMF	International Monetary Fund
INDC	Intended Nationally Determined Contribution
IP	Intellectual Property
IPCC	Intergovernmental Panel on Climate Change
IPSF	International Platform on Sustainable Finance
IRENA	International Renewable Energy Agency
JAES	Joint Africa–EU Strategy

LGX	Luxembourg Green Exchange
MEE	Ministry of Ecology and Environment (China)
MEPs	Member of the European Parliament
MIIT	Ministry of Industry and Information Technology
MOF	Ministry of Finance (of the People's Republic of China)
MOFCOM	Ministry of Commerce (of the People's Republic of China)
NDB	New Development Bank
NDC	National Determined Contribution
NDICI	Neighbourhood, Development and International Cooperation Instrument
NDRC	National Development and Reform Commission
NEA	National Energy Administration
NGFS	Network for Greening the Financial Sector
NLGCPCN	National Leading Group on Carbon Peak and Carbon Neutrality
NPC	National People's Congress
PBoC	People's Bank of China
PRC	People's Republic of China
PV	Photo Voltaic (panels)
QFLP	Qualified Foreign Limited Partner
RCEP	Regional Comprehensive Economic Partnership
R&D	Research and Development
RES	Renewable Energy Sources
RMB	Renminbi
RRF	Recovery and Resilience Facility
RRPs	Recovery and Resilience Plans
SAF	Sustainable Aviation Fuels
SAIC	State Administration for Industry and Commerce
SBG	Sustainability Bond Guidelines
SBP	Social Bond Principles
SC	State Council
SDGs	Sustainable Development Goals
SEEE	Shanghai Environment & Energy Exchange
SEIP	Sustainable Europe Investment Plan
SFDR	EU's Sustainable Finance Disclosure Regulation
SLBP	Sustainability-Linked Bond Principles
SRF	Silk Road Fund
SRI	Socially Responsible Investing
UN	United Nations
UNEP	United Nations Environment Program
UNFCCC	UN Framework Convention on Climate Change

UNSDCF	United Nations Sustainable Development Cooperation Framework
UNSDGs	United Nations Sustainable Development Goals
US	United States of America
VNRs	Voluntary National Reviews
WTO	World Trade Organization

Introduction

This book aims to illustrate the world's transition toward a green economy and the role of green finance in sustaining the transition. In addressing this extremely topical issue, the authors present the policies and measures adopted by the major economies, not only because their actions and choices follow the indication of the United Nation for sustainable development, intended to reach the targets of the Paris Convention on climate change, but also because they are major influencers and the rest of the global community will hopefully follow their example. We start with China which has become a front runner in tackling climate change because of its great interest in changing its development pattern, having realized that, after 40 years of intensive industrialization and exploitation of natural resources at the expense of the environment, only by protecting our environment will it be possible to achieve a sustainable and shared future for mankind. In particular, the continued reform process in China allowed the achievement of the first centenary goal and the preparation to reach the second centenary goal in a timely fashion, which is inevitably linked to the green transition and the shaping of a nature-positive economy to achieve a sustainable and shared future.

China, the EU, and the US are now transforming themselves into more advanced and ecological economies by implementing a series of policies aimed at reaching the objectives of the Paris Agreement and of the United Nations for sustainable development. In doing this, they are turning their attention and efforts toward technologies able to trigger more sustainable and green development, increasing the use of renewable sources of energies and paying greater attention to our environment, because only with a restored environment and by protecting nature and its ecosystems will it be possible to further develop our society in harmony with nature.

The world is on the brink of a climate catastrophe. It is therefore necessary to work together and coordinate efforts to cut emissions, primarily by building a sustainable power sector, phasing out fossil fuels, and raising investment and spending on R&D to deploy new technologies needed to go green in other critical industries. It seems the trend is heading in this direction with a significant increase in the issuance of green bonds and other financial instruments fostering sustainable finance aimed at supporting the 'green transition.' Nevertheless, major funding gaps remain. It is necessary to further develop green finance and foster it by creating a global framework in which it can flourish (adopting a widely accepted taxonomy) to create more confidence among institutional and private investors willing to allocate their resources to restoring ecosystems and financing projects aimed at favoring green transition while also granting them a reasonable return of their investment. Thus, a substantial part of this work analyzes the growing importance of green finance and its many aspects, putting in evidence that this market is destined to grow exponentially considering the financial resources needed to address the many climate and environmental questions and the new technological solutions to be financed in order to shape sustainable development. It is necessary to underline that these new financial resources that have emanated from green finance also validate the need to shift away from non-sustainable sources of energy and further emphasize the important role that the financial service sector and markets play in the sustainable transition process, providing the necessary resources for the greening of our economies. As will emerge from the pages of this book further work needs to be done. It seems that green finance will play a fundamental role in contributing to the preservation of our world. It is therefore necessary to advance toward a new financial system which can respond to all these necessities. A combination of financial innovations, collaboration between governments and this industry, and an harmonized framework in terms of taxonomy, represent an absolutely necessity to allow the green markets to take off. The financial world is now equipping itself with specific measures to grasp this enormous opportunity for issuers and investors putting at their disposal new investment instruments which need to be well disciplined to produce the desired effects and helping the entire global community reaching its carbon neutrality goals and create a nature-positive society. A global problem like climate change needs global solutions; thus, it is desirable that the entire global community works together to tackle this threat which is putting our existence in peril.

Given the weight of China's economy and the environmental questions it needs to address, China is active in the world's major global initiatives to tackle climate change, but its efforts need to be coordinated with the actions of the other major economies. Further, it is also necessary to emphasize that with the growing importance of its green finance and further implementation of policies aimed at favoring this sector, China could position itself to drive a green revolution globally as the country's scale and position in the global economy and supply chains will inevitably trigger and drive transformation in other parts of the world as well. China holds a critical and outsized role in helping the global community achieve the targets of the Paris Agreement and preserve the planet's biosphere. However, a more stringent international cooperation is necessary to accomplish this objective. In this regard, at the 26th UN Climate Change Conference of the Parties (COP26) held in Glasgow, Scotland, from 31 October to 13 November 2021, China and the US agreed to boost climate cooperation over the next decade. In a joint declaration, the two countries called for increased efforts to close the significant gap, which will be necessary if the world is to maintain its target of restricting the average global temperature rise to 1.5°C, as set out in the Paris Agreement of 2015. Noteworthily, COP27 which was held in November 2022 in Egypt, reaffirmed these commitments by all participating nations and also saw the establishment of the so-called *Loss and Damage Fund* (see Chapter 3, paragraph 3, point 3.2) to compensate the more vulnerable countries affected by climate change. Given the importance of this theme, China and the EU also shaped their partnership along the lines of fighting climate change (refer to Chapter 3). All these themes are treated in this manuscript which also presents the climate policies of the major economies, highlighting the steps to be taken to advance toward this necessary green transition and achieve a shared future in harmony with nature for future generations.

Chapter 1

The Elements Stimulating China's Green Development and the Role of 'Green Finance' in Supporting the Transition of China toward a Sustainable, Carbon-Neutral Economy and a Shared Future

> China will strive to peak carbon dioxide emissions before 2030 and achieve carbon neutrality before 2060. This requires tremendous hard work, and we will make every effort to meet these goals.
>
> *The President of the People Republic of China, Xi Jinping*

Statement at the General Debate of the 76th Session of the United Nations General Assembly, September 2021.

China is an integral part of this globalized world, and there is no doubt that it needs to do its part in order to tackle global warming and climate change. But China started to have a role to play only four decades ago when the reform process started. By the end of 1978, China's gross annual value of industrial and agricultural output was RMB￥569 billion, with a population of 975.23 million,[1] and the per capita income was RMB￥583.

[1] See 1978 年 (stats.gov.cn). At that time, China's economy was a plan-oriented one, with no GDP concept.

These data put China among the most underdeveloped countries in the world. However, poverty does not belong in socialism, and to prove it, China started its Reform and Opening-up policy. By the end of 2000, the GDP was RMB￥8940 billion for a population of 1.265 billion,[2] and the per capita income reached RMB￥7063, and thus China was heading toward a moderately prosperous society. However, China at that time remained at a relatively low level of development — it was not inclusive and it was a very unbalanced society in terms of distribution of wellness.[3] In addition, climate change and severe pollution (due to the rapid industrialization) started to cause problems in China. At the beginning of its reform process, China was extensively focused on economic development, which was conducive to high energy consumption, high pollution and contamination of the environment, and high CO_2 emissions. And then China began to build a moderately prosperous society in all respects including historic changes to the eco-environment sphere after realizing that it is only by protecting our environment that it is possible to shape sustainable development and a shared future. On September 22, 2020, at the General Debate of the 76th Session of the United Nations General Assembly, President Xi Jinping announced that "*China will strive to peak carbon dioxide emissions before 2030 and achieve carbon neutrality before 2060.*" From struggling against pollution, China is now turning into a green economy on a magnificent scale.

The target is to achieve carbon neutrality before 2060 and to transform China into a nature-positive economy serving as an example for other countries. In order to reach this objective, China is implementing a series of new policies to limit CO_2 emissions and pushing renewables, with Chinese energy companies massively investing in new technologies which can help in the further development and production of 'clean energy,' thus favoring green transition. China has gained an important role on the international stage and it can now influence the direction in which the entire global community is heading. This was possible thanks to the continued reform process that focused on economic development and the establishment of peaceful relationships with other countries, which allowed China to become what it is today. China has transformed itself from an underdeveloped country into a promising one, and it is

[2] See 第五次全国人口普查公报 (第1号) (stats.gov.cn). Chinese only.

[3] See 中国的全面小康_白皮书_中国政府网 (http://www.gov.cn). Chinese only.

approaching the standards of the most developed and advanced economies, becoming an example for the rest of the underdeveloped world. Therefore, it appears appropriate to begin this work with a brief introduction illustrating the fundamentals of this reform process and the achievements of China starting from the so called 'two centenary goals.' This in fact represents the basis from which China began to shape not only its future but also a shared future for the entire global community by adopting measures which allowed it to move toward a nature-positive economy fostered by the green finance (or sustainable finance). This represents a sector where China made significant progress and there is no doubt it will become the global leading market for these new financial products.

1. China's Economic Success Based on a Continued Reform Process Stimulating Green Development

China has built its success on a continued reform process, initiated in the late 1970s by Deng Xiaoping, the chief architect of China's reform process, opening, and modernization; however some of the old problems have not been resolved completely such as the efficiency of State-Owned Enterprises and the imbalances exacerbated by fast development. Further adjustments in the finance sector are needed, especially now with the advent of the so-called 'green finance,' which is needed to sustain green transition; but the path to follow is clear. Moreover, China faces great challenges in domestic (imbalances between the richest and poorest people) and foreign affairs (trade friction with the US still remains).[4] However, it is evident that reforms have worked well so far, and that is the path to follow to reduce imbalances and continue to foster change in China, to present China to the rest of the world in a stronger position to contribute to solving global issues, especially climate change. There is no doubt that China is planning to strengthen and deepen the country's reform process, considering the positive results of 40 years of reforms. At present, China's leaders' determination for furthering the reform process

[4] A complete analysis of the trade friction between China and the US is offered in the manuscript titled, *China-US Trade Frictions Shaping New Equilibriums with the EU and the US — Towards a New Multilateralism or Tripolarism*, Xugang Yu, Mario Tettamanti, Cristiano Rizzi, World Scientific, 2021.

is clear as some significant measures in the political, economic, and social fields all point in this direction, mirroring in some cases the goals of the United Nations. If these efforts are accompanied by a little flexibility in managing critical issues such as human rights, national reunification, territorial sovereignty, maritime rights and interests, and ethnic separatist forces, the international community will further deepen relations with China. Furthermore, with the Chinese government implementing new reforms to transition the country toward sustainable and green development, which provides the stability the country needs to achieve its goals and shape a shared future, the rest of the global community will only reinforce its relationship with China.

1.1. *Realizing a moderately prosperous society: A bit of history*

China is a very disciplined country which has embraced a developmental mode based on a continued reform process aimed not only at ameliorating how this country is governed but also at raising the living standards of its population. The eradication of extreme poverty was an example of the success of China's reform process. On July 1, 2021, Xi Jinping, general secretary of the CPC (Communist Party of China) Central Committee, announced that China had realized the first centenary goal of building a moderately prosperous society — *Xiaokang Shehui* (小康社会) — in all respects. This achievement is of particular importance because the realization of 'Xiaokang' represents the latest stage in a series of steps in what President Xi has often described as a relay race for China, and has involved generations of CPC leaders and members. Undoubtedly one of the greatest leaders of China, Deng Xiaoping would be extremely delighted with this important achievement as, thanks to his reform process[5] initiated more than 40 years ago, it has been possible for China to reach this incredible success in a relatively short period of time. During the last four decades, something absolutely extraordinary has happened in China to allow the achievement of *Xiaokang*. If we consider where China

[5]The authors of this manuscript in their work titled, *China's Belt and Road — The Initiative and Its Financial Focus*, World Scientific, 2018, at pp. 5–54, have explained in detail the reform process initiated by Deng Xiaoping which formed the basis for China's success, and formed the so-called 'China Model' which is based on the *Beijing Consensus* (see the aforementioned book at pp. 36–50).

was in 1980 and where it is today, it is evident that the reforms introduced have shaped a new China. In 1980, nearly three-fourths of the country's population was living at or below the poverty line, with a vast majority living in extreme poverty in rural areas. Forty years later, extreme poverty has been officially eradicated.

The decisions and development process which led to this success are as follows:

Historically, 'Xiaokang' is an attractive social ideality described by Chinese ancient thinkers and also reflects common people's aspirations for a bounteous and substantial life. This concept was first recorded in *Shi Jing* (The Book of Poetry), the earliest collection of poems and songs in China, collected from the early years of the Western Zhou Dynasty to the middle period of the Spring and Autumn, from 1100 BC to 600 BC, edited by Confucius:

> The people indeed are heavily burdened but perhaps a little ease (Xiaokang) may be got for them.
> Translated by the Scottish Sinologist James Legge.[6]

The Chinese people had been impoverished for thousands of years[7] and had also experienced numerous wars, plagues, natural disasters, and burdensome work under twenty dynasties, literally millennium over a millennium, often most of them leading vagrant lives on account of poverty, including three years of natural disasters from 1959 to 1961 and 10 years of Civilization Revolution from 1966 to 1976, until the Great Reform initiated by Deng Xiaoping and the open door policy (Figure 1).

Historically, it is necessary to put the following in evidence:

From 400 AD to 1000 AD, the annual average compound rate of Asia's GDP excluding Japan was 0, from 1000 AD to 1820 AD 0.20, and from 1820 AD to 1998 AD 1.84.[8] It goes without saying that these statistics also include China. It must be noted that from 1800 AD onward, China's economy declined sharply, far below the level of the period from 400 AD to 1000 AD, to the lowest point in the history of China. This was because of the two Opium Wars, the aggression of the Eight-Power Allied

[6]See Book of Poetry: *Greater Odes of the Kingdom: Decade Of Sheng Min* — Chinese Text Project (ctext.org) (accessed January 28, 2023).

[7]See Deng Xiaoping's southern talk in January of 1992 (news.cctv.com/2013/06/17/VIDE1371456480546660.shtm, China).

[8]See Angus Maddison, The Economy — A Millennial Perspective, 2001, OECD, p. 28.

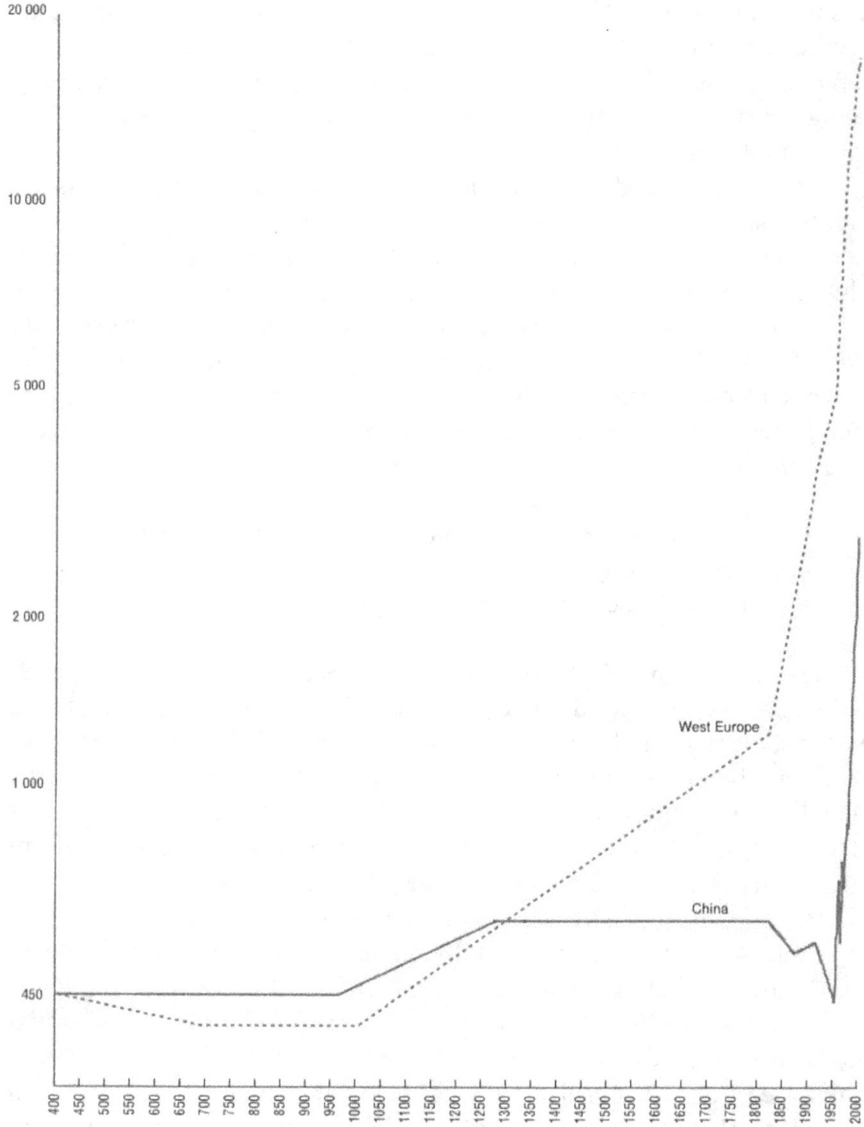

Figure 1: Comparative levels of GDP per capita income: China and West Europe, 400–1998 AD (International Yuan)

Source: Angus Maddison, The Economy — A Millennial Perspective, 2001, OECD, p. 42.

Forces, the Japanese Invasions, the two World Wars, China's War of Liberation, and the Korean War; all these events negatively influenced China's development until the beginning of the Reform and Opening-up, while the West European economy soared at a high speed.

Consequently, from the beginning of the Chinese civilization, the common people have being tending toward the creation of a 'Xiaokang society,' a 'moderately prosperous' or a well-off one, bounteous and substantial, which is the dream of all Chinese people; in most cases, they are not focused on financial standards but on a stable social order, such as in *Liji* (The Book of Rites), the explanatory note by the East Jin Dynasty's historian Mr. Songzhi Pei for the Zhaoda Biography of Wu Kingdom's Record in *The Records of Three Kingdoms*, *Book of Tang*, *History as a Mirror*, and *Jin History*.[9]

On December 6, 1979, Deng Xiaoping propounded that the Chinese should enjoy a bounteous and substantial life based on financial data when he granted an interview to the Japanese Prime Minister Masayoshi Ohira:

> The four modernizations we are striving to achieve are modernizations with Chinese characteristics. Our concept of the four modernizations is different from yours. By achieving the four modernizations, we mean achieving a comparative prosperity. Even if we realize the four modernizations by the end of this century, our per capita income GNP will still be very low. If we want to reach the level of a relatively wealthy country of the Third World with a per capita income GNP US$1,000 for example, we have to make an immense effort. Even if we reach that level, we will still be a backward nation compared to West countries. However, at that point China will be a country with a comparative prosperity and our people will enjoy a much higher standard of living than they do now.[10]

On May 12, 1980, while meeting with the 48th UK Prime Minister Leonard James Callaghan, Deng Xiaoping said the following: "Our concept of modernization is with Chinese characteristics. While talking with

[9]参见崔海英,《"小康"一词经历了怎样的承古创新》,《解放日报》, 2021 年 1 月 5 日版. (Chinese).

[10]See *Selected Works of Deng Xiaoping* (1975–1982), Volume II, Foreign Languages Press, China, 1995, p. 240.

the Japanese Prime Minister Masayoshi Ohira, I had said that this was our objective if each person in China had US$1,000 income per capita income and became a 'Well-off Family.' Within 20 years, by and large, should increase three times, which is not easy."[11]

On April 14, 1981, Deng Xiaoping met with the Chinese delegation of the Association of Dietmen League for Japan China Friendship, saying, "In 1979, I had talk with Prime Minister Masayoshi Ohira that at the end of this century we could only achieve a well-off society, life being not bad. Through our effort, we envisaged to double in one decade, to double twice in two decades, and we would achieve per capita income US$1,000 GNP (Gross National Product). Through our grope in this period, it seems that it's not easy for US$1,000, for example 800, 900, and even if 800, it will be a well-off life."[12]

Deng Xiaoping pondered on the past and future of China. He visited many countries, including the United States of America, Japan, Thailand, Malaysia, Singapore, and North Korean, and also organized a visit for his colleagues to West Europe to explore how to develop China. As a consequence, the 'Xiaokang Society' thought was finalized and became part of the National Policy.

On September 1, 1982, the 12th National Congress of the Communist Party of China was held, and the goal to quadruple the annual industrial and agricultural output of the country[13] was put forth along with the two-step strategy which was officially formed:

---

[11]参见中共中央文献研究室编,《邓小平年谱 1975–1997 (上)》, 中国文献出版社 2004 年 7 月版，第 632 页. (Chinese).

[12]参见中共中央文献研究室编,《邓小平年谱 1975–1997 (下)》, 中国文献出版社 2004 年 7 月版, 第 732 页. (Chinese).

[13]At the 12th National Congress, held in Beijing (September 1, 1982), the Congress outlined the general task of the Party in the new historical period as follows: to unite the people of all ethnic groups in working hard and self-reliantly to achieve, step by step, the modernization of industry, agriculture, national defense, and science and technology and to make China a culturally and ideologically advanced and highly democratic socialist country. It also set the economic goal for the period from 1981 to the end of this century, that is, under the prerequisite of constantly improving economic efficiency, to quadruple the annual industrial and agricultural output value of the country, i.e., from 710 billion yuan in 1980 to about 2,800 billion yuan in the year of 2000, so that people can enjoy a better standard of living. *Source*: China.org.cn, available at: http://www.china.org.cn/china/CPC_90_anniversary/2011-06/16/content_22798387.htm (accessed January 28, 2023).

> The general objective of China's economic construction for the two decades between 1981 and the end of this century is, while steadily working for more and better economic results, to quadruple the gross annual value of industrial and agricultural production — from 710 billion yuan in 1980 to 2,800 billion yuan or so in 2000……
>
> In order to realize our objective for the next two decades, we must take the following two steps in our strategic planning: in the first decade, aim mainly at laying a solid foundation, accumulating strength and creating the necessary conditions; and in the second, usher in a new period of vigorous economic development. This is a major policy decision taken by the Central Committee after a comprehensive analysis of the present conditions of China's economy and the trend of its growth.[14]

On October 6, 1984, while being interviewed with Chinese and foreign delegates at a symposium on China's economic cooperation with foreign countries, Deng Xiaoping said, "Invigorating our domestic economy and opening to the outside world are long-term, not short-term, policies that will remain unchanged for at least 50 or 70 years. Why? Because quadrupling the GNP, which will take 20 years, is only our first step and will be followed by a second, approaching the level of developed countries, which will take 30 or 50, let's say 50, years. That two steps together will take 50 or 70 years."[15] On April 16, 1987, Deng Xiaoping spoke at a meeting with the members of the Committee for Drafting the Basic Law of The Hong Kong Special Administrative Region. By the end of 20th century China's per capita income GNP would reach between US$800 and $1,000. "More important, if with that as a foundation we could continue to develop, in another 50 years, we shall again quadruple our per capita income GNP, which would put China among the moderately developed countries, though its place would still be lower than that of dozens of others."[16] On August 29, 1987, while talking to Leonilde Jotti and Renato Zangheri, the leaders of the Italian Communist Party, Deng Xiaoping brought up his three-step strategy again, reaffirming that "China is developing its economy in three steps. Two steps will be taken in this century, to reach

---

[14] See the 12th Report of National Congress of the Communist Party of China.

[15] See *Selected Works of Deng Xiaoping* (1982–1992), Volume III, Foreign Languages Press, China, 1994, pp. 86–87.

[16] *Selected Works of Deng Xiaoping* (1982–1992), Volume III, Foreign Languages Press, China, 1994, pp. 214–215.

the point where our people have adequate food and clothing and lead a fairly comfortable life. The third step, which will take us 30 to 50 years into the next century, is to reach the level of the moderately developed countries. These are our strategic objectives and our high ambitions."[17]

The abovementioned is known as the 'three-step strategy,' repeatedly explained by Deng Xiaoping to foreign press, which he was able to translate into China's national policy.

On October 25, 1987, the three-step strategy was written in the report of the Thirteenth National Congress of the Communist Party of China:

Ever since the Third Plenary Session of the Eleventh Central Committee, we have been carrying out a strategic plan for economic development. This plan involves three steps. The first step is to double the GNP of 1980 and solve the problem of food and clothing for our people. This task has been largely fulfilled. The second step is to double it again by the end of this century, thus enabling our people to lead a fairly comfortable life. The third step is by the middle of the next century to reach the per capita income GNP level of moderately developed countries. This will mean that modernization has been basically accomplished and that our *people have begun to enjoy a relatively affluent life*.

On September 12, 1997, the new three-step strategy was made clear and retained in the Report of the 15th National Congress of the Communist Party of China: "In the first decade, the gross national product will double that of the year 2000, the people will enjoy an even more comfortable life and a more or less ideal socialist market economy will have come into being. With the efforts to be made in another decade when the Party celebrates its centenary, the national economy will be more developed and the various systems will be further improved. By the middle of the next century when the People's Republic celebrates its centenary, the modernization program will have been accomplished by and large and China will have become a prosperous, strong, democratic and culturally advanced socialist country."

It must be evidenced that in the first two decades of the Reform and Opening-up, focusing on economic development, China's economy impressively accelerated: the GDP was RMB￥8,940.4 billion[18] with a

---

[17] *Selected Works of Deng Xiaoping* (1982–1992), Volume III, Foreign Languages Press, China, 1994, p. 247.

[18] See 2000 年 (stats.gov.cn) (Chinese).

population of 1,265.83 million, not including Taiwan, Hong Kong, and Macao,[19] and the per capita income was RMB￥7,063. Thus, in the year 2000, the first two steps were realized.

The concept of a 'moderately prosperous society' is firmly rooted in traditional Chinese culture and is viewed as the threshold accomplishment necessary to create a great society united in peace and harmony — *Datong Shehui* (大同社会). This is why President Xi placed such great emphasis on the achievement of this goal. In his speech, President Xi summarized the Party's efforts and success in leading a series of revolutions for the country's modernization, particularly in pursuing Reform and Opening-up since 1978 (when the reform process was initiated), which Xi called a "*crucial move in making China what it is today*." President Xi also reviewed the historical background of the CPC's creation and explained the fundamental role it played in the nation's efforts to realize 'rejuvenation, which is intrinsically linked to the two centenary goals and to the continued reform process. This process has allowed China to become a truly advanced country while also improving the living conditions of Chinese people: "*Since the very day of its founding, the Party has made seeking happiness for the Chinese people and rejuvenation for the Chinese nation its aspiration and mission*," Xi said, stressing also that the Party "*has always represented the fundamental interests of all Chinese people.*" As China embarks on a new journey toward socialist modernization, President Xi vowed that the CPC will continue to practice a people-centered philosophy[20] of development, address the people's concerns, and promote common prosperity for all.

---

[19] See 第五次全国人口普查公报（第 1 号) (stats.gov.cn) (Chinese).

[20] The people-centered philosophy of development was raised by President Xi at the fifth plenary session of the 18th CPC Central Committee in October 2015, and it stresses that China's development must be for the people and by the people, and thus its fruits shared among the people. The philosophy has been emphasized again in China's latest development blueprint — the Outline of the 14th Five-Year Plan (2021–2025) for National Economic and Social Development and the Long-Range Objectives Through the Year 2035. The document vows to further improve people's livelihoods by pursuing more balanced, higher-quality development. *Source*: *With 'Xiaokang' goal achieved, CPC vows to lead Chinese people in quest for better life, rejuvenation*, July 1, 2021, available at: https://news.cgtn.com/news/2021-07-01/With-Xiaokang-achieved-CPC-vows-to-lead-people-toward-better-life-11xvkhxk5pe/index.html (accessed January 28, 2023).

The reforms introduced in the past 40 years have proven to be the right recipes to allow China an incredible transformation, reclaim its place as a global economic and political leader, and rightly claim to be a moderately prosperous society.[21] Over the past 40 years, the country has lifted 770 million people out of poverty, meeting the poverty eradication target in the United Nations' 2030 Agenda for Sustainable Development, 10 years ahead of schedule, and resolving its greatest challenge in building a moderately prosperous society in all respects.[22]

1.2. *The fast growth of economy was accompanied by fast degradation of the environment*

Thanks to its reforms, China's economy was able to grow fast; however, it happened at the expense of the environment and with an increase of the greenhouse gas emissions, especially CO_2. This path of development, initially adopted by China, has caused severe pollution of the environment, such as rivers, lakes, land, and the atmosphere. Although China promulgated its Environmental Protection Law in 1979, the Marine Environment Protection Law in 1983, the Law on Prevention and Control of Water Pollution in 1984, and the Law on Air Pollution and Control in 1987, these pieces of legislation have not always produced the desired results. Worsening pollution heavily damaged the environment and in some cases threatened people's health and put in peril further development of the country; for these reasons, China has started shaping dedicated policies to seriously tackle this problem. In fact, only transitioning toward a green economy will grant sustainable development not only for China but also for the entire global community.

Photographic Documentation of the consequences of pollution in China (Figures 2–5):

---

[21] *Source*: *Achieving a Xiaokang society and the first centenary goal*, Jon Taylor, China.org.cn, China focus, July 19, 2021, article available at: http://www.china.org.cn/opinion/2021-07/19/content_77636518.htm (accessed January 18, 2023).

[22] *Source*: *Xi declares China a moderately prosperous society in all respects*, article available at: http://english.scio.gov.cn/topnews/2021-07/01/content_77599525.htm (accessed January 28, 2023).

Figure 2: Songhua river pollution tackled anew (Xinhua News Agency May 11, 2007)[23]

Figure 3: Fish die in suspected pollution in Hangzhou, 2006. *China Daily* (news photo)[24]

[23] *Source*: http://www.china.crg.cn/english/photo/210384.htm (accessed February 8, 2023).
[24] *Source*: http://www.chinadaily.com.cn/photo/2006-06/05/content_608440.htm (accessed February 8, 2023).

Figure 4: Pollutant algae return to Lake Tai[25]

Figure 5: Waste clogs a polluted river in Changsha, Hunan province, February 24, 2013. Nearby factories have been discharging polluted water into the Yangjiawan section of the Liuyang River since the end of 2012 (LONG HONGTAO / XINHUA)[26]

---

[25] *Source*: http://www.china.org.cn/environment/news/2008-04/15/content_14957505.htm (accessed February 8, 2023).

[26] *Source*: https://www.chinadailyhk.com/articles/28/167/242/1501563309733.html (accessed February 8, 2023).

1.3. *Evidence of the threats caused by fast growth with regard to the environment*

The fast growth of the economy was and still is based on the extensive use of fossil fuels (oil and coal), which produce greenhouse gases, especially CO_2. As a result, China has become a major contributor of GHG emissions causing the warming of the earth. Global warming, causing climate change, is a global issue. Unfortunately, notwithstanding the adoption of the so-called Paris Agreement to tackle climate change, the global temperature is still rising, especially in the recent decade. The *WMO Provisional State of the Global Climate 2022* indicates that global temperature in 2022 was estimated to be 1.15 ± 0.13°C above the 1850–1900 average. The eight years from 2015 to 2022 are likely to be the eight warmest years on record, with 2022 most likely to be 5th or 6th warmest (Figure 6).[27]

The continuous warming of the earth engenders extreme weather globally, contributing to a great number of disasters. According to a WMO

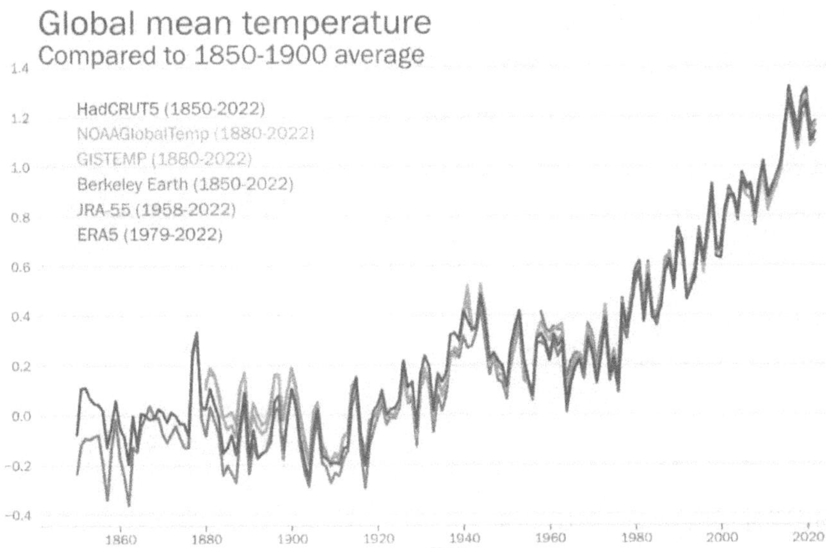

Figure 6: (Color online) Global temperature (1850–1900)

Source: WMO Provisional State of the Global Climate 2022, p. 7.

[27]See WMO Provisional State of the Global Climate 2022, p. 3.

report, from 1970 to 2019, 11,072 disasters have been attributed to extreme weather conditions, climate, and floods. These disasters resulted in 2.06 million deaths and US$3.64 trillion in losses. Thus, over the last 50 years, 50% of all recorded disasters, 45% of related deaths, and 74% of related economic losses were due to extreme weather events, climate change, and its consequences.[28]

The Chinese topography is very complex and multifarious, composed of flatlands, highlands, uplands, hills, and basins, out of which two-thirds is mountainous area; there are also over 1,500 rivers, with each drainage area being over 1,000 square kilometers, 24,800 lakes,[29] 18,000 kilometers of coastline, and 7,600 islands.[30] Extreme weather easily emerges in this kind of topography. In the first two decades of the Reform and Opening-up, the Chinese industrialization process was impressively accelerated, causing the production of huge amount of CO_2 emissions. These emissions have naturally contributed to the rise of global temperature, influencing extreme weather conditions, at least in the Chinese territory. Consequently, the extreme weather severely affects China, and in order to avoid catastrophic damage, China has initiated a new model of development, adopting measures to restore the environment as will be illustrated in the following chapters (Figure 7).

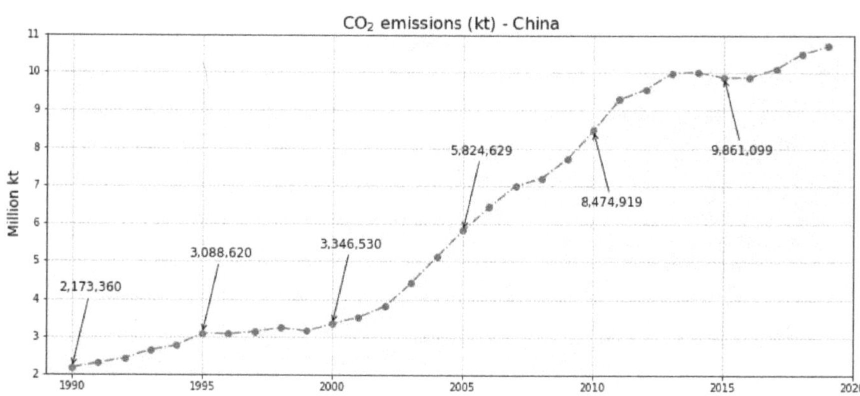

Figure 7: Emissions of GHGs

Source: World Bank.

[28] See WMO Atlas of Mortality and Economic Losses from Weather, Climate and Water Extremes (1970–2019), p. 8.

[29] See 河流和湖泊_自然地理_中国政府网 (www.gov.cn) Chinese (visited on January 21, 2023).

[30] See 国情_中国政府网 (www.gov.cn) Chinese (visited on January 21, 2023).

In 1994, economic losses to China due to drought totaled US$23.72 billion; in 1996, floods resulted in damage amounting to US$20.52 billion; in 1998, again due to floods, this figure soared to US$47.02 billion; in 2008, due to extreme temperatures, the loss was of US$25.06 billion; in 2010, floods amounted to the loss of US$21.1 billion; in 2016, due to floods, damage worth US$22.92 billion was caused.[31] In 2020, the national mean temperature was 0.7°C higher than the average year, the eighth warmest year since 1951[32], and mainly due to floods, geological hazards, wind, hailstorms, and typhoons, the direct losses have amounted to RMB￥370 billion.[33] In 2021, China's mean temperature was 10.53°C, 1.0°C higher than the average year, the highest year since 1951,[34] and again mainly due to floods, wind, hailstorms, drought, typhoons, earthquakes, geological hazards, low temperature and frost, and extreme snow events, the total direct losses amounted to RMB￥334 billion (Figure 8).[35]

Last year, i.e., 2022, extreme weather events once again hit China: Heavy rains in the south and northeast broke the rainfall record in Guangzhou, causing the flooding of 40 rivers in the Songliao Watershed; drought in the central part from the middle and upstream regions of Yangtze River to the middle and lower regions of Yangtze River lasted two seasons from spring to summer and summer to autumn, respectively; and high temperatures in east-central China lasted for 79 days, the highest temperature of 361 national weather stations reaching or surpassing the overall maximum.[36]

Throughout history, China has had the most number of natural disasters in the world. In the last 550 years, flood and drought have always

---

[31] See WMO Atlas of Mortality and Economic Losses from Weather, Climate and Water Extremes (1970–2019), p. 29.

[32] See 2020 年中国气候公报发布！(内附全文) (ncsc.org.cn) Chinese (visited on January 21, 2023).

[33] See 应急部网站: 2020 年全国自然灾害基本情况-中国气象局政府门户网站 (cma.gov.cn) Chinese (visited on January 21, 2023).

[34] See 中国气象局发布 2021 年《中国气候公报》-中国气象局政府门户网站 (cma.gov.cn) Chinese (visited on January 21, 2023).

[35] See 应急管理部发布 2021 年全国自然灾害基本情况--中华人民共和国应急管理部 (mem.gov.cn) Chinese (visited on January 21, 2023).

[36] See 中国气象局: 2022 年夏秋季高温创历史纪录_腾讯新闻 (qq.com). Chinese (visited on January 21, 2023).

Figure 8: Droughts in China

Source: 500 年大数据告诉你: 中国旱涝格局呈现周期性变化-资讯-中国天气网 (weather.com.cn).

emerged frequently. Each year, there are regional or local floods or droughts, some of which are historically the most severe natural disasters in China. Every year has experienced at least one flood; severe floods have hit China in the following years: 1730, 1755, 1823, 1931, 1935, 1954, 1975, 1998, and 2016. The 1998 flood was the biggest in the last 150 years, causing 4.159 deaths and RMB￥455 billion in direct economic losses. These severe and terrible losses need to be avoided with preparedness and specific policies (Figure 9).

Along with the fast development during China's industrialization and urbanization process, the losses from flood and drought were more severe. From 1965 to 1989, the annual losses amounted to RMB$119.2 billion, and from 1990 to 2013, the annual losses leapt to RMB￥307.9 billion, 1.6 times greater, among which the proportion caused by flood was the biggest.[37]

It goes without saying that along with the continuingly rising temperatures, the extreme weather events became more frequent, leading to natural disasters, inexorably damaging the Chinese economy, the Chinese natural environment, and Chinese lives. Consequently, China has had to change its development modality to reduce the emissions of greenhouse

[37]See 500 年大数据告诉你: 中国旱涝格局呈现周期性变化-资讯-中国天气网 (weather.com.cn).

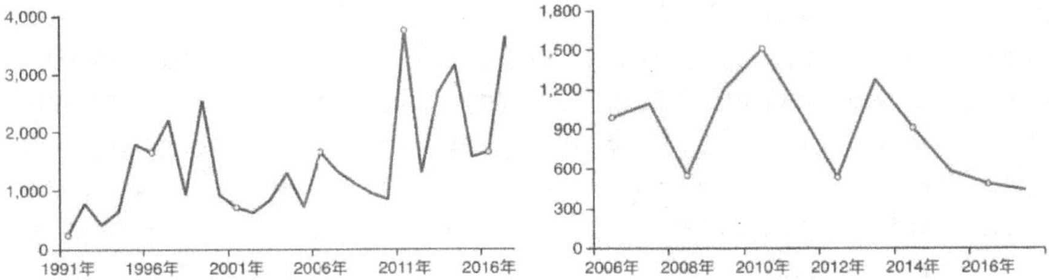

Flood losses from 1950 to 2017 in RMB¥100 million

Drought losses from 1950 to 2017 in RMB¥100 million

Figure 9: Floods and droughts in China

Source: 500 年大数据告 诉你: 中国旱涝格局呈现周期性变化-资讯-中国天气网 (weather.com.cn).

gases. This must be done in a concerted manner with the rest of the global community, hand in hand, honestly, with open minds, and sharing experiences and technologies which can help reduce the emissions affecting our climate. Nature provides the basic conditions for human survival and development. Respecting, adapting to, and protecting nature are essential requirements for building China into a modern socialist country. China must uphold and act on the principle that clear waters and lush mountains are invaluable assets, and must maintain harmony between humanity and nature when planning development.[38]

As evidenced, the first two decades of the Reform and Opening-up process have coincided with two decades of pollution and extreme weather events, and the whole environment in China, including the land, the water, the sea, and the atmosphere, has been severely polluted and contaminated. However, starting with the beginning of the new century, China has come to understand that only by protecting the environment will it be possible to shaped a moderately prosperous society; in fact, this objective is not only based on the GDP of China but also based on the resources the environment offers China (and the rest of the world). Thus, protecting nature and its ecosystems, and the earth where we all live, has become a priority for China. These new targets have been embodied in the UN's goals, which have embraced the idea of clear waters and lush mountains, and a sustainable development to be reached step by step. China has started new green development and is fostering it with its new policies and initiatives as illustrated in the following chapters of this book. This decade

[38] See Xi Jinping, Report to the 20th National Congress of the Communist Party of China, October 16, 2022.

and the next thirty years will be of extreme importance to China because, while advancing toward its carbon goals, i.e., peaking emissions in 2030 and carbon neutrality in 2060, and shaping and fostering a green economy, China is also reinforcing its economy and rethinking its development mode. The rest of the global community is also embracing the same new green development pattern in order to avoid catastrophic consequences for the whole world.

2. Building a Moderately Prosperous Society in All Respects Includes the Historic Change of Making the Protection of the Environment One of the Top Priorities

Severe pollution and extreme weather events not only cause direct economic losses but are also responsible for the loss of people's lives and negative influence on health. For these reasons, China has started to attach greater importance to ecological issues, and environment protection was brought at the center of a new development strategy. China has started the construction of a so-called 'ecological civilization' because everybody needs to contribute to sustainable development in harmony with nature.

2.1. *Recognition of the necessity to protect our environment*

On August 3, 1996, the State Council released the *Decision on Several Issues Concerning Environmental Protection*,[39] with a view to further carry out the basic state policy of environmental protection, implementing the strategy of sustainable development, specifically mentioning the following: "Municipalities directly under the central government, capital cities of provinces, cities within special economic zones, coastal open cities, and key tourist cities should all keep environmental air and environmental quality of surface water up to the corresponding national standards in terms of their functional categories. The Huaihe River and

[39]Decision of the State Council on Several Issues Concerning Environmental Protection, August 3, 1996. Document available at: https://english.mee.gov.cn/Resources/Policies/policies/Frameworkp1/200710/t20071017_111494.shtml (accessed January 28, 2023).

the Taihu Lake should have waters cleared. The Haihe River, the Liaohe River, the Dianchi Lake and the Chaohu Lake should have the quality of surface water markedly improved." The decision also called on the concerned authorities to conduct strict checks and resolutely control new pollution, take effective measures to prohibit the transfer of waste, preserve the ecological balance, protect and rationally exploit natural resources, resolutely enforce environmental protection laws, and strengthen supervision and management of the environment. This decision has put in evidence the necessity and urgency to act in defense of nature and has stimulated further development of legislation in defense of nature.

2.2. *Ecological civilization and nature preservation are now part of the national strategy for green and sustainable development*

The state organs of the People's Republic of China apply the principle of democratic centralism, led by the CPC, and as a result the direction in which the country is heading and the policies shaping its future shall be designed and pushed forward by the Party Central Committee. One of the objectives, as already explained, is the realization of a moderately prosperous society, as designed by Deng Xiaoping, converted into the Party's policy, and then transformed into the national target, which can only be reached by pursuing green development in harmony with nature. This is why ecological civilization and environment protection have become top priorities; in fact, they are an integral part of the new development mode and strategy of China to continue shaping a prosperous, strong, democratic, and culturally advanced socialist country.

A milestone marking this change in China's development process was reached on October 11, 2000, when the Central Committee of the CPC passed the proposal for the 10th Five-Year Plan on National Economy and Social Development, requiring the implementation of a new sustainable development strategy with responsible use of natural resources, with attention paid to nature, accompanied by the construction and strengthening of an ecological civilization needed to protect our environment.

On March 15, 2001, the National People's Congress approved the 10th Five-Year Plan, and in particular, on the environmental issue, it was decided to increase forest coverage to 18.2% and the urban green rate to

35%. The total amount of major urban and rural pollutants discharged had to be reduced by 10% as compared with 2000, and more measures were to be taken to protect and save natural resources.

On November 8, 2002, Jiang Zemin, on behalf of the 15th Central Committee of the Communist Party of China (CPC), delivered a report to the 16th CPC National Congress which opened in Beijing. The report was titled "*Build a Well-off Society in an All-round Way and Creating a New Situation in Building Socialism with Chinese Characteristics.*" Jiang said that the 16th CPC National Congress was the first of its kind convened by the Party to take the third step of the strategic plan for socialist modernization in China. "We must be aware that China is in the primary stage of socialism and will remain so for a long time to come. The well-off life we are leading is still at a low level; it is not all-inclusive and is very uneven." By the 16th National People's Congress of the CPC, the second step of the strategy made by the 15th National People's Congress, i.e., to build a well-off society in an all-round way when the Party celebrates its centenary, was accomplished: "*The capability of sustainable development will be steadily enhanced. The ecological environment will be improved. The efficiency of using resources will be increased significantly. We will enhance harmony between man and nature to push the whole society onto a path to civilized development featuring the growth of production, an affluent life and a sound ecosystem.*" Thus, besides economic development, democracy, and the legal system, the construction of society which includes 'ecological civilization' will be pursued.

Thus, from the 16th National Congress of the CPC, ecological civilization has been integrated into China's objective of building a well-off society, along with other objectives, as covered by United Nations' Sustainable Development Goals.

It also must be noted that during the 17th National Congress of the CPC, the term and concept of 'ecological civilization' (生态文明) was further elaborated and expanded upon, and it now includes the smart use of energy, efficient use of resources in general, environment-friendly structure of industries (greening of industrialization), and greener and more sustainable pattern of growth and mode of consumption. For this reason, China is implementing a large-scale circular economy and will considerably increase the proportion of renewable energy sources in total energy consumption. The discharge of major pollutants shall be brought under effective control, which will have a positive effect on ecosystems and in general on the environment. Awareness of ecological civilization shall be firmly established in the whole of society.

2.3. *Environmental protection has become a national goal*

Environmental protection has now become a national first-level objective, because only by promoting sustainable development and transitioning toward a green economy will China be able to further advance its other goals, contribute to a type of new multilateralism, and play a major role in global issues.

"*Promoting ecological progress is a long-term task of vital importance to the people's wellbeing and China's future. Faced with increasing resource constraints, severe environmental pollution and a deteriorating ecosystems, we must raise our ecological awareness of the need to respect, accommodate and protect nature. We must give high priority to making ecological progress and incorporate it into all aspects and the whole process of advancing economic, political, cultural, and social progress, work hard to build a beautiful country, and achieve lasting and sustainable development of the Chinese nation.*" This is how the concepts of Beautiful China and green development were expressed in a talk delivered at the opening of the 19th CPC National Congress by General Secretary Xi Jinping. During his speech, President Xi affirmed that *the government will put in more effort into improving the environment, and building a 'beautiful China.'* The concept was first mentioned in 2012, when the country faced a series of environmental problems. Achieving this goal of 'beautiful China' includes a set of reforms to develop an 'ecological civilization.' Xi Jinping intended for the reforms to speed up, and brought up four key points during his report: to promote green development, solve prominent environmental problems, intensify the protection of the ecosystem, and reform the environmental regulation system. According to Xi Jinping, this 'beautiful China' will be attained by 2035.[40]

The following is an interest extract from the report:

Man and nature form a community of life; we, as human beings, must respect nature, follow its ways, and protect it. Only by observing the laws

---

[40] *Source*: https://news.cgtn.com/news/3d4d544e334d4464776c6d636a4e6e62684a4856/share_p.html.

of nature can mankind avoid costly blunders in its exploitation. Any harm we inflict on nature will eventually return to haunt us. This is a reality we have to face.

The modernization that we pursue is one characterized by harmonious coexistence between man and nature. In addition to creating more material and cultural wealth to meet people's ever-increasing needs for a better life, we need also to provide more quality ecological goods to meet people's ever-growing demands for a beautiful environment. We should, acting on the principles of prioritizing resource conservation and environmental protection and letting nature restore itself, develop spatial layouts, industrial structures, and ways of work and life that help conserve resources and protect the environment. With this, we can restore the serenity, harmony, and beauty of nature.

1. Promoting green development: "*We will step up efforts to establish a legal and policy framework that promotes green production and consumption, and promote a sound economic structure that facilitates green, low-carbon, and circular development. We will create a market-based system for green technology innovation, develop green finance, and spur the development of energy-saving and environmental protection industries as well as clean production and clean energy industries. We will promote a revolution in energy production and consumption, and build an energy sector that is clean, low-carbon, safe, and efficient.*"[41]

It is evident with these statements that President Xi intends to put the implementation of 'Beautiful China' and 'green development' at the center of the next phase of development, which will inevitably also stimulate the economic field with new investments.

China, thanks to this new impulse led by President Xi, has formulated and enforced a series of stringent measures for environmental protection. This framework applies the principles and methods of the rule of law to promote eco-environmental progress. By enacting the strictest

[41] See full text of Xi Jinping's report at 19th CPC National Congress about Securing a Decisive Victory in Building a Moderately Prosperous Society in All Respects and Striving for the Great Success of Socialism with Chinese Characteristics for a New Era, October 18, 2017, in particular Part IX "Speeding up Reform of the System for Developing an Ecological Civilization, and Building a Beautiful China," available at: https://www.chinadaily.com.cn/china/19thcpcnationalcongress/2017-11/04/content_34115212.htm (accessed January 28, 2023).

environmental protection law in its history, and formulating or amending a range of other laws and regulations, China has created a legal framework that covers all environmental factors in major fields. This must be considered in conjunction with new initiatives such as the 1 + *N* framework (see Chapter 2, n. 2) aimed at improving the efficient use of resources, the conservation and restoration of ecosystems, and in general enhancing environmental protection and favoring green development.

To conclude, it must be underlined that building a moderately prosperous society, for the Chinese leaders and policymakers, does not merely mean implementing economic reforms and thus fostering economic growth but it also involves comprehensive progress in China's long-term plans to develop a great modern socialist country. This means continuing with the reform process, further stimulating the internal economy, and advancing science and education which represent two fundamental elements intrinsically linked to the success of a country. The reforms introduced in the past 40 years in China have proven to be the right recipes to foster an incredible transformation, help China reclaim its place as a global economic power, become an effective member of this global community, and rightly claim to be a moderately prosperous society.[42] Over the past 40 years, the country has lifted 770 million people out of poverty, reaching one of the targets of the United Nations' 2030 Agenda for

Ecosystem Restoration Projects

Since the late 1970s, China has launched six national key restoration projects across the country to protect its environment and restore the degraded ecosystems. The first project was the Three-North Shelter Forest Program, which was initiated in the late 1970s. The project is now known as the "Green Great Wall" because its area spans half of northern China. The fourth term of this project started in 2001 and ended in 2010. The next project was the Yangtze River and Zhujiang River Shelter Forest Projects, launched in 1989 across the southern parts of China with the aim of battling floods and reducing soil erosion. The second term of this project also began in 2001 and ended in 2010. The Natural Forest Protection Project

(*Continued*)

[42]*Source*: *Achieving a Xiaokang society and the first centenary goal*, Jon Taylor, China.org.cn, China focus, July 19, 2021, article available at: http://www.china.org.cn/opinion/2021-07/19/content_77636518.htm (accessed January 8, 2023).

(*Continued*)

was subsequently initiated in 1998 and has shown numerous benefits, including biodiversity conservation, reduction of soil erosion and flood risk, and prevention of other natural disasters associated with deforestation; which has also provided 80% carbon storage, among which the total amount is 9.2 billion ton in the Chinese forest vegetation.[1] The Grain for Green Program, also known as China's Sloping Lands Conversion Project, was initiated in 2000 and has advanced the conversion of croplands in hilly areas to forests. GGP is regarded as the world's largest ecological restoration program in terms of scale and investment and is a typical example of ecological compensation. The Beijing–Tianjin Sand Source Control Project was initiated in 2001 to promote environmental conservation near the capital by controlling the risk of sand and soil erosion. The last project, known as the Returning Grazing Land to Grassland Project, was launched in 2003 to reduce the impact of overgrazing and promote grassland productivity. These projects together cover 44.8% of China's forests and 23.2% of China's grasslands.[43]

Sustainable Development 10 years ahead of schedule, resolving its greatest challenge in building a moderately prosperous society.[44]

2.4. *Concrete results of efforts to build a moderately prosperous society in all respects including paying more attention to the environment*

On July 1, 2021, when President Xi Jinping announced the achievement of the first centenary goal, he stressed the fact that China had made a historic transformation by raising the living standards of its people from bare subsistence to an overall level of moderate prosperity and then had transformed its society into a moderate prosperous society in all respects.[45]

---

[43] *Source*: *Xi declares China a moderately prosperous society in all respects,* article available at: http://english.scio.gov.cn/topnews/2021-07/01/content_77599525.htm (accessed October 8, 2022).

[44] *Source*: https://www.pnas.org/doi/10.1073/pnas.1700294115, Chinese, (accessed January 28, 2023).

[45] See 习近平:在庆祝中国共产党成立 100 周年大会上的讲话 (www.gov.cn).

The achieving of moderate prosperity, or 'Xiaokang,' is measured in terms of multiple aspects, such as the economy, democracy, science and education, culture, society, and people's lives. The requirements include doubling the country's 2010 GDP and per capita income disposable income by 2020. "Last year, the country's GDP exceeded 100 trillion yuan (about $15.45 trillion). Its per capita income disposable income hit 32,189 yuan, double the level in 2010. The country has developed the world's largest social security system and boasts the world's biggest middle-income group — 400 million people. In a historic feat, China has eliminated absolute poverty."[46] This result also signals a historic change regarding environmental protection. Nature needs to be regarded as an important asset for China.

To further secure the interests and well-being of both current and future generations, and guarantee China's sustainable development, the CPC has decreed that "lucid waters and lush mountains are invaluable assets" which need to be protected. For this reason, China has adopted a basic national policy of resource conservation and environmental protection, and worked hard to build a 'Beautiful China.' Its endeavors have made the skies bluer, the lands greener, and the waters clearer across the vast and beautiful landscape of the country, and added more green touches to the planet that is home to all. More awareness about the importance and the protection of nature is the key to advance toward green development and to secure people's well-being, and this awareness also represents a salient feature of moderate prosperity in all respects.

China has formulated and enforced stringent systems for eco-environmental protection (reference must be made to the so-called $1 + N$ framework). It applies the principles and methods of the rule of law into practice in promoting eco-environmental progress. By enacting the strictest environmental protection law in its history, and formulating or amending a range of other laws and regulations, it has created a legal framework on the eco-environment sphere covering all environmental factors in major fields.

China has established a series of eco-environmental protection systems in areas such as efficient use of resources, conservation and restoration, lifelong accountability for damage, responsibility for and performance evaluation of targets, and central government supervision.

---

[46]*Source*: The State Council, available at: http://english.www.gov.cn/news/topnews/202107/01/content_WS60ddd47ec6d0df57f98dc472.html (accessed February 8, 2023).

The most rigid constraints possible imposed by this stringent system have resulted in better outcomes in changing the development model, fostering eco-friendly habits among the people, and promoting environmental protection and governance.

China has paid particular attention to monitoring and managing its rivers, lakes, and forests across the country in a sustainable manner as if they are sub-districts in urban areas, and also to protecting its reservoir areas with the same care as scenic resorts. As a result, designated personnel are in place to tend to mountains, plant trees, protect forests, and take on related responsibilities, thus establishing lasting governance of the eco-environment.

China has involved the whole of society in eco-environmental protection. A better system has been established for public participation, including decision-making, scrutiny, and reporting of environmental violations. Environment-related information has become more transparent and public awareness of environmental protection has been raised. Naturally, this benefits people in terms of living in a better and cleaner environment. Green development is contributing to eco-environmental progress and impacting the whole of society.

"China has made strong headway in preventing and controlling pollution. In its drive to keep the skies blue, the waters clear, and the land pollution-free, China achieved the following in 2020:

- *In cities at or above prefecture level, 87% days reached good or excellent air quality.*
- *In cities at or above prefecture level that fell short of the national standards, average PM2.5 concentrations decreased by 28.8% from 2015.*
- *The proportion of excellent and good-quality surface water reached 83.4%.*
- *Up to 94.5% of the drinking water sources serving urban communities reached the required standards.*
- *Black and foul water bodies in urban built-up areas at or above the prefecture level were largely eliminated.*
- *Approximately 90% of polluted farmland and more than 93% of polluted land plots were rendered safe for use.*
- *The target of bringing down the imports of foreign solid waste to zero was achieved as scheduled.*

In a more beautiful living environment with fresher air, cleaner drinking water, and safer food, the people have enjoyed the pleasures brought by environmental improvements, and registered greater satisfaction with the improved eco-environment and a stronger sense of gain. In 2020, 89.5% of Chinese people were satisfied with the eco-environment."[47]

"In a more beautiful living environment with fresher air, cleaner drinking water, and safer food, the people have enjoyed the pleasures brought by environmental improvements, and registered greater satisfaction with the improved eco-environment and a stronger sense of gain. In 2020, 89.5% of Chinese people were satisfied with the eco-environment." Furthermore, it is necessary to stress that "China has improved the health and stability of its ecosystems. Prioritizing resource conservation and environmental protection, and letting nature restore itself, the country has protected and managed its mountain, river, forest, farmland, lake, grassland, and desert ecosystems with a holistic approach. It has improved its management and inspection systems for nature reserves and eco-environmental protection zones, thereby strengthening eco-environmental security and ensuring China's sustainable development."[48]

3. The Second Centenary Goal: To Build a Modern Socialist Country that is Prosperous, Strong, Democratic, Culturally Advanced, and Harmonious by the Middle of the 21st Century with an Eye on the UN's Goals

Four decades of hard work produced results, and the realization of the so-called *Xiaokang* society is a tangible achievement of the continued reform process, which also means that the Chinese model proved its validity. Now, in order to achieve the next goal by the 100th anniversary of the People's Republic of China in 2049, a lot of work still remains to be done, but the path is clear: The second centenary goal is to build a modern

[47] *Source*: *China Daily*, 'China's Epic Journey from Poverty to Prosperity,' available at: https://global.chinadaily.com.cn/a/202109/29/WS6153c41aa310cdd39bc6c469_10.html (accessed February 8, 2023).

[48] *Ibid.*

socialist country that is prosperous, strong, democratic, culturally advanced, and harmonious by the middle of the 21st century.

According to the report of the 20th National Congress of the CPC dated October 16, 2022, the central task of the CPC will be to lead Chinese people of all ethnic groups in a concerted effort to realize the second centenary goal of building China into a great modern socialist country in all respects and to advance the rejuvenation of the Chinese nation on all fronts through a path of modernization placing emphasis on the green transition.

Chinese modernization has five characteristics: a large population, common prosperity for all, material and cultural-ethical advancement, harmony between humanity and nature, and peaceful development, all of which are identical to the UN's Sustainability Goals.

To build China into a great modern socialist country in all respects, China has adopted a two-step strategic plan: (i) realize socialist modernization from 2020 through 2035; (ii) build China into a great modern socialist country that is prosperous, strong, democratic, culturally advanced, harmonious, and beautiful from 2035 through the middle of this century.

Common prosperity for all is achievable in the terms indicated by President Xi Jinping,[49] but only by continuing to implement further reforms and eliminating internal inequalities among citizen through granting stability and continuity. The CPC is well aware of the necessity to reduce the gaps between the most fortunate and less fortunate people, and it is now addressing this issue by engaging in impactful policy measures like (i) rural revitalization,[50] (ii) national

[49]Xi Jinping, general secretary of the CPC Central Committee, on behalf of the 19th CPC Central Committee, delivered to the Congress opened on the morning of October 16, 2022 at the Great Hall of the People in Beijing, a report titled "*Hold High the Great Banner of Socialism with Chinese Characteristics and Strive in Unity to Build a Modern Socialist Country in All Respects.*" He pointed out that the 20th National Congress of the Communist Party of China is a meeting of great importance. It takes place at a critical time as the entire Party and Chinese people of all ethnic groups embark on a new journey to build China into a modern socialist country in all respects and advance toward the second centenary goal.

[50]Rural vitalization is a critical part of the Chinese government's 2020–2025 work plan and a major component of the government's plan to make China a strong modern country by 2050. In 2017, President Xi Jinping shared the idea of "*implementing the rural revitalization strategy*" during the 19th National Congress of the CPC, which has impacted rural livelihoods. In 2018, the Central Committee of the CPC and State Council issued a

new-type urbanization,[51] and (iii) the dual circulation strategy.[52] The third point is of paramount importance because implementing this strategy will further stimulate the internal economy and also promote international trade. However, in order to further advance on this plan, it is absolutely necessary to attain internal 'stability' and 'continuity,' which are attainable only with a solid leadership, and this is certainly the case with the confirmation of President Xi for a third mandate at the 20th Congress of the CPC.[53] President Xi Jinping at the opening of the

---

comprehensive document "2018–2022 Strategic Planning for Revitalization of Rural Areas" to highlight the process for rural development. For more detail on this theme, see: *China's rural revitalization and development: Theory, technology and management*, Liu Yansui, Zang Yuzhu, Yang Yuanyuan, Journal of Geographical Science, December 2020, article available at: https://www.researchgate.net/publication/347995391_China%27s_rural_revitalization_and_development_Theory_technology_and_management (accessed January 28, 2023).

[51] New-type urbanization and rural revitalization have gradually become national strategies, and are an objective requirement for China to be able to enter into a new era of socialism with Chinese characteristics. A very exhaustive explanation about this theme is contained in the article titled *The Integration of New-Type Urbanization and Rural Revitalization Strategies in China: Origin, Reality and Future Trends*, Mingxing Chen, Yuan Zhou, Xinrong Huang, MDPI, February 18, 2021, article available at: https://www.mdpi.com/2073-445X/10/2/207/htm (accessed January 28, 2023).

[52] The so-called 'dual circulation strategy' was first mentioned at a meeting of the Politburo, China's 25-member policymaking committee, in mid-May 2020, and it aims to create conditions that allow domestic and foreign markets to balance each other. In essence, the country will continue seeking to improve its ability to participate in global trade, finance, and technology, while strengthening domestic consumption, production, and technological capabilities to hedge against global market disruptions. President Xi Jinping later added that China would "*gradually form a new development model in which domestic circulation plays a dominant role*." For a more detailed explanation, see video titled *Special Series on Dual Circulation Ep. 01: An Overview of China's New Economic Strategy*, March 6, 2021, CGTN, available at: https://news.cgtn.com/news/2021-03-06/Dual-Circulation-Ep-01-An-Overview-of-China-s-New-Economic-Strategy-YpfHmPogjS/index.html (accessed January 28, 2023) where a very informative video about the 'dual circulation strategy' is also available.

[53] President Xi Jinping secured a historic third term as China's leader on Sunday October 23, 2022 at the closing of the 20th Congress of the Communist Party. The Central Committee of the Chinese Communist Party elected Xi Jinping as its general secretary for another five-year term, Xinhua reported: article available at: https://english.news.cn/20221023/289564cb819a4af2ba3eb6fb1cad5177/c.html (accessed January 28, 2023).

Congress stressed that "*we must fully and faithfully apply the new development philosophy on all fronts, advance reforms to develop the socialist market economy, adhere to high-standard opening up, and accelerate efforts to foster a new pattern of development that is focused on domestic economy and features positive interplay between domestic and international economic flows.*" On the technological aspects, Xi pointed out that "*we must regard science and technology as our primary productive force, talent as our primary resource, and innovation as our primary driver of growth. We will fully implement the strategy for invigorating China through science and education, the workforce development strategy, and the innovation-driven development strategy.*"[54] It is worth noting that when it comes to innovation, technology, and education, President Xi did not set out detailed policies but set clear goals for the Party that are mission critical to national aspirations, particularly much greater self-reliance in the face of fraught relations with the United States and the West. President Xi also promised that China will not engage in any kind of "expansionism" and affirmed that China is committed to its policy of opening up to the outside world. This is necessary to reinforce international cooperation, especially in the ambit of climate change. This theme is of particular importance for China's future development: President Xi has reiterated that China will favor green and low-carbon development, promoting harmony between humanity and nature, and improve pollution controls (these themes are treated in the following chapters). Xi also promised to use coal in a cleaner and more efficient way; however, no clear plans have been formulated yet. On this aspect, China faces a dilemma about cutting coal use to meet its emissions targets and assuring sufficient energy (especially in winters).

It is evident that President Xi is determined to achieve the second centenary goal not only in a timely fashion but also with the intent to transform China into a leading nation, and also with regard to climate change considering the measures introduced to tackle this issue. In fact, China is acting to shape a more advanced society in harmony with nature,

[54]*Source*: Ministry of Foreign Affairs of the People's Republic of China, 20th National Congress of Communist Party of China opens in Beijing, Xi Jinping delivers report to Congress on behalf of 19th CPC Central Committee, October 16, 2022, available at: https://www.fmprc.gov.cn/eng/zxxx_662805/202210/t20221018_10785042.html (accessed January 28, 2023).

as will clearly emerge from the pages of this book. This objective requires the country to march united with the rest of the global community, adopt a shared vision on the future, rethink multilateralism, and readjust the responsibilities in global governance for the benefit of our planet and all its inhabitants. Readjusting equilibriums in global governance is another priority for China: Only with balanced and shared responsibilities reflecting the capabilities of each single nation will it be possible to shape a new global economy meeting the goals of the UN which are aimed not only at respecting our environment but also at granting a sustainable future.

3.1. *Development of a green China will help achieve the objectives of the UN's 2030 Agenda*

The next five years are critical for China in transforming itself into a leading power, and this should happen by the middle of the century in two stages: first by completing modernization by 2035 and then by becoming a 'pace-setter and goal-setter of global development by 2050' (completing its modernization in all respects). The other goal is to become a carbon-neutral economy before 2060, which perfectly matches not only internal objectives to ameliorate its industrial sector but also international targets to pursue sustainable development. In this regard, quantitative growth cannot be the only measure of China's development. China needs sustainable quality growth, reducing the use of coal and incrementing renewables, to be measured ultimately by self-reliance in many aspects of security, such as energy security, food security, and the narrow concept of military security. There are also reasonable expectations of safety from disease and natural disasters. In terms of CPC's goal of common prosperity in which growth benefits everyone, President Xi is essentially talking about growing the middle class and favoring small businesses, but President Xi also talked about helping the poor with a particular emphasis on job creation. Quality growth includes carbon neutrality and air quality, with pollution in a sense being comparable with poverty. Thus, the new measures introduced to favor the green transition are of extreme importance to reach China's objectives, shape sustainable development, and build a shared future for mankind.

President Xi has pointed out that development is a timeless theme for humanity: Only through continuous development can the people's dream for a better life and social stability be realized. Each country has its own development path suited to its own national realities, but in the end to reach common goals it is necessary to work together and unite efforts, especially with regard to this common threat, i.e., climate change. Today, at a time when the COVID-19 pandemic is eroding decades of gains in global development, the implementation of the UN's 2030 Agenda for Sustainable Development is encountering difficulties. Thus, it is more than necessary to cement international cooperation to reach the UN's goals and adopt the best solution to preserve our environment and resources to shape a sustainable future.

3.2. *China is committed to a peaceful, sustainable, and green development*

China is transforming itself into a carbon-neutral economy because it understands that only by protecting nature and shaping a dual circulation economy is it possible to further develop its economy, reach its objectives, and lead the way to the widespread use of the renewables. China, as a matter of fact, is leading the development of solar and wind energy not only to respond to its own needs but also because this is the only way forward to respond to climate change. Green transition and the use of clean, green, and renewable sources of energy have become a necessary path if we want to avoid the catastrophic of climate change which impacts the entire global community.

It is evident that a world in peace where multilateralism should allow to find acceptable solutions for different situations, and where each nation bears its own responsibilities in global governance, it is the *optimum* scenario for a world on the brink of a climate disaster if the global community do not act united adopting the necessary remedies.

If energy is one of the components of this dramatic international situation, then there is no other choice but to develop alternative sources of energy. This also responds to the needs of the entire world and saves our environment from further degradation. China is gradually introducing, in a very responsible manner, measures to favor the greening of its economy, and thus a green transition, adopting a series of new policies to safeguard the environment. In response to China's new development paradigm and in particular to the new ecological civilization concept, three Strategic Priorities have been identified by China for the period 2021–2025 taking into consideration the United Nations Sustainable Development Cooperation Framework (UNSDCF). The three Strategic Priorities are as follows:

- "***Priority 1*** *— People and Prosperity: Achieving Innovation-driven, Coordinated and Shared Development. Equitable and high-quality economic, social and human development for all throughout the life-course.*
- ***Priority 2*** *— Planet: Achieving Green Development towards a more sustainable and resilient environment.*
- ***Priority 3*** *— Partnerships: Realizing the full potential of China's international engagement to promote its open development and partnerships to accelerate achievement of the SDGs across the world.*"[55]

"Recognizing the synergy between China's vision of high-quality development and the 2030 Agenda, these three Priority Areas will serve as the foundation for all of the UN System's work in and with China over the coming five years, and will support China's high-quality development as well as providing the basis for cooperation with China in assisting other developing countries around the world in achieving the Sustainable Development Goals."[56] President Xi Jinping, at the opening of the 20th National Congress of the Communist Party of China on October 16, 2022, stressed that "*we must uphold and act on the principle that lucid waters and lush mountains are invaluable assets, and we must remember to maintain harmony between humanity and nature when planning our development.*" China will advance the Beautiful China Initiative and take a holistic and systematic approach to the conservation and improvement of mountains, waters, forests, farmlands, grasslands, and deserts. China will carry out coordinated industrial restructuring, pollution control, ecological conservation, and climate response, and will also promote concerted efforts to cut carbon emissions, reduce pollution, and expand green development, while pursuing economic growth. China will prioritize ecological protection, conserve resources and use them efficiently, and pursue green and low-carbon development through the following actions: (1) accelerating the transition to a model of green development; (2) intensifying pollution prevention and control; (3) enhancing diversity, stability, and sustainability in our ecosystems; and (4) working actively and prudently toward the goals of reaching peak carbon emissions and carbon neutrality.[57]

---

[55] *Source*: *United Nations Sustainable Development Cooperation Framework for the People's Republic of China*, 2021–2025, document available at: https://unsdg.un.org/sites/default/files/2021-06/UNSDCF-China-2021-2025.pdf (accessed January 28, 2023).

[56] *Ibid.*

[57] See the Report of the 20th National Congress of the CPC.

President Xi reiterated the nation's commitment to the green transformation of its economy in line with achieving peak carbon emissions by 2030 and carbon neutrality by 2060. These goals will be accomplished by the development of low-carbon industries and a national sustainable lifestyle, which can only come about if the country improves the efficiency of its energy use and promotes further clean energy alternatives. In order to achieve all these goals, it is necessary to generate enough resources to finance such advancements, and for this reason new investment instruments are needed, which need to be calibrated on specific exigencies. Green finance is emerging as an available instrument not only to finance green projects but also as a valid finance source to transition China (and the entire global community) toward a greener and sustainable economy.

3.3. *China's green transition needs to be supported by green finance*

Marching toward a green, nature-positive economy requires a huge amount of financial resources and China is pushing 'green finance' to find these resources. It is evident that China's new investment policies align with the UN Sustainable Development Goals (SDGs), and China is shaping and refining its financial system placing particular emphasis on 'green' to accompany its green revolution. Transforming from a resource- and pollution-intensive economy to a green economy is now a strategic priority for China. Success depends on the implementation of new policies and instruments able to meet these new objectives. As will be explained in the following sections, China has increasingly promoted green finance since the People's Bank of China (PBoC) issued its Guidelines for Establishing the Green Financial System in 2016,[58] which

---

[58] *On August 31, the People's Bank of China, along with six other government agencies, issued the "Guidelines for Establishing the Green Financial System" (Yinfa 2016 Doc No 228), with the approval of the State Council. The Guidelines — issued jointly by the People's Bank of China, the Ministry of Finance, the National Development and Reform Commission, the Ministry of Environmental Protection, China Banking Regulatory Commission, China Securities Regulatory Commission, and China Insurance Regulatory Commission — will provide an essential next step for implementing the overall strategy of promoting ecological civilization, formulated by the Central Party Committee and the State Council. They will also advance the development concepts of innovation, harmony, greenness, openness and sharing, and promote the establishment of China's green*

laid the foundation for this sector. This initiative was followed by other green finance policies and regulations aimed at promoting the issuance of green bonds to start financing green projects in China.

With support from the central and local governments, green finance in China experienced rapid growth. As of the end of 2021, outstanding green loans denominated in yuan and foreign currencies, according to the PBoC's latest green financial report,[59] amounted to 15.9 trillion yuan (approximately US$2.2 trillion), representing a 33% year-on-year increase and ranking China as the world leader in this area.[60] And, in 2021, domestic issuance of green bonds exceeded $68 billion, representing a year-on-year growth rate of 186%, overtaking all the other markets in terms of the annual growth rate according to the report jointly released by international organization 'Climate Bonds Initiative' and China Central Depository & Clearing's research center.[61] According to the aforementioned report, "*financial firms issued $24 billion worth of green bonds in 2021, up 237 percent year-on-year. Green bonds issued by non-financial companies surged 482 percent year-on-year to $31.2 billion, which was about 46 percent of all the green bonds issued last year. It was the first time in China that nonfinancial companies issued more green*

financial system. The Guidelines stress that the primary purpose of establishing the green financial system is to mobilize and incentivize more social (or private) capital to invest in green sectors, while restricting investment in polluting sectors. The green financial system will help facilitate a green transformation for the Chinese economy, promote technological progress in environmental protection, new energy, energy saving and other fields, and accelerate the development of new growth drivers and enhance the potential for economic growth. Source: Bank of China, available at: http://www.pbc.gov.cn/en/3688110/3688172/4048320/3712407/index.html (accessed January 28, 2023).

[59] Bank of China (or "BoC") Green Bonds enables BoC to support environment friendly projects and companies which are particularly active in terms of environment preservation, energy transition, or climate change mitigation. Annual Report on Bank of China's Sustainability Series Bonds as of December 31, 2021, available at: https://www.boc.cn/en/investor/ir10/202203/t20220324_20914249.html (accessed January 28, 2023).

[60] *Source*: The Asset, *Xi stresses China commitment to green economy*, published October 18, 2022, article available at: https://www.theasset.com/article-esg/47849/xi-stresses-china-commitment-to-green-economy (accessed January 28, 2023).

[61] See China Green Bond Market Report 2021, Published jointly by the Climate Bonds Initiative and China Central Depository & Clearing Research Centre (CCDC Research), document available at: https://www.climatebonds.net/files/reports/cbi_china_sotm_2021_0.pdf (accessed January 28, 2023).

bonds than financial service providers. Some 61 percent of the green bond financing was used for the development of renewable energy last year, the report stated. Nearly 19 percent of the financing flowed to the low-carbon transportation sector and another 9 percent to low-carbon construction."[62]

It is also foreseen that in order to reach its goal of carbon neutrality by 2060, China will need to raise about 140 trillion RMB (approximately $22 trillion) from green bonds and other environmentally friendly funding tools, according to a World Economic Forum report.[63] This is why it is so important for China to further develop its green financial market. China needs to further accelerate on a larger scale to provide the funding required to reach its targets of peak carbon by 2030 and carbon neutrality by 2060.

4. China is Shaping a Nature-Positive Economy Fostered by Green Finance in Line with the Sustainable Development Goals of the United Nations

China has always attached great importance to ecological and environmental protection, and recently has made ecological conservation a priority for socialist modernization, people's well-being, and sustainable development in the long run as reiterated by President Xi Jinping at the 20th National Congress of the Communist Party of China. President Xi and the Chinese leadership are well aware that climate change poses a significant threat to China's long-term prosperity. Thus, dedicated measures and policies have been put in place to tackle this delicate issue as explained in the following chapters. President Xi has made statements (e.g., "*lucid waters and lush mountains are as good as mountains of gold and silver*") which evidence the importance China is now giving to the preservation of nature. Under the guidance of Xi Jinping, the concept of 'ecological conservation' has been elevated as one of the top priorities to

[62] *Ibid.*

[63] *Source*: *China's Climate Challenge: Financing the Transition to Net Zero*, Insight report, July 2022, World Economic Forum (in collaboration with Oliver Wyman, document available at: https://www3.weforum.org/docs/WEF_Finance_the_Transition_NewZero_Future_China_2022.pdf (accessed January 28, 2023).

pursue modernization with harmony between man and nature. This new approach has been translated into policies aimed at restoring ecosystems and transitioning China toward a sustainable, eco-friendly model of development. This new development strategy is in line with the goals of sustainable development set out by the United Nations' 2030 Agenda,[64] and at the same time is stimulating China's financial sector. In fact, China's 2060 carbon neutrality goal requires larger-scale investments as mentioned earlier, and green finance is positioned to play an important role to that end given its growing importance. China thus is on the track to further develop its green finance market in order to sustain this green transition.

As China further opens up its capital market, it is evident that international cooperation in green finance also plays a role in facilitating cross-border fund flows, thus helping to create a more harmonious global green financial system through a recognized and accepted international taxonomy. This will be done by covering standards, disclosure, incentives, products, and of course international cooperation to improve the financial policy framework that supports orderly, credible development of green finance in the market. It is noteworthy that China is already cooperating with the EU on Common Ground Taxonomy (CGT) which supports the expansion of China's green bond market and makes it easier for Chinese entities to issue green bonds overseas (refer to Chapter 5).

China's current development vision calls for a shift from the pursuit of rapid growth to high-quality development, in line with the goals of the United Nations for sustainable development. However, China's transition to carbon neutrality presents some challenges: First, internal imbalances need to be addressed, such as the distribution of wealth (this is related to the second centenary goals); second, the greening of the industry requires particular attention and nobody can be left behind. China is generating resources, but in the long run economic costs for this green transition need to remain manageable. Thus, it is necessary to further reform the financial system while advancing toward a low-carbon economy and supporting poor households in the face of higher energy prices. This can be done by training and reskilling workers from the fossil fuel sector and providing

[64]The 2030 Agenda that incorporated 17 sustainable development goals (SDGs) was implemented by all United Nations (UN) member states as a universal plan toward achieving sustainability. Chinese President Xi Jinping on many occasions affirmed that China will take pragmatic steps to give continued support to the UN's 2030 Agenda for Sustainable Development.

targeted assistance to the most affected local communities. Furthermore, this 'innovation-driven development' which needs to be sustained by the government, together with the digitalization of its economy, represents the key components of China's strategy to maintain healthy economic growth by transforming the old model based on traditional factors (intensive use of fossil fuels by and subsidies to inefficient SOEs which generate about half of the country's total GHG emissions[65]) to an innovation-driven model favoring new technologies besides incentivizing the greening of the economy. The new objectives for China are further growth but in harmony with nature, 'coordinated development' which aims to address unbalanced development by focusing on integrated and comprehensive impact, and coordinated development between rural and urban areas and among regions. If green development is now perceived as a top priority, it cannot be achieved without 'open development,' which means achieving sustainable development together with the rest of the global community. Only with joint effort and a shared vision concerning the challenges the world is facing will it be possible to put in place the necessary measures to tackle and solve those global challenges, starting from climate change to food and energy security. International cooperation is a top priority: Only by sharing development benefits with the rest of the global community, based on mutual benefit and "win-win cooperation" is conducive to global goods. This reflects China's strong engagement in global development. China's vision of a 'shared and sustainable development' puts people at the center, pursuing development for the people and by the people and enabling all people to benefit from development. These development concepts are closely aligned with the 17 SDGs in the 2030 Agenda and should be put at the center of political agendas of all governments. China in

[65]According to the contents of the latest World Bank report concerning China, State-owned enterprises (SOEs) continue to play a dominant role in China's economy, especially in carbon-intensive sectors. SOEs are estimated to account for around 25% to 40% of the GDP and around 40% of employment. SOEs control value chains for sectors responsible, directly or indirectly, for the majority of China's emissions: coal, electricity, oil, gas, steel, and cement. It is estimated that SOEs generate about half of the country's total GHG emissions. Addressing emissions generated by SOEs will therefore form a key component of reaching China's goal of carbon neutrality before 2060; *Source*: World Bank Group, China, Country Climate and Development Report, October 2022, document available at: https://openknowledge.worldbank.org/bitstream/handle/10986/38136/FullReport.pdf (accessed January 28, 2023).

implementing its new policies is embracing the concerns of the UN and is also seriously working to accomplish the targets of the Paris Convention, acting as an example for the rest of the global community.

4.1. *Is China's green finance ready to take off?*

China has made substantial progress in the past decade to establish its green financial system, and the results are evident considering the constant growth of this sector. According to the World Bank Group Report,[66] "*at the end of 2021, the outstanding green loans of major Chinese banks reached US$2.3 trillion, up from US$0.85 trillion in 2016, while outstanding green bonds increased to US$254 billion from US$37.6 billion.*" As evidenced by the report, despite this rapid growth, green assets still account for only a fraction of China's financial market, with green loans and bonds making up about 8% and 1%, respectively.[67] This puts in evidence the great potential of green finance in China. However, "green equity markets, especially for early-stage risk capital necessary to spur innovation, remain shallow. The banking and capital market authorities have devised a host of measures to create new markets (such as green bonds) and guide financial institutions toward climate-friendly financing."[68] To this extent, new instruments, such as sustainability-linked bonds and sustainability-labeled investment products, have also emerged and are now ready to rapidly 'conquer' the market simply because there is an increasing demand and need for them. It is also necessary to stress that standards have been developed, updated, and introduced, such as the green project taxonomy[69] — thanks to international cooperation — to

---

[66] *Source*: World Bank Group, China, Country Climate and Development Report, October 2022, document available at: https://openknowledge.worldbank.org/bitstream/handle/10986/38136/FullReport.pdf at p. 73 (accessed January 28, 2023).

[67] *Ibid.*

[68] *Ibid.*

[69] In July 2020, the EU and China initiated a Working Group on taxonomies with the objective of undertaking a comprehensive assessment of the existing taxonomies for environmentally sustainable investments, including identifying the commonalities and differences in their respective approaches and outcomes. The Common Ground Taxonomy (CGT) is a milestone work resulting from an in-depth comparison exercise that puts forward areas of commonality and differences between the EU and China's green taxonomies. As for China, the main significance of green taxonomy reflects the EU's use the EU

reflect the latest international consensus on these new financial products. On this particular aspect, which shows the critical importance of taxonomy to foster the use of green bonds and these new financial instruments, it is worth reporting that on April 21, 2021, in an effort to coordinate green definitions among financial regulators, the BoC, NDRC, and CSRC jointly released an amended version of the Green Bond Endorsed Projects Catalogue (2021 Edition).[70] This represents another major development in China's effort to unify its domestic green definitions. The updated edition of the Green Bond Catalogue,[71] which came into effect on July 1, 2021,

---

does of it; in particular, China's green taxonomy refers to financial services provided for economic activities that are supportive of environment improvement, climate change response, and more efficient resource utilization. These economic activities include the financing, operations, and risk management for projects in areas such as environmental protection, energy savings, clean energy, green transportation, and green buildings. Therefore, the environmental objectives of China's green taxonomy are environmental improvement, climate change response, and more efficient resource utilization. For a comparison between the EU and China taxonomy, refer to the following document: *International Platform on Sustainable Finance — Common Ground Taxonomy — Climate Change Mitigation,* IPSF Taxonomy Working Group Co-chaired by the EU and China, document available at: https://ec.europa.eu/info/sites/default/files/business_economy_euro/banking_and_finance/documents/211104-ipsf-common-ground-taxonomy-instruction-report-2021_en.pdf (accessed January 28, 2023).

[70] On April 21, 2021, in an effort to coordinate green definitions among the financial regulators, the People's Bank of China (PBoC), together with the National Development & Reform Commission (NDRC), and the China Securities & Regulatory Commission (CSRC), jointly released the amended version of the Green Bond Endorsed Projects Catalogue. This represents a major development in China's effort to unify its domestic green definitions. The Green Bond Endorsed Project Catalogue represents the most up-to-date, unified, and clear green definitions at the activity and project level in China. Therefore, the Green Bond Endorsed Projects Catalogue is referred to as the 'Chinese Taxonomy' and used as China's equivalent to the EU Taxonomy for the purposes of comparison.

[71] The Green Bond Endorsed Project Catalogue, 2021 edition: In May 2021, the People's Bank of China (PBoC), China's central bank, the China Securities & Regulatory Commission (CSRC), and the National Development & Reform Commission (NDRC) announced an updated "Green Bonds Endorsed Projects Catalogue" to govern China's green bonds market in a significant consolidation that has implications for investors as the market grows. *Source*: Climate Bonds, document available at: https://www.climatebonds.net/files/files/the-Green-Bond-Endorsed-Project-Catalogue-2021-Edition-110521.pdf (accessed January 28, 2023).

has multiple objectives: (i) building a green financial system, (ii) regulating the green bond market further, (iii) promoting structural transformation, (iv) accelerating the ecological civilization construction, and (v) facilitating sustainable economic development in cohesion with other existing frameworks. The consolidation of the multiple preexisting green bond catalogues means that going forward, the identification of the 'green' attributes of all bonds will be based on the criteria of the updated and domestically harmonized catalogue, regardless of their type or the market in which they are issued. Naturally, this move contributes to the further development of green finance in China although the financial system faces significant challenges in responding to the needs of the market, in particular regarding the green investment demand. As reported in the abovementioned World Bank Group Report, the energy sector and transport infrastructure alone would require US$14-17 trillion worth of additional green investments in 2020–2060 (or 1.14% of GDP) to reach the carbon neutrality goal set by the government. It is worth noting that "*the energy sector, particularly, presents the largest source of climate finance demand, but it has experienced consistently large financing gaps. For example, to support clean power generation, energy storage, and grid investments, the electricity industry is estimated to require 49% of total net-zero financing.*"[72] However, according to the report, less than 28% of green loans and bonds go to clean energy and power sectors currently. Given the current situation, it is evident that the green financial sector in China has great development potential, but this will be possible only upon continuing to foster it with new policies also aimed at pushing the decarbonization of China's economy. New policies should better address the risk of greenwashing. On this point, it is necessary to stress that the regulatory frameworks for climate-related disclosure and the audit and assurance market are yet to be formulated. It appears evident that China, in order to fully express the potential of its green finance, needs to address the unique challenges of this sector and accelerate broader financial sector reforms.

[72] In this sense, see the World Bank Group, China, Country Climate and Development Report, October 2022, document available at: https://openknowledge.worldbank.org/bitstream/handle/10986/38136/FullReport.pdf at p. 74 (accessed January 18, 2023). According to China International Capital Corporation Ltd. (CICC) estimates, the transport sector has the second largest financing need, equivalent to US$5.9 trillion in 2020–2060, or 2% of total net-zero financing, followed by the building sector (US$3.5 trillion, 16%), industrials (US$1.3 trillion, 6%), and agriculture (US$0.6 trillion, 3%).

This will improve capital allocation across the board and will allow a flow of new capital resources for green transition.

It is evident that China is yet to fully harness financial product innovations for green transition. As emphasized in the World Bank report, green loans account for about 95% of total green financing.[73] However, despite this market expansion, the share of bond financing remains small. Moreover, there is a significant shortfall of equity financing. Green equity funding, including from private and public markets, remains very limited and accounts for only 3% of total green-labeled financing (Lan 2021).[74]

Although the Chinese green finance market is very promising, financial product innovations are lacking, and authorities are well aware about the following: (i) the need for these financial instruments to help green transition and help China reach its carbon neutrality goals; (ii) the necessity for further regulatory inputs to expand the market for green financial instruments. It is noteworthy that sustainability-linked bonds were inaugurated in 2021 but authorized in a sub-segment of the bond market only. This is limiting the circulation of these instruments. Financial authorities should work toward ameliorating their regulatory frameworks and guidance, allowing the diffusion of these innovative financial instruments and ensuring that funds are used precisely for their scope.

4.2. *Green finance to support China's decarbonization goals: Priority should be given to the private sector and not only to SOEs*

Green finance has the scope to support China's decarbonization as evidenced in the World Bank Report. However, from the report, it also emerges that the financial sector and credit market favors SOEs,[75] even

---

[73] *Source*: *Develop Green Finance to Support Carbon Neutrality*. Issue No. 2110. Beijing: International Monetary Institute of Renmin University of China (Lan 2021).

[74] *Ibid.*

[75] According to the World Bank report "*State-owned enterprises (SOEs) continue to play a dominant role in China's economy, especially in carbon-intensive sectors. SOEs are estimated to account for around 25 to 40% of GDP and around 40% of employment. SOEs control value chains for sectors responsible, directly or indirectly, for the majority of China's emissions: coal, electricity, oil, gas, steel, and cement. It is estimated that SOEs generate about half of the country's total GHG emissions. Addressing emissions generated by SOEs will therefore form a key component of reaching China's goal of carbon neutrality*

though private firms are more productive in low-carbon transformation. The report by the World Bank affirms that "private firms exhibit significant higher levels of productivity in key decarbonization sectors, but their access to green credit is limited: most renewable energy bank lending has gone to SOEs, which also received more long-term financing than private firms.[76] Private issuers have become an increasingly marginal group in the green bond market, accounting for only 3.3% of issuances and 1.6% of total bonds value in 2021."[77] If China is to reach carbon neutrality before 2060, it is therefore necessary to adjust the growing flow of green investments and give priority to the private sector which can represent a driver for the green transition. It is natural that SOEs will continue to receive the government's support but their green contribution is not as pronounced as it should be, and this emphasizes the necessity for further reforms concerning the SOEs, not only to ameliorate their efficiency but also to respond to the need to transform the Chinese industry into a more sustainable model. SOEs' dominance has some advantages but could also impair efficient decarbonization.[78]

---

before 2060. Source: World Bank Group, China, Country Climate and Development Report, October 2022, at p. 70.

[76] SOEs are estimated to have received 79% of total bank lending for renewable energy projects and 61% more long-term loans (over 10 years) in value terms than unlisted private borrowers (Bloomberg Finance L.P. 2021).

[77] In this sense World Bank Group, China, Country Climate and Development Report, October 2022 (see 'Green Finance,' section).

[78] *State dominance has given the government significant capacity to implement low-carbon policies, including for instance the rapid scale-up of renewable energy in recent years However, there is also evidence that suggests that China's state sector is one of the constraints to faster productivity growth, with SOEs exhibiting large and persistent productivity gaps with private firms. Research has shown that the total factor productivity (TFP) performance gap is greater in key carbon-intensive industries such as utilities, transportation, steelmaking, and chemical manufacturing. Yet, SOEs tend to have easier access to bank credit and more favorable loan terms, compared to private companies. Moreover, dominant market positions of SOEs and an unpredictable regulatory environment may impair dynamic market entry by private sector investors, which can play an important role in driving innovation and diffusion of new technologies. For example, following abrupt regulatory changes to China's renewable subsidy policy and feed-in-tariffs in 2018, the private market share in solar power fell from more than 70% of installed capacity to less than 40% by the end of 2019. Source*: World Bank Group, China, Country Climate and Development Report, October 2022 at p. 70.

In order to allow the private sector to access more resources, the use of 'blended finance' is also suggested,[79] which will mobilize commercial capital for underfinanced climate ventures and sectors. "*Financial sector authorities could explore ways to unlock the catalytic function of available concessional finance, including from domestic policy banks, public capital, donor and philanthropic funds, and international development financial institutions. Given the significant shortfall of early-stage climate financing, supervisors of the investment fund industry (the China Securities Regulatory Commission [CSRC] and the Asset Management Association of China [AMAC]*[80]*) may want to add blended finance to their work priorities, authorize pilots, and devise regulatory measures*."[81] The report also suggests that the authorities should consider relaxing market access for foreign institutional investors, especially those that demonstrate good climate investing records. Numerous local pilots of the Qualified Foreign Limited Partner (QFLP) program[82] could be converted into a national scheme, with a streamlined approval process and larger quota.

---

[79]The World Bank Group in its report evidences the necessity to use blended finance to respond to the needs of the private sectors to meet their climate goals. Document available at: https://openknowledge.worldbank.org/bitstream/handle/10986/38136/FullReport.pdf accessed January 18 (accessed January 28, 2023, see "Green Finance" section).

[80]The Asset Management Association of China (AMAC) was established on June 6, 2012 to be the self-regulatory organization that represents the mutual funds industry of China. The website is available only in Chinese at: https://www.amac.org.cn/.

[81]*Source*: World Bank Group, China, Country Climate and Development Report, October 2022.

[82]The Qualified Foreign Limited Partnership (QFLP) is a pilot program developed by various local authorities serving as an essential channel for foreign investors to invest in China's financial market. Under QFLP, foreign investors are able to participate in the establishment of a foreign-funded equity investment management enterprise (QFLP Manager) or a foreign-funded equity investment enterprise (QFLP Fund) (QFLP Manager and QFLP Fund are collectively referred to as QFLP Enterprises). The most obvious advantage of QFLP is that foreign exchange funds can be settled in RMB at the fund level and make equity investment in RMB; in other words, foreign exchange settlement will be approved in advance at the time when a QFLP enterprise is set up, instead of when the capital is called. China has introduced various forms of foreign investments in the gradual process of opening up its capital market to foreign investors. By taking the form of overseas institutional investors (including qualified foreign institutional investors (QFII) and RMB qualified foreign institutional investors (RQFII)) or QFLPs, foreign capital may invest in China's securities market as well as the equity of private companies and start-ups,

4.3. *China's green finance regulatory framework: A brief introduction*

In order to achieve environmental friendly growth and create an inclusive decarbonization pathway, China is implementing a comprehensive framework (1 + *N* framework, see Chapter 3) including the green and sustainable finance sectors,[83] which need to be fine-tuned to favor their evolution. This section is intended to offer a brief panorama of the main initiatives of the Chinese authorities with regard to green finance. Because green finance and sustainable finance in China are governed by a myriad of measures and policies (also at Municipal level), in this short section, only the most relevant and recent regulatory measures are mentioned.

Green finance is quickly gaining momentum in China driven by both the new environmental goals and the concept of 'ecological civilization' which was endorsed by President Xi. China's objectives to achieve peak carbon emissions by 2030 and carbon neutrality (net-zero greenhouse gas emissions) by 2060, known as the so-called 'Dual Carbon goals,' need to be accompanied by a further evolution of the financial system and a dedicated framework for green and sustainable finance to allow the retrieval of financial resources to ensure that these objectives are met. This specific regulatory framework started to take shape in 2016 with the 'Guidelines

---

which are otherwise inaccessible to foreign investors. More information concerning the Qualified Limited Partnership available at Lexology's website available at: https://www.lexology.com/library/detail.aspx?g=65a2ef79-f9be-46c1-85d1-70c8191c06b7 (accessed January 28, 2023).

[83] Finance supporting the transition to a low-carbon economy includes the following: (i) climate finance: finance in support of low-carbon transition only, so its scope is narrower than green finance; (ii) sustainable finance: finance in support of one or more of the 17 United Nations Sustainable Development Goals (SDGs), and is used and accepted more internationally; (iii) ESG finance: similar to and sometimes used jointly with sustainable finance, it is more specifically in relation to the support of environmental, social, and governance goals; and (iv) transition finance: a relatively new concept, which is finance that helps high-carbon companies to implement long-term changes to become greener or low carbon. Chinese financial sectors are actively exploring ways to develop both green finance and transition finance as well as to enhance the coordination between transition finance and green finance regimes. See PBoC: Achieving a Smooth Coordination Between Green Finance and Transition Finance, available at: https://finance.sina.com.cn/china/gncj/2022-04-07/doc-imcwipii2923633.shtml (accessed January 28, 2023).

for Establishing a Green Financial System' (《关于构建绿色金融体系的指导意见》).[84] Another important step was the adoption of the updated version of the 'Green Bond Project Catalogue' in 2021 to replace the previous version issued in 2015. The catalogue brought some important changes of China's taxonomy to sustainable finance, for example, clean use of coal and removal of several fossil fuel projects from the 2021 Catalogue. The 2021 Catalogue also adopted the internationally accepted principle of 'no adverse material impact' in green-bond-supported projects. This is an important example of China's interest in participating in international initiatives in an effort to align Chinese taxonomies with internationally recognized taxonomy frameworks and principles. Noteworthily, China is also participating in the Network of Central Banks and Supervisors for Greening the Financial System (NGFS)[85] and International Platform on Sustainable Finance (IPSF).[86] Regarding this

---

[84]On August 31, 2016, the People's Bank of China, along with six other government agencies, issued the "Guidelines for Establishing the Green Financial System" (Yinfa 2016 Doc No 228). These guidelines provide an essential next step for implementing the overall strategy of promoting ecological civilization, formulated by the Central Party Committee and the State Council. The Guidelines are the basis of China's green financial system. Visit: http://www.pbc.gov.cn/english/130721/3131759/index.html (accessed January 28, 2023).

[85]The Network of Central Banks and Supervisors for Greening the Financial System (NGFS) was launched at the Paris One Planet Summit on December 12, 2017 and is a group of Central Banks and Supervisors willing, on a voluntary basis, to share best practices and contribute to the development of environment and climate risk management in the financial sector and to mobilize mainstream finance to support the transition toward a sustainable economy. Its purpose is to define, promote, and contribute to the development of best practices to be implemented within and outside of the Membership of the NGFS and to conduct or commission analytical work on green finance. More info available at: https://www.ngfs.net/en (accessed January 28, 2023).

See also: Joint statement by the Founding Members of the Central Banks and Supervisors Network for Greening the Financial System — One Planet Summit at: https://www.banque-france.fr/en/communique-de-presse/joint-statement-founding-members-central-banks-and-supervisors-network-greening-financial-system-one.

[86]The International Platform on Sustainable Finance (IPSF) was launched on October 18, 2019. Its members are public authorities from Argentina, Canada, Chile, China, India, Indonesia, Kenya, Morocco, Norway, Switzerland, and the European Union, representing almost half of the world's greenhouse gas emissions. The International Platform aims to (i) exchange and disseminate information to promote best practices in environmentally

international cooperation, it is worth noting that in November 2021, and with an updated version in June 2022, the EU and China (the EU Commission and the People's Bank of China) published the Common Ground Taxonomy reports[87] with an aim to provide more clarity and transparency about the commonalities and differences between taxonomies and potentially contribute to lowering the transboundary cost of sustainable investments. It was also reported that Bank of China's Frankfurt branch issued the first green bonds under the new China–EU Common Ground Taxonomy.[88]

---

sustainable finance; (ii) compare the different initiatives and identify barriers and opportunities to help scale up environmentally sustainable finance internationally; (iii) respect national and regional contexts, enhance international coordination where appropriate on environmentally sustainable finance issues. Where appropriate, some willing members could strive to align initiatives and approaches. *Source*: https://www.switch-asia.eu/resource/international-platform-on-sustainable-finance-ipsf/ (accessed January 28, 2023).

[87]On November 4, 2021, the International Platform on Sustainable Finance taxonomy working group unveiled the "EU–China Common Ground Taxonomy — Climate Change Mitigation (CGT)." This in-depth comparison identifies commonalities and differences between the EU and China's taxonomies and is expected to improve the comparability and interoperability of global sustainable finance standards. To avoid confusion, China's taxonomy here refers to the China Green Bond Endorsed Projects Catalogue (2021 Edition), released in April 2021. The first report is available at: https://finance.ec.europa.eu/system/files/2021-12/211104-ipsf-common-ground-taxonomy-instruction-report-2021_en.pdf; the second updated report of 3 June 2022 is available at: https://finance.ec.europa.eu/system/files/2022-06/220603-international-platform-sustainable-finance-common-ground-taxonomy-instruction-report_en.pdf; all the working documents of the IPSF are available at: https://finance.ec.europa.eu/sustainable-finance/international-platform-sustainable-finance_en#main (accessed January 28, 2023). A summary of the contents of this first version of the report is available at: https://gsh.cib.natixis.com/our-center-of-expertise/articles/eu-china-common-ground-taxonomy-a-painkiller-to-taxonomy-headaches A more in-depth analysis of the 3 June 2022 report is available at: https://gsh.cib.natixis.com/our-center-of-expertise/articles/updated-common-ground-taxonomy-the-crowbar-of-international-green-capital-flows.

[88]*June 20, 2022, Bank of China (BoC) Frankfurt Branch's first green bonds, aligned with the Common Ground Taxonomy Climate Change Mitigation (CGT Updated Version), is admitted to the Open Market at the Frankfurt Stock Exchange and will be available for trading on the China Europe International Exchange AG (CEINEX) in Frankfurt. This USD 500 million 3-year senior unsecured fixed rate offering, drawdown under BoC's USD 40 billion Medium Term Note Programme, is aligned with the updated version of CGT, which is published by the International Platform for Sustainable Finance (IPSF).*

Green finance industry standardization is also a priority for the government. China in fact has issued multiple green-finance-related industry standards during 2021 and 2022, and although these latest regulatory developments are not for mandatory application, these standards serve as guidelines and institutional capacity building for the green finance system in China. The standards are as follows:

- *"In July 2021, People's Bank of China (PBoC) released the Financial Institutions Environmental Information Disclosure Guideline (JR/T 0227-2021).*[89] *It provided guidelines on how financial institutions should disclose environmental information in a standardized and structured way.*
- *In July 2021, PBoC released the Environmental Rights Financing Tools (JR/T 0228-2021),*[90] *which set out general requirements and process of financing based on environmental rights. The environmental rights included the right to discharge pollutants, rights to emit emissions, right to use water, right to use energy.*
- *In April 2022, China Securities Regulatory Commission (CSRC) released the Carbon Financial Products (JR/T0244-2022).*[91] *It defined*

The Bank has opted a two-day execution strategy to introduce to the market the first offering in alignment with the CGT Updated Version, achieving oversubscription by market participants. The proceeds of this bond will be used to finance and/or refinance 14 green projects in renewable energy, clean transportation, and energy efficiency located both in China and Europe. Source: http://ceinex.sinope.de/press-releases/bank-of-china-frankfurt-branch-successfully-lists-its-first-green-bond-on-ceinex-in-frankfurt.html (accessed January 28, 2023).

[89]PBoC Financial Industry Standard of the People's Republic of China, JR/T 0227-2021, Guidelines on Environmental Information Disclosure for Financial Institutions, document available in English at: https://www.chinadevelopmentbrief.org/wp-content/uploads/2021/08/Guidelines-for-financial-institutions-environmental-information-disclosure.pdf (accessed January 28, 2023).

[90]*PBoC released the Environmental Rights Financing Tools (JR/T 0228—2021*, document available in Chinese at: https://www.cfstc.org/bzgk/gk/view/yulan.jsp?i_id=1926&s_file_id=1868 (accessed (January 28, 2023).

[91]China Securities Regulatory Commission, 'Carbon Financial Products' [*Tan Jinrong Chanpin* 碳金融产品 (JR/T 0244-2022)], Financial Industry Standards of the People's Republic of China, April 12, 2022,: http://www.csrc.gov.cn/csrc/c101954/c2334725/2334725/files/%E9%99%84%E4%BB%B62%EF%BC%9A%E7%A2%B3%E9%87%91%E8%9E%8D%E4%BA%A7%E5%93%81.pdf this document is available in Chinese only (accessed January 28, 2023).

various notions of carbon financial products and classified carbon financial products into three categories: carbon market financing tools, carbon market trading tools (derivatives), and carbon market support tools."[92]

Recently, in China, to 'flank' green finance and give further impetus to initiatives aimed at tackling climate change, a new sector emerged, namely, 'Climate finance.' In October 2020, five departments in China jointly issued the 'Guiding Opinions on Promoting the Investment and Financing in Response to Climate Change'[93] (《关于促进应对气候变化投融资的指导意见》). These guiding opinions stated that climate finance is part of green finance, and climate finance should benefit both climate mitigation and climate adaptation activities.

It is also necessary to stress that in order to thoroughly implement the major strategic decisions of carbon peaking and carbon neutrality and to explore differentiated institutional mechanisms for climate investment and financing, on December 23, 2021, the MEE together with other eight administrative bodies and finance intuitions (i.e., the National Development and Reform Commission (NDRC), Ministry of Industry and Information Technology (MIIT), Ministry of Housing and Urban–Rural Development (MoHURD), PBoC, State Asset Supervision and Administration Commission of the State of Council (SASAC), China Banking and Insurance Regulatory Commission (CBIRC), China Securities Regulatory Commission (CSRC), and the National Government Office Administration) circulated the *Notice of the Pilot Work on Climate Investment and Financing* (and attached the drafted *Climate Investment and Financing Pilot Work Scheme*), which is regarded as the decision to launch the climate finance and investment

---

[92] *Source*: *China's green finance — Key recent development*, Herbert Smith Freehills, document available at: https://hsfnotes.com/fsrandcorpcrime/2022/07/12/chinas-green-finance-key-recent-developments/ (accessed January 18, 2023).

[93] *Guiding Opinions on Promoting Investment and Financing to Address Climate Change* jointly issued by Ministry of Ecology and Environment National Development and Reform Commission People's Bank of China, China Banking and Insurance Regulatory Commission China Securities Regulatory Commission, this document is available at: https://www.sbfnetwork.org/wp-content/assets/policy-library/340_China_Guidance_on_promoting_investment_and_financing_to_address_climate_change_2020_PBOC.pdf (accessed January 28, 2023).

pilot work.[94] Noteworthily, "with Chinese national carbon market entering into full operation in July 2021, new forms of climate or carbon finance might be developed alongside the carbon market. For example, Beijing Green Exchange released in 2016 contract templates for carbon asset repurchase, carbon swaps and carbon options for use in the carbon market."[95]

Finally, it is also worth noting that on 1 June 2022, the China Banking and Insurance Regulatory Commission (CBIRC) issued the *Banking and Insurance Sector Green Finance Guidelines*.[96] This is the first document to use the notion of *Environment, Social, and Governance* (ESG) and to ask banks and insurance agencies to effectively incorporate the concept of ESG into their business. For example, the banks and insurance agencies are required to identify, monitor, and prevent ESG risks in their business, enhance ESG disclosure and stakeholder participation, require its client contracts to include terms to elevate the ESG performance of their

---

[94] Climate Investment and Financing Pilot Working Program (气候投融资试点工作方案). Climate investment and financing refers to the investment and financing of activities which guide and mobilize incremental capital to address climate change in order to achieve the NDC and low-carbon development. Climate investment and financing is an important part of green finance. The scope of support includes both mitigation and adaptation. For more information on this Program visit: https://climatecooperation.cn/climate/mee-and-other-government-bodies-publish-the-notice-of-the-pilot-work-on-climate-investment-and-financing-and-attach-the-drafted-climate-investment-and-financing-pilot-work-scheme/ (accessed January 28, 2023).

[95] *Source*: *China's green finance — Key recent development*, Herbert Smith Freehills, document available at: https://hsfnotes.com/fsrandcorpcrime/2022/07/12/chinas-green-finance-key-recent-developments/ (accessed January 28, 2023).

[96] On June 1, 2022, the China Banking and Insurance Regulatory Commission (CBIRC) issued the "*Green Finance Guidelines for the Banking and Insurance Industry.*" The document consolidates the 2019 Guidelines on the high-quality development for the Banking and Insurance Industry and focuses particularly on green banking (e.g., green loans, green credit) and insurance industry. It addresses banking and insurance institutions "to prevent environmental, social and governance (ESG) risks" and "to strengthen ESG information disclosure and interaction with stakeholders." The document describes how banking and insurance institutions should integrate the ESG requirements into management processes and risk management systems. The entire document is available at: https://www.cbirc.gov.cn/en/view/pages/ItemDetail.html?docId=1055048&itemId=981 (accessed January 28, 2023).

clients, conduct ESG due diligence as part of their investment decision-making.[97]

4.4. *China's international cooperation in green finance shall reinforce its leading position*

There is no doubt that China is consolidating its leading position in green finance: China's green bond issuance has more than doubled in 2021[98] as the nation works on its climate goals. It is evident that in the international context China's green finance will further gain the interest of foreign investors, but to achieve this, it is necessary to continue the harmonization process evidenced by the collaboration with the European Union. This cooperation shall reinforce China's green finance system and instill more confidence among investors because harmonization (in particular, with the adoption of a common taxonomy) is the path to creating a uniform market for new green financial products.

However, besides the harmonization of Chinese and European standards, it is necessary to stress that both blocks are also cooperating to support green finance development globally. The harmonization of green finance systems is of particular relevance and importance for two main reasons: (i) First, environmental risks, particularly climate risks, are global and therefore need to be tackled on a global level with the participation of all nations if we want to reach concrete results; (ii) second, with harmonized standards, it will be possible to accelerate capital flows and, in particular, cross-border capital flows.[99]

The recent developments in the Chinese regulatory framework introducing EGS requirements are focused on real-world outcomes. The new guidelines mentioned earlier (the 'CBIRC Guidelines,' see 2.2) go beyond requiring financial institutions to incorporate ESG factors in investment

---

[97] *Source*: *China's green finance — Key recent development*, Herbert Smith Freehills.

[98] *Source*: *China Green Bond Market Report 2021*. According to the report, China is very likely to reach its carbon peaking goal before 2030. Document available at: https://www.climatebonds.net/resources/reports/china-green-bond-market-report-2021.

[99] *Source*: Green Finance and Development Center, *To meet Global Green Finance Needs, the EU and China Must cooperate*, document available at: https://greenfdc.org/to-meet-global-green-finance-needs-the-eu-and-china-must-cooperate/ (accessed January 28, 2023).

decisions and risk management processes. The guidelines explicitly require the banking and insurance institutions[100] to align portfolios with carbon neutrality goals and prevent and address adverse impacts on the environment and society, but they are not limited to this. In fact, "*the guidelines view institutional investors both as capital providers and as stewards who can support and enable the green transition of the economy and society. This includes driving decarbonisation solutions, enabling the transition of carbon intensive industries and curbing the expansion of high emission projects. Banking and insurance institutions are required to exercise investor rights and embed clauses in investment contracts to ensure adequate ESG risk management at investee companies, setting out milestones and targets for assessing and tracking investees' ESG performance, and establishing channels of engagement for stakeholders.*"[101] In this context, it appears appropriate that the CBIRC guidelines mark a significant step forward on China's road to establishing a robust regulatory framework for sustainable investment. And their impact could go far beyond the banking and insurance sectors, influencing all the other industrial sectors.

By requiring the banking and the insurance sectors to manage ESG-related risks of overseas projects, the guidelines could also have significant impacts beyond China's borders. It is evident that all the recent regulatory developments in China indicate an increasing alignment between Chinese regulators and the international standards on green and sustainable finance. China is creating a more sophisticated framework in line with the expectations of major investor initiatives like the Glasgow Financial Alliance for Net Zero (GFANZ)[102] — which calls on investors to help finance the net-zero transition for the whole economy.

---

[100] It is noted by the financial industry that "*the actions of banking and insurance companies will cascade down the investment chain and influence asset managers and service providers, becoming a key driver for mainstreaming responsible investing. This will help with the ongoing alignment of financial flows with carbon neutrality and sustainable development goals in China.*" *Source*: Principle for Responsible Investment, *China raises the bar on investor regulations to promote green finance*, article published on October 19, 2022, document available at: https://www.unpri.org/pri-blog/china-raises-the-bar-on-investor-regulations-to-promote-green-finance/10659.article.

[101] *Source*: Green Finance and Development Center, *To meet Global Green Finance Needs, the EU and China Must cooperate.*

[102] Glasgow Financial Alliance for Net Zero (GFANZ) was launched in April 2021 by the UN Special Envoy on Climate Action and Finance Mark Carney and the COP26

China is emerging as the leading global market in green and sustainable financing. The new policies that China is adopting to foster its green market will lead to a more sophisticated market thanks to the cooperation with the EU to standardize this sector; also, given the size of its market, there is no doubt that China is destined to become the biggest market for these new financial products. Another factor which is favoring the rise of 'China green finance' is the fact that President Xi Jinping is sustaining China's climate change target pledges, and with his third mandate a new impetus will be given to China's efforts to tackle climate change, pushing the growth of 'Green Finance' further. This is in consideration of the fact that new resources are badly needed to meet its goals of peak carbon emissions by 2030 and carbon neutrality by 2060.

5. China's Green Financial Market is Set to Become the Biggest Green Market in the World

China's green finance development continues to accelerate as shown by data; however, regulatory adjustments are needed in order for the green financial sector to fully express its potential. China's green financial system should strengthen its work in terms of (i) defining clear and unified green finance standards (work in progress); (ii) making green finance more popular; (iii) encouraging innovation and arousing financial markets' interest in green products (harmonizing regulatory frameworks); (iv) improving the information disclosure and supervision mechanism of green projects along with improving risk prevention and control (work in progress); and (v) deepening international cooperation to make green finance a global chorus.

---

presidency, in partnership with the UNFCCC Race to Zero campaign, to coordinate efforts across all sectors of the financial system to accelerate the transition to a net-zero global economy. GFANZ is a global coalition of leading financial institutions committed to accelerating the decarbonization of the economy; for example, it recently recommended that investors develop a net-zero transition plan, setting out goals, actions, and accountability mechanisms to align their business activities with net zero. See https://assets.bbhub.io/company/sites/63/2022/06/GFANZ_Recommendations-and-Guidance-on-Net-zero-Transition-Plans-for-the-Financial-Sector_June2022.pdf. At all points, the emphasis is on delivering emissions reductions in the real economy. Visit: https://www.gfanzero.com/ (accessed January 28, 2023).

China is well aware that still there is a lot of work to do in order to align its financial market to the more advanced economies, and the concerned authorities are working to improve and complete the regulatory framework to achieve this objective and to favor further development of green and sustainable finance. As a matter of fact, China's green finance market presents extremely good growth potential, but it needs to be supported to its complete maturation. To this extent, international cooperation is the best way forward to allow this sector to fully express its full potential. However, the major drive for further development of green finance is represented by the dual carbon strategies (the 2030/2060 pledges) adopted by China. In fact, tremendous investment and financing are needed to achieve these goals which are strictly connected with the green economic transition now embraced by China in its new development phase. Naturally, this will create huge growth opportunities for the entire financial industry, and there is no doubt that China's green financial sector is destined to become the biggest market in the world due to the enormous financial resources needed to transition China toward green and sustainable development.

5.1. *The importance of China's green financial market and its prospects*

It must be stressed that China has built one of the world's largest green financing ecosystems in only a fraction of the time the major economies have developed theirs,[103] but this is still a tiny part of the country's entire financial sector and it will need to grow much further to fund the country's climate change goals as evidenced in the previous sections.

President Xi's carbon neutrality targets are giving further impetus to the green financial market; however, the real driver for the latest developments of green finance in China is its economic growth. It is evident that China's development needs to be converted into a more sustainable and nature-positive modality to meet its goals, and the new resources needed

[103] China has increasingly promoted green finance since the People's Bank of China (PBoC) issued its Guidelines for Establishing the Green Financial System in 2016. China did not have a green bond market in 2015. China's rapidly evolving green finance system over the past few years was underpinned by coordinated macroeconomic policy, regulatory, institutional, and technological developments.

for this transformation will be derived from the green finance sector. China has no choice but to enhance its financial system and thus accelerate sustainable finance and green finance to accompany its green transition. China will accomplish its objectives by increasing its capabilities of financing the necessary measures to mitigate its impact on climate change by reducing its emissions. However, it is evident that in order to produce the desired results at the global level, it will be necessary to act in a concerted manner with the rest of the international financial community, which will equally support the green transition globally with new resources.

5.2. *China is moving to enhance its green finance market*

China's green finance market is set to become one of the most important markets in the world, but improving the policy framework, refining and completing the regulatory measures, is only one part of the job that authorities have to work on. The other part is to incentivize financial institutions, investors, and corporations to allocate their financial resources into this sector. In substance, the task of the Chinese legislator is to favor green investments through incentives and a more clear and transparent regulatory framework. On this particular aspect, it is worth noting and reporting the following observations:

- "*On fiscal incentives, a number of local governments introduced interest subsidies and provided credit guarantee and risk compensation to investors of green loans and green bonds. In 2017, eight cities in five provinces (Zhejiang, Jiangxi, Guangdong, Guizhou and Xinjiang) set up pilot zones of green finance reform and innovation. Sichuan province offered interest subsidies to local financial institutions which issue green financial bonds, while Jiangsu provinces offered 30% interest subsidies for two years on green corporate bonds. Last year, Shenzhen government offered green credit enhancement scheme which compensates lenders for up to 50% of the notional amount of green loans in the event of default, and 50% interest subsidies to the low carbon emission enterprise borrowers.*
- *Additional incentives being considered include the possible relaxation of risk weighting requirement on green assets for commercial banks. This will provide some relief on the capital charge for green loans and*

promote green lending. The next step It is critical to integrate climate with environmental, social and governance (ESG) risks in assessing investment opportunities by corporations and investors to promote sustainability. Enhanced disclosure obligation (ESG disclosure or non-financial disclosure) by corporations, borrowers and investors is therefore a key regulatory requirement to support the growth of China's green finance."[104]

There is no doubt that China will introduce new measures to foster the expansion of its green and sustainable finance sector because it is conducive to the pursuit of its climate goals and thus to development in harmony with nature. As a matter of fact, green finance has become an unstoppable force in the financial sector, and surely it will lead to shaping a green economy in China. To speed up the transition to a green economy, the financial industry must develop green features in its operations and trust financial novelty means to change the investing positioning of businesses.

China's green finance was able to give shape to different products in only a few years and, thanks to these wide ranging products, the green financial market is now more competitive. Foreign investors are looking at this market with growing interest, though, as just mentioned, China needs to further refine its financial system.

International cooperation remains a fundamental aspect which needs to be further expanded in order to favor green finance globally. This will naturally help the global community in shaping sustainable development and a global green economy.

In the following box, experts have expressed their views on how to further promote the development of green finance.

As a very significant move to enhance China's green finance, it would be better to integrate this market into the global green finance market. China is actively collaborating with both advanced and developing countries to further develop the global green finance market because harmonized taxonomy and standards will push green transition at global level

[104]In this sense, see the article by Linan Liu, *China: Green Finance to green transition*, available at: https://www.dbresearch.com/PROD/RPS_EN-PROD/PROD0000000000513737/China%3A_Green_finance_to_green_transition.pdf?undefined&realload=yhTpRtpFMB7CURcxAoK50zgPDHxXuYyCIfWwHsJnVCJ8fkJNyiBkw7v047lfyjMn (accessed January 18, 2023).

How to Promote Further Development of Green Finance

1. *To encourage the development of green finance, governments should use fiscal policies to direct credit funds and social capital into green investments, credit, and securities. Fiscal funding should direct credit funds and social capital into a green investment, credit, and securities.*
2. *In the approval process, green operations must be prioritized and the application procedure must be streamlined for environmentally friendly and low-carbon businesses.*
3. *The government should offer program support for green financial growth in underdeveloped regions, lower the issuance and trading thresholds for green bonds and securities, and prioritize initial public offerings of green concept companies, such as new energy, to encourage green financial development.*
4. *Provincial financial institutions should serve as trailblazers in developing environmentally friendly finance practices. Insurance, credit, and funds for the environment all play a significant role in implementing green finance policies.*
5. *As the primary vehicle for implementation, financial institutions should offer green financial instruments to relevant businesses, while also accelerating the alteration and promotion of usual enterprises.*
6. *Green financing should be efficient, and green loans should be readily available. Banks should also provide financial assistance to environmentally friendly businesses. Other financial institutions should be actively involved in the development and upgradation of financial technology, the support of enterprise financing, and the exploration of enterprise value.*
7. *Financial institutions should first organize internal cooperation, optimize business procedures, and create environmental awareness among their personnel to encourage the development of green financing in enterprises.*[105]

as well. Thus, continued cooperation with international entities such as the G20, the 'Network of Central Banks,' and 'Supervisors for Greening the Financial System' is of fundamental importance. China should continue to

[105] In this sense, see Lining Xing, Jun Li and Zhang Yu, *Green Finance Strategies for the Zero-Carbon Mechanism: Public Spending as New Determinants of Sustainable Development*, in Frontier in Environmental Science, July 8, 2022, full article available at https://www.frontiersin.org/articles/10.3389/fenvs.2022.925678/full (accessed January 18, 2023).

pursue multilateralism and global coordination in green finance by both sharing its own experience and learning from the best practices from other countries. "*This acknowledges that the US and Europe are leading the development of parts of the green finance market. Over the medium term, China's domestic capital market is expected to increasingly open up to foreigners both for financing and investment. As part of this, China is expected to gradually integrate its green finance market with the global market in taxonomy, financial and regulatory incentives, and green products specifications.*"[106]

5.3. *The contribution of China's green finance in shaping a sustainable and nature-friendly economy*

As has emerged from this chapter, China is now one of the world's most active and fast growing green financial markets, and its green finance system is also expected to play an important role in helping China achieving its 'dual carbon goals,' namely, to peak emissions before 2030 and become a carbon-neutral economy before 2060. China is using green finance to transform the country into a sustainable model, greening its industry and pushing renewables in order to reduce emissions derived from fossil fuels. In fact, the main aim of green finance is to reduce carbon emissions through green project financing and providing funds for green environmental protection projects, including funds to develop, or enhance, the technologies needed to produce clean and green energy. This tendency is well evidenced in the most advanced economies where renewables are becoming the new focus for sustainable development (especially after the cost of energy dramatically surged due to the invasion of Ukraine). But the trend is growing globally now. It is evident that we need to change our development models to meet the targets of the Paris Convention[107] on

---

[106]In this sense, see the article by Linan Liu, *China: Green Finance to green transition*, available at: https://www.dbresearch.com/PROD/RPS_EN-PROD/PROD0000000000513737/China%3A_Green_finance_to_green_transition.pdf?undefined&realload=yhTpRtpFMB7CURcxAoK50zgPDHxXuYyCIfWwHsJnVCJ8fkJNyiBkw7v047lfyjMn (accessed January 28, 2023).

[107]The Paris Agreement is a legally binding international treaty on climate change. It was adopted by 196 Parties at COP 21 in Paris, on 12 December 2015, and entered into force on 4 November 2016. Its goal is to limit global warming to well below 2 preferably to 1.5 degrees Celsius, compared to pre-industrial levels. For more information about the

climate change, contain the rise of temperatures, and grant a future to the new generations. It is evident that green financial instruments such as green bonds, blue bonds, and similar products (refer to Chapter 5) can help in shaping a more sustainable economy; this could also serve as an important sign of a company's environmental friendliness and consequently stimulate investors' enthusiasm for investment aimed at restoring our environment. Investing in companies which care about nature can also improve the company's environmental commitments. This is particularly feasible and it is happening in countries where green finance is seen as a fundamental element of the green transition and thus favored and supported by governments whose financial systems are more mature and receptive to new green financial products. China is equipping itself with a more sophisticated framework, introducing incentives, and expanding its green finance. This market is destined to become one of the most important green financial markets in the world, and its further development is certainly destined to sustain green transition internally and will have an influence at the international level, favoring globally sustainable nature-friendly development.

Paris Convention, visit the United Nations Climate Change page at: https://unfccc.int/process-and-meetings/the-paris-agreement/the-paris-agreement#:~:text=The%20Paris%20Agreement%20is%20a,compared%20to%20pre%2Dindustrial%20levels. English version available at: https://unfccc.int/sites/default/files/english_paris_agreement.pdf, Chinese version available at: https://unfccc.int/sites/default/files/chinese_paris_agreement.pdf (accessed January 28, 2023).

Chapter 2

China's Vision for a Community with a Shared Future: Multilateralism as Part of the 'Recipe' to Achieve Common Goals through Sustainable and Green Development

President Xi Jinping's vision is to build a community with a shared future in harmony with nature. In order to reach this goal, it is necessary to shape sustainable development. China has now transformed itself into an economic powerhouse after 40 years of a continuous reform process and needs to transition toward a green economy and readjust its policies to not only meet the UN's goals for sustainable development but also preserve our environment and fight climate change before it is too late. Further, China needs to eliminate imbalances created at home and create a more harmonious society. This presents not only challenges but also opportunities. In fact, China is aware that it is necessary to rapidly cut greenhouse emissions to avoid catastrophic consequences for the entire global community, and move it toward a nature-positive economy. However, collective action is needed as internal policies alone are not sufficient. Naturally, investment opportunities will emerge in this transition phase toward a sustainable and green economy, and China is prone to favor and sustain green investments. China's journey toward sustainable and green development through its commitments and actions will take time before producing the expected results. In the meantime, it is necessary to work with the international community to avoid undesirable consequences.

1. China Reinforced Its Role at the International Level but Needs to Work with the Global Community

China is actively contributing to shaping a new multilateralism whihc can change geo-political equilibriums and influences. Such an epochal mutation of the international status quo seems inevitable because China's influence is growing and not only in economic terms. And it is evident the impossibilities of the old great powers to maintain control over the multitude of problems afflicting the entire global community.

In relation to climate change, the necessity to take further actions in concert with the other members of the international community is evident in order to find common solutions before it is too late. China is a strong supporter of the Paris Agreement (also known as Paris Convention)[1] and a leading force in turning the earth greener. China is acting proactively to build a more advanced society in harmony with nature, but in doing so it is necessary to involve the rest of the global community and thus to advance in a united manner to find common ground to face urgent issues, *in primis* climate change. Naturally, China has its own priorities and is forging new agreements such as the *Regional Comprehensive Economic Partnership* (RCEP)[2] which will serve its interests first, rebalancing international spheres of influences and restructuring globalization, which is based on multilateralism, because this is the only way to advance toward a sustainable and sharable future. Only with balanced and shared responsibilities reflecting the capabilities of each nation will it be possible to shape a new global, nature-positive economy meeting the goals of the UN.

1.1. *China's vision for a community with a shared future*

Since the CPC's 18th National Congress in November 2012, President Xi has called for the building of a human community with a shared future.

[1] Paris Agreement, document available at: https://unfccc.int/process-and-meetings/the-paris-agreement/the-paris-agreement (accessed January 28, 2023).

[2] *Regional Comprehensive Economic Partnership* consists of 15 countries: 10 member states of the ASEAN — Association of Southeast Asian Nations; the most important countries are: China, Japan, South Korea, Australia, and New Zealand. The scope of the RCEP is to stimulate intra-East Asian integration.

Since then, Xi's vision for a community with a shared future has gradually developed into a full-fledged concept. Noteworthily, this concept is based on the profound changes in the international situation, development, cooperation, mutual benefit, and an in-depth reflection of the major questions concerning the future of humanity, and thus what kind of world we should build and how we should build it. China has embraced this concept and *three years later* it was presented to the international community when Xi made a speech at the UN Summit on September 27, 2015, titled, "*Build a New Type of International Relations Featuring Win-Win Cooperation, Create a Community of Common Destiny for Mankind.*"[3] This concept was further elaborated. Xi's keynote speech at the UN Office in Geneva on January 18, 2017 presented a fuller picture of this idea for a global community by identifying five specific goals: (i) lasting peace, (ii) common security, (iii) common prosperity, (iv) an open and inclusive world, and (v) a clean and beautiful low-carbon world.[4] In February 2017, the concept of building a community of shared future for mankind was written into a United Nations resolution for the first time.[5] Then, in October 2017, A Community with Shared Future for Mankind was also written into CPC's constitution and included in the preamble of China's constitution the following year.

President Xi links the concept of a "Community with Shared Future for Mankind" with the peaceful coexistence of nations. Thus the four purposes and seven principles are enshrined in the UN Charter[6] as the

[3]*Source*: *Build a New Type of International Relations Featuring Win-Win Cooperation, Create a Community of Common Destiny for Mankind*, Xinhua, September 30, 2015, http://www.china.org.cn/xivisitus2015/2015-09/30/content_36720941.htm (accessed January 28, 2023).

[4]Xi Jinping, "Work Together to Build a Community of Shared Future for Mankind" (speech, Geneva, January 18, 2017), https://america.cgtn.com/2017/01/18/full-text-of-xi-jinping-keynote-speech-at-the-united-nations-office-in-geneva. (accessed January 28, 2023).

[5]The concept was endorsed by the UN and written into several UN resolutions including resolution 2344, related to promoting peace and stability in Afghanistan and the surrounding region, and two resolutions by the UN Human Rights Council on Question of the realization in all countries of economic, social, and cultural rights, and Right to food.

[6]The four purposes of the United Nations are contained in Article 1 and are as follows: "*(1) To maintain international peace and security, to take effective collective measures for the prevention and removal of threats to the peace, and for the suppression of acts of aggression or other breaches of the peace, and to bring about by peaceful means, and in*

main guidelines in building this community. Naturally, the community of the near future should solve unbalanced development, and other global challenges; change the traditional ways of conceptualizing interstate relations and international security; and encourage all countries to direct their priorities toward a sustainable economic development.[7] This community with a shared future should also focus on solutions to transition global economy toward a green, low-carbon economy and pursue a sustainable development mode in line with the goals proclaimed by the UN which are an expression of the thoughts of the entire international community.

---

conformity with the principles of justice and international law, adjustment or settlement of international disputes or situations which might lead to a breach of the peace; (2) To develop friendly relations among nations based on respect for the principle of equal rights and self-determination of peoples, and to take other appropriate measures to strengthen universal peace; (3) To achieve international co-operation in solving international problems of an economic, social, cultural, or humanitarian character, and in promoting and encouraging respect for human rights and for fundamental freedoms for all without distinction as to race, sex, language, or religion; and (4) To be a centre for harmonizing the actions of nations in the attainment of these common ends." Article 2 contains the 7 principles and they are formulated as it follows: "*(1) The Organization is based on the principle of the sovereign equality of all its Members; (2) All Members, in order to ensure, to all of them the rights and benefits resulting from membership, shall fulfill in good faith the obligations assumed by them in accordance with the present Charter; (3) All Members shall settle their international disputes by peaceful means in such a manner that international peace and security, and justice, are not endangered; (4) All Members shall refrain in their international relations from the* ***threat*** *or* ***use of force*** *against the territorial integrity or political independence of any state, or in any other manner inconsistent with the Purposes of the United Nations; (5) All Members shall give the United Nations every assistance in any action it takes in accordance with the present Charter and shall refrain from giving assistance to any state against which the United Nations is taking preventive or enforcement action; (6) The Organization shall ensure that states which are not Members of the United Nations act in accordance with these Principles so far as may be necessary for the maintenance of international peace and security; (7) Nothing contained in the present Charter shall authorize the United Nations to intervene in matters which are essentially within the domestic jurisdiction of any state or shall require the Members to submit such matters to settlement under the present Charter; but this principle shall not prejudice the application of enforcement measures under Chapter VII of the United Nations Charter.*" *Source*: Art. 2 of the UN Charter.

[7]In this sense, see *Chinese Perspective on International Relations in the Xi Jinping Era*, The International Bureau of Asian Research, NBR Special Report #85, June 2020, by Ren Xiao and Liu Ming.

Mother earth is the only home of all of mankind. "*Clear waters and green mountains are as good as mountains of gold and silver. We must maintain harmony between man and nature and pursue sustainable development,*" said President Xi in his speech in Geneva. Xi also emphasized that to protect the earth, we should pursue green, low-carbon development and advance the 2030 UN Agenda for Sustainable Development in a balanced manner.

China is well aware that it is one of the biggest emitters of carbon dioxide together with the US and the EU, thus joint collaboration on climate change management is of paramount importance and should be included in every discussion to shape a new multilateralism for a community with shared future. A community with a shared future for humankind is not just a representation of Xi's personal vision but is also an expression of China's distinctive scheme for a better world order and its desire to play a more prominent role as an international player considering its augmented influence. China can in fact be considered a problem-solver if involved at the international level assuming its policies decided by the central government are quickly translated into reality. China can play an important role in helping to find common ground, such as to preserve enduring world and regional peace, which requires that all stakeholders consult and cooperate with rather than confront each other. It is not surprising that China is seeking a more pragmatic approach with dialogue and consultation to address global issues.

1.1.1. *China is committed to peaceful development but no interferences in internal affairs will be allowed*

In his speech on July 1, 2021, President Xi Jinping stated that "*the Chinese nation does not carry aggressive or hegemonic traits in its genes*" and that "*China has always worked to safeguard world peace, contribute to global development and preserve international order.*" President Xi added that China will stay committed to the path of peaceful development and it will "*promote high-quality development of the Belt and Road initiative (BRI)*[8] *through joint efforts and use China's new achievements in*

[8]Proposed by Xi in 2013, the BRI, which comprises the Silk Road Economic Belt and the 21st Century Maritime Silk Road, aims to build trade and infrastructure networks connecting Asia with Europe and Africa along and beyond the ancient Silk Road routes. The authors in their previous book titled *Belt and Road Initiative — And Its Financial Focus*,

development to provide the world with new opportunities." Noteworthily, a total of 140 countries and regions have signed cooperation agreements with China under the BRI over the past eight years, and the aggregated trade volume between China and its BRI cooperative partners has exceeded $9.2 trillion. Chinese companies have made direct investments totaling over $130 billion in countries along the Belt and Road routes.

In order for China to continue on its path and prosper with its partners, it is absolutely necessary to maintain internal stability and peaceful coexistence with other nations. On this particular aspect, President Xi has underlined that "*We have never bullied, oppressed or subjugated the people of any other country, and we never will*" and again, "*By the same token, we will never allow any foreign force to bully, oppress or subjugate us.*" It is evident that China is interested in contributing to world stability, because this is a basic condition to stimulate and engage in further international trade relations, and to act in a coordinated manner to tackle climate change. However, it is also clear that China will not allow any country to interfere with its internal affairs and internal measures to safeguard its security. Xi in fact reiterated the CPC's stance on Hong Kong, Macao, and the Taiwan region: "*We will ensure that the central government exercises overall jurisdiction over Hong-Kong and Macao, and implement legal system and enforcement mechanisms for the two special administrative regions to safeguard national security.*" As for Taiwan, he described realizing China's complete reunification as a "*historic mission and an unshakable commitment*" of the CPC. These themes should not be put under discussion; however, the primary concern for China is to maintain peace and to forge a more concrete cooperation with the international community for global public goods as it will be explained in the following sections.

1.2. *China sustains the multilateral system but has its own vision for a new global system*

China's development was influenced, and in a sense favored, by multilateralism and this is one of the reasons why it has become a paladin of

---

Yu Xugang, Cristiano Rizzi, Mario Tettamanti, Fabio E. Ziccardi, Guo Li, World Scientific, 2018, explained how the BRI was conceived and its major characteristics. As evidenced in Chapter 1 (p. 5 to p. 54), the Belt and Road Initiative can be seen as a Continuation of China's Reforms and Opening-up and also as a consequence of the Beijing Consensus.

globalism, and certainly will continue to sustain this process, furthering its own vision. In order to advance toward sustainable development and a nature-positive economy, it is necessary to involve the entire global community and work together to better respond to the continuing evolution of international scenarios, monitoring the consequences on economies and societies of the COVID-19 pandemic and global warming.

China's ascent to the position of the world's second largest economy has stirred fears and concern in the western countries (especially the US) which pride themselves as the architect of the current global order and the sole depository of a unique recipe for global governance; however, recent history proves them wrong.

As a matter of fact, the COVID-19 pandemic has disrupted global economy, accelerated the change in global power dynamics, and evidenced the necessity to coordinate efforts and put in place new instruments and measures to sustain economies to reinforce international cooperation for a strong recovery and green transition which can no longer be postponed if one is to avoid catastrophic consequences for the whole of humanity. It is necessary to start locally, and each nation has an obligation to implement new policies to favor sustainable development which includes the use of alternative and renewable sources of energies and phasing out fossil fuels which are the major cause of emissions of GHG. With the COVID-19 pandemic, the recent events in Afghanistan with regard to the defeat of the US and the return to the government of the Taliban, and the inability of the US to impose its vision, it is possible to affirm that we have entered the third decade of this 21st century witnessing epochal changes in the international geopolitical landscape. This fluid evolution somehow needs to be controlled by the entire global community. China in this context is seeking to fill the space left by the US and of course reinforce its presence in foreign markets with new agreements. It is also trying to reshape the international system in a way that reflects both its values and interests but ensuring the continuation of multilateralism and the involvement of the global community in the definition of common issues and concerns (with climate change as the top priority). Undeniably, the world is 'undergoing profound changes unseen in a century.'[9] Unquestionably, China has acquired major influence at the international level; however, there is a gap between China's material

[9]*Source*: Changes, Challenges and Choices: China is Driven by the Path it Takes, Xinhua, August 28, 2019, article available at: http://www.xinhuanet.com/english/2019-08/28/c_138345879.htm (accessed January 8, 2023).

power and influence[10] and its actual capability or authority over international affairs, because the *status quo* has not been changed yet and traditional powers still retain their control, or influence, when it comes to global governance. It is therefore reasonable that China would want to have a bigger say in reshaping the global order. Rather than dismantling the current system entirely, China seeks to reshape some elements of the existing architecture, including some of its institutions (for example the WTO) and norms, trying to promote the concept of 'right to development' underplaying human rights. But in this context it is necessary to underline that in a country of over 1.4 billion individuals a strong guide it is necessary to grant the targets of the second centenary goal and of China's 2035 vision, which would be an enormous success for China. Thus, China's approach is reformative, not transformative. Its vision of the new global order and the prevailing liberal international order are not mutually exclusive. It is worth mentioning that in President's Xi special address at the Davos World Economic Forum on January 25, 2021, he reiterated that "*We should uphold the common values of humanity, i.e., peace, development, equity, justice, democracy and freedom, rise above ideological prejudice, make the mechanisms, principles and policies of our cooperation as open and inclusive as possible, and jointly safeguard world peace and stability.*"

1.2.1. *President Xi supports multilateralism*

The foundation of the existing international system and order is multilateralism. President Xi is well aware of this truth and he repeatedly called for global efforts to uphold multilateralism and steer the world toward the vision of a community with shared future for humanity. This assumption has been expressed by the Chinese President on many occasions. Xi also repeatedly spoke in defense of multilateralism to make economic globalization more inclusive and sustainable, especially now with climate change. It is also evident that globalization is irreversible and in today's world no country could possibly stay aloof and develop in seclusion.[11]

---

[10] China accounts for more than 16% of world GDP, one that has contributed 30% to global growth in the last 10 years and is expected to overtake the United States to become the largest economy within the next 10 years.

[11] See *China–US Trade Frictions Shaping New Equilibriums with the EU and the US — Towards a New Multilateralism or Tripolarism*, Xugang Yu, Mario Tettamanti, Cristiano Rizzi, World Scientific, 2021. Chapter 1 at p. 26.

Concerning this theme, President Xi affirmed that "*multilateralism is about having international affairs addressed through consultation and the future of the world decided by everyone working together. To build small circles or start a new Cold War, to reject, threaten or intimidate others, to willfully impose decoupling, supply disruption or sanctions, and to create isolation or estrangement will only push the world into division and even confrontation. We cannot tackle common challenges in a divided world, and confrontation will lead us to a dead end. Humanity has learned lessons the hard way, and that history is not long gone. We must not return to the path of the past.*"[12] President Xi also said, "*We should build an open world economy, uphold the multilateral trading regime, discard discriminatory and exclusionary standards, rules and systems, and take down barriers to trade, investment and technological exchanges.*"[13]

In China's view, true multilateralism cannot be achieved without the United Nations and a firm commitment to upholding the UN-centered international system. '*The law is the very foundation of governance*' is a saying in ancient Chinese philosophy. International governance should be based on the rules and consensus reached among nations, not on the order given by one or the few. This assumption is strongly supported by China, and it is evident that with its growing influence it deserves to play a bigger role in global governance.

1.2.2. *Important to stay committed to international law and international rules*

On the topic of International law, the Charter of the United Nations is the basic and universally recognized norm governing state-to-state relations. Without International law and international rules that are formed and recognized by the global community and without international cooperation multilateralism cannot be achieved, and the consequences for the entire world and humanity would be devastating. It is so evident that the world

[12] See *Let the Torch of Multilateralism Light up Humanity's Way Forward*, Special Address by H.E. Xi Jinping, President of the People's Republic of China at the World Economic Forum Virtual Event of the Davos Agenda, January 25, 2021, text of the speech available at: https://www.fmprc.gov.cn/mfa_eng/zxxx_662805/t1848323.shtml (accessed January 28, 2023).

[13] *Ibid.*

needs all these elements otherwise nations cannot coexist. As stated by President Xi, "*The world is undergoing changes unseen in a century, and now is the time for major development and major transformation. To uphold multilateralism in the 21st century, we should promote its fine tradition, take on new perspectives and look to the future. We need to stand by the core values and basic principles of multilateralism. We also need to adapt to the changing international landscape and respond to global challenges as they arise. We need to reform and improve the global governance system on the basis of extensive consultation and consensus-building.*

> *We need to give full play to the role of the World Health Organization in building a global community of health for all.* (This has clearly emerged during the pandemic). *We need to advance reform of the World Trade Organization and the international financial and monetary system in a way that boosts global economic growth and protects the development rights, interests and opportunities of developing countries. We need to follow a people-centered and fact-based policy orientation in exploring and formulating rules on global digital governance.*"[14]

These statements appear particularly timed if we consider where we are today. President Xi Jinping is guiding his country toward a sustainable and green modality. He is also putting in evidence simple truths that are sometimes difficult to accept because of the rivalries among countries. Only with coordinated efforts will it be possible to tackle common problems and pursue sustainable development.

1.3. *China's further growth to sustain its internal economy and international pledges based on new principles*

It is clear that China's further development is necessary not only to reinforce its position but also to lead the way in building a shared and sustainable future, advancing toward a nature-positive economy (not only in China). However, this new development needs to be sustained by a strong recovery, but the old paradigms, and the growth based on numbers, do not work in this new context after the pandemic. It is noteworthy that the government in 2020, at the two Sessions, abandoned a specific growth targets and one of the reasons is because COVID-19 impedes to plan for

---

[14] *Ibid.*

a precise rebound not only of the Chinese, but of the entire global economy. Another factor are the uncertainties derived from internal factors. Premier Li Keqiang explained this change in the following words:

> "*I would like to point out that we have not set a specific target for economic growth this year. This is because our country will face some factors that are difficult to predict in its development due to the great uncertainty regarding the COVID-19 pandemic and the world economic and trade environment. Not setting a specific target for economic growth will enable all of us to concentrate on ensuring stability on the six fronts and security in the six areas.*"[15]

Naturally, this refers to the six stabilizations (六稳 liù wěn), which are stabilizing employment, finance, foreign trade, foreign investment, domestic investment, and the people's expectation, and the six guarantees (六保 liù bǎo), which are that the state should ensure the people's employment, basic livelihood, market order, food and energy security, stability of supply chain, and operation of basic/local government functions.

1.3.1. *The six guarantees (六保 liù bǎo): A brief introduction*

The 'six guarantees'[16] (sometimes also called the 'six priorities') represent the six fundamental aspects of the economy and society that according to the central government must receive priority attention and protection in economic policy to ensure economic recovery post COVID-19. These six guarantees give a strong indication of which issues are the most important for the Chinese government and thus which economic policies will be prioritized.

Thus, China's future development will be certainly based on these six priorities with a particular focus on environment and the transition toward

---

[15] *Source*: Premier Li's speech at the third session of the 13th NPC. The full text of the Chinese Premier's speech is available at: https://news.cgtn.com/news/2020-05-22/Full-text-Premier-Li-s-speech-at-the-third-session-of-the-13th-NPC-QHaP1FpB8k/index.html (accessed January, 28, 2023).

[16] The six guarantees 六保 (liù bǎo) are not very different from Western economic recovery plans as they include the following: (1) create jobs; (2) ensure basic livelihood; (3) protect market players; (4) food and energy security; 5) stability of the industrial supply chain; maintain grassroots operations. https://www.thechinaagenda.com/china-six-guarantees-economic-recovery-plan/ (accessed January 28, 2023).

a nature-positive and green economy which will serve as a stimulus not only for China but also for the rest of the global community to put in place new policies for sustainable development, and common initiatives and efforts to reach global public goods and to meet the goals of the UN for sustainable development.

In order to achieve steady growth, China must not only unswervingly stick to its policy of Reform and Opening-up but also embrace a new economic development modality which the leadership has already launched, i.e., the Dual Circulation Strategy (DCS) (see next paragraph), responding at the same time to the urgent question of preserving our environment for future generations. President Xi Jinping in particular has emphasized that to achieve high-quality development, China must implement a new paradigm based on the principles of "*innovation, coordination, green, openness and sharing*" which represent the 'five major development concepts.'[17]

Before introducing the 'Dual Circulation Strategy' and how China intends to develop a sustainable, green, nature-positive economy, it is necessary to stress that COVID-19 has pushed China to introduce changes in its policies not only to reach its ambitious targets and favor its new priorities but also to change its development mode. The new narrative demonstrates China's resolve to become more realistic and also be flexible, and in particular farsighted, with a vision toward innovative, green, and open development, which should be pursued in a coordinated manner with all its partners because sustainable development in harmony with nature is the only possible way forward for everyone.

2. China Promotes a New Sustainable and Nature-Positive Shared Future under the Concept of 'Ecological Civilization' to be Included in the Dual Circulation Strategy

President Xi Jinping's vision to build a global community with shared future is also guided by the new philosophy of an 'ecological

---

[17]A more precise description of these five major development concepts is contained in an article by Robert Lawrence Kuhn, *China Daily*, online version available at: https://www.chinadaily.com.cn/opinion/2016-09/23/content_26872399.htm (accessed January 28, 2023).

civilization'[18] which is so important not only for the entire global community but also for China, a major emitter of CO_2, now marching toward building a green, low-carbon economy.

The concept of 'ecological civilization'[19] (*shengtai wenming* 生态文明) was included in the Chinese Constitution in 2018[20] and it serves as a vision and also indicates the path toward sustainable development with Chinese characteristics. However, the concept of ecological civilization, where development exists in harmony with nature and promotes environmental protection, has a specific political meaning and it seems to respond to societal demands for further reforms to combat inequalities, for

---

[18]"Ecological civilization" is a social developmental goal enshrined in the Chinese constitution. The term refers to a form of civilization in which human beings and nature 'coexist harmoniously.' The concept was first endorsed by President Xi Jinping's predecessor, President Hu Jintao, in 2007, to help China develop sustainable and ecological industrial structures, growth patterns, and consumption modes. President Xi bolstered the idea after taking office in 2012. President Xi has described the construction of ecological civilization as "building a beautiful China." He used a famous metaphor to explain the goal: "Lucid waters and lush mountains are invaluable assets."

[19]The term "Ecological Civilization" refers to "*the final goal of social and environmental reform within a given society. It implies that the changes required in response to global climate disruption and social injustices are so extensive as to require another form of human civilization, one based on ecological principles. Broadly construed, ecological civilization involves a synthesis of economic, educational, political, agricultural, and other societal reforms toward sustainability. Although the term was first coined in the 1980s, it did not see widespread use until 2007, when* "*ecological civilization*" *became an explicit goal of the* Communist Party of China *(CPC)*." *Source*: https://en.wikipedia.org/wiki/Ecological_civilization (accessed January 28, 2023).

[20]Soon after "ecological civilization' was singled out as a constitutive element of Xi Jinping's *Socialism with Chinese Characteristics for a New Era*, this concept was also ratified in the Constitution of the PRC in 2018. On March 11, 2018, the National People's Congress (NPC) of the People's Republic of China adopted an amendment to the PRC Constitution. The amendment contains 21 articles numbered 32 to 52 (the numbering of the articles continues from article 31 of the previous constitutional amendment). The changes introduced by this amendment, in particular, article 46 among other things, add the protection of the environment to the duties and powers of the State Council under item 6 of Art. 89 of the Constitution, which now reads, "*(6) to direct and administer economic affairs and urban and rural development, as well as the building of an ecological civilization.*" See Art. 89 (6) of the Chinese Constitution (2018), Section 3: The State Council, available at: https://npcobserver.files.wordpress.com/2018/12/PRC-Constitution-2018.pdf (accessed January 28, 2023).

example, respecting the environment, preserving resources, and fighting climate change. Undeniably, China has become an important contributor in the global endeavor for ecological civilization; however, it is necessary to involve the rest of the global community to achieve sustainable and green development.

This vision of sustainable development with particular attention to nature and environment protection is to be found in *China's 14th Five-Year Plan* and *Vision for 2035,* which indicated the path China will take to transition toward a green economy, meeting its ambitious climate goals: to peak emissions before 2030 and achieve carbon neutrality before 2060.

2.1. *China as a 'Global Public Good' player*

China in the last decade has shifted its priorities and become a Global Public Good (GPG) player. Today, in fact, China claims to be a climate leader and it plays a more proactive role in promoting a green development, though it has to balance internal needs with other global issues touching not only climate change but also public health. The COVID-19 crisis, for instance, represents another global emergence in which great powers together with the rest of the global community have to prove they can work together, despite political differences, to find 'integrated rather than fragmented solutions'[21] for global problems. It must be underlined that with reference to COVID-19, China has used the pandemic to revitalize a little-known offshoot of the Belt and Road Initiative (BRI), the Health Silk Road (HSR),[22] as part of its contribution to global health solutions.

---

[21] In this sense, the European Commission in its document titled "EU Focus on Global Public Goods. *The EU at the WSSD, 2002. The European Union (EU) recognises the growing importance of global public goods (GPGs) in the context of international efforts to achieve sustainable development. Often individual countries are unable to subordinate their local interests to the general good. GPGs, however, provide an opportunity for getting to grips with issues of common interest. They highlight the way in which problems overlap and require* ***integrated rather than fragmented solutions****. The EU is convinced therefore that an international, open and transparent process is needed to advance consideration and consensus on this matter.*" The entire text of the document is available at: https://ec.europa.eu/environment/archives/wssd/pdf/publicgoods.pdf. (accessed January 28, 2023).

[22] Health Silk Road (HSR) has garnered little attention compared with other high-profile BRI projects; however, it is part of China's efforts to build an international community in

These are only a couple of examples, and it must be reminded that China is willing to share its success and experience with all the countries willing to listen to new thoughts and paradigms. It must be stressed that caring and sharing are in fact characteristics of Chinese culture: According to an ancient Chinese saying, "*take care of yourself well when you are poor, share the benefits with the world when you become better off*" 穷则独善其身，达则兼济天下 (qióng zé dú shàn qí shēn, dá zé jiān jì tiān xià). There is no doubt that China is ready to share a brilliant future with the rest of the international community, but it needs to proceed with caution considering the internal imbalances and the other priorities and goals it has in its agenda.

2.1.1. *BRI and RCEP as drivers for new sustainable development*

The Belt and Road Initiative and the RCEP in a sense both aim at creating new drivers of common development, especially the first, and they represent China's offer to the world to build not only a new multilateralism but also a new sustainable and nature-positive economy which will lead to a shared future especially if the emphasis is placed on building a green, low-carbon, and circular economic system which can involve all its partners in the more ample sense. China is willing to share its experience and expertise to realize infrastructures in countries involved in the BRI, and in doing so it is also reinforcing its trade relations and ensuring the involvement of developing countries in its plans. In particular, a 'green BRI' is now China's renewed effort to promote its overseas infrastructure agenda in a more environmental friendly modality. It must be noted that with growing concern about climate change and the adoption of the UN 2030 Agenda for a sustainable future, China has made a series of high-profile statements about the BRI, indicating and claiming that this initiative is part of a broader commitment to mitigating climate change and promoting cleaner sources of energy. This initiative is also the manifestation of the

---

particular among the countries which have embraced the BRI, and it is an emerging diplomatic initiative for promoting health cooperation. An interesting article titled "*Toward a Health Silk Road — China's Proposal for Global Health Cooperation,*" by Jiahan Cao, 2020 World Century Publishing Corporation and Shanghai Institutes for International Studies China Quarterly of International Strategic Studies, Vol. 6, No. 1, 19–35 is available at: https://www.worldscientific.com/doi/10.1142/S2377740020500013.

Chinese culture and spirit of '*share the benefits with the world when you are better off*' in the realm of international cooperation. Unfortunately, some important partners of China have misunderstood China's moves as a manifestation of expansionism with the intention of dominate the world with its continuously growing economic power thanks to its continued reform process. However, China has reiterated that its goal is not to rule the world but to create an open world economy, a people-oriented and inclusive society, and a beautiful homeland with harmonious coexistence between humans and nature, nurturing sustainable development to solve global problems, preserving world peace, and promoting common development. All these objectives are reachable but it is necessary to have closer collaboration among nations. In any case, China has adopted specific policies to reach its goals and it seems appropriate to introduce them in order to delineate the framework in which China is advancing toward a green economy.

2.2. *China's 2035 vision and the 14th Five-Year Plan in the context*

China's 2035 vision involves the country developing megacities or metropolitan areas that will help foster stronger regional trade with ASEAN, BRI regions, and developing economies across the world. Beijing also intends to foster higher-quality domestic consumption growth and capacity in order to reduce China's reliance on shrinking exports markets, with more details offered in the 14th Five Years Plan (2021–2025)[23] which also aims to push China toward a nature-positive economy. We need to put China's 2035 vision and the 14th FYP in context to better understand their importance in the framework of a sustainable, green, and nature-positive future for mankind.

The 14th Five-Year Plan is of particular significance due to a confluence of many factors such as (1) China's impressive recovery during the

[23]The 14th Five-Year Plan (2021–2025) for National Economic and Social Development of the People's Republic of China (PRC) was approved on March 2021. The Plan highlights high-quality, green development. Building on the achievements of the 13th Plan, it aims to reduce the carbon intensity of the economy and to peak carbon dioxide emissions before 2030. The Plan emphasizes innovation as the core of modern development, relying on the dual circulation strategy as the growth paradigm coupled with reforms to increase living standards.

pandemic which is seen as a roadmap to advancing forward in the new normal; (2) scientific and technological revolution and industrial reform against the backdrop of swelling geopolitical tensions; and (3) China's rising profile in international affairs and its critical role in the global supply chain. With reference to the 14th FYP, it is worth remembering that the 2021 fifth plenum — the second such plenum presided over by President Xi Jinping — saw the release of two separate blueprints: (a) the aforementioned 14th FYP and (b) '2035 vision' (2021–2035) which embodies a mid-term vision to focus on 'socialist modernization.' The release of the 2035 vision (only the second 15-year plan of this type to ever be released) is heavily laden with political meaning, and for many observers it was also a hint of the intention of President Xi to guide China beyond his second term. The projected national plan signposts the midway point of the centenary anniversary of the People's Republic of China and is a key marker of Xi's national rejuvenation project to build a modern socialist country that is prosperous strong, democratic, culturally advanced, and harmonious by 2049.

2.2.1. *Strengthen domestic economy and promote external relations for public good delivery*

In order to contribute to global public good, China needs to address domestic challenges; thus, part of the new FYP is dedicated to reinforcing the internal economy, changing the paradigms of the growth, and paying more attention to sustainable and ecological development. In particular, with regard to climate change, this theme is recognized by Beijing as a "*huge challenge to the survival and development of the human race.*"[24] China has come to the conclusion that it is necessary to move away from fossil fuels and to promote the use of sustainable, alternative, and clean sources of energy; this is why China has become more willing to participate in global climate and energy discussions, to find adequate solutions together with the global community to transition toward sustainable, green development. China's strategy is very clear and it includes advanced

[24] Su, Wei (2015). "Enhanced Actions on climate change: China's nationally determined contributions," this document is available both in Chinese and English language at the following website: https://www4.unfccc.int/sites/ndcstaging/PublishedDocuments/China%20First/China%27s%20First%20NDC%20Submission.pdf (accessed January 8, 2023).

green technologies useful for China's domestic development. It must be stressed that domestic climate action is regarded as a contributor to GPGs. In fact, China is pledging innovations combining political ecology and digital economy, two elements of extreme importance for China to sustain its green development and foster its economy. In doing so, China is pursuing an upgraded commitment to the Paris Convention. In fact, only by paying more attention to our environment and instilling more awareness about the importance of a green development will it be possible for China to contribute to addressing climate change and reaching its goals, which in some cases coincide with the UN's goals for sustainable development, and maintaining its pace of growth. On this particular aspect, the advancements of China are impressive. The World Bank has announced that China will change its status from an 'emerging market economy' to an 'advanced economy' before the end of its 14th FYP, given that its GDP per capita already reached US$12,536 in 2019. GDP per capita in purchasing power parity (ppp) is much higher at $16,804. The success of China is naturally based on the reform process initiated by Deng and continued by Xi. President Xi started a 'New Era'[25] of China's reforms, and its foundation was laid during the 13th FYP. "The *New Era* for China signifies the overcoming of unbalanced and inadequate development and the transition to harmonious development, respectful of man and the environment, environmentally friendly, which puts qualitative rather than quantitative growth first."[26]

The 14th FYP must be seen as a hinge in China's reforms process: For instance, it aims at deepening the objectives of the 'New Era' that started with the 13th FYP, namely, changing the growth regime from capital-intensive accumulation to an innovation-led economy, coupled with enhancing total factor productivity driven by domestic consumption and

[25]Xi Jinping in his book *The Governance of China*, Vol II, Foreign Languages Press, Beijing, 2017, at p. 597, explains that the "New Era" implies that we leave behind an "old era," that we enter a new phase in the history of China and of the world. And this not only because the history of China cannot but influence the destinies of the world but also because, as Xi writes, the destinies of China and the world are interconnected: "*We in China believe that China will do well only when the world does well, and vice versa.*"

[26]The concept of "New Era" is treated in detail in another manuscript: *China's Continued Reforms in a New Era — Their Impact on Chinese Foreign Direct investment and RMB Internationalization*, Xugang Yu, Mario Tettamanti, Cristiano Rizzi, World Scientific, March 2020, in particular, see pp. 44–47.

development of the services sector. Naturally, drawing mainly on domestic resources would be a fundamental change in China's growth and development mode. In particular, it is necessary to stress that the 14th FYP starts a new phase of development and also aims at addressing long-run challenges both nationally and internationally. In the next section, there will be a focus on the SDGs and the international initiatives to build a more integrated international community. However, before introducing this theme, it is necessary to briefly introduce the concept of *dual circulation* because it is the foundation of this transition toward sustainable and green development.

2.3. *Dual circulation strategy* (双循环) *and its significance for China*

The 'domestic–international dual circulation' strategy (or simply the "Dual Circulation Strategy — DCS") needs to be explained in detail because it is of extreme importance for China in this new phase of development. Basically, the DCS is a two-pronged development strategy that seeks to spur China's domestic demand in addition to catering to export markets. Thus, developing the domestic market for an enlarged Chinese middle class will sustain the local economy, on the one hand, and promoting determined initiatives such as the BRI and the Comprehensive Agreement on Investment (CAI)[27] with the EU (not yet ratified) will cement relationships between China and the EU, and the RCEP, on the other hand, these tools will enhance Chinese presence in international markets.

It is noteworthy that the concept of 'Dual Circulation' (双循环) was discussed and proposed on May 14, 2020, in a high-level meeting chaired by President Xi Jinping:

[27]On December 30, 2020, the EU and China announced that they had reached an Agreement in Principle on investment, the so-called Comprehensive Agreement on Investment (CAI). This was the result of lengthy negotiations, which started in January 2014. However, the CAI was not ratified due to the friction that emerged between the parties regarding human rights violations against the Uyghur and other Muslim ethnic minorities in China's Xinjiang region, and the retaliation by China. For more details, visit: https://www.europarl.europa.eu/news/en/press-room/20210517IPR04123/meps-refuse-any-agreement-with-china-whilst-sanctions-are-in-place (accessed January 28, 2023).

> "*The meeting highlighted the necessity to deepen supply-side structural reform, give full play to the advantages of the country's super-large market and the potential of domestic demand and construct a new development model (or pattern) featuring domestic and international dual circulations that complement each other.*"[28]

In more simple terms, 'Dual Circulation' can be defined as the domestic consumption-driven economic rebalancing to achieve sustainable economic development or a nature-positive economy. The strategy is slowly becoming the underlying policy refrain to accompany China's actions to recoup loss of growth momentum due to the COVID-19 outbreak.[29] However, it is also possible to affirm that this is a signal that China's economy will look inward and reduce its exposure to the vagaries of the global economy. In particular, on the demand side and thus to foster internal consumption, the shift to an advanced economy requires social policies to reduce inequalities between provinces and between social classes in the world's largest domestic consumer market, sustained by a middle class of approximately 400 million; this will serve to reach the 2035 goal of a socialist market economy.

China is placing particular emphasis on new technologies to advance its economy. The 14th FYP envisages self-reliance in critical technologies, and this highlights a growing urgency to protect China from external factors by attaining self-reliance in science and technology. Notably, China's push for self-reliance has been accelerated by the US's ability to cut off certain Chinese companies' access to semiconductors which are a critical component in many advanced technologies. Certainly, the trade

---

[28] *Source*: Xinhua (2020). "The Standing Committee of the political bureau of the CPC Central committee held a meeting chaired by Xi Jinping," available in Chinese at: www.xinhuanet.com/politics/leaders/2020-05/14/c_1125986000.html (accessed January 28, 2023).

[29] The ongoing COVID-19 pandemic has provoked global concerns on supply chain dependency, as different countries have been forced to rethink their reliance on other countries, especially in strategic industries, such as medical supplies and access to pharmaceutical raw ingredients, which will likely accelerate supply chain shifts out of China. China has adopted severe measures and also closed its borders to contain the pandemic, and the vaccination campaign is proceeding. All these measures have allowed the rapid resilience of China's economy.

frictions[30] with the United States and the economic cold war which followed prompted China to change its strategy, and it is now equipping itself to overcome these dependencies.

There is another important element to explain in order to understand China's Dual Circulation strategy, namely, its strong commitment to embark on a major energy transition which is of extreme importance to the entire global community and to the investment opportunities that will emerge. This particular theme is developed in Chapter 3. Here, it is sufficient to mention that this further development would not be complete without reference to the so-called SDGs of the UN (see the dedicated section).

It is evident that further reforms are necessary to reach all the targets set by the Chinese government and to implement all the goals outlined in the 14th FYP and, thus, only in the coming years will it be possible to assess how successfully China is achieving its targets with these new policies. But what is clear from the Five-Year Plan is that China, despite its calls for continued openness and international cooperation, is now looking at internally supporting the transition toward a nature-positive economy to ensure its future development.

2.3.1. *Nature-positive energy system: Brief introduction about the importance of renewable sources of energy*

It is necessary to state that China is the largest energy producer and consumer in the world; in order to further its own development and achieve its targets, China needs to secure energy sources, both traditional and renewable ones. Noteworthily, the Chinese government is focusing on

[30]The trade confrontation between China and the US is well explained by the authors of this book in their other manuscript titled *China-US Trade Frictions Shaping New Equilibriums with the EU and the US — Toward a New Multilateralism or Tripolarism,* Xugang Yu, Mario Tettamanti, Cristiano Rizzi, World Scientific, 2021. Phase-one Agreement signed by parties in January 2020 posed an end to China–US trade frictions initiated by the previous US President, Donald Trump, who embraced the so-called 'America First' policy and adopted the old fashioned 'protectionism' which only caused collateral damage for the US. The signing of the China–US phase-one trade accord, which has both economic and political significance, is good news and will certainly bolster the world economy if the two parties will work together to ensure its efficient implementation.

ensuring a stable and affordable energy supply at low environmental and social cost, as envisaged by the 14th Five-Year Plan (2021–2025). By 2025, one of the main objectives for China is to create a framework for a green, low-carbon, and circular economy, improve the energy efficiency of key industries, and reduce the 'weight' of non-fossil energy (i.e., renewable sources) consumption to 20%.[31] It is evident that China, in transitioning toward a nature-positive economy, will of course continue to utilize its large coal reserves, but will keep its promise to peak emissions by 2030 and at the same time increase investments in renewable energy sources. By 2030, another objective is to see significant accomplishments from comprehensive green transformation both in economic and social development, with energy efficiency in key energy-consuming industries increasing the use of renewable sources. The declared objective is to establish a fully green, low-carbon, and circular economy and a clean, low-carbon, and safe and efficient energy system by 2060. Developing a renewable energy sector has become an increasingly urgent priority for China for two main reasons: (1) to reduce carbon emissions and (2) to enhance energy self-sufficiency as policymakers in China have warned against the overdependence on oil and gas imports. The government also sees stable energy supply as an important condition to maintain growth and employment, especially amid threats to global supply chains posed by the COVID-19-induced lockdowns and globally rising protectionism.

China's energy imports increased by nearly 11.6% annually on average during the past decade, compared with 3.8% growth in energy consumption in the same period, highlighting significant import dependency (Figures 1 and 2).

Concerning the 'dual carbon goals,' i.e., peak carbon emissions before 2030 and achieving carbon neutrality by 2060, intensive investment in sustainable energy resources such as solar and wind power (along with energy storage systems) will be required to meet China's energy demands during the transition period. There is no doubt about China's commitment to transforming its economy into a green, sustainable one, and this implies

---

[31] *Source*: Department of Resource Conservation and Environmental Protection of the National Development and Reform Commission (NDRC) People's Republic of China, see the 'Working Guidance for Carbon Dioxide Peaking and Carbon Neutrality in Full and Faithful Implementation of the New Development Philosophy,' October 24, 2021, document available at: https://en.ndrc.gov.cn/policies/202110/t20211024_1300725.html (accessed January 8, 2023).

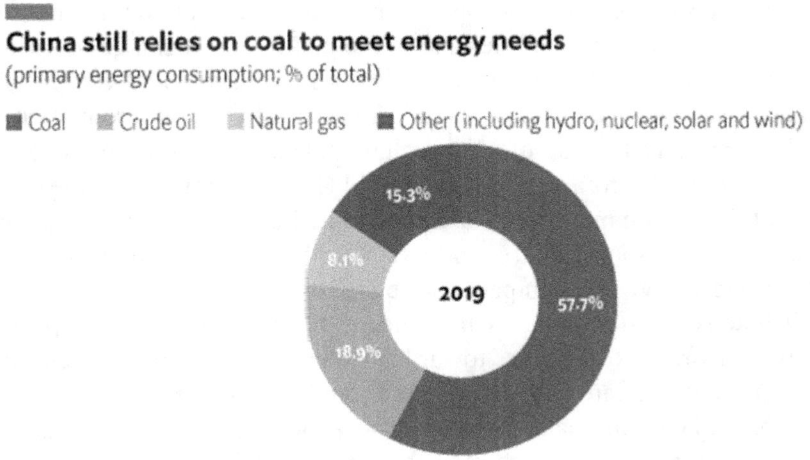

Figure 1: (Color online) China still relies on coal

Sources: National Bureau of Statistics; The Economist Intelligence Unit.

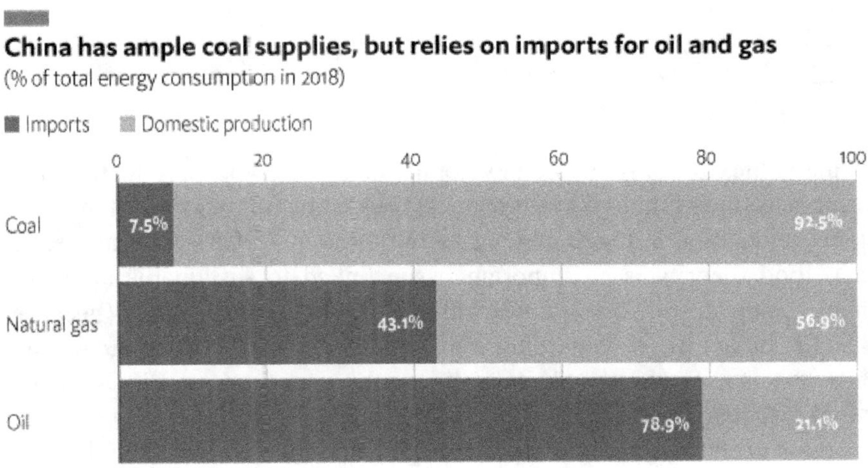

Figure 2: (Color online) China imports oil and gas

Sources: National Bureau of Statistics; The Economist Intelligence Unit.

the increased use of renewable energy sources; however, it is necessary to proceed gradually in order to not disrupt China's growth and in a manner that assures the achievement of China's objectives with particular attention to the conservation of our environment. To this extent, it must be stressed that in the effort to reduce carbon emissions and to develop further renewable energy sources, the risks related to the deployment of new energy generation facilities and to the pollution or damage of natural habitats need to be taken into consideration. Loss of biodiversity is a crucial issue and must be considered. Besides all this, the production of wind energy and the use of photovoltaic panels and other new energy-supporting power storage facilities could lead to a significant increase in demand for certain materials; for example, nickel usage in lithium batteries is expected to increase 16-fold to 1.8 million tons by 2030[32] and this will certainly have some impact on the cost of energy.

There is no doubt that China needs to implement more specific policies in order to advance toward a green, low-carbon, and circular economy and a clean, low-carbon, safe, and efficient energy system to meet its dual carbon goals; therefore, it is appropriate in the next chapter to explain more details concerning the measures China is going to adopt to achieve its carbon neutrality goal as planned. However, before introducing this theme, it is necessary to briefly explain some other factors which are intrinsically linked to China's Dual Circulation Strategy.

2.3.2. *China's DCS is linked to other factors: The importance of food security*

In the context of sustainable development, China's food production and security is one of the links that connect domestic circulation with international circulation in the Dual Circulation Strategy (DCS). As a matter of fact, food security is an important issue linked to sustainable development. China, despite being the world's largest consumer of food (because of its population), is witnessing a decrease in cultivated land areas, and thus imported food plays a vital role in achieving food security and sustainability (Figure 3).

As data show, imported food is surging and this trend is likely to continue in the future. Realizing sustainable agriculture is another key challenge for China in achieving food sustainability, which is of great importance for a sustainable food system for future generations in China.

[32] 'Energy storage material nickel metal may be in short supply in five years,' see https://power.in-en.com/html/power-2329685.shtm (Chinese only) accessed January 8, 2023. *Source*: Seizing Business Opportunities in China's Transition towards a Nature-Positive Economy, p. 55, World Economic Forum, 2022, available at: https://www3.weforum.org/docs/WEF_New_Nature_Economy_Report_China_2022.pdf (accessed January 28, 2023).

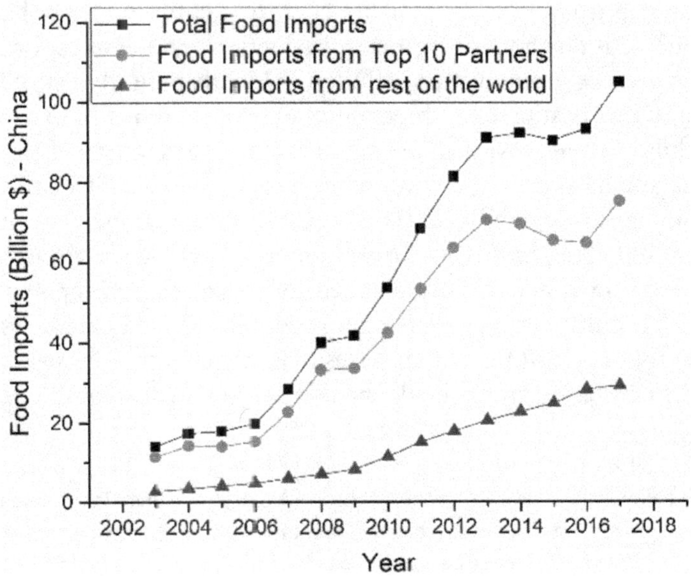

Food Imports in China from 2013 to 2017

Imports	2003	2010	2017
Total food imports (Billion $)	$14 B	$53.7B	$105 B
Imports from top 10 partners	$11.3B (81%)	$42.4B (79%)	$75.3B (72%)
Imports from rest of the world	$2.66B (19%)	$11.3B (21%)	$29.3B (28%)

Figure 3: Food imports to China

Notes: Data from https://chinapower.csis.org/china-food-security/
Source: https://chinapower.csis.org/china-food-security/.

Therefore, the success of the Dual Circulation Strategy in achieving food security through the establishment of a sustainable food system while minimizing the dependence on imported food has an important role to play together with productive and regenerative agriculture. Regenerative agriculture with stable and high yields is another priority for China. Noteworthily, China's 2017 *Bulletin on the Second National Census on Pollution Sources* (a once in a decade survey) revealed large amounts of water pollutants being discharged from the agricultural sector where irrational use of fertilizers and pesticides is leading to degradation of arable land, thus contributing to half of the country's entire water pollutants.[33] It is evident that this not only reduces production and incomes for farmers but also increases groundwater pollution, which is partially caused by the intensive use of pesticides,[34] threatening the physical health of rural residents. Thus, the necessity to further promote agricultural reform with particular attention on the environment clearly emerges. To address this delicate issue, in September 2021, the Chinese government unveiled its *14th Five-Year National Agriculture Green Development Plan*,[35] which for the first time systematically planned for the green development of the country's agriculture sector. This plan is completely dedicated to sustainable and green agriculture and proposes to implement the strictest possible system for protecting arable land, and controlling areas of arable land that

---

[33] See Measured by Chemical Oxygen Demand (COD). *Source*: "Focus on agricultural sources and domestic sources of water pollution control," China Environment News, June 18, 2020, text in Chinese available at: http://www.xinhuanet.com/energy/2020-06/18/c_1126128378.htm (accessed January 28, 2023).

[34] Extensive application of pesticides and fertilizers is a serious problem in China. Before the launch of the *Plan for Zero Growth Rate of Fertilizer Use by 2020*, China consumed one-third of all global fertilizers, with 328 Kg average fertilizer use per hectare of crops — which is 2.5 times the European average. See "Ministry of Agriculture on the issuance of the 'Zero Growth Action Plan for Fertilizer Use by 2020' and 'Zero Growth Action Plan for Pesticide Use by 2020' notices," Ministry of Agriculture and Rural Affairs of the People's Republic of China, 29 November 2017, text in Chinese available at: http://www.moa.gov.cn/nybgb/2015/san/201711/t20171129_5923401.htm (accessed January 28, 2023).

[35] This is not to be confused with the 14th FYP previously mentioned. The Chinese government unveiled its 14th Five-Year National Agriculture Green Development Plan on September 8, 2021. This Plan, jointly issued by six departments, i.e., the Ministry of Agriculture and Rural Affairs (MARA), the National Development and Reform Commission (NDRC), the Ministry of Science and Technology (MOST), the Ministry of Natural Resources (MONR), the Ministry of Ecology and Environment (MEE), and the State Forestry and Grassland Administration (SFGA), identified resource protection, pollution control, restoration of agricultural ecology, and the development of a low-carbon agricultural industrial chains as key goals to be achieved between the years 2021 and 2025. Please refer to the link for the full text of the Plan in Chinese. http://www.gov.cn/zhengce/zhengceku/2021-09/07/content_5635867.htm (accessed January 28, 2023). Additional information available at: https://apps.fas.usda.gov/newgainapi/api/Report/DownloadReportByFileName?fileName=Plan%20for%20Green%20and%20Sustainable%20Ag%20Development_Beijing_China%20-%20People%27s%20Republic%20of_10-21-2021 (accessed January 28, 2023).

are deteriorating. By the year 2025, according to the *National Agriculture Green Development Plan,* China aims to build a total of approximately 70 million hectares of high-standard farmland, treat about 1 million hectares of acidified and salinized arable land, and ameliorate the entire agriculture system. To succeed in these ambitious targets, the Chinese government needs to intensify its efforts in improving the regulations and incentives for green agricultural development, such as revising the rules for crop disease and pest control and ensuring the quality and safety of agricultural products.

Food waste also represents a problem. This issue should be minimized or eliminated through awareness campaigns, promoting an understanding of the importance of healthy diets and practicing nature-compatible consumption. Due to its large population base, one of China's priorities is to develop a sustainable food production system to sustain a growing demand for food. Impressive and disappointing data show that China's urban catering industry alone generates 17–18 million tons of food waste every year which is sufficient to feed between 30 and 50 million people.[36]

2.4. *Reorganization of international relations: The second part of the DCS*

The abovementioned objectives represent the first part of the so-called 'dual circulation' and in relation to nature preservation other aspects are to be considered (see dedicated section); however, there is a second part which needs to be briefly treated in this context, concerning China's view of the reorganization of international relationships. Naturally, this includes new initiatives such as the RCEP and the already mentioned BRI.

2.4.1. *RCEP and BRI as part of China's strategy*

China on the 15th of November 2020 signed the so-called Regional Comprehensive Economic Partnership (hereinafter RCEP). Noteworthily,

[36] "Food Wasted in China Each Year Could Feed 30 Million People, Says Chinese Academy of Sciences," Xinhuanet, December 7, 2016, text in Chinese available at: http://www.xinhuanet.com/politics/2016-12/07/c_129393630.htm (accessed January 28, 2023).

the RCEP is the first free trade agreement between China, Japan, and the South Korea, and is the first multilateral free trade agreement to include the Middle Kingdom. Substantially, RCEP's aim is to unify and deepen economic linkages across East Asia and the eastern Pacific — with China as the region's key driver of economic growth. In this regard, China's 14th Five-Year Plan calls for "*comprehensively improving the level of opening to the outside world and the promotion of trade and investment liberalization and facilitation.*" To this end, China took the lead in ratifying the RCEP (March 2021).

On January 1, 2022, the Regional Comprehensive Economic Partnership agreement entered into force officially.[37] On this occasion, Chinese Premier Li Keqiang described the deal as "*a victory of multilateralism and free trade*" and stated that the new agreement is "*critical to the region's response to the COVID-19 pandemic.*"[38] This agreement, thanks to the post-pandemic recovery, will further reinforce the level of complimentary advantages between China and ASEAN countries. It is also aimed to optimize the regional business and investment environment, and promote the deep integration of the regional industrial chain, supply chain, and value chain, all of which are expected to drive the growth of overall regional economic and trade investment, bringing tangible benefits to all the participants.

As part of its strategy, Beijing aims at strengthening ties with the rest of the world, in particular with emerging countries, and initiatives such as the RCEP and the BRI represent the expression of China in materializing its plans while reorganizing international relations. This is why the second dimension of the double circulation is of utmost importance. The RCEP is the largest trade agreement[39] in the world and it encompasses eastern Asia

---

[37] http://www.chinaembassy.or.th/eng/sgxw/202201/t20220107_10479886.htm (accessed January 30, 2022). See also China's Vision 2035: From Beijing's Forbidden City to Interconnected Eurasian Megacity, Bob Savic, March 24, 2021, article available at: https://www.china-briefing.com/news/chinas-vision-2035-from-beijings-forbidden-city-to-interconnected-eurasian-megacity/ (accessed January 28, 2023).

[38] See World's biggest trade pact signed, "victory of multilateralism, free trade," Xinhua, November 15, 2020, article available at: http://www.xinhuanet.com/english/2020-11/15/c_139518184.htm (accessed January 28, 2023).

[39] The Landmark agreement consists of 15 countries: 10 member states of the Association of Southeast Asian Nations (ASEAN), China, Japan, South Korea, Australia, and New Zealand. The primary aim of the RCEP is to establish a comprehensive economic partnership — building on existing bilateral ASEAN agreements within the region with its

and most of the ASEAN countries (except for India) and extends to Australia and New Zealand. The countries involved do more than half of their foreign trade between them and amount to 30% of the world population. Naturally, China intends to position itself at the center of this trade zone in pursuing its financial opening and the joint internationalization of the renminbi (RMB).

Noteworthily, the "ASEAN economies will be in a unique position to service China's growing domestic economy with value added consumer and intermediate products. At the same time, Japan and South Korea will continue integrating their high-technology production platforms with China's expanding R&D capabilities amid its transformation into a digital, cloud-based, and Artificial Intelligence (AI) economy. Concurrently, Australia and New Zealand are likely to further develop the supply of food, upstream, and value-added downstream resources to China's maturing economy and tap consumption markets."[40]

Besides the RCEP, China will continue to pursue the BRI project because it is of paramount importance for its strategy. This initiative is planned to be the framework of a 'new globalization' and to be a new phase of multilateralism based on reinforced bilateral relations. The BRI has become a strategic part of China's plan to build a community with a shared future and it will result in not only a collection of trade agreements and infrastructure projects throughout the Eurasian region, but also a contribution to fostering the entire global economy, complementing other initiatives such as the RCEP and the Comprehensive Agreement on Investment (CAI) with the EU, which is taking time to be ratified but is of importance for both China and the EU.

As explained in the following sections, China's rise as a moderately prosperous nation and a mature economy by 2035 as envisioned by

---

FTA partners. The RCEP will be guided by a common set of rules and standards, lowered trade barriers, streamlined processes, and improved market access. The RCEP agreement includes 20 chapters covering many of the articles typically found in a free trade agreement. Notably, it makes significant strides by way of harmonizing the rules of origin and strengthening IP measures. But some critics have pointed to the weaker commitments for e-commerce and the omission of a labor and environment protection clause, when compared with the CPTPP. For more details, see RCEP FTA Signed: What Can Foreign Investors in China Expect? In China Briefing, Dorcas Wong, article available at: https://www.china-briefing.com/news/rcep-fta-signed-what-can-foreign-investors-in-china-expect/ (accessed January 28, 2023).

[40] *Ibid.*

President Xi must naturally pass through a modernization and an upgrade of its economy, which needs to follow and apply the principles of the UN as expressed in its 2030 Agenda for Sustainable Development Goals. China can greatly contribute to achieving those goals and it can be an important player in the effort to fight climate change. To this extent, the UN's SDGs play an enormous role in guiding the development of all nations and they will be briefly introduced in the following section.

3. Promoting Sustainable Development and China's Commitment to the UN 2030 Agenda

The UN's goals and the so-called '2030 Agenda'[41] provide an integrated roadmap for sustainable development to end poverty, protect the planet, and bring peace and prosperity to all. These goals perfectly meet the new path China is taking to modernize its society and build a shared future with the rest of the global community. China is a strong supporter of the UN's Sustainable Development Goals and it is aligning its policies to achieve those results.

3.1. *The need to transition toward sustainable growth in line with the UN SDGs*

President Xi on many occasions stressed the necessity to work with the global community for sustainable development, and in particular he affirmed that China will fully implement the 2030 Agenda for Sustainable

[41] The *2030 Agenda for Sustainable Development* was adopted in September 2015 by the UN Members at the United Nations Headquarters in New York as the Organization celebrated its seventieth anniversary. The Heads of States and Government and High Representatives during the meeting have decided on new global Sustainable Development Goals following the principles contained in Agenda 21, a comprehensive plan of action to build a global partnership for sustainable development to improve human lives and protect the environment, adopted in June 1992 at the Earth Summit in Rio de Janeiro, Brazil. The new 2030 Agenda for Sustainable Development contains the 17 Sustainable Development Goals (SDGs), which are an urgent call for action by all countries — developed and developing — in a global partnership. All these Goals recognize that ending poverty and other deprivations must go hand in hand with strategies that improve health and education, reduce inequality, and spur economic growth — all while tackling climate change and working to preserve our oceans and forests. The 2030 Agenda and its Goals are available at the following website: https://sdgs.un.org/2030agenda (accessed January 28, 2023).

Development because it reflects the interests of China. As evidenced, China's commitments on the ecological front are clear, and plans already exist to advance toward a nature-positive economy by transforming China's industrial structure and energy mix at a faster pace promoting a green, low-carbon lifestyle and production with a series of new policies.

In particular, when it comes to climate change, the reference is the Paris Agreement: "*We need to deliver on the Paris Agreement on climate change and promote green development. We need to give continued priority to development, implement the 2030 Agenda for Sustainable Development, and make sure that all countries, especially developing ones, share in the fruits of global development.*"[42] The biggest challenge is to reduce greenhouse emissions. President Xi announced that China's goal is to peak carbon dioxide emissions before 2030 and achieve carbon neutrality before 2060. Though these targets seem too distant — meeting these objectives for China will require tremendous hard work, implementing further reforms to push the industry to take a green path by adopting technologies which can help in this transition — China will become a leading player in providing solutions and technologies to ensure the transition toward net-zero-impact (or at least very low) development. It is evident that in order to achieve this result, it will be necessary to favor investments in green projects. Thus, the importance of green finance naturally follows (see Chapter 5).

3.1.1. *President Xi Jinping and the 2015 UN Sustainable Development Summit*

In September 2015, President Xi Jinping attended the UN Sustainable Development Summit[43] and joined other world leaders in adopting "*Transforming Our World: The 2030 Agenda for Sustainable Development*," which contains 17 Goals.[44]

---

[42] See *Let the Torch of Multilateralism Light up Humanity's Way Forward*, Special Address by H.E. Xi Jinping, President of the People's Republic of China at the World Economic Forum Virtual Event of the Davos Agenda, 25 January 2021, text of the speech available at: https://www.fmprc.gov.cn/mfa_eng/zxxx_662805/t1848323.shtml (accessed January 28, 2023).

[43] The UN Sustainable Development Summit, which adopted the *2030 Agenda for Sustainable Development*, took place from September 25–27, 2015 at UN Headquarters in New York.

[44] The 17 sustainable development goals (SDGs) to transform our world are: Goal 1, No Poverty https://www.un.org/sustainabledevelopment/poverty/; Goal 2, Zero Hunger

By embracing the 17 goals, China is evolving into a more sophisticated society and advanced economy and it is also taking the lead to accompany the entire global community to a new world order in which the themes embodied in the UN SDGs play an enormous role in the further development of our entire society which needs to evolve sustainably and inclusively. This is the only possible path; otherwise, it will not be possible to build an inclusive global community in harmony with nature.

China attaches great importance to the realization of the 2030 Agenda for Sustainable Development because the UN's goals match with its new priorities. In order to favor and stimulate the accomplishment of these goals, China has released the *China's National Plan on Implementation of the 2030 Agenda for Sustainable Development*[45] and a progress Report,[46] which assesses the progress so far. China aligns implementation of the

---

https://www.un.org/sustainabledevelopment/hunger/; Goal 3, Good Health and Well-being https://www.un.org/sustainabledevelopment/health/; Goal 4, Quality Education https://www.un.org/sustainabledevelopment/education/; Goal 5, Gender Equality https://www.un.org/sustainabledevelopment/gender-equality/; Goal 6, Clean Water and Sanitation https://www.un.org/sustainabledevelopment/water-and-sanitation/; Goal 7, Affordable and Clean Energy https://www.un.org/sustainabledevelopment/energy/; Goal 8, Decent Work and Economic Growth https://www.un.org/sustainabledevelopment/economic-growth/; Goal 9, Industry, Innovation and Infrastructure https://www.un.org/sustainabledevelopment/infrastructure-industrialization/; Goal 10, Reduced Inequality https://www.un.org/sustainabledevelopment/inequality/; Goal 11, Sustainable Cities and Communities https://www.un.org/sustainabledevelopment/cities/; Goal 12, Responsible Consumption and Production https://www.un.org/sustainabledevelopment/sustainable-consumption-production/; Goal 13, Climate Action https://www.un.org/sustainabledevelopment/climate-change/; Goal 14, Life Below Water https://www.un.org/sustainabledevelopment/oceans/; Goal 15, Life on Land https://www.un.org/sustainabledevelopment/biodiversity/; Goal 16, Peace and Justice Strong Institutions https://www.un.org/sustainabledevelopment/peace-justice/; Goal 17, Partnerships to achieve the Goal https://www.un.org/sustainabledevelopment/globalpartnerships/ (accessed January 28, 2023).

[45] Document available at: https://www.fmprc.gov.cn/mfa_eng/zxxx_662805/W020161014332600482185.pdf (accessed October 8, 2022). "*The effective implementation of the 2030 Agenda will not only pave the way for China to complete the building of a moderately prosperous society and achieve the "Two Centennial Goals" and national rejuvenation, but also inject strong impetus into international development cooperation and elevate the global development level.*" See document at p. 9.

[46] "China's Progress Report on Implementation of the 2030 Agenda for Sustainable Development (2019)," this document recalls comprehensively the progress made by China to achieve the 17 SDGs; the Report is available at: https://www.fmprc.gov.cn/mfa_eng/topics_665678/2030kcxfzyc/P020190924780823323749.pdf (accessed January 28, 2023).

Agenda with medium- and long-term national development strategies which are contained in its Five-Year Plans, especially the last two, namely, the 13th FYP and the most recent 14th FYP, to promote balanced economic, political, cultural, social, and ecological progress. China has translated the SDGs into its FYPs, upholding the vision of innovative, coordinated, green, open, and shared development. These programmatic plans are the representation of President Xi's vision to shape a modern socialist country that is prosperous, strong, democratic, culturally advanced and harmonious, and build a shared future through sustainable development. Important results are already evident in China: According to the Report of the Ministry of Foreign Affairs, "*the gross domestic product (GDP) reached RMB 90.03 trillion in 2018, up by 6.6% year on year. A total of 13.61 million new urban jobs were created and the surveyed unemployment rate remained at a relatively low level of around 5%. China vigorously implements the innovation-driven development strategy. In 2018, the total research and development expenditure reached 2.18% of the GDP and major innovation results kept emerging. The economic structure has been continuously optimized, with emerging industries developing vigorously, traditional sectors experiencing accelerated transformation and upgrading, infrastructures throughout the country improved in an all-round way and headway being made in building Innovation Demonstration Zones for the Implementation of the 2030 Agenda for Sustainable Development.*"[47]

3.1.2. *China and the UN's Goals: Special emphasis on certain goals*

China released its own national plan to implement the SDGs, namely, "*The National Plan on Implementation of the 2030 Agenda for Sustainable Development*"[48] which serves as the overarching guidance document to prioritize and carry out implementation of the goals in China. The overall aim of China's domestic implementation plan for the SDGs is to bundle its various legacy sustainability efforts and economic

[47] *Ibid.*

[48] *National Plan on Implementation of the 2030 Agenda for Sustainable Development*, document at: https://www.greengrowthknowledge.org/sites/default/files/downloads/policy-database//CHINA%29%20China%27s%20National%20Plan%20on%20Implementation%20of%20the%202030%20Agenda%20for%20Sustainable%20Development.pdf (accessed January 28, 2023).

development plans and align them, as best as possible, with the 17 SDGs and their respective targets.

It must be underlined that the *National Plan* is a high-level document with the purpose of integrating the 17 SDGs and their targets into China's overall mid- and long-term development strategies by linking them to preexisting planning documents on related topics,[49] though China does not prioritize these goals and has its own priorities. For this reason, China heavily emphasizes certain goals or targets, while essentially downplaying others. From China's perspective, the UN SDGs are basically reinforcing what the Chinese leadership is already trying to address domestically (see 13th and 14th FYPs). Some goals constitute clear policy priorities that are backed up with a set of sensible projects and implementation plans (e.g., Goal 1: 'no poverty,' Goal 6: 'clean water and sanitation,' and Goal 7: 'affordable and clean energy'), while others are still largely aspirational. Little information is provided that would help shed light on what areas the government actually intends to focus on, and how, if at all, it intends to move forward with implementation (e.g., Goal 5: 'gender equality' and Goal 16: 'peace, justice, and strong institutions'). President Xi has consistently reiterated three main areas which the Party must concentrate on, namely, (i) poverty alleviation; (ii) pollution control and treatment; and (iii) mitigation of financial system risk. As already explained, China, with the celebration of the first centenary goal, and leadership vision for China 2035, is on its way to becoming a moderately prosperous country and has eradicated extreme poverty. Now, the next priorities are to protect the environment by transitioning toward a nature-positive economy and to establish a more sophisticated financial system in line with the more advanced economies with the introduction of dedicated reforms.

It must be stressed that because of the 2030 Agenda's strong focus on global partnerships for sustainable development, engagement on the SDGs also feeds into China's regional expansion interests (see the RCEP) and its growing geopolitical aspirations, most obviously with further development of the BRI and the start of new trade relations with the EU as soon as the CAI will be ratified. These initiatives will surely reinforce China's soft power. Linking its international initiatives with the implementation of its 14th FYP, which is in line with the SDGs, will help China in gaining more influence and reshaping multilateralism.

---

[49] See Section V Implementation Plan for the 17 Sustainable Development Goals, of the *National Plan on Implementation of the 2030 Agenda for Sustainable Development.*

3.1.3. *China's approach for the implementation of the 2030 Agenda*

China's approach to the implementation of the SDGs consists of the integration of the 17 goals into its development plans,[50] thus achieving the synergy between the 2030 Agenda and China's mid- and long-term development strategy. Then, it is also the responsibility of the local governments (provinces, autonomous regions, and municipalities) to integrate their own five-year plans with the SDGs. China also pushed multilateral mechanisms to formulate action plans for the 2030 Agenda; for example, it played a leading role in urging the G20 to draw up an action plan to implement the SDGs.[51]

China also has put in evidence that the general public's understanding, recognition, and participation are necessary for consistent and effective implementation of the 2030 Agenda. Thus, it is necessary that with more awareness China will help its people fully appreciate the personal and public interest in the implementation of the 2030 Agenda through social mobilization.

To complete its approach and share its achievements, "China will actively participate in follow-up reviews at the international and regional levels." Moreover, China supports the central role of the UN High-Level Political Forum on Sustainable Development and will assist it in regular

---

[50]These plans include the following: The National Outline for Innovation-Driven Development Strategy, the National Sustainable Agricultural Development Plan (2015–2030), and the National Outline for Information Technology Development Strategy. In the social field, it has published the Decision of the Communist Party of China (CPC) Central Committee and the State Council on Winning the Tough Battle in Poverty Reduction and the Healthy China Outline (2030). In the environmental field, China has prepared the China Biodiversity Conservation Strategy and Plan of Action (2011–2030) and the National Climate Change Program (2014–2020). See the *National Plan on Implementation of the 2030 Agenda for Sustainable Development.*

[51]Refer to the G20, 2016, China. On September 4, 2016, the 11th G20 Summit was held at the Hangzhou International Expo Center. President Xi Jinping chaired the summit and delivered the opening speech. Xi Jinping stressed that faced with current challenges, the G20 must keep up with the changing times, fully honor its commitments, make joint efforts and deliver benefits to all, as well as stick together as partners in meeting challenges in order to bring the global economy onto the track of prosperity and stability, and achieve robust, sustainable, balanced, and inclusive growth. For more info, visit: http://www.g20chn.org/English/Dynamic/201609/t20160909_3416.html (accessed January 28, 2023).

reviews of global implementation progress. China will also use the forum as a platform to strengthen exchanges with other countries and solicit opinions and suggestions. "China welcomes enhanced regional cooperation and the positive contributions of the United Nations' regional commissions and specialized agencies. Also China will strengthen cooperation with the United Nations System in China and other international organizations by organizing workshops and compiling and releasing regular reports on China's implementation of the 2030 Agenda to fully review the progress in implementation of all the Sustainable Development Goals in China."[52]

In pursuing the SDGs, China will conduct reviews of its implementation efforts along with assessment of the progress of the 14th FYP. Indeed, a first review was made in 2021 as evidenced in the following section.

3.2 *China's first voluntary national review assessment after the first 5 years*

The UN, as part of its follow-up and review mechanism for its 2030 Agenda, encourages member states to conduct regular and inclusive reviews of progress at the national level. This voluntary National Review aims to facilitate the sharing of experiences with a view toward accelerating the implementation of the 2030 Agenda. After the first five years from the adoption of the 2030 Agenda, 43 countries carried out voluntary national reviews (VNRs) of their implementation of the 2030 Agenda in 2021 including China.

The following is an extract from the UN Economic and Social Council High-level political forum on sustainable development:

> "*Over the past five years, under the strong leadership of President Xi Jinping, China has put people's well-being front and center, followed a new vision of innovative, coordinated, green, open and shared development, and taken comprehensive measures to implement the 2030 Agenda according to its national implementation plan that was among the first*

---

[52] *Source*: China's *National Plan on the Implementation of the 2030 Agenda for Sustainable Development*, document available at: https://www.greengrowthknowledge.org/national-documents/chinas-national-plan-implementation-2030-agenda-sustainable-development (accessed January 28, 2023).

of the kind in the world, and through an inter-ministerial coordination mechanism made up of 45 ministries and agencies, integrating its implementation efforts with the country's 13th Five-Year Plan (and now continued with the 14th FYP) and other medium-to-long-term development strategies. China has also actively participated in international development cooperation to promote global implementation endeavors. All these efforts have yielded remarkable results."[53]

3.2.1. *China has eradicated extreme poverty and ensured food security*

"*At the end of 2020, China won its fight against poverty as scheduled, ending poverty for the 98.99 million rural residents living below the current poverty line, and meeting the targets of SDG 1 ten years ahead of schedule. Building on these achievements, China is prioritizing the development of agriculture and rural areas, and implementing the rural revitalization strategy in a comprehensive manner. In 2020, China reaped bumper harvest in grain production for the 17th year in a row. The 'rice bowl' of the Chinese people is tightly held in the hands of the Chinese themselves.*"

3.2.2. *China has actively taken climate actions and contributed to global green development*

"*Following the philosophy that lucid water and lush mountain are invaluable assets, China has accelerated the transition towards green development. China has won the three critical battles to keep its sky blue, water clear, and soil pollution-free and made remarkable headway in holistic protection and treatment of its mountains, rivers, forests, farmland, lakes, grassland and deserts. China has firmly implemented* the Paris Agreement *and actively participated in global climate governance.*

[53]*Source*: United Nations, Sustainable Development Goals — Knowledge Platform, Voluntary National Review, China, available at: https://sustainabledevelopment.un.org/memberstates/china (accessed January 8, 2023). The entire document containing the 43 voluntary national reviews is available at: https://sustainabledevelopment.un.org/content/documents/27613Compilation_of_main_messages_for_the_2021_VNR.pdf.

Carbon intensity in China has accumulatively dropped by 18.8%. Clean energy now accounts for 23.4% of China's energy mix. China leads the world in installed capacity and output of photovoltaic and wind power generation. China has scaled up its nationally determined contributions and aims to peak its carbon dioxide emissions before 2030 and achieve carbon neutrality before 2060, injecting strong impetus into global climate actions as well as green and low-carbon development worldwide."

3.2.3. *China has met the challenge of the pandemic with success and improved public health governance*

"*Putting people and their lives above everything else, China has scored major strategic achievements in fighting COVID-19 and protected people's rights to life and health. China has increased investment in public health infrastructure and woven the world's largest social safety net with basic medical insurance covering more than 1.3 billion people. With upgraded public health services, Chinese people's sense of fulfillment, happiness and security is steadily increased.*"

3.2.4. *China has registered steady economic growth and enhanced development resilience*

"*China's GDP has increased from less than 70 trillion yuan to over 100 trillion yuan. Steady progress has been made in infrastructure connectivity and sustainable transportation. Pandemic control goes hand in hand with economic and social development. A new development paradigm is forming with domestic circulation as the mainstay and domestic and international circulations reinforcing each other. In 2020, China's GDP grew by 2.3%, making China the only major world economy to grow.*"

3.2.5. *China has shouldered its responsibilities as a major country and advanced international development cooperation*

"*China champions mankind's common values of peace, development, fairness, justice, democracy and freedom, and strives to build a community of shared future for mankind. It has stepped up efforts to promote synergy between the Belt and Road Initiative and the 2030 Agenda, promoted the green BRI, deepened South-South cooperation, and helped other developing countries implement the 2030 Agenda to the best of its capability. China has provided assistance to more than 160 countries and international organizations in combating COVID-19, and donated and exported pandemic response supplies to over 200 countries and regions. China has joined the COVAX, provided or is providing vaccine assistance to more than 80 developing countries most in need, and exported vaccines to more than 40 countries, making its due contribution to the global fight against the pandemic.*

China's remarkable achievements in implementing the 2030 Agenda are attributable to the strong leadership of the CPC (Communist Party of China), to the advantages of socialism with Chinese characteristics, to China's comprehensive drive to deepen reforms and expand opening-up, and to the joint efforts of the people of all ethnic groups in China.

Likewise, the global implementation of the 2030 Agenda calls for strong political leadership, effective institutional guarantees, scientific and technological innovation, extensive social mobilization and pragmatic global partnership. The COVID-19 pandemic has dealt a severe blow to the global implementation of the 2030 Agenda. China stands ready to work with other countries to consolidate political will, put development first, strengthen the means of implementation, take joint actions and address special difficulties of developing countries to leave no one and no country behind."

It is evident that deeper cooperation among all countries is the only possible path to achieving the goals of the UN; thus, China is committed to reinforcing its relationships with the rest of the global community because only through a 'green partnership' will it be possible to pursue sustainable development. Therefore, the entire global community will be involved reshaping multilateralism and improving global governance also.

3.3. *International development cooperation at the core of China's plans*

It is evident that international cooperation is a fundamental element in achieving common goals and President Xi on many occasions has reiterated the fact that "in the age of economic globalization, countries are closely linked in their development and they all rise and fall together. No country could seek development on its own; and the one sure path is through coordination and cooperation."[54] As for international development cooperation, China has been actively promoting an open world economy and a new type of international relations, reshaping global governance and upholding multilateralism and the international system with the UN at the center. China is not only a member of the international community but is also acting proactively to advance international cooperation within the framework of the BRI; for example, it attaches great importance to this initiative not only to better connect China with the West but also to create more solid trade relationships with all the countries involved in this Initiative, thus shaping a reinforced multilateralism with a new element: greater attention to our environment. In this framework, the so-called Comprehensive Agreement on Investment (CAI) with the EU is to be included, currently on standby, as it represents another important piece of the puzzle to create synergies for green recovery and sustainable development. In fact, China and the EU have forged a Green Partnership which is briefly introduced in the following section.

3.3.1. *EU–China green partnership: Introduction*

In the context of international cooperation, it deserves to be mentioned that both China and the EU share commitments toward green and sustainable development, which in turn leads to better global governance on climate change. The two counterparts aim to achieve carbon neutrality, though China has fixed this target for 2060 while the EU has fixed the date for 2050. In order to exchange experiences and pursue joint commitments, and thus forge a more solid 'Green Partnership,' in September 2020, the two sides agreed to establish a High-Level Environment and Climate Dialogue.[55] Notably, this Green Partnership builds on the EU–China

[54] *Source*: Keynote Speech by H.E. Xi Jinping President of the People's Republic of China, at the Opening Ceremony of the G20, Hangzhou, September 3, 2016, document available at: http://www.g20chn.org/English/Dynamic/201609/t20160909_3414.html (accessed January 28, 2023).

[55] *Source*: Multinational Development Policy Dialogue Brussels, *EU–China Green Partnership for Better Global Governance*, document available at: https://www.kas.de/en/web/mned-bruessel/european-green-deal/detail/-/content/eu-china-green-partnership-for-better-global-governance (accessed January 28, 2023).

Partnership on Climate Change[56] and the EU–China Blue Partnership.[57] This bilateral partnership reflects the commitment of both sides to work together to tackle global environmental challenges and to provide an international cooperation model for achieving the 2030 Agenda Goals for sustainable development.

In the next chapters, we present in greater detail the measures adopted by the EU and China to achieve these goals and to transition toward a nature-positive economy. The common objective of a greener and more sustainable global economy needs other elements such as the increased use of renewable and clean sources of energy to reduce greenhouse gasses and green finance to sustain this transition toward a nature-positive economy.

The 14th FYP puts China on the path to reaching its first-phase goal of capping emissions by 2030, which also confirm its interest in developing a green economy and aligning itself with the vision of the EU for green and sustainable development.[58] According to the 14th FYP,

[56]The EU and China Partnership on Climate Change was created in 2005 as one of the major outcomes of the China–EU Summit. "*The focus of the Partnership is on concrete action: the development and deployment of clean energy technology. It demonstrates the EU's determination to tackle climate change at the highest level and in concrete ways.*" *Source*: MEMO/05/298, Brussels, 2 September 2005, document available at: https://ec.europa.eu/clima/system/files/2016-11/joint_declaration_ch_eu_en.pdf (accessed January 28, 2023).

[57]The EU–China Blue Partnership is intended to improve international governance of the world's oceans. The EU and China signed the agreement at the 20th Summit between the EU and China, which took place in Beijing, China, on July 16, 2018. The agreement titled, 'Blue Partnership for the Oceans: Towards Better Ocean Governance,' aims to promote better ocean governance and policy coordination between the two countries. The partnership agreement outlines future areas of collaboration between the EU and China on the conservation and sustainable use of marine biodiversity in the high seas; marine pollution, including marine plastic litter and microplastics; mitigation of and adaptation to climate change impacts on the oceans, including the Arctic ocean; conservation of marine living resources in Antarctica; and fisheries governance and the prevention of illegal, unreported, and unregulated (IUU) fishing. The entire agreement is available at: https://data.consilium.europa.eu/doc/document/ST-10640-2018-INIT/fr/pdf (accessed January 28, 2023).

[58]The 14th FYP puts a particular emphasis on the protection of the environment and climate change and thus it indicates the path toward carbon neutrality: Green development features prominently in the Plan with five of the eight binding targets set in this area. During 2021–2025, energy and carbon intensity are targeted to decline by 13.5% for

"peaking carbon dioxide emissions before 2030 requires more ambitious energy and carbon intensity targets. For instance, a reduction in carbon intensity by 23% from the 2020 level instead of the proposed 18% would increase chances for success. While the Plan does not include a cap on energy consumption, provincial plans could set an ambitious target paired with tighter energy efficiency regulations. Incentives to develop innovative energy efficiency technologies with support from the private sector are critical to reducing energy intensity and should include penalties for industries that fail to meet the benchmark."[59]

Now, let us turn our attention toward how the major economies intend to concentrate their efforts to tackle the common problem of climate change. As will emerge from the next chapters, initiatives are already in place but what is needed is a greater coordination and common platforms in order to better coordinate actions and policies to safeguard our future.

---

energy and 18% for carbon intensity per unit of GDP. Other binding targets include increasing (i) the share of days with good air quality in cities up to 87.5% (from 87% in 2020); (ii) the share of surface water at or better than grade III up to 85% (from 83.4% in 2020); and (iii) forest coverage up to 24.1% (from 23.2% in 2019). As a non-binding indicator, the proportion of non-fossil fuels in primary energy consumption is set at 20% from 15% in the previous plan. The Plan promotes low-carbon development and circular economy with new approaches to transport, energy production, and waste management policies. In this sense, see the 14th Five Year Plan of the People's Republic of China — Fostering High-Quality Development, 中华人民共和国第十四个五年规划 — 推进高质量发展, Observation and Suggestions, Asian Development Bank, No. 2021-01, document available at: https://www.adb.org/sites/default/files/publication/705886/14th-five-year-plan-high-quality-development-prc.pdf (accessed January 28, 2023).

[59] *Ibid.*

Chapter 3

Shared Responsibilities in the Ambit of Climate Change: The Leading Economies' Initiatives for the Transition toward a Carbon-Neutral Economy Need to Converge & the Importance of the Outcome of the COP27

China and the EU have established deep intertwined economic relations and have come to understand that their economic relationships must include a 'Green Partnership' to meet the goals of sustainable development. Both these blocks have implemented specific policies to help their respective economies transition toward a nature-positive economy and this will serve as an example for the rest of the international community. Only with specific new policies and working together[1] will it be possible to reach 'carbon neutrality' and fight climate change and thus build a shared future for mankind.

[1]The USA has adopted a specific framework to fight climate change and it will be illustrated in Section 4.1.

1. China is Building a More Meaningful Partnership with the EU in the Ambit of Climate Change

The new priorities of China have pushed the 'Middle Kingdom' to reinforce its cooperation with the EU, in particular regarding climate change. The so-called 'Green Partnership' is an expression of this renewed cooperation. The fact that the two blocks now pay greater attention to the protection of the nature and environment has awakened the interest of the public and put in evidence the urgency to act as soon as possible in a concerted manner to reduce carbon emissions for the benefit not only of Mother Earth but of the entire global community.

1.1. *Increased commercial relationships with the CAI but also a 'Green Partnership' to contribute to shaping a sustainable development*

In the ambit of investment and trade cooperation, China and the EU, on December 30, 2020 after seven years and 35 rounds of negotiations, reached an agreement in principle on the so-called Comprehensive Agreement on Investment (CAI).[2] One of the main aims of the agreement, not yet in force, is to grant European investors a greater level of access to the Chinese market and to improve the level playing field for those already there. This agreement is also aimed at simplifying the framework for China to invest in the EU because the CAI will replace the bilateral investment treaties (BITs) that all EU Member States, except Ireland, concluded with China. It is noteworthy that the UK exited the European Union and therefore will establish another channel to maintain and continue to attract Chinese investments, though China would have preferred to have had a single instrument to regulate investment in the EU.

The next step is ratification of the CAI. Though the EU has suspended this process amid the ongoing political tensions,[3] it does not necessarily

---

[2]Refer to Section 2.3.

[3]The EU imposed a recent package of sanctions pursuant to Implementing Regulation (EU) 2021/478 which came into force on March 22, 2021, concerning restrictive measures against persons and organizations in mainland China for, according to the EU, serious

mean that the suspension of ratification would lead to its cancellation, which is unlikely.[4] Neither party wants to waste seven years of negotiations. The two blocks are truly interested in having it in place; however, the consequence of the current suspension by the European Commission may lead to several scenarios: (i) The agreement is put on hold indefinitely as a result of its geopolitical significance in the relationship between the EU and mainland China; (ii) once sanctions have been lifted, the EU and mainland China are able to move forward, and ratification of the CAI would take place (the EU's concerns over human rights violations would still present a stumbling block and would therefore present a challenge to get the CAI ratified); and (iii) the EU or mainland China decide to change aspects of the agreement such as the deal's declarations and/or guarantees. In any case, despite the current impasse in the EU–China political relationship, the European Commission will continue to work on the technical aspects of the agreement including the legal scrubbing and translation of the agreement. It seems appropriate at this point to put in evidence that among the main contents of the agreement, besides delineating regulations on open market access, is the section on 'environmental protection.' It is also important to stress that the CAI upholds free trade and multilateralism, and it stresses that the globalization process, which includes trade and investment, cannot be reversed. It is evident that cooperation cannot be limited to economic relations, but it must be extended to other global issues such as climate change, and on this theme the involvement of the entire global community is necessary as will be explained in the following chapters.

---

human rights violations and abuses. The sanctions include asset freezes and travel bans. The sanctions have, for example, targeted four Chinese individuals and a Chinese organization. In consequence, mainland China has taken retaliatory countersanctions against EU officials and entities. The Chinese sanctions imposed in March on several European entities and political representatives, including five Members of the European Parliament and the Subcommittee on Human Rights, were a retaliatory act in response to the EU decision to enact restrictive measures against four Chinese officials over human rights abuses against the Muslim Uyghur minority in the Xinjiang region.

[4]On May 20, 2021, the European Parliament passed a resolution to freeze ratification of the EU–China Comprehensive Agreement on Investment (CAI) in response to Chinese sanctions on European human rights advocates. The vote passed with 599 votes in favor, 30 votes against, and 58 abstentions.

1.1.1. *Green Partnership' respecting multilateralism*

The so-called "Green Partnership" between China and the EU does not mean that the two blocks exclude multilateralism from the solution to climate change and sustainable development; on the contrary, their partnership serves as example for third parties to cement international cooperation. In fact, this 'Green Partnership' is to be interpreted as an important tool in the global search for common and suitable solutions to tackle climate change. It is not possible to ignore the problem anymore, and urgent actions are needed to cut emissions and reach carbon neutrality in order to not worsen the situation. Both the EU and China acknowledge the necessity of involving developing countries, especially those experiencing rapid economic development with a subsequent high rate of greenhouse gases emission, in a comprehensive cooperation framework for greener and sustainable development. Thus, it is necessary to help these countries in tackling environmental problems and include them in global efforts to mitigate climate change. It is evident that this green partnership has a bilateral nature, but it is designed to be backed by a multilateral system where every country has a role to play by recognizing the need for differentiated contributions. In fact, the more advanced economies, and those with technological capabilities, should lead the way and provide technical and concrete aid to the less equipped countries.

1.1.2. *The EU's Emissions Trading System and the Carbon Border Adjustment Mechanism: Brief introduction*

In the context of reducing greenhouse gas emissions and reaching its ambitious target of a 55% reduction in carbon emissions compared to 1990 levels by 2030, and to become a climate-neutral continent by 2050, the EU introduced the so-called 'Emissions Trading System' (ETS)[5] in

[5]The EU's Emissions Trading System is a key pillar of European climate policy. It contributes to the EU's greenhouse gas reduction targets by setting a cap on the maximum level of emissions for the sectors covered and establishing an installation-level market for emission permits, which generates a price for them. This knowledge package traces the history and discusses the main features of EU ETS. Launched in 2005, the ETS is the world's first international emissions trading scheme and the EU's flagship policy to combat climate change. *It sets a cap on the amount of greenhouse gas emissions that can be released from industrial installations in certain sectors. Allowances must be bought on the ETS trading market, though a certain number of free allowances are distributed to prevent carbon leakage. That system has been effective in addressing the risk of leakage but it also dampens*

2005 and in July 2021 the 'Carbon Border Adjustment Mechanism' (CBAM),[6] which is a climate measure mechanism that should prevent the risk of carbon leakage and support the EU's ambition on climate mitigation while ensuring WTO compatibility. However, this system is a controversial element in the framework of the European Green Deal; in fact, the ETS and the CBAM could frustrate developing countries' export trade, resulting in the EU's 'new growth' based on the fact that these 'green trade barriers' will disrupt development of trade with developing countries. Though the EU has implemented a functional system to reduce emissions, there are several concerns to be considered:

(a) *While EU supports the Paris Agreement, the CBAM (also known as Carbon Border Tax — CBT) seems to be at odds with the core of the Paris Agreement, namely the bottom-up INDC approach,*[7] *with all countries declaring their own ambitions. CBAM deviates from the self-determined contribution framework to an approach that features "coercive pressures from some nations towards others." From a critical perspective, the EU's assertion that imposing CBAM could encourage other countries to raise their decarbonization ambition*

(*Continued*)

---

the incentive to invest in greener production at home and abroad. Source: https://ec.europa.eu/commission/presscorner/detail/en/qanda_21_3661 (accessed January 28, 2023).

[6] The Carbon Border Adjustment Mechanism or CBAM system designed in compliance with the World Trade Organization or WTO, will work as follows: *EU importers will buy carbon certificates corresponding to the carbon price that would have been paid had the goods been produced under the EU's carbon pricing rules. Conversely, once a non-EU producer can show that they have already paid a price for the carbon used in the production of the imported goods in a third country, the corresponding cost can be fully deducted for the EU importer. The CBAM will help reduce the risk of carbon leakage by encouraging producers in non-EU countries to green their production processes. Source*: https://ec.europa.eu/commission/presscorner/detail/en/qanda_21_3661 (accessed January 28, 2023).

[7] Intended Nationally Determined Contribution (INDC) is a non-binding national plans highlighting climate change mitigation, including climate-related targets for greenhouse gas emission reduction, policies, and measures governments aim to implement in response to climate change and as a contribution to achieve the global targets set out in the Paris Agreement. https://en.wikipedia.org/wiki/Nationally_determined_contribution (accessed January 28, 2023).

(*Continued*)

might result in a "slippery slope," as it is not convincing that the CBAM- driven result will be better than the INDC-driven counterfactual result. Besides, it may imply that a "sovereignty-seeking" EU places little trust in the efforts of National Determined Contributions from other nations, not to mention that many academic researchers have questioned the so-called "carbon leakage" that serves as the asserted reason for a CBAM (8).

(b) *The EU Green Deal is generally seen as EU's initiative to reclaim global climate governance leadership. Nevertheless, global leadership in the multilateral system must respect existing UN rules and norms. Analysts have raised two major concerns:*
   1. *The CBAM is understood by and large as a protectionist policy which is not yet compatible with WTO legislation.*
   2. *It violates the principle of "common but differentiated responsibilities and respective capabilities" which is endorsed by Paris Agreement and UNFCCC. Therefore, it is understood that if the EU wishes to take the lead in climate policy respecting WTO and UNFCCC principles, then the CBAM should only target developed countries*

(c) *A third concern is that the potential EU–USA alliance on CBT (6) risks becoming a source of conflict on a global scale. In the EU's New EU–US Agenda for Global Change, the EU proposes to re-establish a close and open transatlantic partnership. In the new agenda, the EU affirms the unique nature of EU–US relations, arguing that if Europe and the US join forces, their global influence will be unmatched in terms of both total economic volume and technological innovation capacities. Some analysts raised the concern that if the Biden administration supports the Clean Energy Security Act, the US–EU consensus on a carbon border tax may also become a new trade-protection tool for developed countries against developing countries. If most developing countries practice solidarity in rejecting the CBT, the world economy might split into parallel systems, namely a lower-carbon-intensity economic system (of developed countries) and a higher-carbon-intensity economic system (of developing countries).*[8]

Source: The Multinational Development Policy Dialogue — KAS in Brussels. MDPD Papers: "EU–China Green Partnership for Better Global Governance"

[8]This is an extract from the paper titled "EU–China Green Partnership for Better Global Governance," Yanzhu Zhang — Foreign Environmental Cooperation Center, Ministry of

It is now the right time to introduce 'EU's Green Deal' to better understand the framework in which this Partnership is developing.

1.2. *European Green Deal: EU's commitments for sustainable development*

The 'European Green Deal' (hereinafter EGD), approved in 2020,[9] is the EU's response to the climate crisis and sustainable development. The EGD encompasses a set of policy initiatives aimed at making the EU climate neutral by 2050. Substantially, the EGD resets the Commission's commitment to tackling climate and environmental-related challenges. It recognizes that the EU must act if it is to avoid the most catastrophic consequences for the economy and society, while creating a base for sustainable prosperity for current and future generations. The Green Deal provides a valuable framework for action and a good basis for a new growth strategy for Europe. It acknowledges that changes are needed across sectors, and that these changes toward sustainability will only succeed if the measures taken also enhance competitiveness and 'leave no one behind' according to the EU Commission. At the heart of the EGD is the EU's goal to become climate neutral by 2050, supported by the mid-term target to reduce the EU's GHG emissions by 55% by 2030 (compared to 1990). It is noteworthy that the European Green Deal covers all sectors of the economy — transport, energy, agriculture, buildings, and industries such as steel, cement, Information Communication Technology (ITC), textiles, and chemicals — and it cannot be otherwise if the Green Deal is to ensure a just and inclusive transition toward green and sustainable development.

The European Green Deal *aims to protect, conserve and enhance the EU's natural capital, and protect the health and well-being of citizens from environment-related risks and impacts. At the same time, this*

Ecology and Environment, Beijing, China, document available at: https://www.kas.de/documents/272317/12679503/EU%E2%80%93China+Green+Partnership+for+Better+Global+Governance.pdf/27f58f22-0798-7b2a-d3ad-8b7263c43461?version=1.0&t=1623391813946 (accessed January 28, 2023).

[9]European Commission, Communication From the Commission to the European Parliament, the European Council, the Council, the European Economic and Social Committee and the Committee of the Regions, The European Deal, Brussels, 11.12.2019 COM (2019) 640 final, document available at: https://ec.europa.eu/info/sites/default/files/european-green-deal-communication_en.pdf (accessed January 28, 2023).

transition must be just and inclusive. It must put people first, and pay attention to the regions, industries and workers who will face the greatest challenges. Since it will bring substantial change, active public participation and confidence in the transition is paramount if policies are to work and be accepted. A new pact is needed tobring together citizens in all their diversity, with national, regional, local authorities, civilsociety and industry working closely with the EU's institutions and consultative bodies.[10]

Naturally, the EU Green Deal is to be considered an integral part of the Commission's strategy to implement the United Nation's 2030 Agenda for sustainable development. Consequently, the EGD is focused on sustainability, and the well-being of EU citizens will be at the center of new economic policies. Another important aspect is that the EGD aims to boost the efficient use of resources by moving to a clean, circular economy and reversing biodiversity loss, which is a fundamental element of our environment that is dramatically threatened by climate change.

As clarified in the following sections, the European Green Deal includes a series of political initiatives and strategies which make up a complex and interrelated system of legislation by the EU to make Europe a climate-resilient society by 2050, fully adapted to the unavoidable impacts of climate change.

Before explaining the main initiatives related to the EGD, it is worth noting that the adoption of the European Climate Law (ECL)[11] established a clear binding framework to achieve climate neutrality by 2050 which fully enshrines the 2030 target of at least 55% greenhouse gas reductions.[12] Thus, the ECL writes into law the goals set out in the European Green Deal for Europe's economy and society to become climate neutral by 2050.[13]

---

[10] *Source*: Introduction of the EU Green Deal, COM (2019) 640 final.

[11] Regulation (EU) 2021/1119 of the European Parliament and of the Council of 30 June 2021 establishing the framework for achieving climate neutrality and amending Regulations (EC) No 401/2009 and (EU) 2018/1999 ('European Climate Law'), document available at: https://eur-lex.europa.eu/legal-content/EN/TXT/?uri=CELEX:32021R1119 (accessed January 28, 2023).

[12] A more detailed framework on Climate Actions and about the EU initiatives to deliver the European Green Deal is contained in the following web-page: European Commission, Climate Action: https://ec.europa.eu/clima/eu-action/european-green-deal_en (October January 28, 2023).

[13] Climate neutrality by 2050 means achieving net zero greenhouse gas emissions for EU countries as a whole, mainly by cutting emissions, investing in green technologies, and protecting the natural environment.

1.2.1. *Policies and strategies encompassing the European Green Deal: Brief overview*

The European Green Deal is composed of a series of policies and strategies and it would be necessary to write an entire tome to examine in detail each single aspect; however, it seems appropriate to introduce the main initiatives of this ambitious plan because it has many similarities with the Chinese strategy as will emerge from the following sections.

Notably, the EGD aims at transforming the EU's economy for a sustainable future; in order to achieve its many targets, it was necessary to formulate differentiated strategies and policies touching all the industry sectors and also acting directly to preserve nature with a dedicated initiative. Thus, it seems appropriate to begin with a brief introduction of the so-called 2030 Biodiversity Strategy.[14]

The EU Biodiversity Strategy for 2030[15] is a comprehensive, systemic, and ambitious long-term plan for protecting nature and reversing the degradation of ecosystems. The strategy aims to safeguard Europe's biodiversity and it should serve as an example for other countries. It is a key pillar of the European Green Deal and of EU leadership on international action for global public goods and sustainable development goals (refer to the 2030 Agenda of the UN). With an objective to aid Europe's biodiversity recovery by 2030, the Strategy sets out new ways to implement existing legislation more effectively, with new commitments, measures, targets, and governance mechanisms.

The protection of nature, and investing in its restoration, is not only critical for Europe's economic recovery but also for the rest of the international community. Over half of global GDP depends on nature and the services it provides, with three key economic sectors — construction, agriculture, and food and drink — all highly dependent on it.[16] Another reason why is so urgent to act to protect nature and its biodiversity is

[14] For more information and related actions on Biodiversity visit: https://ec.europa.eu/environment/strategy/biodiversity-strategy-2030_en (accessed October 28, 2022).

[15] The full document COM(2020)380 final, EU Biodiversity Strategy for 2030 — Bringing nature back into our lives, is available at: https://ec.europa.eu/info/sites/default/files/communication-annex-eu-biodiversity-strategy-2030_en.pdf (accessed January 28, 2023).

[16] See COM(2020)380 final, and the document prepared by the World Economic Forum (2020), *Nature Risk Rising: Why the Crisis Engulfing Nature Matters for Business and the*

because biodiversity is also crucial for safeguarding the EU and global food security. As noted in the document from the EU Commission,[17] "*biodiversity loss threatens our food systems, putting our food security and nutrition at risk.*" "*The biodiversity crisis and the climate crisis are intrinsically linked. Climate change accelerates the destruction of the natural world through droughts, flooding and wildfires, while the loss and unsustainable use of nature are in turn key drivers of climate change. But just as the crises are linked, so are the solutions. Nature is a vital ally in the fight against climate change.*"[18] According to the EU Commission and the World Economic Forum, biodiversity loss and with ecosystem collapse represent one of the biggest threats facing humanity in the next decade, and this scenario is supported by the most recent research.[19] Thus, it is extremely urgent to act rapidly to avoid catastrophic consequences and work together with the rest of the international community for sustainable and green development.

The other main strategies and policies include the following:

The Farm to Fork Strategy[20] is also at the core of the EGD, aiming to make food system fair, healthy, and environmentally-friendly. This strategy *addresses comprehensively the challenges of sustainable food systems and recognizes the inextricable links between healthy people, healthy societies and a healthy planet. The strategy is also central to the Commission's agenda to achieve the United Nations' Sustainable Development Goals (SDGs)*.[21] The strategy lays down a new approach to ensure that agriculture, fisheries and aquaculture, and the food value chain

---

Economy, document available at: https://www3.weforum.org/docs/WEF_New_Nature_Economy_Report_2020.pdf (accessed January 28, 2023).

[17] *Source*: COM(2020)380.

[18] *Ibid.*

[19] *Source*: COM(2020)380, see also The Global Risks Report 2020 (15th Edition), World Economic Forum, document available at: https://www3.weforum.org/docs/WEF_Global_Risk_Report_2020.pdf (accessed January 28, 2023).

[20] *Source*: COM(2020)318 final, A Farm to Fork Strategy for a fair, healthy and environmentally-friendly food system, document available at: https://eur-lex.europa.eu/legal-content/EN/TXT/?uri=CELEX:52020DC0381 (accessed October 28, 2022). For additional information on this Strategy visit: https://ec.europa.eu/food/horizontal-topics/farm-fork-strategy_en.

[21] *Ibid.*

contribute appropriately to the objective for a climate-neutral Union in 2050. Food systems remain one of the key drivers of climate change and environmental degradation. The manufacturing, processing, retailing, packaging, and transportation of food are major contributors to GHG emissions, air, soil, and water pollution, and have a profound impact on biodiversity. On the other hand, consumers also need to be empowered to choose sustainable food. The creation of a favorable environment that makes it easier to choose healthy and sustainable diets will benefit consumers' health and quality of life, and reduce health-related costs for society.[22]

Concerning the decarbonization of the EU industry:

The EGD places a particular emphasis on decarbonization of its economy, and in this ambit there is a need to rethink policies for a clean energy supply across the economy, industry, production and consumption, transport, food production, and other sectors. For this reason, decarbonizing the energy system is critical to reach the EU's climate objectives in 2030 and 2050. Thus, an energy sector must be developed that is based on renewable sources, complemented by the rapid phasing out of coal and other fossil fuels. This is why the EU is pushing investment in alternative and renewable sources of energy. This aspect is of particular importance if we take into consideration the conflict in Ukraine: It is absolutely necessary to eliminate the dependence on fossil sources and foster the use of alternative and renewable sources of energy. In this context, it is necessary to state that in 2015 the EU launched its **Energy Union Strategy**[23] which aims to provide secure, affordable, and clean energy for EU citizen and businesses, and to move away from an economy driven by fossil fuels to meet the targets of 2030 and 2050, with the vision to support innovative and competitive European companies that develop the industrial products

[22]*Source*: The EU Green Deal — A roadmap to sustainable economies. Visit: https://www.switchtogreen.eu/the-eu-green-deal-promoting-a-green-notable-circular-economy/ (accessed January 28, 2023).

[23]The Energy Union Strategy was a key priority of the Juncker Commission (2014-2019) with the vision to build an integrated continent-wide energy system where energy flows freely across borders, the best possible use of resources, and a naturally low-carbon and climate friendly economy; see A Framework Strategy for a Resilient Energy Union with a Forward-Looking Climate Change Policy/COM/2015/080 final, the full document is available at: https://eur-lex.europa.eu/legal-content/EN/TXT/?uri=COM:2015:80:FIN (accessed January 28, 2023).

and technology needed to deliver energy efficiency and low-carbon technologies inside and outside the EU. This strategy was flanked by the most recent **Clean Energy Transition Programme**[24] aimed at facilitating the transition toward an energy-efficient, renewable-energy-based, climate-neutral, and climate-resilient economy by funding coordination and support actions across Europe. Periodically, the European Commission publishes its Report on the State of the Energy union, in order to monitor the advancements on the road to climate neutrality by 2050, and the latest one, i.e., COM/2021/950,[25] was published in 2021 putting in evidence the following:

State of the Energy Union: Key findings

- *In 2020, EU* ***greenhouse gas*** *(GHG)* ***emissions*** *(including international aviation) were down 31% compared to 1990 due to the impact of the pandemic on energy consumption but also due to continued decarbonisation trends;*
- ***In 2020, for the first time, renewables overtook fossil fuels as the EU's main power source*** *(38% of EU electricity, fossil fuels 37% and nuclear 25%). The share of renewable energy sources in the overall EU energy mix is expected to have reached at least 22% although some Member States are at risk of failing to meet their national binding target;*
- *Latest available data indicate that EU primary energy consumption declined by 1.9% and final energy consumption by 0.6% in 2019 compared to 2018;*
- ***EU net energy import dependency reached 60.6% in 2019 compared to 58.2% in 2018 and 56% in 2000;*** *the highest level in the past 30 years;*
- *While fossil fuel subsidies fell slightly in 2020, down to EUR 52 billion from EUR56 billion in 2019, this was due to falling consumption amid the COVID-19-related restrictions. Without Member States action, fossil fuel subsidies are likely to rebound as economic activity picks up;*
- *To date, nine Member States have phased out coal, 13 have made national commitments to do so by a certain date, four are considering*

[24] For more information on this theme, visit: https://cinea.ec.europa.eu/life/clean-energy-transition_it.

[25] https://energy.ec.europa.eu/system/files/2021-10/state_of_the_energy_union_report_2021.pdf.

(*Continued*)

possible dates and only one has not yet started national discussions on a phase-out;

- *Energy prices seesawed violently as the economy contracted due to the COVID-19 crisis and then begun to recover. Due to cheaper fuels, subdued demand and rapidly expanding renewable generation, wholesale energy prices fell sharply in 2019. Negative electricity prices became widespread in 2020. This downtrend was abruptly reversed: wholesale electricity prices have increased by 230% on a yearly basis with a more moderate impact on retail prices until September 2021 (+11% EU average). This was largely driven by rising gas prices which had an effect on the electricity price nine times bigger than the effect of the observed carbon price increase over the same period;*
- *More than 98.6% of EU electricity consumption is coupled. Traded volumes on natural gas hubs rose to an all-time high in 2019. This trend continued into 2020;*
- *Public clean energy R&I spending in Member States continues to be lower than in 2010, but national and EU recovery funding that targets clean energy R&I can partially compensate this;*
- *Energy poverty affects up to 31 million people in the EU as of 2019, with persisting differences across Member States and income levels. This underlines the importance of shielding the vulnerable from the current price spike and ensure a just transition towards climate neutrality.*
- *Most, albeit not all, trends are therefore positive but nevertheless still fall short of what is needed to drive the required transformation to achieve the objectives of the Energy Union. An acceleration is required not just to achieve a socially fair transition to climate neutrality by 2050 but also as an insurance against the sort of price shocks the EU is facing today.*
- *The adoption of the European Climate Law and of the "Delivering the European Green Deal" package proposed by the Commission in mid-2021 marked two major steps towards putting in place a credible framework to ensure the above.*
- *Member States' Recovery and Resilience Plans are expected to provide a boost to climate-related investments by at least EUR 177 billion and to foster necessary reforms to support the climate and energy transition.*

Source: Report from the commission to The European Parliament, The Council, The European Economic and Social Committee, and The COMMITTEE of the Regions. State of the Energy Union 2021 — Contributing to the European Green Deal and the Union's recovery. COM(2021)950 final.

The **Circular Economy Action Plan** (CEAP)[26] is another strategy and it represents one of the main building blocks of the European Green Deal. The European Commission in March 2020 adopted this new Circular Economy Action Plan which "*provides a future-oriented agenda for achieving a cleaner and more competitive Europe in co-creation with economic actors, consumers, citizens and civil society organizations. It aims at accelerating the transformational change required by the European Green Deal, while building on circular economy actions implemented since 2015.*"[27] This plan will ensure that the regulatory framework is streamlined and made fit for a sustainable future, and that the new opportunities from the transition are maximized while minimizing burdens on people and businesses.[28] The EU sees this plan as a tool to create sustainable development without depleting the earth's resources; in fact, as noted in the introduction of the new CEAP, "*there is only one planet Earth, yet by 2050, the world will be consuming as if here were three.*"[29] The European circular economy action plan represents a concrete and irreversible transition to a sustainable economic system and it is also an indispensable and integral part of the new EU industrial strategy. It is estimated that applying circular economy principles across the EU economy has the potential to increase EU GDP by an additional 0.5% by 2030, creating around 700,000 new jobs. However, one thing is clear: Europe will not achieve transformative change by acting alone. This is why it is necessary to create synergies with its partners. The EU will continue to lead the way to a circular economy at the global level and use its influence, expertise, and financial resources to implement the 2030

---

[26] COM(2020)98 Final, Communication from The Commission to the European Parliament, The Council, The European Economic and Social Committee and The Committee of The Regions — A new Circular Economy Action Plan For a cleaner and more competitive Europe, document available at: https://eur-lex.europa.eu/resource.html?uri=cellar:9903b325-6388-11ea-b735-01aa75ed71a1.0017.02/DOC_1&format=PDF (accessed January 28, 2023).

[27] *Source*: COM(2015) 614 Final, Communication from The Commission to the European Parliament, The Council, The European Economic and Social Committee and The Committee of The Regions — Closing the loop — An EU action plan for the Circular Economy, document available at: https://ec.europa.eu/transparency/documents-register/detail?ref=COM(2015)614&lang=en (accessed January 28, 2023).

[28] COM(2020)98 Final.

[29] See Introduction of COM(2020)98 and visit: https://www.un.org/sustainabledevelopment/sustainable-consumption-production/.

Sustainable Development Goals. But joint actions are needed at the international level to reach these goals.

Implementing the CEAP will not only reduce pressure on natural resources but it is also a prerequisite to achieve the EU's 2050 climate neutrality target. However, achieving a climate-neutral and circular economy requires concerted mobilization of the industry and correct implementation of all the other policies and strategies.

EU Strategy on Corporate Social Responsibility (CSR) is another tool to involve EU companies in the effort to reach a sustainable development. CSR is important for the sustainability, competitiveness, and innovation of EU enterprises and the EU economy. Generally speaking, the definition of 'Corporate Social Responsibility' according to the European Commission is companies voluntarily going beyond what the law requires to achieve social and environmental objectives while performing their business activities.[30]

In the context of the EGD, the EU Commission has also embraced the so-called **Sustainable and Smart Mobility Strategy**[31] which sets out a roadmap for putting European transport firmly on the right track for a sustainable and smart future. In fact, the EGD calls for a 90% reduction in greenhouse gas emissions from the transport system. This sector in fact accounts for a quarter of the EU's greenhouse gas emission (still growing). The combination of policy measures set out in this strategy can deliver a 90% reduction in the transport sector's emissions by 2050, increasing the efficiency of the transport system and introducing electric vehicles and alternative transport fuels (in particular hydrogen). According to this strategy, by 2025, about 1 million public recharging and refueling stations will be needed for the 13 million zero- and low-emission vehicles expected on European roads. By 2030, at least 30 million zero-emission cars will be in operation on European roads, 100 European cities will be climate neutral, high-speed rail traffic will double across Europe, scheduled collective travel for journeys under 500 Km shall be carbon

---

[30] For more details on the EU Strategy on Corporate Social Responsibility visit: https://www.switchtogreen.eu/eu-strategy-on-corporate-social-responsibility/ (accessed January 8, 2023).

[31] COM(220)789 Sustainable and Smart Mobility Strategy — putting European transport on track for the future, document available at: https://eur-lex.europa.eu/legal-content/EN/TXT/?uri=CELEX%3A52020DC0789 (accessed January 28, 2023).

neutral, automated mobility will be deployed on a large scale, and zero-emission marine vessels will be market ready. By 2035, zero-emission large aircraft will be market ready.[32] By 2050, nearly all cars, vans, buses, as well as new heavy-duty vehicles will be zero emission; rail freight traffic will double; and a fully operational, multimodal Trans-European Transport Network (TEN-T) for sustainable smart transport with high-speed connectivity will be in place.[33]

In this framework, the so-called **Hydrogen Strategy**[34] must be included, the aim of which is to make the widespread use of hydrogen possible by 2050. In fact, hydrogen offers a solution to decarbonize industrial processes and economic sectors where reducing carbon emissions is both urgent and hard to achieve. The use of hydrogen with the proper technology can thus replace fossil fuels. The EU considers hydrogen as a central element of its EGD and its new 'Energy System Integration Strategy.' The priority is to develop clean, renewable hydrogen with cumulative investments between €180 and €470 bn in Europe by 2050.[35] It is worth mentioning that according to the EU Hydrogen Strategy, *Combined with EU's leadership in renewables technologies, the emergence of a hydrogen value chain serving a multitude of industrial sectors*

---

[32] This specific theme was treated by one of the authors in another book titled *Impact of COVID-19 on World Aviation Industry — Challenges and Opportunities*, Paolo Rizzi, Cristiano Rizzi, Mario Tettamanti, see Chapter 2 paragraph 2.6 "The Ultimate technology to decarbonizes air travel: The use of Hydrogen, World Scientific, March 2022).

[33] *Source*: COM(220)789 Sustainable and Smart Mobility Strategy — putting European transport on track for the future, also visit: https://transport.ec.europa.eu/transport-themes/mobility-strategy_it.

[34] In July 2020, the European Commission published the EU Hydrogen Strategy: COM(2020)301 Final — A hydrogen strategy for a climate-neutral Europe. This strategy was designed with a phased approach and its goal is to increase hydrogen shares from less than 2 percent today up to 13–14 percent by 2050. Document available at: https://eur-lex.europa.eu/legal-content/EN/TXT/?uri=CELEX:52020DC0301 (accessed January 28, 2023).

[35] IRENA (International Renewable Energy Agency) estimates that to achieve the Paris agreement around 8% of global energy consumption will be provided by hydrogen (IRENA, Global Renewables Outlook, 2020). For more information, see the publication: Energy Transformation 2050, publication available at: https://irena.org/-/media/Files/IRENA/Agency/Publication/2020/Apr/IRENA_GRO_Summary_2020.pdf?la=en&hash=1F18E445B56228AF8C4893CAEF147ED0163A0E47 (accessed January 28, 2023).

and other end uses could employ up to 1 million people, directly or indirectly. Analysts estimate that clean hydrogen could meet 24% of energy world demand by 2050, with annual sales in the range of €630 billion.[36]

1.2.2. *The completion of the framework with the EU action plan toward zero pollution for air, water, and soil*

The European Commission on May 12, 2021 adopted the so-called *EU Action Plan: Towards a Zero Pollution for Air, Water and Soil*[37] which represents another part of the framework to achieve the goals of the European Green Deal. This Action Plan sets out the vision of a pollution-free world and combines all the ongoing and planned efforts in an integrated strategy that puts pollution prevention first. This zero-pollution ambition is to be seen as an objective contributing to the UN 2030 Agenda for Sustainable Development and complementing the 2050 climate neutrality goal in synergy with the circular economy and restored biodiversity goals. The main objective of this Action Plan is to set out key actions for 2021–2024 to complement the many relevant actions in other European Green Deal initiatives, including the chemicals strategy for sustainability: The EU Commission adopted the **Chemicals strategy for sustainability**[38] to better protect citizens and the environment against hazardous chemicals. The EU already has sophisticated chemicals laws in place, but global chemicals production is expected to double by 2030. This strategy, which is also in line with the EGD, strives for a toxic-free environment, where chemicals are produced and used in a way that maximizes their contribution to society, including achieving green transition, while avoiding harm to the planet and to current and future generations.

---

[36] See in this sense, COM(2020)301 Final.

[37] COM(2021)400 final, Pathway to a Healthy Planet for All — EU Action Plan: Towards Zero Pollution for Air, Water, and Soil, document available at: https://eur-lex.europa.eu/legal-content/EN/TXT/?uri=CELEX%3A52021DC0400&qid=1623311742827 (accessed January 28, 2023).

[38] COM(2020)667 final, Chemicals Strategy for Sustainability Towards a Toxic-Free Environment, document available at: https://ec.europa.eu/environment/pdf/chemicals/2020/10/Strategy.pdf (accessed January 28, 2023).

1.2.3. *The importance of the new technologies as enablers of the European Green Deal*

New technologies, sustainable solutions, and disruptive innovations combined with digital technologies are critical enablers for attaining the sustainability goals of the European Green Deal in many different sectors. **Horizon Europe**[39] facilitates collaboration and strengthens the impact of research and innovation in developing, supporting, and implementing EU policies while tackling global challenges, and in synergy with other EU programs, it will play a pivotal role in leveraging national public and private investments. *At least 35% of the budget of Horizon Europe will fund new solutions for climate, which are relevant for implementing the Green Deal.*[40]

The European Commission will also explore measures to ensure that digital technologies such as artificial intelligence, 5G, cloud and edge computing, and the Internet of Things can accelerate and maximize the impact of policies on climate change and protect the environment.

The initiatives which make up the EGD will be sustained by the EU Commission, creating new financial instruments and making use of the so-called green finance and sustainable finance and also through the 'European Green Deal Investment Plan' (see the next two sections).

1.2.4. *Relevance of the green finance in the ambit of the European Green Deal*

This section is only intended to state the basics of green finance in relation to the EGD. This theme is analyzed in more detail in Chapter 5.

To achieve the goals set by the EGD, there are significant investment needs, and the EU Commission has estimated that achieving the climate and energy targets will require at least €1 trillion in **sustainable**

[39] Horizon Europe is the EU's key funding program for research and innovation; it tackles climate change, helps to achieve the UN's Sustainable Development Goals, and boosts the EU's competitiveness and growth. The detailed description of the content of Horizon Europe — Investing to shape our future, is available at: https://ec.europa.eu/info/sites/default/files/research_and_innovation/strategy_on_research_and_innovation/presentations/horizon_europe/ec_rtd_he-investing-to-shape-our-future.pdf (accessed (January 28, 2023).

[40] See COM(2019) 640 final, The European Green Deal.

investments over the next decade. Green finance and sustainable finance have a key role to play in delivering policy objectives under the EGD as well as the EU's international commitments on climate (we are referring to both the Paris Agreement and the UN Agenda 2030). According to the EU Commission, 'Sustainable finance'[41] is an evolution of green finance, as it takes into consideration environmental, social, and governance (ESG) issues and risks, with the aim of increasing long-term investments in sustainable economic activities and projects. Green finance, on the one hand, involves collecting funds for addressing climate and environmental issues (green financing) and, on the other hand, it aims to improve the management of financial risk related to climate and the environment (greening finance).

'Green financing' stands for 'financing the green economy' or 'financing the green transition,' and corresponds to the aim of increasing the level of financial flows toward green investment. The role of finance in the green transition and its importance for climate action is recognized in Article 2.1(c) of the Paris Agreement,[42] which calls for "making finance flows consistent with a pathway towards low greenhouse gas emissions."[43]

---

[41] *Sustainable finance refers to the process of taking* ***environmental, social, and governance (ESG) considerations*** *into account when making investment decisions in the financial sector, leading to more long-term investments in sustainable economic activities and projects.* ***Environmental considerations*** *might include climate change mitigation and adaptation, as well as the environment more broadly, for instance, the preservation of biodiversity, pollution prevention, and the circular economy.* ***Social considerations*** *could refer to issues of inequality, inclusiveness, labour relations, investment in human capital and communities, as well as human rights issues. The* ***governance*** *of public and private institutions — including management structures, employee relations, and executive remuneration — plays a fundamental role in ensuring the inclusion of social and environmental considerations in the decision-making process.* In this sense, see European Commission, Overview of sustainable finance, visit: https://ec.europa.eu/info/business-economy-euro/banking-and-finance/sustainable-finance/overview-sustainable-finance_en (accessed January 28, 2023).

[42] See Paris Agreement, United Nations 2015, Art. 2, 1(c). Making finance flows consistent with a pathway towards low greenhouse gas emission and climate-resilient development. Document available at: https://unfccc.int/sites/default/files/english_paris_agreement.pdf (accessed January 28, 2023).

[43] *Source*: Green and sustainable finance, European Commission, document available at: https://www.europarl.europa.eu/RegData/etudes/BRIE/2021/679081/EPRS_BRI(2021)679081_EN.pdf (accessed January 28, 2023).

In the framework of the European Green Deal, among other initiatives, the Commission announced its intention to put forward a renewed sustainable finance strategy, a legislative proposal for an EU green bond standard, and a review of the Non-financial Reporting Directive. The renewed sustainable finance strategy will build on the 2018 action plan and, according to the Commission, help to create an enabling framework for private investors and the public sector to facilitate sustainable investment.

It is noteworthy that the Commission has already put in place the **European Green Deal Investment Plan (EGDIP)**, also referred to as Sustainable Europe Investment Plan (SEIP), illustrated in the next section, as part of the Green Deal. This includes the **Just Transition Mechanism**, which focuses on ensuring a fair and just transition to a green economy.

1.2.5. *The European Green Deal investment plan: Overview*

In order to finance the EGD and this green transition, the European Commission presented on January 14, 2020 the European Green Deal Investment Plan (EGDIP),[44] also referred to as *Sustainable Europe Investment Plan* (SEIP). This plan will mobilize at least €1 trillion of private and public sustainable investments over the next decade. This massive investment plan will create an 'enabling the framework' to facilitate and stimulate the public and private investments needed for the transition to a climate-neutral, green, competitive, and inclusive economy which should be realized by 2050. In order to reach this ambitious goal, part of the needed funds will come from the European budget. The EU budget will in fact devote a greater share of public spending to climate and environment than even before; in any case, private funding will be needed too.

As part of the plan, the 'Just Transition Mechanism' (hereinafter 'JTM')[45] will be utilized to realize a fair and just green transition. It will

---

[44] *Source*: COM(2020)21 final, Sustainable Europe Investment Plan — European Green Deal Investment Plan, this plan represents the pillar of the green deal. The full document is available at: https://ec.europa.eu/commission/presscorner/api/files/attachment/860462/Commission%20Communication%20on%20the%20European%20Green%20Deal%20Investment%20Plan_EN.pdf (accessed January 28, 2023).

[45] Just Transition Mechanism refers to the Proposal for a Regulation of the European Parliament and of the Council in establishing the Just Transition Fund, COM(2020)22 final, document available at: https://ec.europa.eu/commission/presscorner/api/files/

Main Objectives of the European Green Deal Investment Plan

The European Green Deal Investment Plan will mobilize EU funding and create an enabling framework to facilitate and stimulate the public and private investments needed for the transition to a climate-neutral, green, competitive, and inclusive economy. Complementing other initiatives announced under the Green Deal, the European Green Deal Investment Plan has three main objectives:

"(1) *The EGDIP will increase funding for the transition, and mobilize at least €1 trillion to support sustainable investments over the next decade through the EU budget and associated instruments, in particular InvestEU;*
(2) *The EGDIP will create an enabling framework for private investors and the public sector to facilitate sustainable investments;*
(3) *The EGDIP will provide support to public administrations and project promoters in identifying, structuring, and executing sustainable projects.*"

mobilize at least €100 billion in investments over the period 2021–2027 to support workers and citizens of the regions most impacted by the transition. The mechanism will create the necessary investment to help workers and communities which rely on the fossil fuel value chain. This is in addition to the substantial contribution of the EU budget through all instruments directly relevant to the transition. In particular, the JTM will consist of three main sources: "(1) ***A Just Transition Fund****, which will receive €7.5 billion of fresh EU funds, coming on top of the Commission's proposal for the next long-term EU budget. In order to tap into their share of the Fund, Member States will, in dialogue with the Commission, have to identify the eligible territories through dedicated territorial just transition plans.* (2) ***A dedicated just transition scheme under InvestEU*** *to mobilize up to €45 billion of investments. It will seek to attract private investments,*

attachment/860470/Proposal%20for%20a%20regulation%20establishing%20the%20Just%20Transition%20Fund%20and%20annexes_EN.pdf (accessed January 28, 2023).

including in sustainable energy and transport that benefit those regions and help their economies find new sources of growth. (3) ***A public sector loan facility with the European Investment Bank backed by the EU budget*** *to mobilize between €25 and €30 billion of investments. It will be used for loans to the public sector, for instance for investments in district heating networks and renovation of buildings*."[46]

Financing elements making up at least EUR 1 trillion over the next decade under the Sustainable Europe Investment Plan (Figure 1).

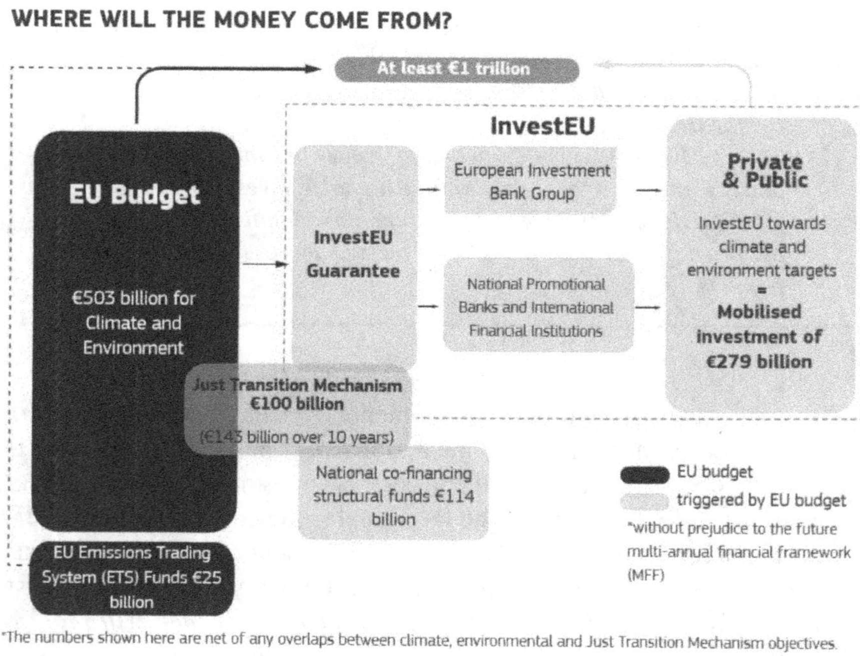

Figure 1: How Will the European Green Deal Investment Plan be Financed?

Source: European Commission, COM(2020)21 Final, Sustainable Europe Investment Plan.

[46]For more references, visit: Financing the green transition: The European Green Deal Investment Plan and Just Transition Mechanism, available at: https://ec.europa.eu/regional_policy/en/newsroom/news/2020/01/14-01-2020-financing-the-green-transition-the-european-green-deal-investment-plan-and-just-transition-mechanism (accessed January 28, 2023).

The Following Explanation is Extrapolated from the Sustainable Europe Investment Plan

Mobilizing at least EUR 1 trillion over the next decade requires a combination of funds provided by the EU budget as proposed by the Commission and further public and private investments triggered by it.

Climate and environmental spending under the EU budget will provide EUR 503 billion from 2021 to 2030, in line with the 25% climate mainstreaming target proposed for the 2021–2027 multiannual financial framework (MFF) and including spending on the environment across all programmes. This will trigger additional national co-financing of EUR 114 billion over this timeframe on climate and environment.

The InvestEU Fund will leverage around EUR 279 billion of private and public climate and environmentally related investments over the period 2021–2030 by providing an EU budget guarantee to reduce the risk in financing and investment operations.

To leave no one behind, the Just Transition Mechanism will include financing from the EU budget, co-financing from the Member States as well as contributions from InvestEU and the EIB to reach EUR 100 billion of investments to be mobilized over 2021–2027, which, extrapolated over 10 years, will reach EUR 143 billion to ensure a just transition. The Innovation and Modernization funds, which are not part of the EU budget but are financed through a part of the revenues from the auctioning of carbon allowances under the Emissions Trading Scheme, will provide at least some EUR 25 billion for EU transition to climate neutrality.

1.2.6. *Similarities with China's strategy*

Undeniably, the EGD presents many similarities with China's new plans for a transition toward a green development. As a matter of fact, the Middle Kingdom, with its 14th FYP, is entering a 'green modality' to transform its economy into a more advanced one by heavily investing in new technologies. The 14th FYP gives an insight into the main goals China is pursuing in the period 2021–2025 and also about its longer-term goals (2035, and 2060). Substantially, the new FYP was conceived to accompany China into a new development pattern by adopting sustainable strategies which improve the coordination mechanism for enhancing ecological civilization and promoting the establishment of a green economy and a green society. This FYP is aimed at building a beautiful China (see Introduction of Section 11 of the 14th FYP).[47] It is noteworthy that this part appears in the text after the goals on economic reform and society, and before those on public welfare and governance, thus showing the importance of this theme for China.

Energy and climate indicators are included under 'new progress of ecological civilization,' which is one of the six overarching economic and social development goals of the 14th FYP. In particular, concerning climate change, the Chinese Plan paves the way to peak carbon emission before 2030 and reach carbon neutrality before 2060.[48] With this FYP, the government plans to increase the share of non-fossil fuel in total energy consumption to 20% by 2025, compared to 15.9% in 2020. However, these are only general data and targets fixed by the FYP; China, in fact, has elaborated specific policies, like the EU, which are recounted in the following sections, to tackle climate change and to transition toward a green and natural-neutral economy.

2. China's '1+N' Framework for a Greener Development Reflects the EU Green Deal

China is the world's top emitter: It produces more than a quarter of the world's annual greenhouse gas emissions due to its dependence on fossil fuels. It is noteworthy that coal alone makes up nearly two-thirds of China's energy consumption.

China has come to understand that protecting the environment, and reducing emissions, is the only path to advance toward a sustainable

---

[47]The 14th Five-Year Plan (FYP), covering the years 2021 to 2025, was officially endorsed by the National People's Congress (NPC) on March 11, 2021. The Plan is divided into 19 sections and 65 chapters, touching on all aspects of development over the next five years, as well as presenting China's 2035 vision. Section 11, from Chapter XXXVII to Chapter XXXIX, deals with environmental issues: "Promote green development and facilitate the harmonious coexistence of people and nature." An English version of the 14th FYP is available at: https://cset.georgetown.edu/wp-content/uploads/t0284_14th_Five_Year_Plan_EN.pdf, Although in this document, Chapters are named as Articles! A bilingual version of the 14th FYP is available at: http://extwprlegs1.fao.org/docs/pdf/chn205796.pdf (accessed January 28, 2023).

[48]See 14th FYP, Chapter XXXVIII, Continue to improve environmental quality, Section 4. Actively respond to climate change.

development and to render its economy more competitive with the introduction of innovative technologies which help in limiting emissions. China has committed itself to cutting emissions under the Paris Agreement, to reduce coal use, and thus to invest massively in renewable sources of energy in order to become a leading player when it comes to tackling climate change. There is no doubt that China will dominate in the renewables market as it is already the number one producer of wind and solar energy (as will be explained); however, some contradictions need to be addressed: In fact, the Belt and Road Initiative still finances coal-fired power plants abroad. Nonetheless, the path China has taken is clear and irreversible: Many strategies and initiatives have been adopted, as stated in the following section, and they are now furthering the greening of China's economy. The new initiatives China is implementing to reach its goal of a nature-positive economy will offer new opportunities of investment through green finance.

2.1. *Environmental protection in China: A brief overview*

'Nature protection' and 'climate change' were neglected in China until the election of President Xi (2013). These two themes have now become a priority for China. Since 2014, China has entered a new era of proactive climate policymaking under the direct leadership of President Xi Jinping. The rapid economic development of China was made possible at the expense of the environment, which now President Xi sees as an important element for a sustainable and green development. President Xi is perfectly aware that the relationship between 'environmental action' and 'economic growth' is not an 'either/or' question — these two factors are intrinsically connected, and China may achieve lasting economic growth while addressing environmental problems and climate change. This is the reason why it is so important to transition toward a nature-positive economy. Moreover, this transition offers investment opportunities, especially with regard to renewable sources of energy. President Xi sees climate change as an opportunity for China to establish a leading role in global climate governance. China is not only a strong supporter of the Paris Agreement but is also introducing initiatives which should induce the rest of the international community to adopt a more concerted action to protect and preserve nature and the environment. The fact that President Xi gives particular attention to environmental issues was marked by his statement that *China would aim to hit peak emissions before 2030 and for carbon neutrality by 2060,* representing the so-called dual carbon goals or 'targets,' arguably the most important milestone in China's history of climate policymaking. The announcement was made before Biden won the US presidential election in November 2020, and this demonstrates China's independent, resolute climate policymaking.

As explained in the following sections, China has established a precise framework to reach its objectives for sustainable development and now finds itself confronted with the dual task of developing its economy in a sustainable manner and protecting the environment. To this extent, China has now established an environmental statutory framework[49] that takes the constitution of the People's Republic of China[50] as the foundation, and the environmental protection law of the People's Republic of China[51] as the main body.

---

[49] This framework includes the following pieces of legislation: the Law on the Prevention and Control of Water Pollution, Law on the Prevention and Control of Air Pollution, Law on the Prevention and Control of Environmental Pollution by Solid Wastes, Marine Environment Protection Law, Forestry Law, Grassland Law, Fisheries Law, Mineral Resources Law, Land Administration Law, Water Resources Law, Law on the Protection of Wild Animals, Law on Water and Soil Conservation, and Agriculture Law. The Chinese government has also enacted more than 30 administrative decrees regarding environmental protection. To implement the State's environmental protection laws and regulations, people's congresses and people's governments at local levels, proceeding from specific conditions in their own areas, have enacted and promulgated more than 600 local laws on environmental protection. See Environmental Protection in China (mfa.gov.cn) (accessed January 28, 2023).

[50] Article 26 of the Constitution of the People's Republic of China stipulates, "*'The state protects and improves the living environment and the ecological environment, and prevents and remedies pollution and other public hazards,*" and Article 9 also states that the state ensures the rational use of natural resources and protects rare animals and plants. The appropriation or damage of natural resources by any organization or individual by whatever means is prohibited. See Constitution of the People's Republic of China, available at: http://www.npc.gov.cn/englishnpc/constitution2019/201911/1f65146fb6104dd3a2793875d19b5b29.shtml (accessed January 28, 2023).

[51] The Environmental Protection Law of the People's Republic of China is the cardinal law for environmental protection in China. The law has established the basic principle for coordinated development between economic construction, social progress, and environmental protection, and defined the rights and duties of governments at all levels, all units and individuals as regards environmental protection. Chinese and English versions of the Environmental Protection Law of the People's Republic of China (2014 revision)

2.1.1. *China's climate goals and the relevance of the 14th FYP*

China has come to understand that only by transitioning toward a sustainable development will it be possible to build a shared future for the global community while meeting its economic development plans and linking them to its long-term climate goals. Thus, it is evident that China's recent commitment to achieving carbon neutrality by 2060 has become a priority, which has even been included in its political agenda. The growing importance of this theme was put in evidence by the latest 14th Five-Year Plan, issued in 2021. The 14th FYP has indicated the path for the implementation of the dual carbon goals and has also indicated the response to climate change, which has already been fully laid out thanks to the introduction of the initiatives explained in the following sections (1+N framework). This framework provides a strong anchor for the carbon neutrality goal. China intends to peak its emissions before 2030, and if it succeeds in reaching this target during its 14th Five-Year Plan (by 2025), i.e., making the transition earlier, it will enhance its international influence, its competitiveness in growing new markets (thanks to its green technologies), and the results will help in setting a strong example for the rest of the global community. As a matter of fact, if the global community does not succeed in reducing carbon emissions, it increases the profound risk of irreversible damage to the world's climate. China's 14th FYP and post-pandemic recovery present an important opportunity to accelerate the transformation to a carbon-neutral economy. Thus, dedicated measures, as will be explained (refer to the 1+N framework in 2.2.1.), have been introduced to reach this objective. If China succeeds in implementing all its new climate policies, its carbon dioxide emissions can peak by the end of the 14th Five-Year Plan period. Accelerating investments and reaching the first target of peaking emissions before 2030 would put China in a better position to reach the carbon neutrality target by 2060. *Early peaking could be achieved by accelerating many of the actions and investments that China will be making in order to make the transition to sustainable growth. This acceleration during the period of the 14th Five-Year Plan would allow China to enjoy the economic benefits of these actions and investments earlier.*[52]

---

are available at: http://www.lawinfochina.com/Display.aspx?lib=law&Cgid=223979 (accessed January 28, 2023).

[52] *Source*: Towards carbon neutrality and China's 14th Five Years Plan: Clean energy transition, sustainable urban development, and investment priorities, in *Environmental Science*

2.1.2. *Role of Ministry of Ecology and Environment: Basic introduction*

It is necessary to put in evidence that although the function of climate policy implementation at the national level officially shifted from the National Development and Regulatory Commission (NDRC) to the newly established Ministry of Ecology and Environment (MEE)[53] in 2018, the NDRC has regained its primacy as the highest-level climate policy agency in China since 2020, as it takes overall responsibility for carbon peaking and neutrality. The MEE, on the other hand, is now playing the role as the implementer of specific policies and programs such as supervising the national carbon market launched in July 2021, i.e., the so-called national Emissions Trading System (ETS).[54] It is noteworthy that 'carbon emissions allowances' (CEAs), traded at the ETS, were initially permitted to trade in 2011, when the NDRC approved the trading of CEAs in local exchanges of seven provinces/cities in China (Shanghai, Beijing, Tianjin, Chongqing, Hubei Province, Guangdong Province, and Shenzhen) under a pilot program.[55]

---

and Ecotechnology, Vol. 8, October 2021 multi authors, article available at: https://www.sciencedirect.com/science/article/pii/S2666498421000545 (accessed January 28, 2023).

[53]The Ministry of Ecology and Environment was officially inaugurated in April 2018 derived directly from the State Environmental Protection Administration which was first transformed into the Ministry of Environmental Protection. *As the most powerful dedicated environmental regulatory body in the history of China, the MEE is responsible for compiling and implementing China's ecological environment policies, plans and standards as well as monitoring the environment. More specifically, the MEE is responsible for pollution control and ecological protection, including the soil and subsurface, the shore and the water, the land and the sea, the city and the countryside, carbon monoxide and carbon dioxide. Moreover, the MEE regulates nuclear and radiation safety, and organizes inspections of central authorities on environmental protection.* See Reform of China's Environmental Governance: The creation of a Ministry of Ecology and Environment, Jinpeng Wang, Chinese Journal of Environment, CJEL https://brill.com/view/journals/cjel/2/1/article-p112_8.xml?language=en, for more specific information about the MEE visit: https://english.mee.gov.cn/About_MEE/Mandates/ (accessed January 28, 2023).

[54]On 16 July 2021, China's nationwide carbon trading officially kicked off at the Shanghai Environment & Energy Exchange (SEEE).

[55]Under the pilot program, each approved local exchange can only trade CEAs held by covered carbon emission enterprises in the relevant local region and other qualified investors according to the rules of the relevant local exchange. For example, SEEE can only

As this theme would require an entire new book, we just conclude this short introduction by stating that there is as yet no absolute cap in China's ETS,[56] and this is its biggest difference with the EU ETS.

The establishment of MEE represents a milestone in China's climate governance and it reflects the fact that China is trying to unify fragmented responsibilities for environment governance into a single body and to practice the idea of ecosystem-based management in the institutional setup at the national level. To flank the MEE to develop more specific policies, a new group was formed, i.e., the National Leading Group on Carbon Peak and Carbon Neutrality.

2.2. *Implementing the national strategy for actively responding to climate change: China's policies and actions against nature loss and climate change*

In May 2021, the State Council created the 'National Leading Group on Carbon Peak and Carbon Neutrality' (NLGCPCN)[57] responsible for

---

host trading of CEAs registered at SEEE (also known as **SHEAs**). CEAs in different exchanges cannot be traded on a cross-exchange basis; hence, these local exchanges are all segregated markets. In 2018, the Ministry of Ecology and Environment (**MEE**) was set up to play a key role in supervising the carbon emissions regime in China. According to *Measures for the Administration of Carbon Emissions Trading (for Trial Implementation)* issued by MEE which took effect from 1 February 2021 (the **MEE 2021 Measures**), MEE was formally authorized to establish a national platform to register CEAs and a national platform to trade CEAs (collectively, the **National CEA Platforms**).

[56] For a more precise functioning about the Chinese carbon trading system and a comparison with the EU, please visit: https://www.energymonitor.ai/policy/carbon-markets/carbon-trading-the-chinese-way and: https://www.energymonitor.ai/policy/carbon-markets/eu-bets-big-on-its-flagship-carbon-market (accessed January 28, 2023).

[57] In May 2021, China established the Leading Group on Carbon Peak and Carbon Neutrality, with Vice Premier Han Zheng as the group leader and an office set within National Development and Reform Commission to further strengthen coordination, deployment, and promotion of work on carbon peak and carbon neutrality. Provinces (autonomous regions, municipalities) successively established leading groups on carbon peak and carbon neutrality to reinforce the coordination of work on CO_2 emission peak and carbon neutrality. Meanwhile, supporting agencies represented by the National Expert Committee on Climate Change continued to play advisory roles. See *China's Achievements, New Goals and Measures for Nationally Determined Contributions,*

Climate Change Policymaking in China (2020–2021)

- President Xi announced the dual carbon targets: Hit peak emissions before 2030 and for carbon neutrality by 2060;
- Created the National Leading Group on Carbon Peak and Carbon Neutrality (NLGCPCN);
- Launched the national carbon market, i.e., the national Emissions Trading System (ETS);
- Started formulating the '1+N' policy framework for carbon peaking and neutrality;
- Climate policy becomes the main plank of China's policy agenda.

macro-strategic planning, organization, and coordination for the dual carbon targets. The NLGCPCN directly reports to the Central Committee of the Chinese Communist Party instead of the State Council, which shows the increasing level of priority attached to climate change in China.

It is noteworthy that the NDRC has formulated (and still developing) the so-called *1+N policy framework* for carbon peaking and neutrality. Then, we have the 'Working Guidance for Carbon Dioxide Peaking and Carbon Neutrality in Full and Faithful Implementation of the New Development Philosophy' (Working Guidance) containing the principles guiding China's transformation. The Working Guidance provides the directions on where to intervene and thus plays the leading role in the '1+N' framework. This principal document envisions a fully established green, low-carbon, circular economy by 2060.

2.2.1. *China's '1+N' framework for reaching its carbon targets of peak carbon by 2030 and net zero by 2060*

The 1+N framework contains clear key indicators for China's green transition. For China, transforming its economy 'into a sustainable green

https://www4.unfccc.int/sites/ndcstaging/PublishedDocuments/China%20First/China%E2%80%99s%20Achievements,%20New%20Goals%20and%20New%20Measures%20for%20Nationally%20Determined%20Contributions.pdf, also see Explainer: China creates new 'leaders group' to help deliver its climate goals, CarbonBrief, article available at: https://www.carbonbrief.org/explainer-china-creates-new-leaders-group-to-help-deliver-its-climate-goals (accessed January 28, 2023).

economy' means increasing the use of renewable sources of energy. The target is to reach an 80% share of non-fossil energy consumption by 2060, though the objectives of these policies are not limited to this goal.

Concerning the strategy adopted by China to achieve its climate goals by implementing the abovementioned 1+N framework, it is useful to clarify that the '1' indicates the overarching 'dual carbon strategy' which was released on September 22, 2021 contained in the *Working Guidance for Carbon Dioxide Peaking and Carbon Neutrality in Full and Faithful Implementation of the New Development Philosophy,* and 'N' indicates the implementation plans for key areas and sectors, such as energy, industry, transportation, and urban–rural construction, and supporting measures in terms of technological support, energy security, carbon sink capacity, fiscal and financial price policies, standard measurement systems, and supervision and evaluation. The first implementation plan came out on 26 October 2021 in the form of the *Action Plan for Carbon Dioxide Peaking before 2030.*[58]

2.2.2. *Working guidance for carbon dioxide peaking and carbon neutrality: Outline*

The extensive 37-article-long policy document titled *Working Guidance for Carbon Dioxide Peaking and Carbon Neutrality in Full and Faithful Implementation of the new Development Philosophy* (Working Guidance)[59] represents the '1' part of the policy framework. The Working Guidance

[58] See in this sense article by Zhao, X.; Qi, Y. *Three Decades of Climate Policymaking in China: A View of Learning. Sustainability* 2022, 14, 2202 see Section 2.3. Elevating the Leadership on Climate Change Policymaking to the Head of State (2014–Present) https://mdpi-res.com/d_attachment/sustainability/sustainability-14-02202/article_deploy/sustainability-14-02202-v2.pdf (accessed January 28, 2023).

[59] The 'Working Guidance,' which is composed of 37 articles divided into 13 sections, was jointly released by the Communist Party of China Central Committee and the State Council, and was an important breakthrough ahead of COP 26 in Glasgow. It is the '1' in the so-called '1+N' policy framework, setting out the overarching principles for a number (N) of forthcoming policies to facilitate China's peaking and neutrality goal. The new development philosophy (mentioned in the title of the document) refers to the concept of innovative, coordinated, green, open, and shared development. The full text of this document is available at the official website of the NDRC: visit: https://en.ndrc.gov.cn/policies/202110/t20211024_1300725.html (accessed January 28, 2023).

outlines specific areas of the economy and society that need to be changed in order to meet China's carbon targets. The Working Guidance outlines five major tasks: (1) creating a green, low-carbon, and circular economy, (2) improving energy efficiency, (3) increasing the share of non-fossil energy consumption, (4) lowering CO_2 emissions, and (5) boosting the carbon sink capacity of ecosystems (see box).

Objectives of the Working Guidance

By 2025, China will have created an initial framework for a green, low-carbon and circular economy and greatly improved the energy efficiency of key industries. Energy consumption per unit of GDP will be lowered by 13.5% from the 2020 level; carbon dioxide (CO_2) emissions per unit of GDP will be lowered by 18% from the 2020 level; the share of non-fossil energy consumption will have reached around 20%; the forest coverage rate will have reached 24.1%, and the forest stock volume will have risen to 18 billion cubic meters. All the above will lay a solid foundation for carbon dioxide peaking and carbon neutrality.

By 2030, China will see significant accomplishments from the comprehensive green transformation in economic and social development, with energy efficiency in key energy-consuming industries reaching advanced international levels. Energy consumption per unit of GDP will have declined significantly; CO_2 emissions per unit of GDP will have dropped by more than 65% compared with the 2005 level; the share of non-fossil energy consumption will have reached around 25%, with the total installed capacity of wind power and solar power reaching over 1200 gigawatts; the forest coverage rate will have reached about 25%, and the forest stock volume will have reached 19 billion cubic meters. CO_2 emissions will reach peak and stabilization and then decline.

By 2060, China will have fully established a green, low-carbon and circular economy and a clean, low-carbon, safe and efficient energy system. Energy efficiency will be at the advanced international level, and the share of non-fossil energy consumption will be over 80%. China will be carbon neutral, and it will have achieved fruitful results in ecological civilization and reached a new level of harmony between humanity and nature.

Source: Working Guidance for Carbon Dioxide Peaking and Carbon Neutrality in Full and Faithful Implementation of the new Development Philosophy, Section II.

The 'Working Guidance' in its 13 Sections gives the 'directions' for how China should reach its climate goals, and it encompasses green transition and economic and social development. The path China has chosen is clearly explained and it touches upon several areas:

- Promoting Comprehensive Green Transformation in Economic and Social Development (Section III, Arts. 3–5);
- In-Depth Industrial Restructuring (Section IV, Arts. 6–9);
- Accelerating the Development of a Clean, Low-Carbon, Safe, and Efficient Energy System (Section V, Arts. 9–13);
- Accelerating the Construction of a Low-Carbon Transportation System (Section VI, Arts. 14–16);
- Improving the Quality of Green and Low-Carbon Development of Urban and Rural Areas (Section VII, Arts. 17–19);
- Strengthening research on Green and Low-Carbon Technologies and Promoting Their Application (Section VIII, Art. 20–21);
- Continuing to Consolidate and Improving Carbon Sink Capacity (Section IX, Arts. 22–23);
- Promoting a Green and Low-Carbon Mode of Opening Up (Section X, Arts. 24–26);
- Improving Laws, Regulations, Standards, and Statistical monitoring systems (Section XI, Arts. 27–29);
- Improving Policy Mechanisms (Section XII, Arts. 30–33);
- Strengthening Organization and Implementation (Section XIII, Arts. 34–37).[60]

The 'Working Guidance' is a programmatic document of particular relevance for China because like the European Green Deal, it specifies all the sectors involved in this green transition, it evidences China's commitments to reach its climate goals, and it indicates the path for emission reduction. In particular, Article 33 of the Guidance specifically addresses the development of market-based mechanisms (Section XII 'Improving Policy Mechanisms') and confirms the planned coverage expansion,[61] the diversification of trading instruments, and the improvement of the allocation and management of allowances for the national ETS. This particular

---

[60] See the content of the Working Guidance.

[61] For more specific information on this theme, visit: International Carbon Action Partnership (ICAP) — China launches national carbon market (icapcarbonaction.com) (accessed January 28, 2023).

provision is in line with previous policy documents such as the trading rules[62] and the new draft national ETS legislation.[63]

It is noteworthy that 'Green Finance' is mentioned in the Working Guidance, and this highlights the importance of green finance products and services which will allow China the passage to a green and sustainable economy. Article 31 of the Working Guidance (Section XII — Improving Policy Mechanisms) specifically states that China intends to *support qualified enterprises in going public and refinancing for the purpose of developing and running green and low-carbon projects, and we will increase green bonds. We need to carry out exploratory work on establishing a national fund for low-carbon transformation. Nongovernmental capital will be encouraged to set up green and low-carbon industrial investment funds. We will establish a sound system of standards for green finance*[64] (Green Finance is treated in more details in Chapter 5).

The Essence of the Working Guidance

- *It sets out the key objectives around establishing (i) a green, low-carbon, and circular economy and (ii) a clean, low-carbon, safe, and efficient energy system by 2025, 2030, and 2060;*
- *The Working Guidance stresses the need for a comprehensive green transformation in economic and social development; and*
- *The Working Guidance sets out the proposed approaches to achieving such objectives (which summarises the steps set out below under the Action Plan).*

---

[62] See article at icap website titled "China publishes rules for national ETS registry and trading," available at: https://icapcarbonaction.com/en/news-archive/779-china-publishes-rules-for-national-ets-registry-and-trading (accessed January 28, 2023).

[63] On March 30, 2021, the Ministry of Ecology and Environment (MEE) of China published new draft national ETS legislation that refines existing measures and places them on a higher level in the Chinese legal hierarchy. See article at icap website titled "China publishes new draft national ETS legislation," available at: https://icapcarbonaction.com/en/news-archive/766-china-publishes-new-draft-national-ets-legislation (accessed January 28, 2023).

[64] In this sense Art. 31 Section XII of the Working Guidance.

The 'Working Guidance' and the *Action Plan for Reaching Carbon Dioxide Peak Before 2030* (the 'Action Plan')[65] represent the basis of China's '1+N' framework for reaching its carbon targets of peak carbon by 2030 and net-zero by 2060. In the following section, we have delineated the main features of the Action Plan which in many aspects realizes the Working Guidance.

2.2.3. *Action Plan for reaching carbon dioxide peak before 2030*

The Action Plan, released on October 24, 2021, is the first of the 'N' documents and will be followed by several more in the months and years to come. According to its introduction, *This Action Plan is formulated to advance actions on carbon dioxide peaking in further implementing the major strategic decisions by the Central Committee of the Communist Party of China (CPC) and the State Council to peak carbon dioxide emissions and achieve carbon neutrality.*

The main objectives of the Action Plan are contained in Section II:

> *Over the 14th Five-Year Plan period, notable progress will be made in adjustment and optimization of the industrial structure and the energy mix. Energy efficiency will be largely improved in key industries, strict controls will be placed upon coal consumption growth, construction of new electric power systems based upon new energy resources will speed up, new progress will be made in the R&D and broad application of green and low-carbon technologies environment-friendly production modes and living patterns will become widespread, and further improvement will be made in the policy framework for green, low-carbon and circular development. By 2025, the share of non-fossil fuels in total energy consumption will reach around 20%, while energy consumption and carbon dioxide emissions per*
>
> (*Continued*)

[65] Action Plan for Carbon Dioxide Peaking Before 2030, National Development and Reform Commission (NDRC), document available at: https://en.ndrc.gov.cn/policies/202110/t20211027_1301020.html (accessed January 28, 2023).

(*Continued*)

unit of GDP will drop by 13.5% and 18%, respectively, compared with 2020 levels, laying a solid foundation for carbon dioxide peaking.

During the 15th Five-Year Plan period, major progress will be made in adjustment of the industrial structure, a clean, safe, efficient and low-carbon energy system will be preliminary established, low-carbon development models will have largely taken shape in key fields, energy efficiency among China's key energy consumption industries will reach advanced international standards, non-fossil fuels will account for a larger share of energy consumption, coal consumption will gradually fall, crucial breakthroughs will be made in green and low-carbon technology, the public will opt for environment-friendly living patterns, and formulation of the policy framework for green, low-carbon and circular development will be mostly complete. By 2030, the share of non-fossil energy consumption will reach around 25%, and carbon dioxide emissions per unit of GDP will have dropped by more than 65% compared with the 2005 level, successfully achieving carbon dioxide peaking before 2030.

The Action Plan outlines key tasks in ten fields (see next paragraph) and 43 items covering power, industry, building, transport, circular economy, carbon sinks, and others as illustrated in the brief summary in the following. These tasks (10 Actions) represent the core of the **Action Plan** to achieve peak carbon emissions by 2030:

1. The action for green and low-carbon energy transition focuses on reducing coal consumption and 'vigorously developing' new energy resources (i.e., renewable energy) through large-scale high-quality development of wind and solar power generation, accelerating the construction of wind and solar farms, further developing biomass power generation, and utilizing geothermal energy as well as new marine energy sources such as wave, tidal, and ocean thermal energy. The action also focuses on developing hydropower (particularly in southwest China); developing nuclear power (including demonstration projects for advanced reactor nuclear power); regulating the consumption of oil and gas (including promoting alternative sustainable fuels); and increasing the pace of the development of the new electricity power system (including optimizing electricity transmission, distribution, and energy storage, and speeding up the development of a unified national electricity market).[66] The fundamental importance, and the primary role, of this task is clear: In fact, only reducing the use of fossil resources and embracing the development of green and low-carbon energy will allow China to shape a green economy.

2. The action for energy saving, carbon emission mitigation, and efficiency improvement focuses on implementing measures to monitor the carbon emissions of 'key energy users,' encourage energy-saving technologies, and support energy conservation and carbon reduction projects across different sectors. Energy saving is of particular importance, and the Action Plan *will step up energy conservation checks and regular oversight on major energy consuming equipment, strengthen full-chain management covering production, marketing, sales, utilization, and disposal, cracking down hard on activities that violate laws and regulations, and thus ensure full execution of energy efficiency standards and energy conservation requirements*. It is evident that the Action Plan aims at raising the share of non-fossil fuels in total energy consumption.[67]

3. The action for peaking carbon dioxide emissions in the industry sector focuses on (i) promoting green and low-carbon development, accelerating efforts to eliminate outdated production capacity, vigorously developing strategic emerging industries, and speeding up green and low-carbon transformation in traditional industries. It also involves pushing the steel industry to peak carbon dioxide emissions, spurring structural optimization for steel industry and the substitution of clean energy, vigorously promoting demonstrations of non-blast furnace technology, improving recycling and reuse of steel scrap, and advancing the use of electric furnaces which can be completely charged with steel scrap. The same strategy will be adopted for the non-ferrous metal industry, the building materials industry, and the petrochemical industry to peak their carbon

[66] See Action Plan, Section III, number 1, from letter (a) to letter (f), document (English version) available at: https://en.ndrc.gov.cn/policies/202110/t20211027_1301020.html, National Development and Reform Commission (NDRC) People's Republic of China, (accessed January 28, 2023)

[67] See Action Plan, Section III, number 2, from letter (a) to letter (d).

dioxide emissions and *firmly curbing the irrational expansion of energy-intensive and high-emission projects.*[68]

4. The action for peaking carbon dioxide emissions in urban–rural development areas focuses on promoting green and low-carbon transformation of urban and rural areas; accelerating energy efficiency improvement in building and municipal infrastructure, instituting higher requirements for saving energy, and reducing carbon emissions so that by 2025 all newly constructed buildings in urban areas will meet green building standards, including increasing the use of small-scale renewable energy in heating/cooling systems. The action also focuses on promoting a low-carbon transition in the development of rural areas.[69]

5. The action for promoting green and low-carbon transportation focuses on promoting low-carbon transformation of transportation vehicles and equipment so that by 2030, 40% of new vehicles would be powered by clean energy such as electricity, hydrogen power, natural gas, and advanced liquid biofuels. The action also focuses on developing green, high-efficiency transportation systems. The aim here is to develop public transport service systems that are fast, convenient, comfortable, and linked efficiently, and actively encourage people to choose green and low-carbon means of transportation. The action further stresses on accelerating the construction of green transport infrastructure, i.e., to carry out green and low-carbon transformation of transport infrastructure, and utilizing the infrastructure more efficiently by coordinating the use of route, land, and airspace resources in comprehensive transportation corridors and integrating waterfront and anchorage resources.[70]

6. The action for promoting a circular economy for carbon mitigation purposes focuses on requiring industrial parks to develop in line with the concept of a circular economy: Circular production in enterprises and circular organization of industries in these parks will be encouraged as well, and arrangements will be made for enterprises to conduct retrofits for clean production. According to the plan, by 2030, all key industrial parks at the provincial level or above will be upgraded to support circular

---

[68] See Action Plan, Section III, number 3, from letter (a) to letter (f).

[69] See Action Plan, Section III, number 4, from letter (a) to letter (d).

[70] See Action Plan, Section III, number 5, from letter (a) to letter (c).

operations and strengthen the use of bulk solid waste. By 2025, the total amount of the nine major reusable resources recycled, i.e., steel scrap, cooper, aluminum, lead, zinc, waste paper, plastic, rubber, and glass, will top 450 million metric tons, reaching 510 million by 2030. The action also involves refining systems for resource recycling, driving high-quality development of remanufacturing industries, and 'vigorously promoting' efforts to reduce and recycle household waste. *By 2025, a basic sorting system for urban household waste will be established, with the reclamation rate up to about 60%. By 2030, the sorting system for urban household waste will cover all cities, and the reclamation rate will rise to 65%.*[71]

7. The action for advancing green and low-carbon technology innovation focuses on putting in place mechanisms and systems which encourage the development of innovative low-carbon technologies. The Action Plan in particular states that "major R&D and demonstration projects for key technologies related to the achievement of peaking carbon dioxide emissions and achieving carbon neutrality will be set up in national key R&D programs, making use of open competition mechanisms to select the best candidates to lead the projects, and intensifying core technology research for reaching low carbon, zero carbon, and carbon negative; enhancing the talent pool, training and capability; launching *major national projects for forward-looking, strategically important cutting-edge technologies…*; and accelerating the research and development of innovative low-carbon technologies."[72]

8. The action for consolidating and enhancing the carbon sink focuses on consolidating the carbon sequestration capacity of ecosystems. This will be achieved by making and implementing China's territorial space plans to form a new model of development and protection, which is conducive to peaking carbon dioxide emissions and achieving carbon neutrality. Also, China will *enforce red lines in ecological conservation, control the use of ecological spaces, and build a nature reserve system centered on national parks, to stabilize the carbon sequestration ability of forests, grasslands, rivers and lakes, wetlands, oceans, soil, permafrost, and karst areas.* The action also focuses on enhancing the carbon sink

---

[71] See Action Plan, Section III, number 6, from letter (a) to letter (d).

[72] See Action Plan, Section III, number 7, from letter (a) to letter (d).

capacity of ecosystems by strengthening forest protection, restoring grassland ecosystems, strengthening the protection and restoration of rivers, lakes, and wetlands, protecting and restoring marine ecosystems, strengthening the foundation of ecological system carbon sinks, and promoting carbon emission reduction and carbon sequestration in agricultural and rural areas.[73]

9. The action for green and low-carbon society focuses on strengthening publicity and education for 'ecological civilization' to raise public awareness of green and low-carbon development and spur public enthusiasm for ecological civilization. It also focuses on advocating green and low-carbon living patterns by expanding green consumption, promoting green and low-carbon products, encouraging enterprises to fulfill their social responsibilities, encouraging enterprises to take proactive steps to meet needs for green and low-carbon development, shouldering more responsibility for environmental protection, strengthening energy and resource conservation, and increasing training. State-owned enterprises in key areas, especially those managed by the central government, should draw up peaking carbon dioxide emissions action plans and strengthen their ability to take the lead and offer guidance. Major energy consumers should review and account for their own carbon emissions, explore ways to further cut emissions, and formulate dedicated work plans tailored to their specific conditions to advance efforts in energy conservation and emissions reduction.[74]

10. The action for promoting peaking carbon dioxide emissions in all regions hierarchically and in an orderly manner focuses on setting sound, systematic targets, and promoting green and low-carbon development according to local conditions. In light of major regional strategies along with the strategy for coordinated regional development and the functional zoning, all local governments should promote green and low-carbon development that is based on their own local realities. The action also focuses on formulating local peaking carbon dioxide emissions plans through coordination between central and local authorities. The governments of provinces, autonomous regions, and municipalities directly under the central government will follow the overall plans and

[73] See Action Plan, Section III, number 8, from letter (a) to letter (d).

[74] See Action Plan, Section III, number 9, from letter (a) to letter (d).

requirements of the state and take into consideration local resource endowments, industrial layouts, and development stages, taking into consideration a whole-of-nation approach while avoiding 'jumping the gun,' to formulate their peaking carbon dioxide emissions action plans and set out pragmatic timetables, road maps, and blueprints. The action also involves carrying out pilot projects. A total of 100 pilot cities and industrial parks will be designated and given support in terms of policy, funding, and technology to launch peaking carbon dioxide emissions trials, so that they can move faster toward their green and low-carbon goals and provide a transferable experience that can be applied elsewhere in China.[75]

In addition to these ten key actions, the plan also stresses the importance of international cooperation (Section IV) and it includes a commitment to *uphold multilateralism, safeguard the UN-centered international system, and urge all parties to fulfill the United Nations Framework Convention on Climate Change and the Paris Agreement* and to *intensify green finance cooperation across the world, actively participate in carbon pricing and global macro policy coordination on green finance standards.* There is also a statement that the Belt and Road Initiative will be a green initiative: *We will follow the principle of extensive consultation, joint contribution and shared benefits, uphold openness, green development, and integrity in advancing the Belt and Road Initiative (BRI), and strengthen cooperation with other participants on green infrastructure, green energy, and green finance. We will make overseas projects more environmentally sustainable, develop a BRI energy partnership characterized by green development and inclusiveness, and expand the export of new energy technology and products.*[76]

In the Action Plan, the importance of 'Green Finance' emerges clearly; in fact, in the document, it is established that China will improve the evaluation mechanism and standards for green finance and establish a sound green finance standard system. This shows the important role green finance is going to play in shaping sustainable development. But other details are also offered: It appears that the Chinese authorities will make an all-out effort to develop green credit, equity, bonds, insurance, funds, and other financial instruments. But the efforts are not limited to those areas. In fact, the introduction of tools which support carbon emission

[75] See Action Plan, Section III, number 10, from letter (a) to letter (d).

[76] See Section IV of the Action Plan — International Cooperation.

reduction is planned. Authorities will also guide financial institutions in providing long-term, low-cost funding for green and low-carbon projects, and encourage development and policy-backed financial institutions to provide continued long-term financial support for peaking carbon dioxide emissions initiatives by employing market-oriented and law-based measures. An expansion the green bond market is also planned and the government intends to support qualified green enterprises in their efforts to go public and refinance.

The Action Plan specifically refers to the carbon trading system, stating that China will give full play to the role of the national carbon emission trading market, further refine supporting systems, and expand the trading scope in due course. China takes this theme very seriously. It intends to build a national market for energy use rights, improve the system for the paid use and trading of energy use rights, and ensure compatibility with the system to control both the total amount and intensity of energy consumption.

It is evident that all these programmatic objectives need more precise 'directions' and in fact the National Leading Group on Carbon Peaking and Carbon Neutrality (NLGCPCN), as stated in the action plan, will formulate specific policies and make overall plans and systematic steps to reach all the targets contained in the Plan: *The members of the Leading Group will make solid efforts in line with the decisions and plans of the CPC Central Committee and the State Council and relevant requirements defined by the Leading Group. The Leading Group Office will strengthen planning and coordination, examine and coordinate work in all regions and key areas and industries on a regular basis, and scientifically put forward the timetable and road map for carbon dioxide peaking step by step so as to ensure the thorough and effective implementation of all targets and tasks.*[77]

One of the most challenging tasks for peaking emissions before 2030 is to reduce the consumption of coal which is still China's biggest source of power. Although China has cut its overall share of energy derived from coal to 56.8% in 2020 from 72.4% in 2005 (according to the Ministry of Ecology and Environment), the total consumption of coal rose by 19% during the 14th FYP period, resulting in China now accounting for 53% of the world's total consumption of coal as reported by climate and energy

[77] See Section VI — Implementation, 1, of the Action Plan.

think tank Ember.[73] The main alternatives to fossil fuels mentioned in the Action Plan are solar, wind, hydroelectric, and other renewable energy sources. China has already taken significant measures in transitioning to renewable energy and this theme will be explained in greater detail in Chapter 4.

2.2.4. *The white paper: Responding to climate change: China's policies and actions*

On October 27, 2021, the State Council Information Office of the People's Republic of China released a white paper (hereinafter WP) titled *Responding to Climate Change: China's Policies and Actions*[79] to document the progress of the Chinese government in mitigating climate change, with the intent to share its experience and approaches with the rest of the international community.

This WP describes in detail all the initiatives adopted by China to tackle climate change and take part in global climate governance. The WP is divided into four sections:

- Section I — China's New Response to Climate Change;
- Section II — Implementing a National strategy of Actively Responding to Climate Change;
- Section III — Significant Changes in China's Response to Climate Change;
- Section IV — Building a Fair and Rational Global Climate Governance System for Win-Win Results.

---

[78] "Global Electricity Review 2021." report by Ember. This report showcases a global dataset for electricity generation and demand across 217 countries from 2000 to 2020. Data for 2020 contained in the report cover 90 percent of the world's electricity production. Visit: https://ember-climate.org/insights/research/global-electricity-review-2021/ and "G20 Profile — China — Global Electricity Review 2021," document available at: https://ember-climate.org/app/uploads/2022/02/Global-Electricity-Review-2021-China.pdf (accessed January 28, 2023).

[79] Responding to Climate Change: China's Policies and Actions, prepared by The State Council Information Office of the People's Republic of China. The White Pater was released on October 27 2021, and the English version of this document is available at: http://www.news.cn/english/2021-10/27/c_1310272455.htm (accessed January 28, 2023).

In the first section, the WP substantially underlines the new principles that form the basis for tackling climate change:

- **Building a Strong Sense of Common Community:** Here, China advocates a joint effort to build a global community of shared future. China also advocates a community of harmony between humanity and nature.[80]
- **Implementing the New Development Philosophy:** *China pursues a philosophy that development must be innovative, coordinated, green, open and shared, and accelerates the pace in creating a new development dynamic. Among the five axes of the new philosophy, green development is a necessary condition for sustainability.*[81]
- **Taking a People-Centered Approach:** *China puts people and lives first, and cherishes the life, value and dignity of every individual. Taking into full consideration the people's aspiration for a better life, their expectation of a sound eco-environment, and their responsibility for future generations, China is pioneering a new approach that synergizes the efforts to fight climate change, develop the economy, generate employment, eliminate poverty, and protect the environment. It guarantees and improves people's wellbeing through development, strives for social equity and justice in the process of green transition, and increases people's sense of gain, happiness and security.*[82]
- **Striving for Carbon Neutrality:** Achieving the goals of peaking carbon emissions and subsequent carbon neutrality is one of China's major strategies.[83] This important objective was stressed in the Action Plan (see Section 2.2.3).
- **Synergizing the Reduction of Pollution and Carbon Emissions:** It is evident that reducing emissions means reducing the utilization of fossil fuels and this will be conducive to mitigating climate change and fostering green transition. China sees pollution prevention and control as an integral part of the response to climate change. Thus, efforts to reduce pollution and carbon emissions are planned and carried out in tandem, and the performance assessment of the two is also conducted jointly.[84]

---

[80] See Section I of the White Paper, 1.

[81] See Section I of the White Paper, 2.

[82] See Section I of the White Paper, 3.

[83] See Section I of the White Paper, 4.

[84] See Section I of the White Paper, 5.

The rest of the White Paper reassembles the initiatives taken by the government to respond to climate change (Section II), including the intent to continuing to update the NDC targets (see the next paragraph) and accelerate the work on the so-called 1+N policies for peaking carbon emissions and achieving carbon neutrality. But the WP also emphasizes China's contributions to the global response to climate change (Section III). China is a strong supporter of the green transition and it now follows the path of green, low-carbon, and sustainable development, and thus the Middle Kingdom is committed to integrating green development into the whole process of economic development. Section III of the WP relates the efforts China has made to reduce its carbon footprint and how China has accelerated the transformation and transition to a clean and low-carbon energy consumption structure. Naturally, more detailed policies will follow according to the content of the Action Plan (see Section 2.2.3). In its last section, the WP evidences the necessity of concerted global efforts to tackle climate change due to the complexity of the issue and its global character. China calls on the international community to take immediate action, strengthen solidarity and cooperation, and remain committed to multilateralism (see Section 3).

2.2.5. *China's achievements, new goals, and new measures for Nationally Determined Contribution (NDC)*

In October 2021, China updated its **Nationally Determined Contribution (NDC)** targets for 2030, and issued a new document, i.e., the *China's Achievements, New Goals and New Measures for Nationally Determined Contributions,*[85] which contains the new objectives and describes the positive results achieved in the implementation of NDC, as well as the new measures to implement the updated NDC Goals.

[85] *China's Achievements, New Goals and New Measures for Nationally Determined Contributions* represents China's concrete action in implementing the Paris Agreement and reflects the country's determination and efforts in promoting green, low-carbon development and addressing global climate change. The document has summed up China's policies, measures, and results in implementing its NDCs since 2015, as well as key policies and measures for its new goals. The full document is available at https://www4.unfccc.int/sites/ndcstaging/PublishedDocuments/China%20First/China%E2%80%99s%20Achievements,%20New%20Goals%20and%20New%20Measures%20for%20Nationally%20Determined%20Contributions.pdf (accessed January 28, 2023).

It is noteworthy that in June 2015, the Chinese government submitted the *Enhanced Actions on Climate Change: China's Intended Nationally Determined Contributions*. In it, China delineated its actions to achieve the peaking of CO_2 emissions around 2030 and make the best efforts to peak early; to lower CO_2 emissions per unit of GDP by 60% to 65% from the 2005 level; to increase the share of non-fossil fuels in primary energy consumption to around 20%; to increase the forest stock volume by around 4.5 billion cubic meters on the 2005 level; and to take adaptive actions to enhance mechanisms and capacities to effectively defend against climate change risks.

Now, China's updated NDC goals are as follows: China aims to have CO_2 emissions peak before 2030 and achieve carbon neutrality before 2060, lower CO_2 emissions per unit of GDP by over 65% from the 2005 level, increase the share of non-fossil fuels in primary energy consumption to around 25%, increase the forest stock volume by 6 billion cubic meters from the 2005 level, and bring its total installed capacity of wind and solar power to over 1.2 billion kilowatts by 2030.

The updated Nationally Determined Contribution substantially reaffirms the targets outlined in the Working Guidance. The updated NDC also highlights the importance of China's carbon market and the commitment to improve and expand it. Both the Action Plan and the NDC also emphasize the importance of coordinating the various market-based approaches to climate and energy in China: In fact, alongside the ETS scheme, these include electricity trading and energy use rights trading (based on tradable units of total energy consumption).

2.2.6. *China's Mid-Century Long-Term Low Greenhouse Gas Emission Development Strategy*

On October 28, 2021, China issued another document, i.e., the *China's Mid-Century Long-Term Low Greenhouse Gas Emission Development Strategy*[86] (hereinafter 'Low-Emission Development Strategy'), which is part of the China's 1+N policy. This document, while summarizing China's key progress in controlling greenhouse gas emissions, puts

[86] *China's Mid-Century Long-Term Low Greenhouse Gas Emission Development Strategy the full document is available at:* https://unfccc.int/sites/default/files/resource/China%E2%80%99s%20Mid-Century%20Long-Term%20Low%20Greenhouse%20Gas%20Emission%20Development%20Strategy.pdf (accessed January 28, 2023).

forward China's guiding principles, strategic visions, strategic priorities, and policy orientations on its mid-century long-term low greenhouse gas emissions development, its approaches, and the advocacies for promoting global climate governance.

The roll-out of new policies, which are presented in the Low-Emission Development Strategy,[87] and measures which China intends to adopt reflects the constant progress made by China in tackling climate change. The objectives are the same as established in the Working Guidance and in the Action Plan; however, the intent is to accelerate green and low-carbon transformation of China's economy and society. The introduction of this 'strategy,' which is again a programmatic document and needs more specific 'directions' from the authority in charge of implementing concrete measures (i.e., the National Leading Group on Carbon Peak and Carbon Neutrality), demonstrates in any case China's role as a responsible major player in the transition toward sustainable and green development.

The Low-Emission Development Strategy is naturally based on national conditions and it counts on future development in green technologies; it also encourages the active participation of all parties, including the industry sector and the common people, thereby enhancing the public's awareness of the necessity to transition toward a green and low-carbon society. The Low-Emission Development Strategy puts forward the basic principles already explained in the other documents, the strategic priorities for China's long-term low-emission development, as well as the concepts and propositions for promoting global climate governance.

2.2.7. *The role of the People's Bank of China in green transition: Brief introduction*

On November 8, 2021 the People's Bank of China announced that it has rolled out a supporting tool for carbon reduction as part of the efforts to

[87] See Chapter 3 of the *China's Mid-Century Long-Term Low Greenhouse Gas Emission Development Strategy*, where the strategic priorities and policy orientation are listed as follows: Foster a green, low-carbon, and circular economic system; build a clean, low-carbon, safe, and efficient energy system; establish a low GHG emission industrial system; impel urban and rural construction in green and low-carbon manner; form a low-carbon comprehensive transportation system; achieve a substantial reduction in non-carbon dioxide GHG emission; implement low-emission technology innovation; create a new pattern of nationwide participation; and promote the modernization of climate governance system and governance capacity.

facilitate the country's goal of carbon neutrality.[88] To help meet the ambitious goals, the bank will provide low-cost loans for financial institutions through this carbon reduction supporting tool, and will guide those institutions to provide loans to firms in key carbon reduction fields on the premise of independent decision-making and risk-taking. It was affirmed that the creation and launch of such a structural monetary policy tool will support the development of key fields, such as clean energy, energy conservation, and environmental protection, in a steady, orderly, targeted, and direct manner. The People's Bank of China will adopt 'the system for direct funds,' which means financial institutions could apply for the low-cost funding from the central bank after the loans for carbon reductions are made. The PBoC will provide 60% of the loan principal made by financial institutions for carbon-emission cuts, with a one-year lending rate of 1.75%."[89]

PBoC's overall approach to contributing to green transition is outlined in a set of guidelines for establishing a green financial system (i.e., 'Guidelines for Establishing the Green Financial System,' Yinfa 2016 Doc No 228), issued by the central bank and a number of other agencies.[90] These guidelines underline that the primary purpose of establishing the green financial system is to mobilize and incentivize more social (or private) capital to invest in green sectors, while restricting investment in polluting sectors. Naturally, more resources will be allocated by the government through its web of national entities; in fact, green transition is something involving the entire country at all levels. The green financial

---

[88] China's central bank rolls out new lending tool for carbon reduction. *Source*: Xinhua, article available at: http://www.news.cn/english/2021-11/08/c_1310299035.htm (accessed January 28, 2023).

[89] *Ibid.*

[90] On August 31, 2016 the People's Bank of China, along with six other government agencies, issued the "Guidelines for Establishing the Green Financial System" (Yinfa 2016 Doc No. 228), with the approval of the State Council. The Guidelines — issued jointly by the People's Bank of China, the Ministry of Finance, the National Development and Reform Commission, the Ministry of Environmental Protection, China Banking Regulatory Commission, China Securities Regulatory Commission, and China Insurance Regulatory Commission — will provide an essential next step for implementing the overall strategy of promoting ecological civilization, formulated by the Central Party Committee and the State Council. They will also advance the development concepts of innovation, harmony, greenness, openness, and sharing, and promote the establishment of China's green financial system. http://www.pbc.gov.cn/english/130721/3131759/index.html.

system, fostered by the government, will facilitate the green transformation of the Chinese economy. Green finance will promote technological progress in environmental protection, new energy sources, energy saving, and other fields as specified in the Working Guidance and Action Plan.

PBoC's Guidelines for Establishing the Green Financial System include a series of policy incentives to support and incentivize green investment. These incentives include, among others, relending operations by the People's Bank of China, specialized green guarantee programs, interest subsides for green-loan-supported projects, and the launch of a national-level green development fund. It is noteworthy that the PBoC and China Banking Regulatory Commission (CBRC) are unusual among the G20 central banks and supervisors with regard to their willingness to influence banks' credit allocation to support green transition. A working paper published in May 2021 by the Grantham Institute at the London School of Economics underlined China's use of a green window guidance policy[91] from 2006 onward incorporating target setting for bank lending based on sustainable objectives. This working paper concludes that the Chinese experience suggests that directed lending through window guidance can be a useful instrument to help align the financial system with climate and other sustainability goals. But it adds that such policies need to be fitted to the specific context in which they are used. Thus, Chinese authorities will closely monitor the impact of the changes introduced and will adjust their policy to offer not only the most updated system but also the most appropriate tools to help green transition.

To conclude this short introduction about green finance, it is necessary to stress that China's financial system has some characteristics that set it apart from other developed economies. China's economy is in fact more dependent on bank lending than market-based finance, and all of its major banks are state owned. This means that initiatives to pursue

[91] *Source*: *Out of the window? Green monetary policy in China: window guidance and the promotion of sustainable lending investment*, LSE and Grantham Research Institute on Climate Change and the Environment, Working paper, 14 May 2021, document available at: https://www.lse.ac.uk/granthaminstitute/publication/out-of-the-window-green-monetary-policy-in-china-window-guidance-and-the-promotion-of-sustainable-lending-and-investment/ (accessed January 8, 2023). This working paper examines the use by Chinese monetary and financial authorities of 'window guidance,' a tool designed to encourage financial institutions to expand credit to sustainable activities and curb lending to heavy-polluting industries.

innovative climate-friendly policies by green finance need to be taken at the central government level.

2.2.8. *The BRI in the new context*

The Belt and Road Initiative (BRI), which is a global infrastructure development strategy adopted by the Chinese government in 2013 aimed at better connecting China with Europe reviving the ancient Silk Road,[92] was initially focused on the construction of coal-fired power projects in several countries along the BRI.[93] However, due to the change in direction of China's development, and the implementation of the concept of 'ecological civilization' (introduced in the Constitution in 2012), China has adopted a more green approach. Thus, in 2016, President Xi Jinping committed to creating a green and sustainable BRI. It is important to underline that both the Working Guidance and the Action Plan push the BRI and they aim at greening this Initiative in line with the new low-carbon development mode and with the acceleration of the development of a green trade system. The Working Guidance in its Section X, Promoting a green and low-carbon mode of opening up, uses the following wording to proclaim China's commitments:

Accelerating the development of a green trade system: *As we continue to improve the composition of trade, we need to make great efforts to promote the trading of green products that are high-quality, high value-added, and technologically advanced. Our export policies will be improved to exercise strict regulation over exports of energy-intensive and high-emission products. We will expand imports of green and low-carbon products, environmental services, and services for energy conservation and environmental protection.*[94] As for the greening of the BRI, the Working Guidance states the following:

---

[92] Refer to the book titled "*China's Belt and Road The Initiative and its Financial Focus*," which the three authors published in 2018 with World Scientific, describing in detail the characteristics of the Initiative and its many facets.

[93] *Source*: *China's Involvement in Coal-Fired Power Projects Along the Belt and Road*, Ren Peng, Liu Chang and Zhang Liwen, Global Environmental Institute, May 2017, http://www.geichina.org/_upload/file/report/China's_Involvement_in_Coal-fired_Power_Projects_OBOR_EN.pdf (accessed January 28, 2023).

[94] See number 24, Section X — Promoting a Green and Low-Carbon Mode of Opening-up of the *Working Guidance for Carbon Dioxide Peaking and Carbon Neutrality in Full and*

Promoting the development of green Belt and Road: *We will accelerate a green transformation in Belt and Road investment and cooperation practices and support the development and use of clean energy in participant countries. We will strive to promote South-South cooperation to help other developing countries better address climate change. We will deepen exchanges and cooperation with other countries on environment-friendly technology, equipment, services and infrastructure construction, actively encourage China's new-energy and other green and low-carbon technologies and products to go global, and make green development a defining feature in the joint pursuit of the Belt and Road Initiative.*[95]

On the other hand, the Action Plan also promotes a green BRI in the ambit of a renewed international cooperation and it states that China "*will follow the principle of extensive consultation, joint contribution and shared benefits, uphold openness, green development, and integrity in advancing the Belt and Road Initiative (BRI), and strengthen cooperation with other participants on green infrastructure, green energy, and green finance.* It is also stated that China *will make overseas projects more environmentally sustainable, develop a BRI energy partnership characterized by green development and inclusiveness, and expand the export of new energy technology and products.* China is determined in *bring into full play the role of cooperation platforms such as the BRI International Green Development Coalition, advocate the Green Investment Principles, advance the implementation of the Belt and Road South-South Cooperation Initiative on Climate Change and the Belt and Road Science, Technology, and Innovation Cooperation Action Plan.*"[96]

It is evident that China's policy shift toward a greener BRI reflects China's own commitment to reach net-zero carbon emissions by 2060. Its efforts to implement and export green transition to other countries participating in the BRI are also evident now. Considering the importance and the implications of green economy for China, and the necessity to shape more sustainable development, China's green action initiatives now encourage green infrastructures and investment in green and renewable

Faithful Implementation of the New Development Philosophy, the full text of this document is available at the official website of the NDRC: visit: https://en.ndrc.gov.cn/policies/202110/t20211024_1300725.html (accessed January 28, 2023).

[95] See Working Guidance at number 25.

[96] See the Action Plan — Section IV International Cooperation number 3. Making the Belt and Road Initiative a green initiative.

energies, as well as in technologies favoring this transition with the use of green finance, under the entire BRI framework. In this new modality, the BRI will contribute to the global fight against climate change.

The Chinese government has rightly decided not to build any more coal-fired power stations overseas embracing the concept of a green BRI, placing a particular emphasis on investments in sustainable projects, and in particular on renewable energy projects,[97] through green finance, and this is a true 'paradigm shift' aimed to sustain the green transition and meet the UN's development goals.

The new eco-friendly policies and initiatives adopted by China will have a considerable impact in greening the BRI and in achieving China's new priorities together with its partners. This will contribute to shaping a new multilateralism taking our environment into greater consideration.

3. Promoting International Cooperation on Climate Change

It is evident that China attaches great importance to international cooperation on climate change and consequently to global climate governance. This stance emerges from every single document analyzed. It is important to remember that China is *de facto* an active participant in climate talks and has contributed to the conclusion and implementation of the Paris Agreement of which China is a strong supporter. As a developing country, China adheres to the principles of common but differentiated responsibilities, respective capabilities, and fairness, and safeguards its development rights and interests. China in implementing its climate policies will follow the United Nations Framework Convention on Climate Change and the Paris Agreement.[98] It is worth noting that the Working Guidance affirms

[97]To further strengthen the concept of Green BRI, 57% of China's investment in BRI partner countries went to renewable energy projects during 2020–2021 up from 38% in 2019, and this is in line with China's new commitments expressed ahead of Glasgow, COP26, and the United Nations Conference of Parties on Climate Change. See China's BRI — new global green investment, article available at: China's BRI — New global green investment — China Environment (china-environment-news.com) (accessed January 28, 2023).

[98]In this sense, see Section X of the *Working Guidance for Carbon Dioxide Peaking and Carbon Neutrality in Full and Faithful Implementation of the New Development Philosophy*, — n. 26.

that China will actively participate in formulating international rules and standards and promote the establishment of a fair and rational system for global climate governance based on mutually beneficial cooperation.[99]

The Action Plan contains a section, i.e., Section IV — International Cooperation, where it is stated that *in enthusiastically communicating to the public Xi Jinping's thought on ecological civilization, China is willing to share with others our concept and practices of pursuing ecological progress and green development, and strength to building a clean and beautiful world, and to work together toward building a community of life for humankind and nature*.[100] The Action Plan continues affirming that China will actively participate in the development of the global green governance system, and adhere to the principle of common but differentiated responsibilities and respective capabilities as well as the principle of fairness. Furthermore, China will uphold multilateralism, safeguard the UN-centered international system, and urge all parties to fulfill the United Nations Framework Convention on Climate Change and the Paris Agreement. The interest of China in reaching all these goals is evident and the Action Plan also stresses that China will take an active part in the negotiations on reducing greenhouse gas emissions in international aviation and shipping[101] as these two sectors substantially contribute to GHG emissions.

3.1. *Shaping an equitable and mutually beneficial global climate governance system*

As China has gradually moved onto the center stage of global climate governance and it is now promoting a new multilateralism mutually beneficial to global climate governance (based on the principle of differentiated responsibilities, equity, and respective capabilities), China firmly believes that coordinated action is the only solution to climate change. Thus, it opposes all forms of unilateralism and protectionism.

From China's point of view, a comprehensive and accurate understanding of the Paris Convention, and of its goals and principles, it is the

---

[99] *Ibid.*

[100] In this sense, see Section IV — International Cooperation, n. 1 Participating in global climate governance of the Action Plan For Carbon Dioxide Peaking Before 2030.

[101] *Ibid.*

only way to tackle climate change along with implementing common policies to safeguard our environment. China has become a paladin of the Paris Convention because it understands that only by shaping a society in harmony with nature will it be possible to grant sustainable development and a shared future. It is therefore imperative to share experiences and formulate adequate plans to tackle climate change, in a coordinated fashion, and gradually shape a global green economy.

3.1.1. *Multilevel climate governance*

The current system of climate governance is based on multilevel climate governance which involves a diverse group of national and local governments, international organizations, NGOs, and the private sector in a continuous process of discussions and negotiations to promote initiatives and prompt actions to address climate change. Given the global, national, and local reach of the effects of climate change, this multilevel governance is of paramount importance in addressing its impacts, and the participation of all these actors is necessary to provide an effective response. The nature of this system strengthens and promotes innovation, problem-solving capability, and thus stimulates the research of solutions which can be applied to specific contexts.

As the UN Framework Convention on Climate Change (UNFCCC) (i.e., the Paris Convention) remains the only universal platform on climate,[102] the UNFCCC needs to be protected and valued through more coordinated efforts, and even if the climate governance system evolves to become more inclusive, there is still a necessity to promote new financial instruments to be used to achieve the goals contained in the Paris Convention and those contained in the UN's 2030 Agenda. In this context, the development of green finance is of extreme importance because it can provide the necessary resources to tackle climate change and protect our environment. Green finance (and new forms of it) can also help the less developed countries which have strong nationally determined contributions, and are eager to act, but have little capacity to put the climate agenda into action because of a lack of financial resources.

[102] See *Is the Global Climate Governance System Working*? Jimera Leiva Roesch, Julia Almeida Nobre, and Eimer Curtin, IPI Global Observatory, November 23, 2021, article available at: https://theglobalobservatory.org/2021/11/is-the-global-climate-governance-system-working/ (accessed January 28, 2023).

3.1.2. *Expanding international cooperation and accelerating climate action*

Since the signing of the Paris Convention in 2015, progress has been made and new political initiatives have been introduced to tackle climate change. Because no country is immune from such a threat and no country can act singularly, the whole world needs to work in solidarity and engage in win-win cooperation. However, key actions, such as the phasing out of the use of fossil fuels to reduce global warming, have yet to be taken, though the transition toward the use of clean and renewable energy is advancing.

It is thus imperative to accelerate and implement concerted climate actions (refer to the COP27, see next section), and it requires strong commitment by the global community, especially in the ambit of global climate governance. The many targets posed by the Climate Convention and by the UN with the 2030 Agenda for a Sustainable Development require greater cooperation among nations, and proper solutions should be studied and taken promptly, through consultations among nations, so as to avoid catastrophic consequences for humanity. Climate change needs to become a top priority for every government just like energy and national security are.

The latest COP27 was held in Egypt in November 2022, and it seems appropriate to highlight the outcomes of this meeting because of extreme interest in it and the consequences for the entire global community. Emissions remain one of the most critical elements in all contexts; therefore, the transition toward renewables and clean sources of energy is also at the core of our next sections and chapter.

3.2. *The outcome of the latest COP27*

The United Nations Climate Change Conference, or 'COP27,'[103] which took place in Sharm el-Sheikh (Egypt) from 6 to 20 November 2022, brought together almost 200 countries with the aim to take actions toward achieving the world's collective climate goals as agreed under the Paris Convention. One of the most notable outcomes was the breakthrough agreement to provide 'loss and damage' funding for vulnerable countries hit hard by climate disasters. Before delving further, it is worth noting the following text:

---

[103] See https://unfccc.int/cop27 to retrieve all official documents.

Statement by the EU, Reassembling the Main Outcomes of COP27

At the COP27 UN Climate Change Conference the European Commission showed ambition and flexibility to keep the goal of limiting global warming to 1.5 degrees within reach. After a difficult week of negotiations, a strong and united European effort helped secure a hard-fought deal to keep the targets of the Paris Agreement alive. The EU's bridge-building also helped to put in place balanced new funding arrangements, with an expanded donor base, to help vulnerable communities to face loss and damage caused by climate change.

On mitigation, Parties agreed that limiting global warming to 1.5C requires rapid, deep and sustained reductions in global greenhouse gas emissions, reducing them by 43% by 2030 relative to the 2019 level. They also recognized that this requires accelerated action in this critical decade, and reiterated the call from the Glasgow Climate Pact for nationally determined contributions (NDCs) to be updated as necessary to align with the Paris Agreement temperature goal, by the end of 2023. They also affirmed that the Glasgow Climate Pact will guide a new Mitigation Work Programme to encourage Parties to align their targets and actions towards net zero.[104]

This gives a glimpse of the results reached at the Conference. The other important outcome, as mentioned above, was the decision to establish the so-called 'Loss and Damage' Fund[105] for nations most vulnerable to the climate crisis. Developing countries have made strong and repeated appeals that were finally heard for the establishment of a loss and damage fund to compensate the countries that are the most vulnerable to climate disasters[106] yet have contributed little to the climate crisis. The decision to establish the fund was transposed in the *Sharm el-Sheikh Implementation*

[104] https://ec.europa.eu/commission/presscorner/detail/en/ip_22_7064 (accessed January 28, 2023).

[105] The decision to establish the *Loss and Damage* fund was incorporated into Decision CP.27 titled *Sharm el-Sheiks Implementation Plan*, Section VI, document available at: https://unfccc.int/sites/default/files/resource/cop27_auv_2_cover%20decision.pdf (accessed January 28, 2023).

[106] Adapting to the climate crisis — which could require everything from building sea walls to creating drought-resistant crops — could cost developing countries anywhere from US$160-US$340 billion annually by 2030. That number could swell to as much as

Plan[107] (see Section VI of the Plan). Section IX on finance, at point 30, states that *about USD 4 trillion per year needs to be invested in renewable energy up until 2030 to be able to reach net zero emissions by 2050,*[108] *and that, furthermore, a global transformation to a low-carbon economy is expected to require investment of at least USD 4–6 trillion per year.*[109]

Delivering such funding will require a swift and a comprehensive transformation of the financial system and of its structures and processes, plus engaging governments, central banks, commercial banks, institutional investors, and other financial actors to concretize the needed resources. Though not mentioned directly, the reference to sustainable and green finance is clear. Only by further developing green finance will it be possible to find all the necessary financial resources to tackle climate change and the related environmental issues.

It must be noted that *Serious concern was expressed that the goal of developed country Parties to mobilize jointly USD 100 billion per year by 2020 has not yet been met, with developed countries urged to meet the goal, and multilateral development banks and international financial institutions called on to mobilize climate finance.*[110]

Creating a specific fund for loss and damage marked an important point of progress.[111] However, while agreement on these issues was seen

---

US$565 billion by 2050 if climate change accelerates, found UN Environment Programme's (UNEP's) 2022 Adaptation Gap Report.

[107] Document available at: https://unfccc.int/sites/default/files/resource/cop27_auv_2_cover%20decision.pdf.

[108] See https://iea.blob.core.windows.net/assets/830fe099-5530-48f2-a7c1-11f35d510983/WorldEnergyOutlook2022.pdf.

[109] See also the United Nations Environment Programme. 2022. Emissions Gap Report 2022: The Closing Window — Climate crisis calls for rapid transformation of societies. Nairobi: United Nations Environment Programme. Available at: https://www.unep.org/resources/emissions-gap-report-2022.

[110] *Source*: COP27 Reaches Breakthrough Agreement on New "Loss and Damage" Fund for Vulnerable Countries, 20 November 2022) document available at: https://unfccc.int/news/cop27-reaches-breakthrough-agreement-on-new-loss-and-damage-fund-for-vulnerable-countries (accessed January 28, 2023).

[111] Governments took the ground-breaking decision to assist developing countries in responding to loss and damage caused by climate change as evidenced in the *Sharm el-Sheikh Implementation Plan.* Governments also agreed to establish a 'transitional committee' to make recommendations on how to operationalize both the new funding arrangements and the fund at COP28 next year.

as a welcome step in the right direction, there appeared to be little forward movement on other key issues, particularly on the phasing out of fossil fuels. On this particular aspect, it is worth evidencing the use of language when it comes to limiting global warming to 1.5 degrees Celsius. In fact, while the necessity to limit global warming to the aforementioned limit is recognized to avoid catastrophic consequences, in the *Sharm el-Sheikh Implementation Plan*, we read the following when it comes to 'Energy' (III) and 'Mitigation' (IV):

Informative Box: Extract from the *Sharm el-Sheikh Implementation Plan*

III. Energy

8. *Emphasizes the urgent need for immediate, deep, rapid and sustained reductions in global greenhouse gas emissions by Parties across all applicable sectors, including through increase in low-emission and renewable energy, just energy transition partnerships and other cooperative actions;.*[112]

.. Omissis

10. *Stresses the importance of enhancing a clean energy mix, including low-emission and renewable energy, at all levels as part of diversifying energy mixes and systems, in line with national circumstances and recognizing the need for support towards just transitions;*

IV. Mitigation

11. *Recognizes that limiting global warming to 1.5 °C requires rapid, deep and sustained reductions in global greenhouse gas emissions of 43% by 2030 relative to the 2019 level;*
12. *Also recognizes that this requires accelerated action in this critical decade, on the basis of equity and the best available scientific knowledge, reflecting common but differentiated responsibilities and respective capabilities, in the light of different national circumstances and in the context of sustainable development and efforts to eradicate poverty;*
13. *Calls upon Parties to accelerate the development, deployment and dissemination of technologies, and the adoption of policies, to transition towards low-emission energy systems, including by rapidly scaling up the deployment of clean power generation and energy efficiency measures,*

[112] In this sense, see *Sharm el-Sheikh Implementation Plan,* Section IIII. Energy 8.

(*Continued*)

including accelerating efforts towards the phasedown of unabated coal power and phase-out of inefficient fossil fuel subsidies, while providing targeted support to the poorest and most vulnerable in line with national circumstances and recognizing the need for support towards a just transition;

... Omissis

The wording of these statements prompted observers to warn that the language used in the document, which includes 'low-emission' energy alongside 'renewable' as the energy sources of the future, leaves a significant loophole, as the undefined terms could be used to justify new fossil fuel development against the clear guidance of the UN Intergovernmental Panel on Climate Change (IPCC)[113] and the International Energy Agency (IEA).[114]

Noteworthily, COP27 saw significant progress on adaptation,[115] with governments agreeing on the way to move forward on the Global Goal on Adaptation, which will conclude at COP28 and inform the first Global Stocktake, improving resilience among the most vulnerable.[116] The UN Climate Change Standing Committee on Finance was requested to prepare a report on doubling adaptation finance for consideration at COP28.

Simon Stiell, UN Climate Change Executive Secretary, reminded delegates in the closing plenary that the world is in a critical decade for climate action.

[113] The Intergovernmental Panel on Climate change (IPCC) was present at the UN Climate Change Conference (COP27) with a broad program of its own events as well as taking part in the official activities of the meeting. *Source*: Outreach — Event (ipcc.ch).

[114] See in this sense the comments on "COP27 closes with deal on loss and damage: 'A step towards justice,' says UN chief," published November 20, 2022. Available at: https://news.un.org/en/story/2022/11/1130832 (accessed January 28, 2023).

[115] Refer to the *Sharm el-Sheikh Implementation Plan (V. Adaptation).*

[116] New pledges, totaling more than USD 230 million, were made to the Adaptation Fund at COP27. These pledges will help many more vulnerable communities adapt to climate change through concrete adaptation solutions. COP27 President Sameh Shoukry announced the Sharm el-Sheikh Adaptation Agenda, enhancing resilience for people living in the most climate-vulnerable communities by 2030.

A lot remains to be done to reach the goals of the Paris Convention, but with a shared vision on the actions to be taken the global community can reach these goals and grant a sustainable and shared future for the whole of humanity.

To conclude, it is worth reporting what COP27 President Sameh Shoukry said at the conclusion of the meeting: *The work that we've managed to do here in the past two weeks, and the results we have together achieved, are a testament to our collective will, as a community of nations, to voice a clear message that rings loudly today, here in this room and around the world: that multilateral diplomacy still works.... despite the difficulties and challenges of our times, the divergence of views, level of ambition or apprehension, we remain committed to the fight against climate change.... we rose to the occasion, upheld our responsibilities and undertook the important decisive political decisions that millions around the world expect from us.*

Chapter 4

Advancing toward a Green Economy Needs the Special Focus of the Entire Global Community on the Development of Green and Low-Carbon Energy Sources and More Pronounced Green Finance

As evidenced by the Intergovernmental Panel on Climate Change (IPCC),[1] the time for action is now: According to IPCC's latest Assessment Report, "in 2010–2019 average annual global greenhouse gas emissions were at their highest levels in human history, but the rate of growth has slowed."[2] The IPCC stresses that without immediate and

[1]The Intergovernmental Panel on Climate Change, IPCC, is the United Nations body for assessing the science related to climate change. The IPCC prepares comprehensive Assessment Reports about the state of scientific, technical, and socioeconomic knowledge on climate change, its impacts and future risks, and options for reducing the rate at which climate change is taking place. For more information, visit: About the IPCC at https://www.ipcc.ch/about/ (accessed January 28, 2023).

[2]IPCC, *The evidence is clear: the time for action is now. We can halve emissions by 2030*, April 4, 2022, available at: https://www.ipcc.ch/2022/04/04/ipcc-ar6-wgiii-pressrelease/ (accessed January 8, 2023). The IPCC is now in its sixth assessment cycle, in which the IPCC is producing the 6th Assessment Report (AR6) with contributions by its three Working Groups. The contribution of Working Group I to the Sixth Assessment Report, Climate Change 2021: The Physical Science Basis, was released on August 9, 2021; the

deep emission reductions across all sectors, limiting global warming to 1.5°C is beyond reach. Considering that around two-third of global greenhouse gas emissions stem from energy production and use, it is necessary to concentrate efforts in this sector to reduce emissions and to combat climate change by pushing the transition toward green, renewable sources of energy to meet climate goals. It is clear that progress in the power sector to ameliorate efficiency needs to be further accelerated, and clean and renewable sources have to scale up, while decarbonization in other sectors, for example, in the transport sector,[3] must pick up steam to at least halve emissions by 2030. As evidenced by the IPCC Working Group III Co-Chair Priyadarshi Shukla, "Having the right policies, infrastructure and technology in place to enable changes to our lifestyles and behavior can result in a 40–70% reduction in greenhouse gas emissions by 2050. This offers significant untapped potential," Moreover "The evidence also shows that these lifestyle changes can improve our health and wellbeing."[4]

This chapter aims at illustrating the importance of renewables and how the major economies intend to foster their use.

1. Alternative Renewable and Clean Sources of Energy are Part of the Solution to Climate Change

The major cause of global warming is the use of fossil fuels. Our society has relied on the use of these resources such as coal and oil, and has based its development on the exploitation of natural resources. This model not

---

contribution of Working Group II, Climate Change 2022: Impacts, Adaptation, and Vulnerability, was released on February 28, 2022; and the contribution of Working Group III, Climate Change 2022: Mitigation of Climate Change, was released on April 4, 2022. The Synthesis Report will be the last of the AR6 products and was scheduled to be released in September 2022.

[3] The transport sector accounted for 23% of global energy-related CO2 emissions in 2019 according to IPCC AR6 Working Group III, see Chapter 10: Transport, Working Group III contribution to the Sixth Assessment Report, available at: https://report.ipcc.ch/ar6wg3/pdf/IPCC_AR6_WGIII_FinalDraft_Chapter10.pdf (accessed January 28, 2023).

[4] See IPCC newsroom, The Evidence is clear: the time for action is now, We can halve emission by 2030. Presentation of its latest Climate Change Report, April 4, 2022.

only threatened the environment but also brought our planet to the brink of an irreversible catastrophic change if we do not act now and opt for more sustainable and green development. Studies (refer to the IPCC's Reports) have demonstrated that the earth is under unprecedented stress from supporting a growing population and degradation, coupled with the rapid depletion of its natural resources. We need to immediately adopt a more sustainable and eco-friendly development, wisely using the remaining resources and pushing for the adoption of green technologies and environmentally compatible processes of production, coupled with the use of renewables.

As put in evidence by IRENA in its report,[5] a decarbonized energy sector, dominated by renewable sources, is at the core of the transition to a sustainable energy future. This would be the first step. Eliminating CO_2 emissions in fact does not solve the problem of global warming. It would take centuries to eliminate greenhouse gas from the atmosphere and thus completely reverse the damage caused to our environment. However, we do not have other options but to change our development mode.

In order to limit global warming and try to reverse the degradation of our environment, the entire global community has no choice but to use renewable energy sources. The great challenge is thus energy transition, which refers to the global energy sector's shift from fossil-based systems of energy production and consumption to a more sustainable mode based on the use of renewables, for example, solar, wind, and hydropower. All these are green, sustainable, clean, and renewable sources and their use will certainly help in reaching the goals of the Paris Convention. The increasing use of renewable energy sources in energy supply, the increase of efficiency, and the smart use of electricity (including improvements in energy storage with the use of new technologies) are all key drivers of energy transition. For more sustainable development, the International Energy Agency predicted the world's total renewable-based power capacity to increase 50 percent between 2019 and 2024. In response to this epochal shift sustained by three of the major consumers of energy, namely, the US, China, and the EU, energy utilities have begun a rapid energy transition away from fossil resources (the EU in particular with its

[5] *Global Energy Transformation — A Roadmap to 2050*, International Renewable Energy Agency (IRENA), 2018, document available at https://www.irena.org/-/media/Files/IRENA/Agency/Publication/2018/Apr/IRENA_Report_GET_2018.pdf (accessed January 28, 2023).

Green Deal is pushing renewables). A very important signal of this transition is the fact that many major oil companies are accelerating their spending on, and diversifying into, renewables and low-carbon energy in response to growing concerns over climate change and also in order to meet the new directions and strategies expressed by many governments to implement the use of sustainable and renewable sources of energy. Before illustrating the different policies and initiatives adopted by the major economies, the following sections explain why it is so important to transition toward green energy and briefly define 'renewable sources of energy.'

1.1. *Introduction: Why green energy is so important?*

Our society has relied on sources such as coal and oil to provide us with the energy we need, and our development has been based on the use of NON-renewable sources of energy which produce and expel pollution (greenhouse gases and in particular CO_2) into our atmosphere and environment. These resources are limited in nature and will eventually run out, causing worry about shortages and access to them; but what is worse is the environmental harm they inflict. The use of these sources of energy contributes to global warming, and burning coal and oil releases toxic gases into the atmosphere, impacting our health especially in industrialized areas, causing respiratory problems for those people who are particularly sensitive to these agents. These are only a few of the consequences of using fossil resources, so it is evident that the transition toward green energy and renewable, clean, and sustainable sources will help mitigate these effects. The quicker we move to renewable, clean, and sustainable sources of energy, the better.

1.1.1. *Combination of green energy and UN's sustainable goals*

It is not only renewable and sustainable sources of energy that are part of a common global strategy to help preserve our environment and fight climate change but also Sustainable Development Goals: According to the declaration contained in the 2030 Agenda for Sustainable Development, "*Natural resource depletion and adverse impacts of environmental degradation, including desertification, drought, land degradation, freshwater scarcity and loss of biodiversity, add to and exacerbate the list of challenges which humanity faces. Climate change is one of the greatest challenges of our time and its adverse impacts undermine the ability of all countries to achieve sustainable development. Increases in global temperature, sea level rise, ocean acidification and other climate change impacts are seriously affecting coastal areas and low-lying coastal countries, including many least developed countries and small island developing States. The survival of many societies, and of the biological support systems of the planet, is at risk.*" This evidences the urgent necessity to take action and adopt a more sustainable model of development. The leading role must be played by the energy sector; thus, the use of green and renewable sources of energy needs to be pushed further. The widespread use of green energy will also favor the transformation of our economies into green economies. Before introducing the initiatives of the major economies in sustaining renewable and green sources of energy, the next section briefly defines those sources of energy.

1.2. *Defining green, renewable sources of energy: Brief introduction*

Some forms of green energy have been around for years, but the technology to exploit those forms of energy was not mature. Today, governments are incentivizing and supporting investments in new technologies to improve efficiency in using these alternative renewable green sources of energy. Especially with the signing of the Paris Agreement and its entry into force in 2016, a vast majority of the countries around the world are now committed to limiting carbon emissions and implementing all the measures and goals contained in the Agreement coupled with the goals of the UN's Agenda 2030 for sustainable development.

But what is green energy, and what are these renewable sources?

Generally speaking, green energy refers to a form of energy that emits a small amount of pollution in terms of greenhouse gases or other contaminants when we produce it. Substantially, green energy provides the highest environmental benefit and includes power (electricity) produced by solar (photovoltaic), wind, geothermal, low-impact hydroelectric, and certain eligible biomass sources. These forms of energy are also called sustainable sources and they renew themselves automatically.

1.2.1. *Wind and solar energy*

Wind and solar energy are two examples of green, clean, renewable energy which are present in nature and cannot be depleted by mankind because they always have existed and are constantly being replenished. Wind was used since men started sailing, and thanks to the evolution of technology, wind now can be used to produce energy. In this case, three-blade wind turbines are used to produce electricity. These work on a rather simple principle: Wind turns the blades of the turbine, which turn an internal rotor, which then moves the main shaft, which spins a generator and creates electricity. On the other hand, solar power was used by Archimedes as a weapon with mirrors acting collectively as a parabolic reflector to burn ships which were attacking Syracuse. Now, solar power can be used to produce energy but it took a long time before we invented the technology (photovoltaic panels) to use the sun to produce energy. Solar energy is a clean source of energy which comes directly from the sun and we just need to capture it. Solar panels are the most common form of solar energy harvesting.

Noteworthily, according to IRENA, wind and solar power together accounted for approximately 8% of the total energy generated in 2019.[6] This also means a 23% increase in solar power generation and a 12% increase in wind power generation compared to 2018.

1.2.2. *Hydropower*

Hydropower or hydroelectric power is produced by capturing the kinetic energy contained within flowing water in rivers, streams, or dams. This is commonly achieved by storing water in a reservoir or dam and selectively purging water by opening an intake. When water is released, the flow spins a turbine which once again activates a generator creating electricity.

---

[6]According to the data gathered by IRENA, in 2019, the total amount of electricity generated from renewable was 6963 TWh, and wind and solar contributions were 1412 TWh and 693 TWh, respectively. IRENA's data show a 26% renewable share of generation in 2019, of this 20% was wind power and 10% solar power, which correspond to about 8% of the total energy generated. See Renewable energy statistics 2021, Renewable energy highlights, document available at: https://irena.org/publications/2021/Aug/Renewable-energy-statistics-2021 (accessed January 28, 2023).

Though hydropower nowadays provides about 16 percent[7] of energy used around the world, some people argue that this source of energy has too many social and environmental costs to be considered a sustainable or 'green' resource. In fact, dams can cause permanent destruction to local habitats. Thus, hydropower that could damage the environment is not to be considered green, renewable, or sustainable. Hydropower designed not to damage the environment, on the other hand, can be considered green, clean, and sustainable.

1.2.3. *Other sources of renewable energy*

Biomass is another source of renewable energy. Biomass energy is the oldest energy source used by humans. It is derived from organic matter present in nature and it comprises animal manure (dung), herbaceous plant material (non-wood), and peat (partially decomposed plant and animal tissues). Today, biomass can also be converted into liquid biofuels such as ethanol and methanol.

Geothermal energy is a source of green, clean, and sustainable energy and it is derived from the heat of earth's internal geologic process, but this source is only exploitable in certain determined regions. The mantle of the earth, under the crust, will always give off heat from the core. Thanks to specific technology, we can access this source of heat and use it. In Iceland, which is located in an active volcanic region near a mid-ocean ridge, geothermal energy supplies ninety percent of residents' electricity needs for entire cities.

These two sources of renewable energy, according to the latest data by IRENA, accounted 8% and 1%, respectively, of the renewable electricity generated in 2019.[8]

---

[7]According to the latest data by IRENA (2021), Renewable energy highlights, in 2019, the total amount of electricity generated from renewables was 6963 TWh, and hydroelectricity accounted for about 61% of this, i.e., 4207 TWh. In terms of total electricity generation, IRENA's data show a 26% renewable share of generation in 2019; thus, the 61% of hydropower corresponds to 16% of the total. See Renewable energy statistics 2021, Renewable energy highlights, document available at: https://irena.org/publications/2021/Aug/Renewable-energy-statistics-2021 (accessed January 28, 2023).

[8]In 2019, the total amount of electricity generated from renewables was 6963 TWh, of which 558TWh was bioenergy and 92TWh geothermal energy. See Renewable energy

1.3. *Hydrogen: An alternative which deserves particular attention*

As a matter of fact, hydrogen is the most abundant chemical element in nature, and it can be used to produce energy in vast quantities and for a myriad of sectors. It is considered a renewable source of energy. However, only 'green' hydrogen can be considered a clean source; in fact, this element can be produced from a wide variety of sources even from fossil fuels. Hydrogen can be produced using multiple processes and energy sources. From this, a color code nomenclature has been developed (Figure 1).

Noteworthily, the vast majority of hydrogen used today is 'grey' hydrogen, produced using fossil fuels, emitting carbon dioxide in the process. 'Blue' and 'Turquoise' hydrogen are made using natural gas by capturing carbon dioxide, making it cleaner than grey hydrogen but not completely climate-friendly. This is why attention is on 'green' hydrogen, which is a carbon-free product. Green hydrogen is made using electricity (the scientific term is 'electrolysis') by splitting the hydrogen molecules from oxygen molecules in water. In this process, the byproduct after hydrogen combustion is not carbon dioxide, but water. Green hydrogen is forecast to fill 15% to 20% of the world's energy needs that will not be easily met by wind or solar power (see IRENA data).

1.3.1. *Increasing role of green hydrogen but still barriers to overcome*

The demand for hydrogen continues to increase because of its use in many different industry sectors such as the steel industry, chemical industry, and refineries; however, because today's hydrogen production is mostly based on natural gas and coal, which together account for more than 90% of production, there is a necessity to increase the production of green hydrogen. Today, green hydrogen faces barriers that prevent its full contribution to the green transition including the following: (i) high production costs (two to three times more than grey hydrogen); (ii) lack of dedicated infrastructures; (iii) energy losses (green hydrogen incurs significant energy losses at each stage of the value chain, i.e., about 30–35% of the energy

---

statistics 2021, Renewable energy highlights, document available at: https://irena.org/publications/2021/Aug/Renewable-energy-statistics-2021 (accessed October 28, 2022).

GREY HYDROGEN[1] is produced with fossil fuels (i.e. hydrogen produced from methane using steam methane reforming (SMR) or coal gasification). The use of grey hydrogen entails substantial CO_2 emissions, which makes these hydrogen technologies unsuitable for a route toward net-zero emissions.

During early stages of the energy transition, the use of **BLUE HYDROGEN** (i.e. grey hydrogen with carbon capture and storage [CCS]) could facilitate the growth of a hydrogen market. Around three-quarters of hydrogen is currently produced from natural gas. Retrofitting with CCS would allow the continued use of existing assets while still achieving lower GHG emissions. This is an option is to produce hydrogen with lower GHG emissions while reducing pressure on the renewable energy capacity installation rate to produce green hydrogen. Notably, industrial processes like steel production may require a continuous flow of hydrogen; blue hydrogen could be an initial solution while green hydrogen ramps up production and storage capacity to meet the continuous flow requirement.

However, blue hydrogen has limitations that have so far restricted its deployment: it uses finite resources, is exposed to fossil fuel price fluctuations, and does not support the goals of energy security. Moreover, blue hydrogen faces social acceptance issues, as it is associated with additional costs for CO_2 transport and storage and requires monitoring of stored CO_2. In addition, CCS capture efficiencies are expected to reach 85-95% at best,[2] which means that 5-15% of the CO_2 will still be emitted. And these high capture rates have yet to be achieved.

In sum, the carbon emissions from hydrogen generation could be reduced by CCS but not eliminated. Moreover, these processes use methane, which brings leakages upstream, and methane is a much more potent GHG per molecule than CO_2. This means that while blue hydrogen could reduce CO_2 emissions, it does not meet the requirements of a net-zero future. For these reasons, blue hydrogen should be seen only as a short-term transition to facilitate the uptake of green hydrogen on the path to net-zero emissions.

TURQUOISE HYDROGEN combines the use of natural gas as feedstock with no CO_2 production. Through the process of pyrolysis, the carbon in the methane becomes solid carbon black. A market for carbon black already exists, which provides an additional revenue stream. Carbon black can be more easily stored than gaseous CO_2. At the moment, turquoise hydrogen is still at the pilot stage. (Philibert, 2020; Monolith, 2020).

Among the different shades of hydrogen, **GREEN HYDROGEN** – meaning hydrogen produced from renewable energy – is the most suitable one for a fully sustainable energy transition. The most established technology options for producing green hydrogen is water electrolysis fuelled by renewable electricity. This technology is the focus of this report. Other renewables-based solutions to produce hydrogen exist.[3] However, except for SMR with biogases, these are not mature technologies at commercial scale yet (IRENA, 2018). Green hydrogen production through electrolysis is consistent with the net-zero route, allows the exploitation of synergies from sector coupling, thus decreasing technology costs and providing flexibility to the power system. Low VRE costs and technological improvement are decreasing the cost of production of green hydrogen. For these reasons, green hydrogen from water electrolysis has been gaining increased interest.

1 Sometimes referred to as black or brown hydrogen.

2 An alternative route to SMR could be a process called autothermal reforming, for which it is estimated that a possible capture rate up to 94.5% of the CO_2 emitted is possible (H-Vision, 2019).

3 For example, biomass gasification and pyrolysis, thermochemical water splitting, photocatalysis, supercritical water gasification of biomass, combined dark fermentation and anaerobic digestion.

Figure 1: Types of hydrogen

Source: Green Hydrogen — A Guide to Policy Making, IRENA, November 2020, document available at: https://irena.org/publications/2020/Nov/Green-hydrogen.

used to produce hydrogen through electrolysis is lost (see IRENA's report));[9] and (iv) the need to ensure sustainability: According to IRENA, "electricity can be supplied from a renewable energy plant directly connected to the electrolyzer, from the grid, or from a mix of the two. Using only electricity from a renewable energy plant ensures that the hydrogen is 'green' in any given moment. Grid-connected electrolyzers can produce for more hours, reducing the cost of hydrogen. However, grid electricity may include electricity produced from fossil fuel plants, so any CO_2 emissions associated with that electricity will have to be considered when evaluating the sustainability of hydrogen."[10]

Green hydrogen to be used as a renewable source in energy transition still faces challenges which can be solved by investing in technology. Naturally, policymakers have to implement energy strategies which include the wide use of green hydrogen coupling them with incentives while the green hydrogen era is gaining grip. All major economies have included hydrogen in their energy plans and it will definitely play its part in reaching the carbon neutrality goals.

To conclude this section, it is worth emphasizing that green hydrogen is of great importance and has a fundamental role to play in the transport system, including the aviation sector. However, solutions need to be found for safely storing hydrogen on aircrafts and building infrastructure for alternative fuel at airports. Nevertheless, technology is advancing and proper solutions will be adopted to overcome those challenges. Green hydrogen will play a significant role in decreasing emissions from air travel to reach zero impact on climate change following the new path indicated by the International Air Transport Association (IATA), which major manufacturers are pursuing. The aviation industry, including all major manufacturers, has committed to an industry-wide decarbonization or 'green aviation' drive, which was a result of the crisis caused by COVID-19 to this industry.[11] At its 77th Annual General Meeting, IATA

---

[9] *Source*: Green Hydrogen — A guide to Policy Making, IRENA, report available at: https://irena.org/-/media/Files/IRENA/Agency/Publication/2020/Nov/IRENA_Green_hydrogen_policy_2020.pdf (accessed January 28, 2023).

[10] *Ibid.*

[11] A more detailed analysis of this theme is contained in the book titled, The Impact of COVID-19 on World Aviation Industry — Challenges and Opportunities, Paolo Rizzi, Cristiano Rizzi, Mario Tettamanti, World Scientific, April 2022, which examines also the use of hydrogen for aviation.

approved a resolution for the global air transport industry to achieve net-zero carbon emissions by 2050. This commitment will align with the Paris Convention goal for global warming not to exceed 1.5°C.[12]

In the following sections, we explain the initiatives of the major economies in relation to their advancements in green transition of the energy sector. It is evident that reaching carbon neutrality means implementing plans to introduce more renewable sources of energy, and clearly all major economies have put in place specific strategies to integrate their current and growing need of energy with sustainable and green alternatives, which will have a positive impact on our environment and will help to mitigate the effects of climate change.

2. China's Green Transition Needs a Special Focus on the Development of Green and Low-Carbon Energy

Given the fact that China is the world's largest energy consumer and carbon emitter, accounting for one-third of global CO_2 emissions, its push for renewables which is a basic element of the green transition is not surprising. China's objective to reach carbon neutrality by 2060 has hinged on a major acceleration in green and clean energy innovation, which means more investment and public spending on low-carbon energy research and development. Such innovation, which is expected to be one of the major drivers of China's future economic growth, stands at the core of three major strategies China is pursuing:

- **Technological leadership:** to become 'the top innovation-oriented country by 2035' and 'the world's major science center and a highland of innovation.'[13]

---

[12] See Net-Zero Carbon Emissions by 2050, IATA, Press Release No. 66, October 4, 2021, document available at: https://www.iata.org/en/pressroom/2021-releases/2021-10-04-03/ (accessed January 28, 2023).

[13] References: Strive to become the world's major science center and innovation highland [translated], President Xi Jinping, document available at: http://www.gov.cn/xinwen/2021-03/15/content_5593022.htm (accessed January 28, 2023); and Speeches at the 20th Academician Conference of the Chinese Academy of Sciences, the 15th Academician Conference of the Chinese Academy of Engineering, and the 10th National Congress of the

- **Innovation-driven growth:** to build a 'new momentum' for high-quality economic development, with scientific and technological achievements as the 'main battlefield of the economy and society.'[14]
- **Tackle environmental challenges:** to achieve the vision of an 'ecological civilization,' including a peak in CO_2 emissions before 2030, carbon neutrality before 2060, and tackling air, water, and land pollution.

China's commitment to reduce its carbon emissions is evidenced in all the programmatic policy documents that we have analyzed in the previous chapters. Now, the pace of China's emissions reductions over the next three decades will be important in determining if the world succeeds in preventing global warming from exceeding 1.5°C.

The key solutions lie in technologies, including those related to energy storage, and not just renewable energy sources. China is fully aware of the necessity to accelerate investment in research; in fact, it takes time for technology to mature and achieve large-scale applications, which in turn will lead to the lowering of emissions and will help in establishing a green energy sector. However, the starting point is enhancing the current capability of the production of the renewables like solar and wind power, where China has gained substantial experience, and thus expanding their usage.

2.1. *China is well positioned to become a leading player in renewable energy*

At the top of its agenda, China has put the reduction of emissions and the transition toward cleaner forms of energy as the main paths to reach carbon neutrality by 2060. To this extent, China has made major contributions to energy technology development since 2000, and it is possible to affirm that China is leading the innovation in renewable sources. As a matter of fact, China is now becoming a hub for manufacturing

---

Chinese Association for Science and Technology [translated], http://www.xinhuanet.com/politics/leaders/2021-05/28/c_1127505377.htm (accessed January 28, 2023).

[14] *Source*: Accelerate the construction of an innovative country to fully support the new development pattern [translated], http://www.scio.gov.cn/xwfbh/xwbfbh/wqfbh/44687/44975/wz44977/Document/1699260/1699260.htm (accessed January 28, 2023).

'innovations' to help green transition. Innovation and investment in technology in China have had an impressive impact on the clean energy sector, especially in helping to reduce the costs of solar Photo Voltaic (PV) panels by over 90% since 2005.[15] The experience with solar PV, and also with batteries and light-emitting diodes (LEDs) which allow a more efficient use of energy, has certainly changed energy technology expectations for further advancements, and at the same time has raised confidence that innovation will lower the economic and political barriers to tackling climate change with solutions contributing to the reduction of carbon emissions in other sectors. This is why it is so important to invest in research and new technologies. Notably, China accounted for one-quarter of global public spending on energy R&D and 15% of spending on low-carbon energy R&D in 2020.[16]

2.1.1. *China is taking the worldwide lead in wind power*

Before entering into more details concerning China's wind power capability, it is interesting to note that globally onshore wind additions through 2026 are set to be almost 25% higher on average than in the 2015–2020 period. In fact, global onshore wind additions doubled in 2020, but this was driven by an acceleration in China as developers rushed to complete projects before subsidies expired. According to the report by the International Energy Agency (IEA),[17] while annual additions in the coming years are not expected to match 2020's record, the Agency forecasts that onshore capability will average 75 GW per year over the 2021–2026 period and the offshore wind capability is forecast to more than triple by 2026.

It has been put in evidence that "although the pledge of reaching carbon neutrality in 2060 represents an enormous challenge that could be

---

[15] *Source*: *An Energy Sector Roadmap to Carbon Neutrality in China*, report by IEA (International Energy Agency), 2021, p. 231. Document available at: https://iea.blob.core.windows.net/assets/6689062e-43fc-40c8-9659-01cf96150318/AnenergysectorroadmaptocarbonneutralityinChina.pdf (accessed January 28, 2023).

[16] *Ibid.*, p. 232.

[17] *Source*: International Energy Agency, Renewables 2021 — Analysis and forecast to 2026. Document available at: https://iea.blob.core.windows.net/assets/5ae32253-7409-4f9a-a91d-1493ffb9777a/Renewables2021-Analysisandforecastto2026.pdf (accessed January 28, 2023).

difficult to meet, this official long-term goal still commits China to an ambitious investment path in the production of renewable energy[18] and electricity distribution, low-carbon transport and housing renovation, agricultural production and the restoration of natural habitats."[19] China intends to produce 50% of its energy from non-fossil sources, including nuclear and renewable sources, by 2030 and this will be possible by investing more in green energy. To this extent, it must be noted that a leading position in green energy is conducive to exporting solutions and technology, which China is actively pursuing. Noteworthily, China's wind and solar power generation accounted for 30% of the world's total in 2020, and the installed capacity of these two renewable sources is expected to double to more than 1.2 billion kilowatts by 2030.[20] Also, it must be stressed that "*To ensure such an ambitious transition does not come at the expense of nature, the transition requires a thoughtful approach to avoid any unintended consequences, for example through a heavy reliance on rare-earth minerals for batteries or the disruption of land- and ocean-based ecosystems through the installation of wind and solar farms. The adoption of natural climate solutions should balance the climate benefits brought by new energy (e.g., biomass) with its impact on nature*."[21]

In particular, wind power in China is scaling up: According to data from 2021 offshore wind power capacity saw a 16.9 gigawatt (GW)

---

[18] Renewable energy demand and capacity are growing at an impressive rate in China, meeting the objectives of the government to transition toward a more sustainable development. "*China is now the world leader in production, export, and installation of solar panels, wind turbines, batteries, and electric vehicles.*" *Source*: SingularityHub, *China is taking the worldwide lead in wind power*, Marc Prosser, April 4, 2019, article available at: https://singularityhub.com/2019/04/04/china-is-taking-the-worldwide-lead-in-wind-power/ (accessed January 28, 2023).

[19] See *The 14th Five-Year Plan in the New Era of China's Reform — Asian Integration, Belt and Road Initiative and Safeguarding Multilateralism*, Michel Aglietta, Guo Bai and Camille Macaire, in Policy Brief, CEPII, No. 2020-36, May 2021.

[20] "China's renewable energy power generation installed capacity of over one billion kilowatts of hydropower, wind power, solar power and biomass power generation capacity are ranked first in the world," State-owned Assets Supervision and Administration Commission of the State Council, Chinese version available at: http://www.sasac.gov.cn/n2588025/n2588139/c21975690/content.html (accessed January 28, 2023).

[21] *Source*: *Seizing Business Opportunities in China's Transition Towards a Nature-Positive Economy*, p. 57, World Economic Forum, 2022, available at: https://www3.weforum.org/docs/WEF_New_Nature_Economy_Report_China_2022.pdf (accessed January 28, 2023).

increase, greater than every other country combined in the past five years. These data come from the statistics from the state energy regulator, i.e., the National Energy Administration (NEA).[22] Noteworthily, China's current installed capacity of offshore wind (reported as 26,4 GW) corresponds to approximately two and a half that of the previous world leader, the U.K., which has an offshore wind capacity of 11GW (as of the third quarter of 2021). China is planning to further expand its offshore wind capacity in the coming years and increase its solar capacity to meet its dual carbon goals. Solar power and wind power now account for 635 GW of power (by the end of 2021), making up 26.7% of China's total national capacity.[23] This green energy capacity is expected to increase to 1.200 GW by 2030 (presumably even before the end of the 14th Five-Year Plan).

2.1.2. *China's solar power capacity expected to grow*

Again, it is worth noting that solar PV alone accounts for more than half of all renewable power in China. According to the data reported by the IEA, solar power accounted for 60% of all renewable capacity additions in 2021 followed by wind and hydropower. The growth of renewable power capacity in China is forecast to accelerate in the next five years, accounting for almost 95% of the increase in global power capacity through 2026.[24]

As for China alone, the renewable electricity capacity is expected to increase by almost 800GW or 85% over the period 2021–2026, led by solar PV (and followed by wind power). In the next five years, solar PV coupled and wind power are expected to provide two-third of China's renewable capacity.[25] According to the Chinese National Energy

---

[22] The National Energy Administration (NEA) is a state administration under the National Development and Reform Commission (NDRC). The NEA drafts China's national energy strategy, implements energy policy, and regulate energy sectors. For more information, visit: www.nea.gov.cn (Chinese only).

[23] *Source*: Energy Tracker Asia, *What the 2021 China Wind Power Boom Means for the World*, article available at: https://energytracker.asia/what-the-2021-china-wind-power-boom-means-for-the-world/ (accessed January 28, 2023).

[24] In this sense: *International Energy Agency, Renewables 2021 — Analysis and forecast to 2026*. Document available at: https://iea.blob.core.windows.net/assets/5ae32253-7409-4f9a-a91d-1493ffb9777a/Renewables2021-Analysisandforecastto2026.pdf (accessed January 28, 2023).

[25] *Ibid.*

Administration (NEA), the newly installed PV capacity reached 54 GW in 2021, and of this capacity around 29 GW comes from distributed generation projects, with large-scale solar plants accounting for the remaining share. The country's cumulative installed power reached 306 GW, despite a supply disruption of raw material at the end of December (2021), which can cover the power generation of Germany based on NEA information. It is worth noting that the main demand drivers of China's solar industry growth are the growing domestic demand, government stimulus, and an increased environmental awareness. The future of solar power in China looks bright. In this context, it is sufficient to mention that out of the 75 GW solar power projects currently under construction in China, 45 GW of capacity is expected to be connected to the grid by the end of 2022, while the remaining capacity is to be completed by the end of 2023.

The solar energy market growth in China will continue to increase as the development of the solar photovoltaic systems will also continue to improve, and this China will remain the global leader in terms of renewable energy production over the next five years. However, according to solar energy analysts, upon the elimination of some solar energy subsidies and incentives, the reliance of China on coal for power generation is still unavoidable in 2022. Furthermore, the NEA stated in their solar forecast that the country's annual target capacity of solar power generation is bound to increase over the next five years, with an aim to achieve nearly 16.5% of total power generation by the end of 2025.[26]

2.1.3. *Hydropower and China: Global interests and not just a national priority*

It must first be underlined that hydropower supplied one-sixth of global electricity generation and it is the third largest source of energy after coal and natural gas. Its importance in green transition in thus evident. According to the IEA's latest report, hydropower's total capacity over the last 20 years rose 70% globally, but its share of total generation stayed stable due to the growth of wind, solar PV, coal, and natural gas.[27] Global

---

[26]*Sources*: Solar Energy Statistics — Solar Power Statistics in China 2021, Solar Feeds, March 9, 2022, article available at: https://www.solarfeeds.com/mag/solar-power-statistics-in-china-2021/ (accessed January 28, 2023).

[27]*Source*: International Energy Agency, Hydropower Special Market Report — Analysis and forecast to 2030, revised version, July 2021, document available at:

capacity is expected to increase further between the period 2021 and 2030, contributing to reaching carbon neutrality by 2050, however, net capacity additions over this period are forecast to decrease compared with the previous decade because of the aging of the hydro plants. A great portion of the existing plants around the globe are over 50 years old and thus it would be necessary to modernize them to ensure they can contribute to electricity security in a sustainable manner for the decades to come. According to the report by the IEA, the modernization of all aging plants worldwide would require USD 300 billion in investment between 2021 and 2030. This certainly offers an opportunity, but the limited visibility on long-term revenues, as evidenced by the IEA, makes it difficult to secure the necessary financing. Another aspect which needs to be explained is that globally around half of hydropower's economically viable potential is untapped. This offers huge potential to add further clean energy, particularly in emerging economies and developing economies, especially in China where hydropower is seen as a fundamental part of the energy policy.

China is in fact the world's largest producer of hydropower: Net electricity generated by hydropower plants in China reached 1,323,741.1 GWh in 2021, growing 1.1% year on year. In 2021, the China's National Energy Administration announced plans to double its generating capacity from pumped storage hydropower (PSH) in five years, and to double it again by 2030.[28] But what is more interesting is that Chinese investment accounts for most hydropower growth in emerging and developing countries. According to the IEA, over half of the new hydropower projects in Sub-Saharan Africa, Southeast Asia, and Latin America through 2030 are set to be either built, financed, partially financed, or owned by Chinese firms.[29] In Asia only (excluding India), nearly 45% of all hydropower

https://iea.blob.core.windows.net/assets/4d2d4365-08c6-4171-9ea2-8549fabd1c8d/HydropowerSpecialMarketReport_corr.pdf (accessed January 28, 2023).

[28] Hydropower capability in China represented around 18% According to the International Hydropower Association's 2020 Hydropower Status Report. Document available at: https://hydropower-assets.s3.eu-west-2.amazonaws.com/publications-docs/2020_hydropower_status_report.pdf (accessed January 28, 2023).

[29] International Energy Agency, Hydropower Special Market Report — Analysis and forecast to 2030, revised version, July 2021, document available at: https://iea.blob.core.windows.net/assets/4d2d4365-08c6-4171-9ea2-8549fabd1c8d/HydropowerSpecialMarketReport_corr.pdf (accessed January 28, 2023).

plants that are set to be built through 2030 involve a Chinese company. China's interest to invest in this sector and export its technology is clear, and this will also allow it to increase its influence in BRI countries where these projects are to be realized, hopefully pushing the share of renewables in these countries.

2.1.4. *The contribution of biomass energy*

China has pledged to boost the high-quality development of the biomass power generation sector in 2021, as part of the government's ongoing efforts to peak carbon emissions by 2030 and achieve carbon neutrality by 2060. On 14 September 2021, the China Biomass Energy Industry Promotion Association (BEIPA) launched the China Low-Carbon Biomass Development Blue Paper assessing the potential of China's biomass sector to contribute to the country's 2030 carbon peaking and 2060 carbon neutrality goals. According to the report, China's biomass sector can help to reduce over 900 million tons and 2 billion tons of carbon dioxide emissions until 2030 and 2060, respectively.[30] "The development of the biomass energy industry in China has ushered in an important window period under China's strong green commitment and the industry has great potential for further growth," said Zhang Dayong, secretary-general of China's Biomass Energy Industry Promotion Association.[31]

Noteworthily, China already makes considerable use of waste and residues: "Since 2017, China has been the world leader in building bio-energy power plants, contributing 60% of global capacity additions in 2019. Roughly half of these are waste-to-energy (WTE) plants mainly fueled by municipal solid waste (MSW), a proportion of which is biomass material, e.g., food waste, wood, paper and cardboard, and which are concentrated around large population centers. The remaining capacity is fueled by agriculture and forestry residues, and, to a lesser extent, by biogas. China also uses significant volumes of solid biomass and biogas for heating."[32]

---

[30] *Source*: Report sheds light on potential of China's biomass sector to contribute to carbon neutrality — SUSTAINABLE TRANSITION CHINA (transition-china.org) document (Chinese only) available at: China_Low-Carbon_Biomass_Development_Blue_Paper_CN.pdf (energypartnership.cn) (accessed January 28, 2023).

[31] *Source*: The State Council — The People's Republic of China, Biomass energy to provide heat, fuel, article available at: http://english.www.gov.cn/news/topnews/202104/15/content_WS60778ff2c6d0df57f98d7d92.html.

[32] *Source*: https://iea.blob.core.windows.net/assets/bcf51d31-b7c6-4183-944f-707d05021356/AnenergysectorroadmaptocarbonneutralityinChina.pdf (accessed January 28, 2023).

China accounts for roughly one-third of global wood pellet production, using it domestically for large-scale heating systems. Biogas, on the other hand, is mostly produced and consumed by households, mainly for cooking. China is also the world's third largest producer of liquid biofuels after the United States and Brazil, with ethanol derived mainly from corn in the northeastern provinces and renewable diesel from used cooking oils (UCO) (IEA, 2020c).[33]

2.1.5. *China is set to accelerate its green energy transition*

China is clearly accelerating its green energy transition to meet the goals set by the government. The policy challenge is to ensure sufficient investment to grant the realization of new projects which will help in reaching carbon neutrality by 2060. This target represents a priority for China, and in order to achieve it China is fostering and incrementing the use of green financial instruments and thus pushing the so called green finance which is the main theme of chapter 5. In this paragraph, it is necessary to put in evidence that by accelerating its green energy transition, China will secure its economic development and innovation in technology, while helping the entire world move close to achieving shared climate goals, regardless of the fact that China is giving itself more time to reach carbon neutrality. Because the energy sector is the source of almost 90% of China's greenhouse gases, it is obvious that energy policies are at the heart of the country's transition to carbon neutrality and for advancement toward a green economy. As stressed by the IEA Executive Director Faith Birol, "*China's efforts to achieve its ambition of carbon neutrality will result in even greater flourishing across a wider array of low-carbon technologies and a significant decline in fossil fuel use in the coming decades.*"[34] This means China needs to invest more in green technologies and further increase the use of renewables. However, as the IEA report shows ('An

---

[33]*Source*: International Energy Agency (IEA), An Energy Sector Roadmap to Carbon Neutrality in China, September 2021, document available at: https://iea.blob.core.windows.net/assets/bcf51d31-b7c6-4183-944f-707d05021356/AnenergysectorroadmaptocarbonneutralityinChina.pdf (accessed January 28, 2023).

[34]*Source*: Press release by IEA, "China has clear pathway to build a more sustainable, secure and inclusive energy future," September 29, 2021, available at: https://www.iea.org/news/china-has-a-clear-pathway-to-build-a-more-sustainable-secure-and-inclusive-energy-future (accessed January 28, 2023).

energy sector roadmap to carbon neutrality in China'),[35] the country has the means and capabilities to accomplish an even faster clean energy transition that would result in greater social and economic benefits for the Chinese people and also increase the world's chances of limiting the rise in global temperatures to 1.5°C. Dr. Birol added that "*This accelerated transition would put China's CO_2 emissions into marked decline after 2025, opening up the possibility of China reaching carbon neutrality well before 2060. This would be both good for China and good for the world.*" There is no doubt China has made significant progress in its green energy transition and this is evidenced by the increase of solar, hydro, and wind power, but coal still accounts for over 60% of electricity generation and China is still the second largest oil consumer in the world; but at the same time, China is also home to 70% of global manufacturing capacity for electric vehicle batteries.[36] These contradictions need to be addressed by the government, which is already working to reach China's climate targets. These targets can be achieved but only if China is to address and introduce new measures to drastically reduce its emissions from its huge existing fleet of fossil-fuel-based power plants, steel mills, cement kilns, and other industrial facilities with the help of new technologies and the increased use of renewables. The main drivers of emission reductions between now and 2030 in this pathway are energy efficiency improvements, reduction in coal use, and the expansion of renewables.[37] Electricity generation from renewables, mainly wind and solar PV, must increase sevenfold between 2020 and 2060, to reach carbon neutrality. It means that renewables will account for almost 80% of China's power mix by then. In order for China to reach its targets, the role of emerging innovative technologies in improving energy efficiency and carbon capture

[35] International Energy Agency report "An energy sector roadmap to carbon neutrality in China," Country report — September 2021, document available at: https://www.iea.org/reports/an-energy-sector-roadmap-to-carbon-neutrality-in-china (accessed January 28, 2023).

[36] In this sense, see the Press release of the IEA, China has a clear pathway to build a more sustainable, secure and inclusive energy future, https://www.iea.org/news/china-has-a-clear-pathway-to-build-a-more-sustainable-secure-and-inclusive-energy-future.

[37] *Ibid.*

technologies, together with the wider use of new sustainable sources (such as green hydrogen) must growth strongly after 2030 and produce expected results before 2060. Naturally, these innovations and changes will boost China's labor market because new jobs will be created in specialized areas which do not exist today. Substantially more new jobs will be created in the growing low-carbon energy technologies than are lost in declining fossil fuel industries. Policies to reach these goals are set out in the '1+N' framework examined in Chapter 3; however, achieving a faster transition to green and sustainable energy over the period to 2030 is expected to enhance socioeconomic benefits to China beyond those associated with alleviating the impact of climate change. One of the most remarkable benefits of the transition to carbon neutrality is that the number of jobs in energy and energy-related sectors will increase, and these jobs offer safer working conditions and better salaries compared with traditional energy sector, in particular coal mining. It is evident that this transition, if accompanied by other policies to support China's objectives for industrial restructuring, will favor socioeconomic development (Figure 2).

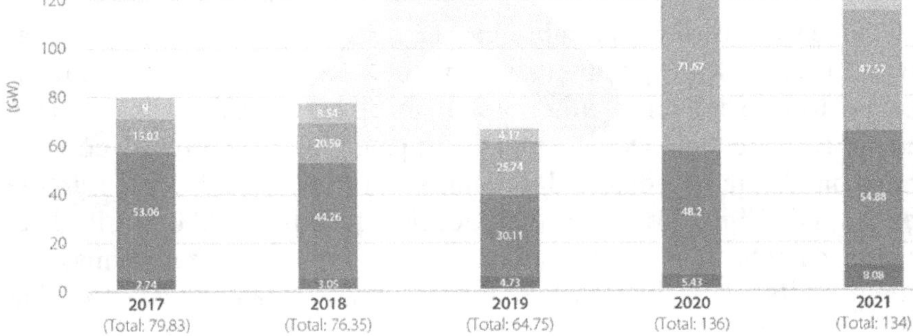

Figure 2: (Color online) Renewable energy capacity

Source: National Energy Administration, State Council Information Office

2.2. *China's green energy transition and the need for international collaboration*

Energy transition should be structured in a manner to deliver continued economic growth and grant affordable and clean energy (UN's SDG 7) while contributing to achieving the decarbonization targets contained in the Paris Convention. To achieve this, it is clear that we need to not only rely on all technologically feasible and economically affordable solutions for reducing emissions to net zero, by 2050 or before 2060 according to China's plans, but also enhance international collaboration. All countries will benefit from innovations deriving from new technologies aimed at reducing emissions, but this also means sharing experiences and putting in place coordinated actions. In fact, reaching the target of net-zero emissions requires an unprecedented level of international collaboration. Thus, global coordination will be required to be more effective. Naturally, each country needs to implement its own specific measures which are indicated in programmatic documents of the respective government, but in the end the result will be achieved together by adopting and implementing more incisive initiatives.

As the International Energy Agency has put in evidence, China will struggle to reach its 2060 carbon neutrality target without international collaboration, just as other countries will struggle to meet their own goals.[38]

2.2.1. *The importance of innovation and of knowledge sharing*

As evidenced, carbon neutrality can be achieved with a mix of initiatives, but it is clear that innovation and new technologies play a fundamental role in reducing emissions. It must be underlined that 'Clean energy Research and Development' and patenting are currently concentrated in the most advanced economies, i.e., United States, Europe, Japan, and China. Together, they account for about 90% of all clean energy patents. It is evident that progress toward net-zero emissions would be boosted by sharing these innovations and thus extending

[38]*Source*: "An Energy Sector Roadmap to Carbon Neutrality in China, report by the International Energy Agency," document available at: https://iea.blob.core.windows.net/assets/9448bd6e-670e-4cfd-953c-32e822a80f77/AnenergysectorroadmaptocarbonneutralityinChina.pdf (accessed January 28, 2023).

experience and knowledge of clean energy technologies in countries that are not involved in their initial development but where these innovations are badly needed to reduce emissions. This is important if rich, developed countries expect poorer countries to contribute to fighting climate change and wish these developing countries to reduce the use of fossil fuel and polluting sources of energy. Facilitating knowledge exchange should be the top priority for the most developed economies because only with the widespread implementation of new technologies harnessing green and clean energy will the rest of the world also contribute to reaching carbon neutrality.

2.2.2. *China's cooperation with third-world countries for energy transition*

Under the necessity of uniting efforts to fight climate change, a progressive international cooperation among countries is emerging in terms of energy transition, and China has all the reasons to give impetus to this international cooperation as one of the bigger emitters of CO_2. China has put in motion an ambitious plan to reach the carbon neutrality before 2060 by expanding the use of renewables and instilling in its population the concept of 'ecological civilization' which is of extreme importance to educate people about the importance of sustainable development for a shared future.

China has launched a series of cooperative projects with other countries which are summarized in the following Table 1. It must be underlined that at the very beginning, the purposes of cooperation were focused on the following three main points: "*(1) Cooperation should help both China and other countries achieve the goal of energy security and environmental protection. (2) Cooperation should help improve the energy efficiency of traditional fossil energy in both China and other countries. (3) Cooperation should help promote the technological progress and improve the economies of scale in new energy (renewable or clean energy) between China and other countries.*"[39]

---

[39] See *Strategic analysis and framework design on international cooperation for energy transition: A perspective from China*, Pingkuo Liu, Zhaohui Hei, *Energy Reports* 8 (2022) pp. 2601–2616, document available at: https://www.sciencedirect.com/science/article/pii/S2352484722001743#tbl1 (accessed January 28, 2023).

It is worth noting that China has in place numerous international cooperative programs in the energy sector, and probably the most important one is the platform with the EU which will be examined later in the chapter. However, many other projects have been started with both the G7 members and the BRICS members as deftly summarized by other scholars in the following tables (Table 1).

From this short list, it might appear that the energy cooperation between China and the G7 countries is mostly focused on energy efficiency management; however, during the most recent times, new initiatives and platforms have been developed, especially with the EU (i.e., the *EU–China Energy Cooperation Platform* which was launched on May 15, 2019) to further expand the ambit of these cooperative initiatives. It is evident that with the current crisis in Ukraine new initiatives will be studied and cooperation will be strengthened to develop the sector of renewable energies faster and improve their efficiency.

In the ambit of the BRICS, it is worth reporting that China has initiated the initiatives mentioned in Table 2, and that for the same reason explained earlier, the cooperation among Asian countries will be reinforced in the ambit of renewables. It seems that even if China has good relationships with Russia, the move to invade Ukraine put China in an 'uncomfortable' position though China will continue to import gas from its partner. But the path for China is clear: to expand the use of renewables and thus reinforce cooperation with the EU and the remaining members of the G20[40] to achieve not only energy sustainability but also sustain

---

[40]The G20 Energy Transition Working Group (ETWG), organized by the Ministry of Energy and Mineral Resources of the Republic of Indonesia, is one of the 13 working groups that are part of the G20 Sherpa track. Working within the energy transitions pillar, the ETWG aims to strengthen global sustainable energy systems and just transitions, while accelerating efforts for achieving SDGs and mitigating the adverse impacts of climate change. The first ETWG meeting was held in Yogyakarta (Indonesia) from March 24 to 25, 2022 in a hybrid format. The meeting was attended by delegates from all G20 member countries, invited countries, and several international organizations, namely ERIA, the Asian Development Bank (ADB), the International Energy Agency (IEA), the International Energy Forum (IEF), the International Renewable Energy Agency (IRENA), the Organization for Economic Co-operation and Development (OECD), the Organization of Petroleum Exporting Countries (OPEC), Sustainable Energy for All (SE4ALL), and the United Nations Economic and Social Commission for Asia and the Pacific (UN ESCAP). Following the ETWG's objective, the first ETWG was divided into three sessions to discuss priority issues: first, Securing Energy Accessibility, second, Smart and Clean Energy

Table 1: China–G7 Cooperation in the Energy Sector, Most Important Initiatives from 2009

Partner country	Cooperation field	Time	Cooperation document/Cooperative project	Key content
The United States	Clean energy	2009	"*Ten-Year Framework for Energy and Environment Cooperation between China and the United States*"	China and the United States should establish five priority cooperation goals for ten-year cooperation.
	Renewable energy	2009	"*Memorandum of Understanding on China-US Cooperation in Clean Energy and Climate Change*"	China and the United States have focused on renewable energy and grid modernization as important areas.
		2009	"*Memorandum of Cooperation on the Establishment of a renewable energy Partnership between China and the United States*"	China and the US will strengthen cooperation in renewable energy and advanced grid solutions.
	Shale gas	2009	"*Sino-US Memorandum of Understanding (MOU) on the Cooperation of Shale Gas Development*"	The document upgrades the cooperation between the two countries to the national level.
	Clean energy	2011	"*Memorandum of understanding on promoting the construction of China-US energy cooperation projects*"	China and the United States will deepen cooperation in the field of clean energy and strengthen liaison between government agencies.
	Natural gas	2019	"'*Grant Agreement' on the Sino-American Energy Cooperation Project Natural Gas Series Seminar*"	The USTDA would provide full funding support for the conference in the form of grants.

(Continued)

Table 1: (*Continued*)

Partner country	Cooperation field	Time	Cooperation document/Cooperative project	Key content
France	Nuclear energy	2015	"*Joint statement on deepening civil nuclear energy cooperation*"	China and France will cooperate to design a safe and competitive third-generation new reactor.
		2017	"*Agreements on nuclear energy and science*"	Both sides will deepen cooperation in the whole industrial chain of nuclear energy.
Japan	Renewable energy	2011	"*The second China-Japan high-level economic dialogue*"	Both parties will strengthen cooperation in promoting energy conservation and environmental protection.
Canada	Clean energy	2012	"*CNOOC takes over Nexen*"	The CNOOC successfully obtained the exclusive right to an LNG terminal.
Germany	Efficiency	2012	"'*Sino-German passive low energy consumption building demonstration Project,' Qinghuangdao's 'Beside the River' Housing*"	The cooperation project would be equipped with energy and heat recovery devices to meet the requirements, and use the renewable energy to reduce primary energy consumption.
	Renewable energy	2012	"*Joint Statement on the second Sino-German government consultations — Looking forward to the Future Sino-German Strategic Partnership [Effective]*"	China and Germany will establish a strategic partnership in regard to renewable energy.
		2011	"*Sino-German Climate Partnership*"	The two sides will conduct a dialogue on climate protection and low-carbon economy.

	Energy transition	2015	*"Sino-German cooperation on low carbon transport"*	The two sides will strengthen cooperation in the development of a climate-friendly transport sector.
		2013	*"German Chinese Sustainable Fuel Partnership"*	The two sides will strengthen cooperation in alternative energy supply and technology in the travel sector.
Britain	Nuclear energy	2014	*"Joint Statement between the Government of the People's Republic of China and the Government of the United Kingdom of Great Britain and Northern Ireland on Civil Nuclear Energy Cooperation"*	China and Britain would strengthen strategic cooperation in the field of civil nuclear energy, and jointly develop nuclear energy projects in the United Kingdom and China.
			"Joint Statement from Government of the People's Republic of China & Government of the United Kingdom of Great Britain and Northern Ireland"	China and Britain had unanimously decided to deepen the civil nuclear energy industry research and development and next-generation nuclear power technology cooperation, and establish a long-term mutually beneficial partnership.
Italy	Renewable energy and smart grid	2019	*"State Grid Co., Ltd. and the National Gas Distribution Company of Italy signed a cooperation framework agreement"*	Both sides will continue to deepen cooperation in the field of energy infrastructure.

Source: Strategic analysis and framework design on international cooperation for energy transition: A perspective from China, Pingkuo Liu and Zhaohui Hei.

Table 2: China–BRICs Countries Cooperation in the Energy Sector, Main Initiatives

Partner country	Cooperation field	Time	Cooperation document/Cooperative project	Key content
Russia	Natural gas	2014	*"The China-Russia east-route natural gas pipeline project"*	Russia will provide China with natural gas for a long time.
		2017	*"Amur Gas Processing Plant construction project"*	The P1 section of the Amur natural gas processing plant was contracted by GEZHOUBA CORPORATION.
	Clean energy	2015	*"Yamal LNG Project"*	PetroChina and the Silk Road Fund (SRF) hold 20% and 20% of the shares in the project, respectively.
India	Efficiency	2009	*"Agreement on Cooperation on Addressing Climate Change between the Government of the Peoples Republic of China and the Government of the Republic of India"*	China and India will strengthen cooperation in the field of energy efficiency, renewable energy, and clean energy technologies.
South Africa	Various types of energy	2007	*"Agreement between the Government of the People's Republic of China and the Government of the Republic of South Africa on Cooperation in the Field of Minerals and Energy"*	China and South Africa had unanimously decided to conduct all-round exchanges in the energy and mineral fields.

		2010	*"Memorandum of Understanding between the Government of the People's Republic of China and the Government of the Republic of South Africa on Cooperation in the Energy Field"*	China and South Africa will promote cooperation between state-owned oil enterprises and oil and gas enterprises.
Brazil	Various types of energy	2009	*"Tsinghua-UFRJ China-Brazil Center for Climate Change and Energy Technology Innovation"*	The two sides agreed to actively encourage and support the relevant departments and enterprises of the two countries to carry out two-way investment and cooperation in energy and other fields including bioenergy.
		2011	*"Joint Communiqué Between the People's Republic of China and The Federative Republic of Brazil on Further Strengthening China-Brazil Strategic Partnership"*	The two sides expressed their willingness to deepen cooperation in the peaceful use of nuclear energy and new energy sources including biofuels.
	New energy	2015	*"2015–2021 Joint Action Plan Between the Government of the People's Republic of China and the Government of the Federal Republic of Brazil"*	China and Brazil would regard bioenergy technology as a priority area of scientific and technological cooperation.

Source: Strategic analysis and framework design on international cooperation for energy transition: A perspective from China, Pingkuo Liu and Zhaohui Hei.

green transition, which represents a fundamental objective not only for China but also for the entire global community.

It is evident that Russia has become unpredictable, but international efforts to fight climate change and the cooperation to develop green technologies to reduce emissions and thus initiatives to further cooperate in this direction will continue with more intensity among the rest of the global community.

China is intensifying the use of renewables, in particular solar and wind energy, and there is no doubt it is imposing itself as a leading example; however, to be more influential, its participation in various existing international platforms, such as the IEA, to propose its solutions to ameliorate global energy governance should be intensified. This should be accompanied by promoting the reform of international energy government with the help of the G20 platform. China, while playing the role of paladin in the use of the renewables, is also bringing forward a green transition by exporting its experiences under the framework of its BRI. In its new vest, China possesses the ability to create a vast community for energy cooperation. Naturally, the development of these plans will be accompanied by the increased use of the so-called 'green finance' which is accompanying this green transition. Thus, in the next section, the basic elements of green finance and its role in China are explained before introducing the initiatives of the EU and of the US in the ambit of the green transition.

2.3. *China's transformation into a green economy needs to elevate the role of green finance*

The concept of 'green finance' has emerged since the global community has started discussions about building a green and sustainable economic system, and its significance has continued to expand. Green Finance is a multifaceted concept which encompasses the requirement for financial institutions to give full consideration to the environmental impacts of their investments, thus cutting off financial support to polluting projects, and instead increasing support for environment restoration projects. Green finance also means promoting green and inclusive economic growth through reshaping existing financial systems, and allowing new forms of investment to sustain green transition. It is undeniable that the concept of green finance is gaining traction globally and its importance is now widely recognized by numerous

---

Technologies Scaling Up, and third, Advancing Energy Financing. https://www.eria.org/news-and-views/eria-presents-at-the-first-g20-energy-transition-working-group-meeting-in-yogyakarta/ (accessed January 28, 2023).

institutions as will emerge in the following sections. Now, an increasing number of countries begin to include green finance into their policy framework. Institutional investors in developed countries have already become a major force in advancing green finance agendas.

China's experience in developing its own green finance system has attracted wider attention from the international community. China in order to sustain its transformation into a nature-positive economy has come to understand the necessity of elevating the role of green finance. While developing its own green financial system, China is also seeking international cooperation to improve the function of green finance itself and adapt it to the necessities of sustainable growth. China's green finance system should not limit itself to sustaining green transition and must thus contribute to reducing emissions, focusing on clean energy and energy-efficient low-carbon transportation; it should also expand its scope to provide financial support for the restructuring of China's industrial sector, thereby contributing to the green transformation of traditional enterprises. Projects involving the cleanup and safeguarding of the environment constitute only one area of interest, and China's green finance system should have an impact on the entire financial system and help the entire economy. The transformation from a resource- and pollution-intensive economy to a green economy is now a strategic priority for China. Success naturally depends on the development of green industries and the transformation and reduced importance of many traditional industries with the help of new green investment which the government has already planned.[41]

2.3.1. *Green economy and green finance: Two faces of the same coin*

China has clearly indicated its target to reach carbon neutrality before 2060 in its '1+N framework' and has made significant progress since the implementation and development of 'green finance,' specifically aimed at financing this green transition. It is worth noting that the first Chinese policy relating to 'green finance' was issued by the People's Bank of China

[41]The Chinese government is now focused on 'greening' its financial system to align it with the systems of the most advanced economies and to sustain its green transition. More details about this process are offered in the publication titled *Greening China's Financial System*, DRC — Financial Research Institute and IISD International Institute for Sustainable Development, 2015, document available at: https://www.iisd.org/system/files/publications/greening-chinas-financial-system.pdf (accessed January 28, 2023).

(PBoC) in 1995 — "*Notice on Credit Policy for Environmental Protection.*"[42] In 2007, the Banking Regulator CRBC released the '*Green Credit Guideline*' (also known as '*Green Credit policy*'),[43] encouraging banks to promote environmental objectives and consider environmental risks in their lending. However, this first attempt to start shaping a green financial system did not work well because of technical barriers and problem in its application (the Chinese financial system was not mature enough). It was with China's impetus, during its presidency of the G20 in 2016, that green finance was added to the agenda of the G20, showing the importance of this theme for China in particular. The creation of the 'Green Finance Task Force'[44] in 2014, under the authority of the People's Bank of

---

[42]The first Chinese government policy relating to green finance can be dated back to 1995, when the People's Bank of China issued the 'Notice on Credit Policy for Environmental Protection.' It offered provisions for the financial sector to implement the national environmental policy in credit-related work, requiring financial departments at all levels to protect natural resources and the environment in credit-related work and to make supporting ecological resources protection and pollution prevention and control as two of the considerations in issuing bank credit. https://journals.plos.org/plosone/article?id=10.1371/journal.pone.0261311 (accessed January 28, 2023).

[43]The beginning of China's green credit policies can be traced back to 2007, when the green credit policy was jointly issued by the Ministry of Environmental Protection (now MEE), PBoC, and CBRC (now CBIRC). It initially set out that the bank lending should flow toward green projects and away from polluting and energy-intensive projects, substantially encouraging finance institutions to consider environmental risks when lending. See *Green Finance in China: Overview, Experience and Outlook*, Tsinghua University National Institute of Financial Research, January 20, 2021 document available at: http://eng.pbcsf.tsinghua.edu.cn/upload/default/20210120/a9d979c5405c2e5b461afa03f7925b36.pdf (accessed January 28, 2023).

[44]The *Green Finance Task Force* is co-sponsored by the Research Bureau of the People's Bank of China (PBC) and the United Nations Environment Programme Inquiry into the Design of a Sustainable Financial System (UNEP Inquiry). The Task Force is assembled from more than 40 experts from the PBC, the China Banking Regulatory Commission, the Ministry of Finance, policy banks, commercial banks, credit rating agencies, stock exchanges, insurance companies, fund companies, the Chinese Academy of Social Sciences, universities, and non-governmental think-tanks, with additional support and contribution coming from a number of foreign experts. Pan Gongsheng, the Deputy Governor of PBC, serves as the advisor to the Task Force; Chief Economist Ma Jun at the PBC Research Bureau acts as the domestic convener while Simon Zadek, the Co-Director of the UNEP Inquiry, acts as the international convener. A number of organizations have lent great support to this Task Force, chief among which are Chongyang Institute for

China (PBoC) fostered by the UN, played a very important and critical role in developing a consensus on green finance both at the ministry level and among the most senior policymakers.[45] As a result in 2016, the 'Guidelines for Establishing the Green Financial System'[46] document was published with the endorsement of China's State Council — the highest governing body. Thus, China's commitment to developing green finance by supporting the development of a large domestic green bond market to sustain China's objective of carbon neutrality is evident. It is also evident that green finance accompanies green transition, and these two elements are undeniably correlated and indispensable to the future sustainable development.

The development of green finance in China will certainly contribute to the achievement of carbon neutrality goals, but advancements toward international standards seem necessary; in fact, this will help green finance evolve further. Green finance has to respond to the needs of the investors and recipients, and if green finance can converge to the same standards globally, it will favor its maturation and attract more resources. Noteworthily, another branch of green finance has recently emerged, i.e., Blue Finance,[47] which can be regarded as a further offshoot of green

---

Financial Studies of Renmin University, the Ecological Finance Research Center at the Renmin University of China, the Eco Forum Global, the International Institute for Sustainable Development, the Green Credit Special Committee of China Banking Association, and China Finance 40 Forum. See *Establishing China's Green Financial System* (构建中国绿色金融体系), this is the preliminary version published in March 2015, document available at: https://www.unepfi.org/fileadmin/communications/EstablishingChinasGreenFinancialSystem.pdf (accessed January 28, 2023).

[45] People's Bank of China & UN Environment Program (2014). *China Green Finance Task Force Report: Establishing China's Green Financial System.* Document available at: https://www.unepfi.org/psi/wp-content/uploads/2015/07/Establishing-Chinas-Green-Financial-System_PBoC_UNEP_Inquiry.pdf This is the April 2015 version which is the complete version. See also Green Finance Info, International Institute of Green Finance, article available at: https://iigf-china.com/green-finance-info-2 (accessed January 28, 2023).

[46] *Guidelines for Establishing the Green Financial System*, this is the full version published on April 2015. The guidelines are available at: https://www.cbd.int/financial/privatesector/china-Green%20Task%20Force%20Report.pdf (accessed January 28, 2023).

[47] Blue Finance, as described by the International Finance Corporation (World Bank Group), is an emerging new area, within Green Finance, which is attracting increasing interest from investors, financial institutions, and issuers globally. Blue Finance offers tremendous opportunities and helps address pressing challenges by contributing to

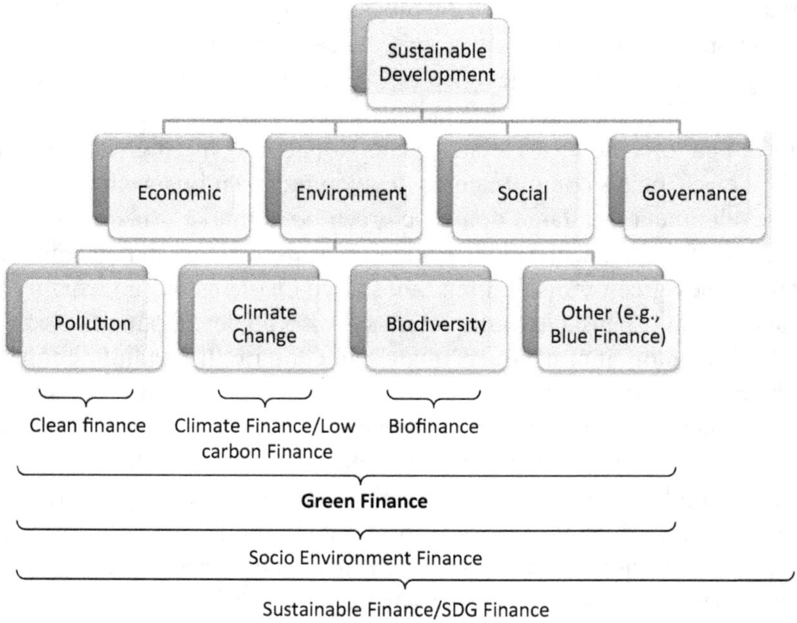

Figure 3: Understanding the subdivision of green finance

Source: International Institute of Green Finance, China. See https://iigf-china.com/green-finance-info-2.

finance like Clean Finance, Climate Finance, and Bio-Finance (see Figure 3).

2.3.2. *Evolving significance of green finance*

The significance of green finance has developed fast and now it comprehends different facets or specialized areas; moreover, green finance in

---

economic growth, improved livelihood, and the health of marine ecosystems. The ocean economy is expected to double to $3 trillion by 2030, employing 40 million people, as compared to 2010. Innovative financing solutions are key to enhancing ocean and coastal preservation and increasing clean water resources, and Blue Finance has huge potential to help realize these goals. See Guidance for financing the Blue Economy, building on the Green Bond Principles and the Green Loan Principles, International Finance Corporation — Guidelines for Blue Finance, document available at: https://www.ifc.org/wps/wcm/connect/industry_ext_content/ifc_external_corporate_site/financial+institutions/resources/guidelines-for-blue-finance (accessed January 28, 2023).

China is becoming a mainstream trend in the domestic financial industry. Though this is also happening in the other more advanced economies, in China, this trend is particularly pronounced. In China, policies that uphold environmental, social, and corporate governance investment concepts, linked to the SDGs, are fostered by the government, and consequently the financial industry is focusing on green financial products. Many banking financial institutions in China have gradually established and improved strategic planning, organizational structure, incentives and constraints, resource allocation, and information disclosure for the development of green finance, which has become a complex system (which includes the abovementioned 'Blue Finance' and other areas such as Clean Finance,[48] Climate Finance,[49] and Bio Finance[50]).

As a consequence of this new trend, China has been enriched with financial products in the fields of green finance and climate finance. The main green financial products in China include the following:

[48]Clean Finance basically 'serves' pollution prevention, and its scope is to sustain any practice that reduces, eliminates, or prevents pollution at its source. Thus, a natural goal of many investors is to target investment toward companies and opportunities that are working on solutions to reduce the emission of greenhouse gases.

[49]Climate Finance is a broad term that can refer either to the role of finance in facilitating efforts to address climate change or to the obligations owed by richer nations to transfer capitals to developing nations to help them address problems related to climate change. Climate finance is used to incentivize investment and development in renewable energy infrastructure, sustainable agriculture, or other adaptations to climate change. Many argue that developed economies should subsidize the adoption of environmentally friendly energy sources by developing nations, along with other such investments. The topic of climate finance is growing in international importance, as countries and companies become increasingly aware of the risks and opportunities associated with climate change. By 2023, developed countries will have spent up to $100 billion on climate finance initiatives, according to the OECD. In this sense, visit: https://www.investopedia.com/terms/c/climate-finance.asp (accessed January 28, 2023).

[50]The term 'Bio-Finance' is self-explanatory: Capitals in this case are used to protect and preserve biodiversity. Biodiversity protection is different from climate protection in one crucial point: greenhouse gas emissions in one place have climate impacts around the whole world. As a consequence, only global solutions are really effective to deal with climate change, but biodiversity protection is much more localized depending on local actions to be taken to protect the habitat for specific species, and species located in determined areas. More on this theme at: Biodiversity Finance Research https://iigf-china.com/biodiversity-finance-research (accessed January 28, 2023).

- *"green bonds — where capital is raised on public markets in the form of bonds and the proceeds are earmarked for funding climate and environmentally friendly projects;*
- *sustainability-linked loans — where the interest rate of the loan is linked to the ESG performance of the borrower;*
- *green loans — where capital is given between the lender and the borrower without a public market;*
- *green insurance — which covers economic compensation liabilities caused by environmental accidents. Mandatory insurance can increase returns and lower risks on green finance."*[51]

As a matter of fact, China has advanced rapidly in developing its green financial system and markets. The proliferation of green financial products is increasing the necessity for international green finance cooperation to standardize rules regulating this market. In the following sections, we have introduced this aspect evidencing the initiatives of the major economies in transitioning toward a nature-positive economy with the help of green finance. The ongoing global green transition requires substantial funding to support the transformation of the industrial sectors which shall participate to the reduction of the global emissions, and a majority of these resources will come from green finance. As for China alone, "*official data show*[52] *an outstanding green credit of RMB 15.1 trillion (US$2.37 trillion) at the end of 2021. To achieve the country's carbon peak by 2030 and carbon neutrality target by 2060, it is estimated*[53] *that*

---

[51] *Source*: Green Finance Info, International Institute of Green Finance, visit: https://iigf-china.com/green-finance-info-2 (accessed January 28, 2023).

[52] *Source*: Xinhua, China's green credit balance tops 15 trillion yuan, article available at: https://english.news.cn/20220327/e747f4f597ed4caf8dbcf443d67521b2/c.html (accessed January 28, 2023).

[53] *Source*: Green Finance & Development Center — China's "Two Sessions" 2022 — What it means for economy, climate, biodiversity, green finance and the Belt and Road Initiative (BRI0. "*China's green transition is inextricably linked to green finance. According to Wu Gang, a member of the National Committee of the CPPCC and Chairman of Xinjiang Goldwind Science & Technology, the green finance industry has been highly valued by the government, which provides important financial support for the development of the renewable energy industry and supports steps towards the "dual carbon" target. It is estimated that RMB 3-4 trillion of green investment is needed annually to achieve the country's carbon peak by 2030 and the carbon neutrality target by 2060.*" Full article available at: https://greenfdc.org/chinas-two-sessions-2022-what-it-means-for-economy-climate-biodiversity-green-finance-and-the-belt-and-road-initiative-bri/ (accessed January 28, 2023).

RMB 3–4 trillion (US$ 450–570 billion) of green investment is needed annually."[54]

2.3.3. *The need for standardization and diverse forms of green cooperation*

The development of green finance in China which is aimed at accompanying this green transition, must be guided by common principles and rules because it represents an important and growing part of the financial international system, and green financial instruments are now used by a growing number of investors (institutional and private) all around the world. Thus, the interoperability between the financial markets treating these financial investment instruments is inevitable. The cooperation of domestic and foreign parties with financial institutions is becoming more evident and more frequent and it has shown a trend of normalization and diversification. For example, "*the Sino-British Financial Dialogue, led by the Green and Gold Council and the City of London, has strengthened exchanges and cooperation between the two sides and promoted environmental information disclosure by pilot financial institutions, achieving remarkable results*. And again "*Cooperation between financial institutions and the government and financial technology companies can help smooth the path of access to corporate environmental data information, establish a risk sharing mechanism, and solve key problems faced by green finance, such as information asymmetry and low market liquidity.*"[55]

Discussions during the Two Sessions (the political meeting held in March 2022) emphasized the importance of unifying green finance standards, as the coexistence of different standards (both locals and international) makes it more complex to protect the rights and interests of market participants.[56]

---

[54] *Source*: *China's Green Financial Market: Policies, Incentives, Investment Opportunities*, Yi Wu, China Briefing, article available at: https://www.china-briefing.com/news/chinas-green-finance-market-policies-incentives-investment-opportunities/ (accessed January 28, 2023).

[55] *Source*: A better understanding of the role of new energy and green finance to help achieve carbon neutrality goals, with special reference to China, by Feng Kong, *Science Progress* 2022, Vol. 105(1) 1–23, article available at: https://Journals.sagepub.com/doi/epub/10.1177/00368504221086361 (accessed January 28, 2023).

[56] "Various standards coexist in China, for instance green credit standards issued by the China Banking and Insurance Regulatory Commission, different green bond standards

Where China's Green Financial System Should be Strengthened (Two Sessions, March 2022)

- "*Defining clear and unified green finance standards;*
- *Improving the mechanism to make green finance more popular;*
- *Encouraging innovation and arousing financial markets interest in green products;*
- *Improving the information disclosure and supervision mechanism of green projects;*
- *Developing the carbon financial market;*
- *Studying how to integrate the national carbon trading market with the international market;*
- *Supporting energy and transport projects along the Belt and Road Initiative;*
- *Improving risk prevention and control; and*
- *Deepening cooperation to make green finance a global chorus.*"

3. The EU's Green Transition Focuses on Renewables and Efficiency: Crisis in Ukraine Accelerates the Transition and the Cooperation with the Major World Economies

As previously explained, the EU adopted and is implementing the so-called 'European Green Deal,' composed of a number of policies, aimed at enabling the European Union to achieve carbon neutrality by 2050. As the production and use of energy account for more than 75% of the EU's greenhouse gas emissions, it is evident that the decarbonization of the EU's energy system is critical to reach its climate objectives.

issued by the People's Bank of China, the National Development and Reform Commission and the China Securities Regulatory Commission, and green standards set by local governments." See *Green Finance & Development Center — China's "Two Sessions" 2022 — What it means for economy, climate, biodiversity, green finance and the Belt and Road Initiative* (BRI0. https://greenfdc.org/chinas-two-sessions-2022-what-it-means-for-economy-climate-biodiversity-green-finance-and-the-belt-and-road-initiative-bri/ (accessed January 28, 2023).

The European Green Deal focuses on 3 key principles for clean energy transition, which will help reduce greenhouse gas emissions and enhance the quality of life of EU citizens. The three principles are as follows:

(i) ensuring a secure and affordable EU energy supply;
(ii) developing a fully integrated, interconnected, and digitalized EU energy market; and
(iii) prioritizing energy efficiency, which includes improving the energy performance of buildings and developing a power sector based largely on renewable sources.

It is through the effective implementation of the Green Deal that Europe will be the first climate-neutral continent by 2050. To achieve this objective, the EU is actively transforming its energy system to make it greener (pushing on renewables), smart, which means fully integrated and interconnected, and affordable (in line with the Sustainable Development Goal 7 of the UN).[57] The European energy system of the future will be more efficient and circular using waste heat, among other clean and renewable sources, to create energy, and integrating low-carbon fuels (e.g., hydrogen) in sectors that cannot be electrified.[58]

3.1. *The EU's objectives in the energy sector and the crisis in Ukraine*

The reduction of emissions in the energy sector is a fundamental step to reach the climate objectives. The European Commission adopted a set of initiatives to adjust the EU's climate, energy, transport, and taxation policies for reducing net greenhouse gas emissions by at least 55% by 2030,[59]

---

[57] Goal 7, ensuring universal access to affordable electricity by 2030, means investing in clean energy sources such as solar, wind, and thermal. Adopting cost-effective standards for a wider range of technologies can facilitate the use of renewable sources. https://www.unep.org/explore-topics/sustainable-development-goals/why-do-sustainable-development-goals-matter/goal-7 (accessed January 28, 2023).

[58] For more detailed information on Energy strategies and the Green Deal, visit the European Commission web-page at: https://ec.europa.eu/info/strategy/priorities-2019-2024/european-green-deal/energy-and-green-deal_en#relatedlinks (accessed January 28, 2023).

[59] On July 14, 2021, the European Commission adopted the 'fit for 55' package, adapting existing climate and energy legislation to meet the new EU objective of a minimum 55%

compared to 1990 levels. Among these, there is the so-called *'fit for 55'* package,[60] which is part of the European Green Deal, a flagship of the Von der Leyen Commission that aims to put the EU firmly on the path toward climate neutrality by 2050, as set out in the recently agreed European Climate Law[61] (July 2021).

As pointed out in the following sections, the crisis in Ukraine makes it more urgent for the EU Member States to invest in renewable energies and to accelerate the green transition. New legislative initiatives on renewables and energy efficiency will help in reaching these objectives.

3.1.1. *The role of renewables in the EU's clean energy transition*

The European Union has invigorated the role of *renewable energy* sources (RES) among the measures set to favor a low-carbon emission economy. The European Commission in April 2022 adopted the REPowerEU Plan,[62]

reduction in greenhouse gas (GHG) emissions by 2030 compared with 1990 levels, thereby setting the EU more firmly on the path toward meeting its long-term goal of climate neutrality, i.e., net zero GHG emissions by 2050. See https://www.europarl.europa.eu/RegData/etudes/BRIE/2021/698781/EPRS_BRI(2021)698781_EN.pdf (accessed January 28, 2023).

[60] The Fit for 55 Package encompasses a suite of legislative initiatives across various sectors, including energy, transport, and buildings, which are intended to fundamentally overhaul the EU's climate policy framework and put the EU on track to deliver on its 2030 climate target of 55% emission reduction. The Fit 55 Package is to be regarded as an integral part of the EU Green Deal: https://ec.europa.eu/info/strategy/priorities-2019-2024/european-green-deal/delivering-european-green-deal_en (accessed January 28, 2023).

[61] Regulation (EU) 2021/1119 of the European Parliament and of the Council of 30 June 2021 establishing the framework for achieving climate neutrality and amending Regulations (EC) No 401/2009 and (EU) 2018/1999 ('European Climate Law'). It writes both the 2030 and 2050 targets into EU law, available at: https://eur-lex.europa.eu/eli/reg/2021/1119/oj (accessed January 28, 2023).

[62] See European Commission, COMMUNICATION FROM THE COMMISSION TO THE EUROPEAN PARLIAMENT, THE EUROPEAN COUNCIL, THE COUNCIL, THE EUROPEAN ECONOMIC AND SOCIAL COMMITTEE AND THE COMMITTEE OF THE REGIONS, REPowerEU Plan, Brussels, May 18, 2022, COM(2022) 230 final, document available at: https://eur-lex.europa.eu/legal-content/EN/TXT/?uri=COM%253A2022%253A230%253AFIN&qid=1653033742483 (accessed January 28, 2023).

which is not only the EU's response to the hardships and global energy market disruption caused by Russia's invasion of Ukraine but also a stimulus in fast-forwarding clean transition and joining forces to achieve a more resilient energy system and a true Energy Union. The measures in the REPowerEU Plan can respond to this ambition through energy savings, diversification of energy supplies, and an accelerated rollout of renewable energy to replace fossil fuels in homes, industry, and power generation. "*REPowerEU builds on the full implementation of the Fit for 55 proposals tabled last year without modifying the ambition of achieving at least –55 % net GHG emissions by 2030 and climate neutrality by 2050 in line with the European Green Deal.*"[63]

3.1.2. *The new REPowerEU is an integral part of the EU Green Deal: Energy savings and renewables as the main focus*

The REPowerEU initiative can be seen as an integral part of the UE Green Deal. More importantly, it gives impetus to the entire EU energy system to become more rational and efficient, and it also evidences the necessity to accelerate the development of renewable sources to meet the ambitious climate targets and thus phase out fossil fuels.[64] This new EU initiative in the energy sector emphasizes 'energy saving' and the development of renewable sources, further supporting clean transition with new investment.

---

[63] *Ibid.*

[64] On June 7, 2022, the European Parliament voted to mandate that all new car and van sales should be zero emissions from 2035 as part of efforts to clean up road transport. Lawmakers backed the final report on revised vehicle CO2 emission standards legislation with 339 in favor, 249 against, and 24 abstentions. The legislation is a key part of the Fit for 55 package and mandates that carmakers should reduce their fleet-wide emission averages by 100 percent from 2035, with interim steps in 2025 and 2030. The Parliament's position maintains the Commission's original 2035 phase-out date. See EU Parliament passes ban on new petrol, diesel cars by 2035, article available at: https://www.euractiv.com/section/transport/news/eu-parliament-passes-ban-on-new-petrol-diesel-cars-by-2035/; See Official EU Reference document at: https://www.europarl.europa.eu/RegData/docs_autres_institutions/commission_europeenne/com/2021/0556/COM_COM(2021)0556_EN.pdf (accessed January 28, 2023).

"Energy savings are the quickest and cheapest way to address the current energy crisis, and reduce bills. The Commission proposes to enhance long-term energy efficiency measures, including an ***increase from 9% to 13% of the binding Energy Efficiency Target*** *under the 'Fit for 55' package of European Green Deal legislation."*[65] The EU Commission in the REPowerEU proposes to increase the binding target in the Energy Efficiency Directive to 13%.[66] Member States are also encouraged to use fiscal measures to encourage energy savings, such as reduced VAT rates on energy-efficient heating systems, building insulation, and appliances and products.

The EU in order to cut the gas and oil demand further intends to accelerate the rollout of renewable sources. A massive scaling up and speeding up of renewable energy in power generation, industry, buildings, and transport will accelerate the EU's independence and will give a boost to the green transition, favoring the reduction of prices over time. The Commission in its 'REPower EU initiative' proposes to increase the headline 2030 target for renewables from 40% to 45%[67] under the 'Fit for 55 package.' It is interesting to note that in this ambit solar energy plays a particularly important role: Solar photovoltaic is one of the fastest technologies to roll out. This clean source of energy if adequately developed has enormous potential. This is why the Commission set the REPowerEU target to over 320 GW of solar photovoltaic newly installed by 2025, which is over twice today's level, and almost 600 GW by 2030. The EU

---

[65] EU Press release, May 18, 2022, at: https://ec.europa.eu/commission/presscorner/detail/en/IP_22_3131.

[66] See European Commission, COM(2021)558 final, Proposal for a DIRECTIVE OF THE EUROPEAN PARLIAMENT AND OF THE COUNCIL on Energy Efficiency, official document available at: https://eur-lex.europa.eu/resource.html?uri=cellar:a214c850-e574-11eb-a1a5-01aa75ed71a1.0001.02/DOC_1&format=PDF (accessed January 28, 2023).

[67] Based on its modeling of impacts and feasibility (see the 'Commission Staff Working Document Implementing the REPowerEU Action Plan: Investment needs, Hydrogen Accelerator and Biomethane Targets, accompanying this communication'), the Commission is proposing to increase the target in the Renewable Energy Directive to 45% by 2030, up from 40% in last year's proposal. This would bring the total renewable energy generation capacities to 1236 GW by 2030, in comparison to 1067 GW by 2030 envisaged under Fit for 55 for 2030. See in this sense, the content of the REPower EU initiative.

solar strategy[68] also includes the so called 'Solar Rooftop Initiative'[69] with a phased-in legal obligation to install solar panels on new public and commercial buildings and new residential buildings.

For the EU, another clean, renewable, important source is wind energy.[70] In particular, offshore renewable energy plays an important role

---

[68] '*EU solar strategy,*' see COM(2022) 221, (18.05.2022), official document available at: https://eur-lex.europa.eu/legal-content/EN/TXT/?uri=COM%3A2022%3A221%3AFIN&qid=1653034500503 (accessed October 8, 2022). "*As part of the REPowerEU plan, this strategy aims to bring online over 320 GW of solar photovoltaic by 2025 (more than doubling compared to 2020) and almost 600 GW by 2030. This is because solar energy costs have decreased spectacularly over time. The EU's renewable energy policies helped bring PV costs down by 82% over the last decade, turning it into one of the most competitive source of electricity in the EU. Solar energy, combined with energy efficiency, protects European citizens from the volatility of fossil fuel prices.*"

[69] The EU-wide European Solar Rooftops Initiative, announced in the Commission's REPowerEU Communication, aims at unlocking the vast, underutilized solar generation potential of rooftops to make energy cleaner, more secure, and affordable. To achieve this swiftly, immediate action is necessary by end 2022. According to some estimates, rooftop PV could provide almost 25% of the EU's electricity consumption. 'European Solar Rooftops Initiative"' contained in the EU solar energy strategy.

[70] European companies have invaluable experience by being first movers — the first offshore wind farm was installed in Denmark in 1991. With already around 16 GW of grid-connected capacity to explore offshore sites further out to sea with stronger and more consistent winds, several European developers are working on floating offshore wind turbines. The first pilot projects are now up and running, with deployment expected to accelerate toward the end of this decade. See *Floating offshore wind — Delivering climate neutrality*, document available at: https://etipwind.eu/files/reports/ETIPWind-floating-offshore-wind-factsheet.pdf (accessed January 28, 2023). To harness the full potential of offshore wind in the North Sea and the Baltic Sea and boost cooperation between countries in these regions, the EU is also part of the North Seas Energy Cooperation (see https://energy.ec.europa.eu/topics/infrastructure/high-level-groups/north-seas-energy-cooperation_en) and the Baltic Energy Market Interconnection Plan (see https://energy.ec.europa.eu/topics/infrastructure/high-level-groups/baltic-energy-market-interconnection-plan_en). The Mediterranean Sea has a high potential for offshore wind energy (mostly floating), good potential for wave energy, and localized potential for tidal energy (see 32 to 75 GW potential according to the Study on the offshore grid potential in the Mediterranean region (Guidehouse, 2020–11) — https://data.europa.eu/doi10.2833/742284). Regional cooperation on offshore renewables is organized under the Barcelona Convention (environment) and the WestMed initiative (visit: www.westmed-initiative.eu). Recently, the MED7 Alliance also specifically referred to support for the development of

for the EU. Offshore energy consists of many different sources that are abundant, natural, and clean, and besides wind it includes wave and tidal.[71] Offshore energy represents a significant future opportunity: Resources are stable and abundant, and public acceptance is higher. In order to ensure that these forms of renewable and clean energy can help reach the EU's ambitious energy and climate targets, the Commission published a dedicated 'EU strategy on offshore renewable energy' on 19 November 2020[72] that assessed its potential contribution and proposed ways forward to support the long-term sustainable development of this sector.

This EU strategy aims to make offshore renewable energy a core component of Europe's energy system by 2050. But because there exist different sources and methods to harness energy, it requires taking a diversified approach tailored to different situations, and thus different technologies are requested depending on the source we want to exploit. It is for this reason that this EU strategy presents a general enabling framework, addressing barriers and challenges common to all offshore renewable energy technologies[73] and setting out specific policy solutions adapted to the different states of development of technologies and regional contexts.

Noteworthily, the EU industry is also the global leader for developing ocean energy technologies, mainly wave and tidal. According to the

---

offshore renewable energy in the Mediterranean Sea and in the Atlantic (see www.diplomatie.gouv.fr/en/french-foreign-policy/europe/news/article/ajaccio-declaration-after-the-7th-summit-of-the-southern-eu-countries-med7-10 (accessed January 28, 2023).

[71] The energy of the oceans can be harnessed by modern technologies without emitting any greenhouse gases, making offshore renewable energy a potential cornerstone of the clean energy transition in the EU.

[72] "*An EU Strategy to harness the potential of offshore renewable energy for a climate neutral future,*" COM(2020)741 final, document available at: https://eur-lex.europa.eu/legal-content/EN/TXT/?uri=COM:2020:741:FIN&qid=1605792629666 (accessed January 28, 2023).

[73] "*The term 'offshore renewable energy technology' encompasses a number of clean energy technologies that are at different stages of maturity. Large commercial-scale projects are currently operating in European waters for bottom-fixed wind turbines but other technologies are starting to catch up. Large commercial floating wind energy projects are being announced in some Member States and ocean energy is reaching a level of maturity that makes them attractive to future applications.*" *Source*: An EU Strategy to harness the potential of offshore renewable energy for a climate neutral future, see https://eur-lex.europa.eu/legal-content/EN/TXT/?uri=COM:2020:741:FIN&qid=1605792629666 (accessed January 28, 2023).

'offshore renewable energy strategy,' the EU companies hold 66% of patents in tidal and 44% of patents in wave energy, and 70% of the global ocean energy capacity has been developed by EU27-based companies.[74] Currently, all projects worldwide use EU technology. Ocean energy technologies are relatively stable and predictable and can complement wind and solar PV (photovoltaic).

The EU is leading in offshore wind deployment, and it is currently a global leader in the manufacturing of key wind turbine components, as well as in the foundations and cables industry. Almost half of the active companies in the wind sector (onshore and offshore) are headquartered in the EU. To further strengthen the EU wind sector's global competitiveness, and achieve the REPowerEU ambition with fast wind energy deployment, supply chains need to be strengthened and drastically accelerated.[75]

The EU is evidently pushing renewable energy in the ambit of the Green Deal and several funding possibilities in the energy sector exist in order to favor green transition as will explained in the next section. However, it is worth noting that in the ambit of offshore renewable energy the EU has helped develop wind power thanks to its ambitious policies and investments which are now destined to increase. According to the EU strategy for offshore renewable energy, the needed investment for the large-scale deployment of **offshore renewable energy technologies by 2050 is estimated to be almost EUR 800 billion**, around two-third to fund the associated grid infrastructure and a third for offshore generation.[76] Private capital is expected to provide a great part of this amount through green investment products (see Chapter 5); however, the EU sustainable finance taxonomy will guide investment in these activities in line with European long-term ambitions. Naturally, the EU has in place other programs which contribute to the realization of the Green Deal and in the following we offer a brief panorama of these instruments. It is foreseen that efficient and well-targeted use of EU support for new technologies will also play a strategic catalytic role.

---

[74] In this sense, see *An EU Strategy to harness the potential of offshore renewable energy for a climate neutral future*. COM(2020)741 final.

[75] *Source*: https://energy.ec europa.eu/topics/renewable-energy/eu-strategy-offshore-renewable-energy_en (accessed January 28, 2023).

[76] Financing of offshore hybrid assets in the North Sea (Guidehouse, 2020–11), visit: https://data.europa.eu/doi10.2833/269908 (accessed January 28, 2023).

3.1.2.1. Different funding sources to facilitate the green transition

The following funding sources represent the main programs initiated by the EU to sustain the green transition. Among them, the new *InvestEU program*[77] provides support and guarantees for emerging technologies to accelerate private investment through its different windows, for example, supporting research and innovation, infrastructure development, and strategic industries. More specific funding resources targeting clean energy and thus climate change are as follows:

Horizon 2020 and Horizon Europe: Horizon 2020 was the EU's research and innovation funding program from 2014 to 2020 with a budget of nearly €80 billion. Now, this program has been succeeded by Horizon Europe. Horizon Europe is the EU's key funding program for research and innovation with a budget of €95.5 billion.[78] It tackles climate change, helps to achieve the UN's Sustainable Development Goals, and boosts the EU's competitiveness and growth.

The European Commission established 'The European Climate, Infrastructure and Environment Executive Agency' (CINEA),[79] which is

---

[77]The *InvestEU Programme* (UK English is used in official documents) gives an additional boost to investment, innovation and job creation in Europe over the period 2021–2027. It builds on the successful model of the Investment Plan for Europe, the Juncker Plan, which mobilized more than €500 billion in the period 2015–2020, with the aim of triggering a new wave — more than €372 billion — in investments using an EU budget guarantee. More info at: https://investeu.europa.eu/about-investeu_en; https://energy.ec.europa.eu/topics/funding-and-financing/eu-funding-possibilities-energy-sector_en (accessed January 28, 2023).

[78]"*Horizon Europe has a budget of EUR 95.5 billion for the period from 2021–2027. This includes EUR 5.4 billion from the Next Generation EU instrument, particularly to support the green and digital recovery from the COVID crisis. The budget is divided amongst four pillars and 15 components to create a programme that will support all the areas of research and innovation: excellent science, global challenges and industrial competitiveness, innovative Europe and widening participation and strengthening the European Research Area.*" *Source*: European Commission, Directorate-General for Research and Innovation, *Horizon Europe, budget: Horizon Europe — the most ambitious EU research & innovation programme ever*, Publications Office, 2021, https://data.europa.eu/doi/10.2777/202859 (accessed January 28, 2023).

[79]CINEA started its activities on 1 April 2021. It has a budget of 56 billion Euro for the period 2021–2027. The Agency supports vital transport and energy infrastructure actions

the successor organization of the Innovation and Networks Executive Agency (INEA), in order to implement parts of certain EU programs and it plays a key role in supporting the EU Green Deal and thus Europe transition to climate neutrality by 2050.

LIFE: Clean Energy Transition: "*A new sub-programme of the LIFE Programme will be dedicated to clean energy transition.*[80] *It will offer support to deliver on sustainable energy-related polices that contribute to reach the European Green Deal objectives. With a budget close to € 1 billion for the period 2021–2027, the sub-programme aims to facilitate the transition towards an energy efficient, renewable energy based and resilient economy by funding coordination and support actions across Europe. It is managed by CINEA.*"[81]

---

under the connecting Europe Facility program and under the Horizon Europe program and it also implements research and innovation projects aimed to strengthen climate actions, as well as the quality the services they bring to societies; it also manages the implementation of the innovation fund, one of the world largest funding programs for commercial demonstrations of innovative low-carbon technologies. The Agency also implements the renewable energy financing mechanism. CENIA also advances environmental, nature conservation, climate actions, and clean energy projects as it takes over the implementation of the *LIFE programme*. It is also in charge of the maritime, fishery, and aquaculture fund which supports the common fishery policy, the Union's maritime policy, and the EU Agenda for international ocean governance. For further information, visit the 'European Climate, Infrastructure and Environment Executive Agency' at: https://cinea.ec.europa.eu/index_en (accessed January 28, 2023).

[80] LIFE Clean Energy Transition sub-program has a budget of nearly EUR 1 billion over the period of 2021–2027 and aims at facilitating the transition toward an energy-efficient, renewable energy-based, climate-neutral, and resilient economy by funding coordination and support actions (Other Action Grants) across Europe. These are actions of high EU added-value, which are targeted at breaking market barriers that hamper the socioeconomic transition to sustainable energy, and typically engage multiple small and medium-sized stakeholders, multiple actors including local and regional public authorities, and non-profit organizations, as well as consumers. More info at: https://cinea.ec.europa.eu/programmes/life/clean-energy-transition_en (accessed January 28, 2023).

[81] In this sense, see the European Commission, Energy, EU funding possibilities in the energy sector at: https://energy.ec.europa.eu/topics/funding-and-financing/eu-funding-possibilities-energy-sector_da#european-regional-development-fund (accessed January 28, 2023).

The Innovation Fund: The Innovation Fund,[82] which is the successor of the *NER 300 programme*,[83] is one of the largest funding programs in the world that is dedicated to the demonstration of use innovative low-carbon technologies. The Innovation Fund will provide around **EUR 38 billion of support from 2020 to 2030** (at EUR 75/tCO_2), depending on the carbon price, for the commercial demonstration of innovative low-carbon technologies, aiming to bring to market industrial solutions to decarbonize Europe and support its transition.[84] The Innovation Fund is managed by the European Climate, Infrastructure and Environment Executive Agency (CINEA), and there will be regular calls for proposals in the lifetime of the fund.

Recovery and Resilience Facility[85]: The Recovery and Resilience Facility (RRF) is the key instrument at the heart of NextGenerationEU, the EU's plan for emerging stronger from the COVID-19 pandemic; it is also a further stimulus for reaching climate goals. It is structured around six pillars:

---

[82] The Innovation Fund, which is managed by the CINEA, focuses on technologies and big flagship projects that can bring significant emissions reductions, including innovative low-carbon technologies and processes in energy-intensive industries, carbon capture and utilization, carbon capture and storage, renewable energy generation, and energy storage. Visit: https://ec.europa.eu/clima/eu-action/funding-climate-action/innovation-fund_en (accessed January 28, 2023).

[83] NER 300 was a funding program pooling together about EUR 2 billion for innovative low-carbon technology, focusing on the demonstration of environmentally safe Carbon Capture and Storage (CCS) and innovative renewable energy technologies on a commercial scale within the EU.

[84] Visit: https://ec.europa.eu/clima/eu-action/funding-climate-action/innovation-fund/policy-development_en.

[85] In the context of the NextGenerationEU recovery plan, the Recovery and Resilience Facility (RRF) of EUR 672.5 billion channels 37% to the green transition and thus could support reforms and investments in offshore renewable energy under the 'Power up' flagship initiative. Regulation (EU) 2021/241 of the European Parliament and of the Council from 12 February 2021 establishing the Recovery and Resilience Facility, document available at: https://eur-lex.europa.eu/legal-content/EN/TXT/?uri=CELEX%3A32021R0241 (accessed January 28, 2023).

Informative Box: The Six Pillars

1. Green transition: *Reflecting the European Green Deal as Europe's sustainable growth strategy and the importance to achieve climate neutrality by 2050, the RRF contributes to the mainstreaming of climate action and environmental sustainability. To that end, the measures supported by the RRF should contribute to the green transition, including biodiversity. Member States have put forward reforms and investments in green technologies and capacities, including in sustainable mobility, energy efficiency, renewable energy, climate change adaptation, circular economy, and biodiversity.*[86]

2. Digital transformation: *Reforms and investments in digital technologies, infrastructures and processes are essential for increasing the Union's resilience and innovative potential. They are also instrumental in reducing the EU's external dependencies by diversifying key supply chains. The RRF supports reforms and investments aiming to promote the roll-out of very high capacity networks, the digitalisation of public services and government processes, the digitalisation of businesses, in particular SMEs, the development of basic and advanced digital skills as well as measures supporting digital-related R&D and the deployment of advanced technologies.*[87]

3. Smart, sustainable and inclusive growth: *Member States will use RRF funds to implement ambitious reforms and investments to make their economies more resilient and competitive and enable a sustainable recovery. The RRF supports measures to promote smart, sustainable and inclusive growth, entrepreneurship, competitiveness, industrialisation and reindustrialisation, renovate buildings, improve the business environment, foster research, development and innovation, and support SMEs.*[88]

(*Continued*)

---

[86] Pillar 1, Green transition. Data available at: https://ec.europa.eu/economy_finance/recovery-and-resilience-scoreboard/green.html (accessed January 28, 2023).

[87] Pillar 2, Digital transformation. Data available at: https://ec.europa.eu/economy_finance/recovery-and-resilience-scoreboard/digital.html (accessed January 28, 2023).

[88] Pillar 3, Smart, sustainable and inclusive growth, including economic cohesion, jobs, productivity, competitiveness, research, development and innovation, and a well-functioning internal market with strong SMEs. Data available at: https://ec.europa.eu/economy_finance/recovery-and-resilience-scoreboard/smart.html.

(Continued)

4. Social and territorial cohesion: *One of the key objectives of the RRF is to promote social and territorial cohesion and to mitigate the social impact of the crisis. This should also contribute to fighting poverty and tackling unemployment, enabling Member States to rebound while leaving nobody behind. The reforms and investments supported by the RRF should contribute to improving social and territorial infrastructure and services, including social protection and welfare systems, the inclusion of disadvantaged groups, support employment and skills development, and lead to the creation of high-quality and stable jobs.*[89]

5. Health, economic, social and institutional resilience: *The COVID-19 crisis has highlighted the importance of reforms and investments in health. It will also be crucial to invest in economic, social and institutional resilience to increase crisis preparedness and response capacity. Member States have included in their plans reforms and investments to improve the resilience, accessibility and quality of health and long-term care, including measures to advance their digitalisation, and to increase the effectiveness of public administration and judicial systems.*[90]

6. Policies for the next generation: *Reforms and investments for children and the youth are essential to mitigate the impact of the COVID-19 crisis on the next generation of Europeans and to ensure that the generational gap is reduced. The RRF supports reforms and investments aimed at improving access to general, vocational, and higher education, as well as its quality and inclusiveness, focusing on digital education, early childhood education and care, and youth employment support.*"[91]

---

[89] Pillar 4, Social & territorial cohesion. Data available at: https://ec.europa.eu/economy_finance/recovery-and-resilience-scoreboard/social.html (accessed January 28, 2023).

[90] Pillar 5, Health, and economic, social and institutional resilience with the aim of, *inter alia*, increasing crisis preparedness and crisis response capacity. Data available at: https://ec.europa.eu/economy_finance/recovery-and-resilience-scoreboard/health.html (accessed January 28, 2023).

[91] Pillar 6, Policies for the next generation, children and youth, such as education and skills. Data available at: https://ec.europa.eu/economy_finance/recovery-and-resilience-scoreboard/policies.html (accessed January 28, 2023).

The RRF, which makes available the astonishing amount of 723.8 billion euros, will help member states implement reforms and investments that are in line with the EU's priorities and that address the challenges identified in country-specific recommendations under the European Semester framework of economic and social policy coordination; it will also help the EU achieve its target of climate neutrality by 2050.[92]

3.1.3. *The recovery and resilience facility and its relevance for the REPowerEU plan*

To support REPowerEU, **€225 billion is already available** in **loans under the RRF**. The Commission adopted legislation[93] and guidance[94] for member states to modify and complement their RRPs[95] in the context of REPowerEU. Delivering the REPowerEU objectives requires an **additional investment of €210 billion**[96] between now and 2027. Member

---

[92] In this sense, the European Commission, EU funding possibilities in the energy sector. Visit: https://energy.ec.europa.eu/topics/funding-and-financing/eu-funding-possibilities-energy-sector_da#european-regional-development-fund (accessed January 28, 2023).

[93] Proposal for a Regulation of the European Parliament and of the Council amending Regulation (EU) 2021/241 as regards REPowerEU chapters in recovery and resilience plans and amending Regulation 2021/1060, 2021/2115, 2003/87/EC and Decision 2015/1814, available at: https://ec.europa.eu/info/system/files/com-2022-231_en.pdf (accessed January 28, 2023).

[94] See Commission Notice — Guidance on Recovery and Resilience Plans in the context of REPowerEU, document available at: https://ec.europa.eu/info/sites/default/files/c_2022_3300_1_en_0.pdf (accessed January 28, 2023).

[95] See the section titled 'National recovery and resilience plans" where the 27 Members states plans are available at: https://ec.europa.eu/info/business-economy-euro/recovery-coronavirus/recovery-and-resilience-facility_en#close-links-to-the-european-semeste (accessed January 28, 2023)

[96] "*The Commission's analysis indicates that REPowerEU entails additional investment of 210 billion euro between now and 2027, on top of what is needed to realise the objectives of the Fit for 55 proposals. Such investment will pay off. Implementation of the Fit for 55 framework and the REPowerEU plan will save the EU EUR 80 billion in gas import expenditures, EUR 12 bn in oil import expenditures and EUR 1.7 bn in coal import expenditures per year by 2030.*" See REPowerEU Plan: https://eur-lex.europa.eu/legal-content/EN/TXT/?uri=COM%3A2022%3A230%3AFIN&qid=1653033742483 (accessed January 28, 2023).

states will use the funds provided by the RRF to implement ambitious reforms and investment to make their economies and societies more sustainable, resilient, and prepared for the green and digital transitions. To accelerate the green and digital transitions, each member state in their Recovery and Resilience Plans "*must dedicate at least 37% of the expenditures of its recovery and resilience plan to measures contributing to climate objectives and at least 20% of the expenditure to digital objectives. It seems that the reforms and investments proposed by Member States have exceeded these targets: for the RRF as a whole, estimated climate expenditure amounts to about 40$ and digital expenditure to about 26%.*"[97]

The Recovery and Resilience Plans (RRPs) have proven highly suitable to implement urgent priorities in a joint EU framework, based on needs by member states and with a strong result orientation. They are already providing a set of ambitious reforms[98] and investment projects to deliver on the green transition and sustainable development. The Commission invites member states to add to their existing RRPs a dedicated chapter with new actions to deliver on the REPowerEU objectives of diversifying energy supplies and reducing dependence on fossil fuels. Technical support to member states is available under the Technical Support Instrument.[99]

---

[97] European Commission: Recovery and Resilience Scoreboard, visit: https://ec.europa.eu/economy_finance/recovery-and-resilience-scoreboard/index.html#:~:text=Recovery%20and%20resilience%20plans%20also%20aim%20to%20support,or%20on%20gender%20equality%20in%20the%20endorsed%20plans (accessed January 28, 2023).

[98] Each Member State has prepared its own plan. At the section 'National recovery and resilience plans" of the following website: https://ec.europa.eu/info/business-economy-euro/recovery-coronavirus/recovery-and-resilience-facility_en#close-links-to-the-european-semester. The flags in this section of the web-page contain a link which will guide you to the Member State's sub-page. The links contain all relevant country-specific information, such as the recovery and resilience plans and key points about them, and where available, the legal texts approving the plan and accompanying press material.

[99] The Technical Support Instrument — TSI — is the EU program that provides tailor-made technical expertise to EU Member States to design and implement reforms at the national level, with emphasis on green and digital transition. Initiated in 2021, the TSI is the successor of the Structural Reform Support Programme (SRSP). Since 2017, both programs have helped design, develop, and implement over 1400 reform projects in 27 Member States. Visit: https://ec.europa.eu/info/funding-tenders/find-funding/eu-funding-programmes/technical-support-instrument/technical-support-instrument-tsi/technical-support-instrument-2022-country-factsheets_en (accessed January 28, 2023).

Before the Ukraine crisis erupted, the EU was already implementing energy policies aimed at phasing out fossil fuels and reaching carbon neutrality; however, this event prompted the adoption of new more incisive measures which are intended to accelerate Europe's clean energy transition and the green transition in general. Nevertheless, it is not possible to end the dependence on fossil fuels and Russia's gas completely in a few months, unless renewable sources are further sustained to be fully deployed to thus reach their full potential. As we have explained, the EU is developing a series of policies in order to achieve carbon neutrality and green sustainable development in line with the SDGs, which are mirrored by Chinese initiatives and can serve as a further example for third countries. Before examining how the major economies are progressing in their coordinated efforts to reach climate goals, it seems appropriate to conclude this part by emphasizing the necessity for the EU to establish a common market for energy in order to stop the dependence on Russia's supply.

3.2. *The Ukraine crisis has accelerated the green transition*

It is evident that following the crisis in Ukraine that began at the end of February 2022, caused by the invasion of its territory by Russia, the case for a rapid clean energy transition has never been stronger and clearer. It is worth remembering that before the crisis the EU was importing 90% of its gas consumption in varying levels across member states, with Russia providing around 45% of those imports. The sudden, unexpected, and brutal change in the relations between the EU and Russia has provoked a surge in the prices of energy related in particular to gas and oil and has exposed the absolute necessity to drastically accelerate the clean energy transition and increase Europe's energy independence from unreliable suppliers and volatile fossil fuels. The revised and enhanced EU energy policy, in the long run, will trigger a new surge in renewable energy developments in Europe and this will certainly benefit green transition not only in the old continent but also worldwide. In fact, this acceleration in the EU will boost the capacity of its wind and solar power sectors and other renewables, which can in turn help scale up future investments in renewable energy infrastructure abroad.

3.2.1. *Improvements and investment in renewables*

A tangible result of the conflict in Ukraine was the 'wake-up call' for a faster transition to green energy for Europe. The EU responded by reinforcing its policies on energy and climate with the introduction of the REPowerEU; in fact, the European Union can do nothing less than ensuring its energy security in a manner compatible with its climate objectives. As evidenced, the green transformation of Europe's energy system will strengthen its economic growth and reinforce its industrial leadership with new investments, which will also arrive from the private sector (green financial instruments to accompany the green transition, see Chapter 5). The new updated and reinforced energy system will put the EU on a speedy path toward climate neutrality by 2050. As evidenced by the European Commission, "*there is a double urgency to reduce Europe's energy dependence: the climate crisis, severely compounded by Russia's aggression against Ukraine, and EU's dependence on fossil fuels, which Russia uses as an economic and political weapon.*"[100] What is also evident is that there are no easy answers, and a short-term and temporary deviation from purely climate considerations must be accepted in the interests of finding structural solutions to Europe's energy security. Fortunately, in the medium and long term, the goals of the European Green Deal coincide with those related to the EU's energy security. It is for this reason that the European Commission calls on leaders, member states, regional and local authorities, every citizen of the EU, and every business to reduce energy dependence on Russia through the implementation of the REPowerEU plan and also by adopting a more responsible attitude when it comes to our environment.

3.2.2. *Strengthening cooperation with the other world major economies with a focus on climate change*

Considering what is happening in the middle of continental Europe with the invasion of Ukraine by Russia — which is not only threatening Ukraine's sovereignty and territorial integrity but also marking a new defining moment for the continent and naturally impacting the relationships with the rest of the world — it is expected for the rest of Europe to discuss how to strengthening cooperation with other major economies. The EU is in fact intensifying talks with both the USA and China to find constructive solutions to the Ukraine crisis, including the climate change and energy security questions.

[100] *Source*: European Commission, REPowerEU Plan.

Since China is an important commercial partner for the EU, these two blocks have everything to gain from working together to favor a rapid solution of the crisis. The European Union and China held their 23rd bilateral Summit via videoconference on April 1, 2022.[101] President of the European Council, Charles Michel, and President of the European Commission, Ursula Von der Leyen, held the Summit meeting with China's Prime Minister Li Keqiang, followed by exchanges with China's President Xi Jinping. The main focus of the Summit was seeking common ground regarding the crisis in Ukraine and bridging the deepening gulf between them. In the context of the COVID-19 pandemic,[102] and given the central role which energy plays in the Ukraine crisis, they also tackled "the state of bilateral relations and areas of shared interest such as climate change, biodiversity and health, as well as ways to ensure a more balanced and reciprocal trade relationship between China and Europe."[103] Despite the ongoing crises, fighting climate change, preserving biodiversity, and implementing better regulations at the international level were still included in the Summit's agenda and discussed. For instance, the parties agreed to continue cooperation on climate change and energy transition, which is necessary to tackle this urgent global challenge. Climate change has particularly important implications for the entire global community and must be addressed properly with coordinated efforts. The EU stressed the importance of additional measures, including phasing down coal, in the run up to COP 27 in Sharm-El Sheikh[104] (see Section 3.2) to

[101] *EU–China Summit: Restoring peace and stability in Ukraine is a shared responsibility*, available at: https://ec.europa.eu/commission/presscorner/detail/en/IP_22_2214 (accessed January 28, 2023).

[102] The recovery from the COVID-19 pandemic remains a shared priority. Leaders discussed cooperation on the vaccination campaign and reopening of the economy. The EU confirmed its commitment to work with China and other member states of the World Health Organization on a new agreement on pandemic prevention, preparedness, and response. See EU–China Summit report, available at: https://ec.europa.eu/commission/presscorner/detail/en/IP_22_2214 (accessed January 28, 2023).

[103] *Source*: Global Times, China, EU should seek further cooperation, strengthen policy coordination: Premier Li, article available at: https://www.globaltimes.cn/page/202204/1257427.shtml (accessed January 28, 2023).

[104] The 27th Session of the Conference of the Parties to the United Nations Framework Convention on Climate Change (UNFCCC COP27) was held in Egypt, Sharm El Sheikh, from **6 to 20 November 2022.** "*The hosting of COP27 in the green city of Sharm el-Sheikh this year marks the 30th anniversary of the adoption of the United Nations Framework*

meet climate goals and, in particular, carbon neutrality by 2050. Moreover, during the Summit, it was also decided that the EU and China will work together to secure a robust and ambitious new global biodiversity framework as it was envisioned at the COP15 in Kunming.[105] Noteworthily, during part I of this conference, CBD parties (Convention on Biological Diversity) adopted the Kunming Declaration[106] through which they committed to negotiating an effective post-2020 Global Biodiversity Framework that can bend the curve of biodiversity loss. As reported by the official site, "*The goal of the framework is to create a plan that would enable the implementation of a broad transformation in society. It aims to create a shared vision of living in harmony with nature by 2050.*"[107] To support biodiversity protection in developing countries, the

Convention on Climate Change. In the thirty years since, the world has come a long way in the fight against climate change and its negative impacts on our planet; we are now able to better understand the science behind climate change, better assess its impacts, and better develop tools to address its causes and consequences." This is first part of the welcome message from H.E. Abdel Fattah el-Sisi, President of the Arab Republic of Egypt, full message available at: https://cop27.eg/en/President-Speech. For the official host country website, visit: https://cop27.eg/. The Road to Sharm el-Sheikh: Informal consultations by the COP 26 Presidency and the COP 27 incoming Presidency, visit: https://unfccc.int/process-and-meetings/conferences/the-road-to-sharm-el-sheikh-informal-consultations-by-the-cop-26-presidency-and-the-cop-27-incoming (accessed January 28, 2023).

[105] The first segment of the Fifteenth Meeting of the Conference of the Parties to the Convention on Biological Diversity (CBD COP15) took place in the Chinese city of Kunming and online from October 11 to 15, 2021. This was the biggest biodiversity conference in a decade. It included the participation of over 2900 delegates in Kunming, and 2400 connecting virtually. CBD COP15, part 2, initially planned for April 25–May 8, 2022 but now most likely to be rescheduled for later, expected to take place in Kunming though a back-up location will be secured.

[106] Kunming Declaration: Declaration from the High-Level Segment of the UN Biodiversity Conference 2020 (Part I) under the theme: "Ecological Civilization: Building a Shared Future for All Life on Earth" (final Draft), document available at: https://www.cbd.int/doc/c/df35/4b94/5e86e1ee09bc8c7d4b35aaf0/kunmingdeclaration-en.pdf (accessed January 28, 2023).

[107] *Source*: "The 15th Conference of the UN Biological Diversity in Kunming, China: The establishment of the Kunming Declaration and the Role for Financial Institutions," document available at: https://greenfdc.org/the-15th-conference-of-the-un-biological-diversity-in-kunming-china-the-establishment-of-the-kunming-declaration-and-the-role-for-financial-institutions/ (accessed January 28, 2023).

Chinese President announced the creation of the Kunming Biodiversity Fund[108] to support biodiversity protection in developing countries.

This event naturally put in evidence the extreme importance for China of the surrounding issues concerning climate change[109] for sustainable development and a shared future. But biodiversity is only one of the concerns China is trying to address while meeting its climate goals. It is worth remembering that the EU and China have in place a *Strategic agenda for cooperation*[110] which is still valid, notwithstanding the recent slowdown due to China's countermeasures to EU sanctions on human rights, economic coercion, trade measures against the single market, and China's ambiguous position with respect to the conflict in Ukraine.

3.3. *EU–China 'expanded' cooperation*

The commitments contained in the 'EU–China 2020 Strategic Agenda for Cooperation' (战略合作) — which was adopted to facilitate exchange of views in the aforementioned climate and biodiversity matters engaging the two blocks in the so-called EU–China Environment Project

[108] See Press Release: UN Biodiversity Conference's High-Level Segment sees creation of Kunming Biodiversity Fund, adoption of Kunming Declaration, building political impetus for adoption of ambitious post-2020 global biodiversity framework, document available at: https://www.cbd.int/doc/press/2021/pr-2021-10-13-cop15-hls-en.pdf (accessed January 28, 2023).

[109] Among the most important commitments and initiatives presented during the meeting were the announcement made by Chinese President Xi Jinping of the 1.5 billion-yuan (about EUR 205 million) Kunming Biodiversity Fund; the EU's commitment to double external funding for biodiversity; the commitment of President Macron of France to dedicate 30% of its climate funds to biodiversity; the announcement by the Government of Japan of a EUR 15 million extension to the Japan Biodiversity Fund; and the commitment made by the coalition of financial institutions, with assets of 12 trillion euros, to protect and restore biodiversity through its activities and investments. *Source*: European Commission, Newsroom, First segment of the 15th United Nations Conference on Biological Diversity (CBD COP 15), Kunming and online, October 11–15, 2021, available at: https://ec.europa.eu/newsroom/env/items/731542/en (accessed January 28, 2023).

[110] EU–China 2020 Strategic Agenda for Cooperation, available at: https://eeas.europa.eu/archives/docs/china/docs/eu-china_2020_strategic_agenda_en.pdf (accessed January 28, 2023).

and[111] also aimed to promote common standards and integration in environmental governance — are more expanded and they comprehend not only cooperation in the environmental context but also in several

[111] The EU–China environment project, "*funded by the EU Foreign Policy Instrument, supports cooperation between the EU and China on environmental policy, aiming to improve environmental protection standards and increase integration between the EU and China on environmental governance. Phase 1 of the project was implemented from January 2018 to June 2021, while Phase 2, which runs from July 2021 to June 2024 is currently ongoing. The project is implemented by a consortium including GOPA, Policy Research Center for Environment and Economy (PRCEE) of China's Ministry of Ecology and Environment, and ClientEarth. This project supports the ministerial-level EU–China Environmental Policy Dialogue (EPD), as well as the EU–China High Level Dialogue on Climate and Environment, which was established in September 2020, just before China's President Xi Jinping made the pledge to achieve carbon neutrality by 2060. Some highlights of the project to date include: EU–China biodiversity dialogue ahead of Kunming COP: The project, in cooperation with the Office of the Executive Committee for CBD COP15 co-hosted six workshops towards the post-2020 Global Biodiversity Framework to be agreed upon at COP15 in Kunming; Integrated environmental policies for a green economy: The project carried out an in-depth study, a policy visit to Europe, and two online workshops, focusing on how to ensure the integration of environmental policies, and integrating environmental considerations into broader economic policies, planning and legislation. This has supported the drafting of the environmental chapter of the 14th Five Year Plan, the establishment of a new department in the Ministry of Ecology and Environment, and a policy document on 'Integrating and Strengthening Efforts in Climate Action and Ecological and Environmental Protection'; Global environmental governance: The project organized a series of workshops and short papers on climate change, biodiversity, marine protection, environment and trade, green economic recovery and other key topics related to global environmental governance. By bringing together policymakers and broader stakeholders, the project supported China in playing a more active role in global environmental governance.*" https://www.clientearth.org/projects/eu-china-environment-project/ (accessed June 13, 2022). The main drivers for cooperation in the environment field have been the Environment Policy Dialogue (EPD) implemented in 2003, and the Bilateral Coordination Mechanism (BCM) implemented in 2009, dealing with Forest Law Enforcement and Governance (FLEG). In addition to the usual bilateral summits, several other tools were elaborated such as the China-Europe Water Platform (CEWP) (accessed January 28, 2023).

areas such as 'Peace and Security,'[112] 'Prosperity,'[113] and 'Sustainable Development'[114] as the first, second, and third priorities, respectively. It is

---

[112] 'Peace and Security' is the first area of cooperation indicated in the EU–China 2020 Strategic Agenda for Cooperation, where it is stated that "*peace, development, cooperation and mutual benefit have become the trend of the times. Promoting multilateralism remains crucial to ensure effective, coordinated and coherent responses to pressing global challenges. As important actors in a multipolar world, the EU and China commit to enhancing dialogue and coordination at bilateral, regional and global levels, to meet regional and global challenges together, and work to make the international order and system more just and equitable.*" See Peace and Security, document available at https://eeas.europa.eu/archives/docs/china/docs/eu-china_2020_strategic_agenda_en.pdf (accessed January 28, 2023).

[113] 'Prosperity' is the second area indicated by the EU–China 2020 Strategic Agenda for Cooperation: "*The EU and China enjoy one of the world's biggest and most dynamic trading relationships. Their trade and investment exchanges have become a major engine driving their respective economic development and innovation. Both sides share responsibility for ensuring that their economies remain key drivers for global economic growth and providing prosperity for all. They are committed to building a world economy where all countries enjoy development and innovation, interconnected growth, interests converging, and firmly safeguarding and developing an open world economy. In that perspective, they are determined to enhance further their trade and investment relationship towards 2020 in a spirit of mutual benefit, by promoting open, transparent markets and a level-playing field. Particular importance will be paid to improving opportunities for Small and Medium Sized Enterprises (SMEs)*"; *Ibid.*

[114] Energy is inserted in the third area of cooperation, namely, 'Sustainable Development' of the EU–China 2020 Strategic Agenda; this part states the following: "1. *Reinforce cooperation on energy issues, with a special emphasis on global energy security within the framework of the Energy Dialogue. 2. Implement a roadmap for EU–China energy cooperation, in order to reinforce exchanges and cooperation in fields of energy legislation, policy and standard formulation. 3. Further explore cooperation in low-carbon energy technologies, which will support sustainable economic growth. 4. Bring into play such existing cooperation platforms as the EU–China Clean Energy Centre (EC2), encourage enterprises to take part in EC2 enterprise alliance and cooperate on pilot projects. 5. Address the issue of nuclear energy development in a safe and secure manner through a general EURATOM agreement and closer scientific cooperation. 6. Reinforce cooperation in energy regulation in order to share experience and promote best practices both regionally and internationally, thereby enhancing consistency in energy policy-making in each country as well as the efficiency of the energy market. China as an observer to the Energy*

precisely this area of cooperation that contains a programmatic statement which concertized itself with the '*Energy Cooperation Platform*' briefly explained in the following section. The fourth and last area of cooperation in the Strategic Agenda is people-to-people exchange.[115]

High-Level Trade and Economic Dialogue (HED) deserves a particular note.[116] Given the importance of trade relationships between the two blocks, it was natural to establish a body to coordinate trade relations and regulate investments. In this framework, the new bilateral investment agreement or the so-called *Comprehensive Agreement on Investment* (CAI) must be included, which was concluded by China and the EU at the end of 2020 but not yet ratified by the parties.[117]

It is therefore evident that the two blocks were able to forge multiple *fora* of discussions in order to duly negotiate better environmental,

---

Charter Conference by invitation will further develop its relationship with the Energy Charter." This area of cooperation includes Climate change and environmental protection (Section V). *Ibid.*

[115] People-to-People Exchange is the fourth area of cooperation contained in the EU–China 2020 Strategic Agenda for cooperation. In the introduction of this part, the following is stated: "*People-to-people exchanges are an essential vector of peace, while contributing to economic development. Together the EU and China represent over a quarter of the world's population. Expanding contacts between peoples on both sides is crucial to enhance common understanding and foster cross-fertilisation between societies.*" *Ibid.* The EU–China High-Level People-to-People Dialogue (HPD) was established at the 14th EU–China Summit held in Beijing on February 14, 2012. The HPPD forms the third pillar of EU–China relations, alongside the High-Level Economic and Trade Dialogue and the High-Level Strategic Dialogue. The first HPPD Joint Declaration was signed in Brussels on April 18, 2012. *Source*: https://euecran.eu/high-level-people-to-people-dialogue (accessed January 28, 2023).

[116] The 'High-Level Economic and Trade Dialogue,' which is also mentioned in the EU–China 2020 Strategic Agenda (Prosperity — I Trade and investment section), was launched in Beijing in April 2008 and it deals with issues of strategic importance to EU–China trade, investment, and economic relations, and provides the impetus for concrete progress in sectoral dialogues.

[117] On December 30, 2020, the EU and China announced that they had reached an Agreement in Principle on investment. The text is the result of lengthy negotiations, which started in January 2014. The EU–China comprehensive Agreement on Investment (CAI) however was not ratified due to the friction that emerged between the parties regarding human rights violations against the Uyghur and other Muslim ethnic minorities in China's Xinjiang region, and retaliation decided by China. More information available at: https://www.europarl.europa.eu/news/en/press-room/20210517IPR04123/meps-refuse-any-agreement-with-china-whilst-sanctions-are-in-place (accessed January 28, 2023).

economic, and financial practices favoring both the planet and its inhabitants. Energy is an area of particular importance, as explained in the following section.

3.3.1. *EU–China energy cooperation platform*

EU–China Energy Cooperation Platform (ECECP) was launched on May 15, 2019 to support the implementation of activities announced in the 'Joint Statement on the Implementation of EU–China Energy Cooperation.'[118] The overall objective of the ECECP is to "enhance EU–China cooperation on energy. In line with the EU's Energy Union, the Clean Energy for All European initiative, the Paris Agreement on Climate Change and the EU's Global Strategy, this enhanced cooperation will help increase mutual trust and understanding between EU and China and contribute to a global transition towards clean energy on the basis of a common vision of a sustainable, reliable and secure energy system."[119]

The EU and China share the same objectives for sustainable development and climate goals, and in order to reach those goals they both are investing in renewable and clean sources to reach carbon neutrality and shape a green economy which will benefit the entire global community. The aim of the platform is to share experiences and advance together toward a carbon neutral economy and align policies to reduce emissions.

3.3.2. *Harmonization of the carbon markets: Is it a feasible solution?*

Though the two parties have in place different legislations and methodologies, one of the issues the two parties are examining is the possibility to

[118]The Joint Statement was signed during the 8th EU–China Energy Dialogue that was held in Brussels on April 9 between Commissioner for Climate Action and Energy Miguel Arias Cañete and the Administrator of the National Energy Administration of China ZHANG Jianhua, with the 21st EU–China Leaders' Summit on April 9, 2019, and was witnessed by Jean-Claude Juncker, President of the European Commission, Donald Tusk, President of the Council of Europe, and Dr. Li Keqiang, Premier of China. The full document is available at: https://energy.ec.europa.eu/system/files/2019-04/joint_statement_on_the_implementation_of_the_eu-china_cooperation_on_energy_en_0.pdf (accessed January 28, 2023).

[119]*Source*: EU–China Energy Cooperation Platform, see http://www.ececp.eu/en/about-eu-china-energy-cooperation-platform-ececp/ (accessed January 28, 2023).

align their respective emissions trading systems (ETSs). This would signal a great leap forward. However, China's ETS, being at an earlier stage of development, differs from the EU ETS, which is more sophisticated.

China's national ETS was launched on July 16, 2021,[120] and so far it covers only one sector, power generation. However, the 2.162 companies it includes produce an estimated 4.5 billion tons of CO_2 emissions annually. On the other hand, the EU launched its emissions trading system in 2005 and it now covers 11.000 emitters and almost half of the European emissions. It uses a market-based cap-and-trade system to reduce greenhouse gas emissions from large power stations, industrial plants, and flights within Europe.[121] "*Since then, several other national or sub-national carbon markets have either been fully launched or partly developed — notably in Canada, Japan, New Zealand, South Korea, Switzerland and the United States. But the EU has worked particularly hard to build a collaborative relationship with China — to help develop the carbon market concept — because China's size makes it the obvious market leader in Asia.* And again: *The rationale underpinning this EU–China cooperation is that by sharing its experience with China, the market with the greatest potential to reduce global emissions, the most established carbon trading system, the EU, can expedite progress in the fight against global warming.*"[122]

---

[120]The key objective of China's ETS is to cover the majority of energy-related emissions and provide cost-effective, market-driven support to greenhouse gas (GHG) emission reduction targets that are integral to China's plan to peak its emissions by 2030 and become climate neutral by 2060. *Source*: https://www.energymonitor.ai/policy/carbon-markets/carbon-trading-the-chinese-way (accessed January 28, 2023).

[121]The EU ETS legislation provides for the possibility to link the EU ETS with other compatible emissions trading systems in the world at the national or regional level. Conditions for linking include (1) system compatibility (the systems have the same basic environmental integrity, and a tonne of CO_2 in one system is a tonne in the other system); (2) the mandatory nature of the system, and (3) the existence of an absolute cap on emission. Further documentation is available at: https://ec.europa.eu/clima/eu-action/eu-emissions-trading-system-eu-ets/international-carbon-market_mt (accessed January 28, 2023).

[122]*Source*: China Dialogue, see https://chinadialogue.net/en/climate/can-the-eu-and-china-align-their-carbon-markets/ "*In the article it is stated that 'the introduction of a global carbon market is an ideal scenario that, however, seems unrealistic at present. Several hurdles must first be overcome, as the different ETSs, especially those of China and the EU, are at different stages of development and use different approaches and mechanisms that are currently difficult to align.*"

In this context, with a proliferation of carbon markets around the world, it would be wise and logical to establish a unique market to gain synergy and efficiency. The EU has, for example, linked up with Switzerland.[123] China, too, is working with its neighbors to develop a regional carbon market, leveraging trade relations built over the years with the ASEAN block. But this is hard work for policymakers because of the many differences. Though regional ETS harmonization makes sense, analysts at the Green Finance and Development Center say this is difficult to achieve in the short term as the development of individual carbon markets in Vietnam, Indonesia, Thailand, and the Philippines is still at an early stage.[124]

It is worth noting that the EU Commission is a founding member of the International Carbon Action Partnership (ICAP),[125] aimed at facilitating international exchange and sharing experience on emission trading which brings together countries and regions[126] with mandatory cap-and-trade systems.

International cooperation in the green energy sector is key to accelerating the development of clean energy solutions in order to contribute to mitigating climate change, reducing emissions, and advancing global

---

[123] In 2017, the **EU and Switzerland** signed an agreement to link their systems. The agreement entered into force on January 1, 2020 following the exchange of the instruments of ratification or approval between the EU and Switzerland. Visit: *Notice concerning the entry into force of the Agreement between the European Union and the Swiss Confederation on the linking of their greenhouse gas emissions trading systems,* available at: *https://eur-lex.europa.eu/legal-content/EN/TXT/?uri=uriserv:OJ.L_.2019.330.01.0001.01.ENG* consolidated version: https://eur-lex europa.eu/legal-content/EN/TXT/?uri=CELEX:02017A1207(01)-20200101 (accessed January 28, 2023).

[124] See Potential Harmonization of emission trading systems: China and Southeast Asia, available at: https://greenfdc.org/potential-harmonization-of-emission-trading-systems-ets-china-and-southeast-asia/ (accessed January 28, 2023).

[125] The International Carbon Action Partnership (ICAP) is an international forum for governments and public authorities that have implemented or are planning to implement emissions trading systems (ETS), facilitating cooperation between countries, sub-national jurisdictions, and supranational institutions that have established or are actively pursuing carbon markets through mandatory cap and trade systems, *Source*: https://icapcarbonaction.com/en (accessed January 28, 2023).

[126] Founded in 2007 in Lisbon, Portugal, by the leaders of more than 15 governments, ICAP currently counts **33 full Members and 7 Observers**. The full list of Members and Observers is available at: https://icapcarbonaction.com/en/members-observers (accessed January 28, 2023).

commitments under the Paris Convention and the United Nations 2030 Agenda for Sustainable Development. Global efforts are underway to reach the goals indicated by the UN and carbon neutrality is one of the most important and challenging targets to reach. As we have explained, the energy sector plays an enormous role, and major financial efforts and coordination will be needed to transition toward sustainable and green development for the entire global community. The following section of this chapter puts in evidence this expanded cooperation in the energy sector, and the necessity to harmonize the so-called 'green finance.' The latest in fact will growth of importance globally, and this is of paramount importance because it will generate resources to implements projects which will contribute to shape a green economy, and grant a sharable future for the entire global community, putting at the disposal of the investors new instruments to invest in.

4. EU, China, and the US Energy and Climate Cooperation: A Necessity to Reach Climate Goals and the Importance of an Harmonized Green Finance

The European Union, China, and the US are responsible for around 40% of global greenhouse gas emissions and together they consume nearly half of the world's energy. Therefore, decisions made in Brussels, Beijing, and Washington have significant implications for the world's climate and energy security. These three blocks alone can change the path of our development and indeed they are already shaping a green future, though their approaches do not always coincide. As we have explained, the EU is fighting climate change through its 'Green Deal,' which includes a series of ambitious policies to cut emissions by at least 55% by 2030, and with the scope of rendering Europe the world's first climate-neutral continent by 2050. China has adopted its '1+N' framework to reach targets of peak carbon by 2030 and net zero by 2060, which includes an action plan, which reflects the EU Green Deal in a sense, but with its own priorities and characteristics. Considering that China is the world's largest emitter, this was a huge move for global climate action and will be regarded as an example for third-world countries. This is especially the case for the BRI community because China will export its experience in this ambit too. The US, on the contrary, does not have a comprehensive legal framework to address climate change, and its climate change policy is developed at the local, state, and federal levels of government. Noteworthily, only 22 states (of 50) in the United States have climate action plans, and of these, only six consider carbon mitigation, negative emissions, and equity issues. It is also necessary to underline that under the Trump Administration the US withdrew from the Paris Convention and only after the election of President Biden did the US rejoined it. Furthermore, President Joe Biden has set a target of reaching net-zero emissions by 2050, a move that mirrors Europe's own commitments. The following section explains in further detail the US policy on climate change and initiatives currently in place to reach climate goals in particular in the green finance sector to foster the green transition.

4.1. *How the US made progress on climate change without ever passing a bill*

In 2009, President Barack Obama was unable to have a comprehensive energy and climate bill approved.[127] In any case, the US emissions of the last decade outperformed the Obama bill's target.[128] US emissions from 2012 to 2020 were more than 1 billion tons below what the bill would have required according to data from the Rhodium Group.[129] It is interesting to analyze the US's model because, though it lacks a precise

[127] Shortly after being elected, President-elect Barack Obama declared a comprehensive climate and energy bill among his top legislative priorities. The US House of Representatives passed the American Clean Energy and Security Act of 2009 by a vote of 219 to 212 in June 2009. The legislation, written by Reps. Henry Waxman (D-Calif.) and Edward Markey (D-Mass.), would have established an economy-wide greenhouse gas cap-and-trade system and critical complementary measures. However, the bill was never brought to the floor of the Senate for discussion or a vote. https://en.wikipedia.org/wiki/American_Clean_Energy_and_Security_Act (accessed January 28, 2023).

[128] The Obama bill would have required the US to cut greenhouse gas emissions 17 percent by 2020 as compared with their all-time high; however, the emissions were down 21 percent: https://rhg.com/research/preliminary-us-emissions-2020/ (accessed January 28, 2023). The same bill said that the US had to generate 20 percent of its electricity from renewables by 2020. In 2020, the US met that target: https://www.eia.gov/energyexplained/electricity/electricity-in-the-us.php (accessed January 28, 2023).

[129] Rhodium Group is an independent research provider combining economic data and policy insight to analyze global trends, visit: Home | Rhodium Group (rhg.com) (accessed January 28, 2023).

framework (like the 'Green Deal' in the EU and the '1+N Framework' in China), it was able to shape its climate policy, which President Biden is now pushing forward, along with financial incentives and technological advancements driving decarbonization. It seems that these advancements were triggered by a self-accelerating process and helped by the new legislation.[130] The industry in fact is advancing toward a greener modality. If we look at the example of the car industry, Ford is already producing more electric *Mustang Mach-Es* than gas-powered Mustangs;[131] moreover, General Motors, Honda, Volvo, and Jaguar have promised to stop selling gas cars altogether by 2040. Royal Dutch Shell was court-ordered to cut its emissions, and shareholders forced Exxon[132] to replace a quarter of its board with climate-concerned activist investors. It is also interesting to note that the costs of solar and batteries have declined in the United States by a factor of 10 over the past decade, and the cost of wind has fallen 70 percent. All this is pushing the US into a green transition which will be more evident with the development of the climate policy that President Biden has relaunched since the beginning of his mandate.

4.1.1. *The US climate policy: Brief introduction*

Historically, the United States has demonstrated varying approaches and intents with regard to addressing climate change; numerous legislative proposals have been discussed and some of them even passed.[133] At the international level, the US adhered to some important initiatives, such as

---

[130] https://www.c2es.org/content/congress-climate-history/ (accessed January 28, 2023).

[131] *Source*: Ford Production of Electric Mustang Exceeds Gas-Powered Pony Car — Bloomberg, article available at: https://www.bloomberg.com/news/articles/2021-06-03/ford-production-of-electric-mustang-exceeds-gas-powered-pony-car (accessed January 28, 2023).

[132] *Source*: Wall Street's Skirmish With Big Oil: Exxon's Climate Fight — The Atlantic. Article available at: https://www.theatlantic.com/science/archive/2021/06/wall-streets-skirmish-with-big-oil-exxons-climate-fight/619070/ (accessed January 28, 2023).

[133] Congress has debated climate change for nearly 30 years with varying results. Laws and congressionally approved funding have led to new programs to reduce emissions and incentives to speed the deployment of clean energy. Other efforts to address climate change more holistically, including by using market-based approaches, have not advanced. A brief US Congress Climate legislative initiatives history is available at: https://www.c2es.org/content/congress-climate-history/ (accessed January 28, 2023).

the 1992 'United Nations Framework Convention on Climate Change' (UNFCCC) and the Paris Agreement (or 'Paris Convention') in 2015. Here, it is worth remembering that although President Trump during his term announced the US withdrawal from the Paris Convention in June 2017 (which became effective in November 2020), on day one of his presidency, Biden fulfilled his promise to rejoin the Paris Agreement and the United States again became a party on February 19, 2021. Noteworthily, President Biden set a course for the United States to tackle the climate crisis at home and abroad, reaching net-zero emissions economy-wide by no later than 2050.

As part of reentering the Paris Agreement, President Biden also launched a whole-of-government process, organized through his National Climate Task Force,[134] to establish a new intermediate 2030 emissions target. The United States has established a new pledge to reduce its economy-wide net GHG emissions by 50–52% below the 2005 level by 2030. This is the new 'nationally determined contribution' (NDC) by the US, a key requirement of the Paris Agreement.[135] According to the Biden Administration, the NDC exceeds a straight-line path to achieve net-zero

---

[134]The National Climate Task Force is chaired by the National Climate Advisor and includes Cabinet-level leaders from 21 federal agencies and senior White House officials, and its task is to implement the Biden–Harris Administration's policies tackling climate change, creating good-paying, union jobs, and achieving environmental justice. *Source*: Readout of the First National Climate Task Force Meeting available at: https://www.whitehouse.gov/briefing-room/statements-releases/2021/02/11/readout-of-the-first-national-climate-task-force-meeting/; see also https://www.whitehouse.gov/climate/ (accessed January 8, 2023). The 'Mission and Work' of the Task Force as stated in Executive order 14008 on Tackling the Climate Crisis at Home and Abroad, January 27, 2021, is as follows: *The Task Force shall facilitate the organization and deployment of a Government-wide approach to combat the climate crisis. This Task Force shall facilitate planning and implementation of key Federal actions to reduce climate pollution; increase resilience to the impacts of climate change; protect public health; conserve our lands, waters, oceans, and biodiversity; deliver environmental justice; and spur well-paying union jobs and economic growth. As necessary and appropriate, members of the Task Force will engage on these matters with State, local, Tribal, and territorial governments; workers and communities; and leaders across the various sectors of our economy.* https://www.whitehouse.gov/briefing-room/presidential-actions/2021/01/27/executive-order-on-tackling-the-climate-crisis-at-home-and-abroad/ (accessed January 28, 2023).

[135]After the United States rejoined the Paris Agreement, the Biden Administration communicated a new Nationally Determined Contribution (NDC) to the Paris Agreement, a

emissions economy-wide by no later than 2050. "*For comparison, the previous US NDC, released in 2015, set a target of 26–28% below 2005 levels by 2025, which President Obama had indicated was on a straight-line trajectory to a reduction of 80% below 2005 levels by 2050. The content of NDCs is nationally determined and nonbinding, but it should reflect what a Party to the Paris Agreement intends to achieve.*"[136]

The US also aims to obtain 100% carbon-pollution-free electricity by 2035[137] and deliver 40% of the benefits from federal investments in climate and clean energy to disadvantaged communities.[138]

4.1.2. *President Biden's actions to tackle the climate crisis*

President Biden campaigned and won his presidency on a bold vision for clean energy in the future which was translated into '*US Climate Change Policy*' briefly introduced in the previous section. In formulating this Climate Change Policy, the US has recognized the urgency of the climate crisis and the necessity to tackle it with adequate measures which include economic and environmental justice for all,[139] making investments to achieve true energy security and create millions of good-paying jobs in

---

formal submission to the United Nations Framework Convention on Climate Change (UNFCCC).

[136] See *US Climate Change Policy*, October 28, 2021. A document prepared by the Congressional Research Service which contains an explanation of the US policy on Climate Change is available at: https://crsreports.congress.gov/product/pdf/R/R46947 (accessed January 28, 2023).

[137] The 2021 NDC also sets a goal to eliminate carbon emissions from the electricity sector by 2035. The Biden Administration reports that it will seek to decarbonize the energy sector in various ways, "including by cutting energy waste; shifting to carbon pollution-free electricity; electrifying and driving efficiency in vehicles, buildings, and parts of industry; and scaling up new energy sources and carriers." See US Climate Change Policy, October 28, 2021.

[138] These targets are contained in the US Climate Change Policy, and are also specified in President Biden's Actions to Tackle the Climate Crisis, see related document at: https://www.whitehouse.gov/climate/.

[139] The Biden–Harris Administration is committed to continually fighting for environmental justice through meaningful and sustained partnership with communities and dedicated

clean energy generation,[140] reinforcing international cooperation to confront climate change more efficiently and avoid the worst, irreversible impacts of this crisis on global economy, and thus fostering a sustainable development.

All these bold goals are to be achieved through coordinated actions and executive orders[141] which are included in the 'US Climate Change Policy' where it is also indicated that "*early executive orders and actions directed by the Biden Administration may be viewed as reinstatement and expansion of policies of the Obama Administration on climate change, with some important differences. In his first three months in office, President Biden rejoined the Paris Agreement, announced US GHG reduction targets, and centralized executive branch organizations to identify and coordinate climate-related actions.*"[142] It is evident that these

leadership in Federal agencies. For more info on Environmental Justice, visit: https://www.whitehouse.gov/environmentaljustice/ (accessed January 28, 2023).

[140]Clean energy is by far the biggest job creator in America's energy sector, with over 3 million Americans employed in clean energy jobs during 2021, earning wages 25% over the national median. *Ibid.*

[141]The 'US Climate Change Policy' (October 28, 2021), contains a series of executive orders by President Joe Biden, which are an integral part of the US policy on Climate change; they are as follows: Executive Order 13990, Protecting Public Health and the Environment and Restoring Science to Tackle the Climate Crisis, January 20, 2021 — Presidential Actions, document available at: https://www.whitehouse.gov/briefing-room/presidential-actions/2021/01/20/executive-order-protecting-public-health-and-environment-and-restoring-science-to-tackle-climate-crisis/; Executive Order Executive Order 14008, Tackling the Climate Crisis at Home and Abroad, January 27, 2021 — Presidential Actions, document available at: https://www.whitehouse.gov/briefing-room/presidential-actions/2021/01/27/executive-order-on-tackling-the-climate-crisis-at-home-and-abroad/; Executive Order 14027, Establishment of the Climate Change Support Office, May 7, 2021, document available at: https://www.govinfo.gov/content/pkg/DCPD-202100388/pdf/DCPD-202100388.pdf; Executive Order 14030, Climate-Related Financial Risk, May 20, 2021 — Presidential Actions, document available at: https://www.whitehouse.gov/briefing-room/presidential-actions/2021/05/20/executive-order-on-climate-related-financial-risk/; Executive Order 14037, Strengthening American Leadership in Clean Cars and Trucks, August 5, 2021 — Presidential Actions, document available at: https://www.whitehouse.gov/briefing-room/presidential-actions/2021/08/05/executive-order-on-strengthening-american-leadership-in-clean-cars-and-trucks/ (accessed January 28, 2023).

[142]*Source*: US Climate Change Policy, see Announced Policies and Rulemakings, p. 20.

executive orders[143] and the content of the 'US Climate Change Policy' represent only a portion of the initiatives President Biden has adopted to tackle the climate crisis and thus reduce emissions and accelerate the transition toward clean energy economy. In fact, President Biden and Vice President Harris have mobilized the whole of the government in every sector of the economy with each sector developing its own framework.

Document: Regulatory Frameworks by Sector to Tackle the Climate Crisis

The following content contains extracts from the White House website and related links

Power Sector

- "***Launched the American offshore wind industry****, approving the first large-scale projects*[144]*, identifying new wind energy areas in the Atlantic and the Pacific,*[145] *and holding a record-breaking $4.3 Billion lease sale*[146] *in the New York Bight — putting this major new industry*

---

[143] Executive Order 14030, included in the US Climate Change Policy, is of particular importance because it delineates as the document itself says, "A roadmap to build a climate-resilient economy" touching several delicate aspects of the US economy while examining climate-related risks. See US Climate-Related Financial Risk, Executive Order 14030, A Roadmap to Build a Climate-Resilient Economy, October 14, 2021, document available at: https://www.whitehouse.gov/wp-content/uploads/2021/10/Climate-Finance-Report.pdf (accessed January 28, 2023).

[144] *Source*: US Department of the Interior, Interior Department Approves Second Major Offshore Wind Project in US Federal Waters, see Press releases 24/11/2021, visit: https://www.doi.gov/pressreleases/interior-department-approves-second-major-offshore-wind-project-us-federal-waters (accessed January 28, 2023).

[145] Fact Sheet: Biden Administration Open Pacific Coast to New Jobs and Clean Energy Production with Offshore Wind Department, May 25, 2021, available at: https://www.whitehouse.gov/briefing-room/statements-releases/2021/05/25/fact-sheet-biden-administration-opens-pacific-coast-to-new-jobs-and-clean-energy-production-with-offshore-wind-development/ (accessed January 28, 2023).

[146] *Source*: US Department of the Interior, Biden-Harris Administration Sets Offshore Energy Records with $4.37 Billion in Winning Bids for Wind Sale, see Press releases 24/11/2021, visit https://www.doi.gov/pressreleases/biden-harris-administration-sets-offshore-energy-records-437-billion-winning-bids-wind (accessed January 28, 2023).

on track to achieve the President's bold goal[147] *of deploying 30 gigawatts of offshore wind by 2030, all while creating good-paying union jobs up and down the supply chain.*

- *Fast-tracked clean energy projects to bring jobs and savings to communities, by approving record levels of solar and other renewables on public lands,*[148] *helping local governments advance community solar projects*[149] *and rooftop installations, and launching a new initiative to deploy distributed energy resources*[150] *in disadvantaged communities.*
- *Advanced power grid upgrades to increase reliability, lower costs, and unlock more clean energy*[151] *through the "Building a Better Grid" initiative*[152] *to deploy more than $15 billion from the Bipartisan Infrastructure Law and build out long-distance transmission lines, and by helping Puerto Rico harness $12 billion in federal recovery funds to strengthen grid resilience and achieve its 100% clean electricity target.*

---

[147] Fact Sheet: Biden Administration Jumpstarts Offshore Wind Energy Projects to Create Jobs, March 29, 2021, available at: https://www.whitehouse.gov/briefing-room/statements-releases/2021/03/29/fact-sheet-biden-administration-jumpstarts-offshore-wind-energy-projects-to-create-jobs/ (accessed January 28, 2023).

[148] Fact Sheet: Biden-Harris Administration Races to Deploy Energy that Creates Jobs and Lowers Costs, January 12, 2022, available https://www.whitehouse.gov/briefing-room/statements-releases/2022/01/12/fact-sheet-biden-harris-administration-races-to-deploy-clean-energy-that-creates-jobs-and-lowers-costs/ (accessed January 28, 2023).

[149] See Department of Energy, DOE Sets 2025 Community Solar Target to Power 5 Million Homes, October 8, 2021, available at: https://www.energy.gov/articles/doe-sets-2025-community-solar-target-power-5-million-homes (accessed January 28, 2023).

[150] Fact Sheet: A Year Advancing Environmental Justice, January 26, 2022, available https://www.whitehouse.gov/briefing-room/statements-releases/2022/01/12/fact-sheet-biden-harris-administration-races-to-deploy-clean-energy-that-creates-jobs-and-lowers-costs/; see 'Delivering Clean, Affordable Energy' section (accessed January 28, 2023).

[151] Fact Sheet: Biden Administration Advances Expansion & Modernization of the Electric Grid, April 27, 2021, available https://www.whitehouse.gov/briefing-room/statements-releases/2021/04/27/fact-sheet-biden-administration-advances-expansion-modernization-of-the-electric-grids (accessed January 28, 2023).

[152] See Department of Energy, DOE Launches New Initiative from President Biden's Bipartisan Infrastructure Law To Modernize National Grid, January 12, 2022, available at: https://www.energy.gov/articles/doe-sets-2025-community-solar-target-power-5-million-homes (accessed January 28, 2023).

- *Invested in rural electric infrastructure through a $464 million investment from USDA*[153] *to expand smart grid technologies and help agricultural producers and rural small businesses install clean energy systems.*
- *Accelerated innovation by creating an Energy Earth shots Initiative*[154] *to drive clean energy breakthroughs and dramatically reduce the cost of critical technologies, hosting the first White House Fusion Summit,*[155] *and launching a new DOE Office of Clean Energy Demonstrations*[156] *to oversee more than $20 billion from the Bipartisan Infrastructure Law."*

Transportation Sector

- "*Rallied automakers and autoworkers around an electric transportation future, setting a national target*[157] *of 50% electric vehicle sales share in 2030 and spurring investments in new American factories*[158] *to manufacture EVs, batteries, and chargers.*

---

[153] See US Department of Agriculture, USDA Invest $464 Million in Renewable Energy Infrastructure to Help Rural Communities, Businesses and Ag Producers Build Back Better, September 9, 2021, available at: https://www.usda.gov/media/press-releases/2021/09/09/usda-invests-464-million-renewable-energy-infrastructure-help-rural (accessed January 28, 2023).

[154] See Department of Energy, Energy Earthshots Initiative, available at: https://www.energy.gov/policy/energy-earthshots-initiative (accessed January 28, 2023).

[155] Fact Sheet: Developing a Bold Vision for Commercial Fusion Energy, March 15, 2022, available https://www.whitehouse.gov/ostp/news-updates/2022/03/15/fact-sheet-developing-a-bold-vision-for-commercial-fusion-energy/ (accessed January 28, 2023).

[156] See Department of Energy, DOE Establishes New Office of Clean Energy Demonstrations Under the Bipartisan Infrastructure Law, December 21, 2021, available at: https://www.energy.gov/articles/doe-establishes-new-office-clean-energy-demonstrations-under-bipartisan-infrastructure-law (accessed January 28, 2023).

[157] Fact Sheet: President Biden Announces steps to Drive American Leadership Forward on Clean Cars and Trucks, August 5, 2021, available at: https://www.whitehouse.gov/briefing-room/statements-releases/2021/08/05/fact-sheet-president-biden-announces-steps-to-drive-american-leadership-forward-on-clean-cars-and-trucks/ (accessed January 28, 2023).

[158] Fact Sheet: Biden-Harris Administration Ensuring Future is Made in America, February 8, 2022, available https://www.whitehouse.gov/briefing-room/statements-releases/2022/02/08/fact-sheet-biden-harris-administration-ensuring-future-is-made-in-america/ (accessed January 28, 2023).

- *Launched EV Charging Action Plan to deploy*[159] *$7.5 billion from the Bipartisan Infrastructure Law to build out a national charging network that is convenient, reliable, and equitable, through a new Joint Office of Energy and Transportation.*[160]
- *Finalized strongest passenger vehicle standards in American history to increase average fuel economy*[161] *to 49 miles per gallon, reduce greenhouse gas emissions,*[162] *protect communities from pollution, and save drivers money at the pump.*
- *Accelerated clean buses, trucks, and ports with Vice President Harris announcing actions*[163] *to reduce pollution from heavy-duty transportation and invest in electric vehicle models for public transit, school bus fleets, freight and port operations — providing relief to fenceline communities who bear the brunt of these dirty emissions.*
- *Strengthened battery supply chains by invoking the Defense Production Act*[164] *to support American production of critical minerals and materials such as lithium, securing nearly $7 billion in*

---

[159] Fact Sheet: The Biden-Harris Electric Vehicle Charging Action Plan, December 15, 2021, available at: https://www.whitehouse.gov/briefing-room/statements-releases/2021/12/13/fact-sheet-the-biden-harris-electric-vehicle-charging-action-plan/ (accessed January 28, 2023).

[160] Visit: Home Page · Joint Office of Energy and Transportation (driveelectric.gov).

[161] See US Department of Transportation, USDOT Announces New Vehicle Fuel Economy Standards for Model Year 2024–2026, April 1, 2022, available at: https://www.transportation.gov/briefing-room/usdot-announces-new-vehicle-fuel-economy-standards-model-year-2024-2026 (accessed January 28, 2023).

[162] See United States Environmental Protection Agency, EPA Finalizes Greenhouse Gas Standards for Passenger Vehicles, Paving Way for a Zero Emissions Future, December 20, 2021, available at: https://www.epa.gov/newsreleases/epa-finalizes-greenhouse-gas-standards-passenger-vehicles-paving-way-zero-emissions (accessed January 28, 2023).

[163] Fact Sheet: Vice President Harris Announces Actions to Accelerate Clean Transit Buses, School Buses, and Trucks, March 7, 2022, available https://www.whitehouse.gov/briefing-room/statements-releases/2022/03/07/fact-sheet-vice-president-harris-announces-actions-to-accelerate-clean-transit-buses-school-buses-and-trucks/ (accessed January 28, 2023).

[164] White House: Memorandum on Presidential Determination Pursuant to Section 303 of the Defense Production Act of 1950, as amended, March 31, 2022, available at: https://www.whitehouse.gov/briefing-room/presidential-actions/2022/03/31/memorandum-on-presidential-determination-pursuant-to-section-303-of-the-defense-production-act-of-1950-as-amended/ (accessed January 28, 2023).

the Bipartisan Infrastructure Law[165] *for domestic battery manufacturing and recycling—all while adhering to strong sustainability and community engagement standards.*[166]
- *Advanced the future of American aviation, coordinating leadership and innovation*[167] *across the federal government, aircraft manufacturers, airlines, fuel producers, and more to produce three billion gallons of sustainable fuel and reduce aviation emissions by 20% in 2030.*"

Buildings Sector

- "*Expanded a program to help families weatherize homes with a $3 billion Bipartisan Infrastructure Law investment in the Weatherization Assistance Program*[168] *to increase energy efficiency, make homes healthier, and lower energy bills for thousands of American families.*
- *Updated energy-saving appliance and equipment standards with a roadmap*[169] *for 100 actions by the end of 2022 that will save households an average of $100 dollars a year through more efficient air conditioners, stoves, refrigerators, and more.*

---

[165] Department of Energy, Biden Administration, DOE Invest $3 Billion to Strengthen US Supply Chain for Advanced Batteries for Vehicles and Energy Storage, February 11, 2022, https://www.energy.gov/articles/biden-administration-doe-invest-3-billion-strengthen-us-supply-chain-advanced-batteries#:~:text=President%20Biden's%20Bipartisan%20Infrastructure%20Law,sourcing%20materials%20for%20domestic%20manufacturing (accessed January 28, 2023).

[166] Biden-Harris Administration Fundamental Principles for Domestic Mining Reform, February 22, 2022, document available at: https://www.doi.gov/sites/doi.gov/files/biden-harris-administration-fundamental-principles-for-domestic-mining-reform.pdf (accessed January 28, 2023).

[167] Fact Sheet: Biden Administration Advances the Future of Sustainable Fuels in America Aviation, September 9, 2021, https://www.whitehouse.gov/briefing-room/statements-releases/2021/09/09/fact-sheet-biden-administration-advances-the-future-of-sustainable-fuels-in-american-aviation/ (accessed January 28, 2023).

[168] Department of Energy, Biden Administration Announces Investments to Make Homes More Energy Efficient and Lower Costs for American Families, March 30, 2022, https://www.energy.gov/articles/biden-administration-announces-investments-make-homes-more-energy-efficient-and-lower (accessed January 28, 2023).

[169] Department of Energy, DOE Releases Energy-Saving Rules for Federal Buildings and Proposes New Standards for Consumer Appliances, March 30, 2022, https://www.energy.gov/articles/doe-releases-energy-saving-rules-federal-buildings-and-proposes-new-standards-consumer (accessed January 28, 2023).

- *Supported subnational action, launching a new Building Performance Standards Coalition*[170] *of over 30 states and local governments to reduce building emissions, create good-paying union jobs in energy efficiency and electrification, and lower energy bills.*
- *Invested in school facility upgrades with Vice President Harris announcing a new Biden-Harris Action Plan for Building Better School Infrastructure*[171] *to support energy efficiency retrofits and other improvements that save school districts money and deliver health and education benefits to students, educators and school staff.*
- *Accelerated innovation with the launch of the Initiative for Better Energy, Emissions, and Equity on RDD&D of clean heating and cooling systems to support sustainable buildings and updated ENERGY STAR standards*[172] *to promote innovative heat pump technologies and encourage electric appliances.*"

Industry Sector

- "*Advanced clean domestic manufacturing, with major announcements*[173] *on using trade policy to reward American manufacturers of clean steel and aluminum, a Buy Clean Task Force for federal*

[170] Fact Sheet: Biden-Harris Administration Launches Coalition of States and Local Governments to Strengthen Building Performance Standards, January 21, 2022, document available at: https://www.whitehouse.gov/briefing-room/statements-releases/2022/01/21/fact-sheet-biden-harris-administration-launches-coalition-of-states-and-local-governments-to-strengthen-building-performance-standards/ (accessed January 28, 2023).

[171] Fact Sheet: The Biden-Harris Action Plan for Building Better School Infrastructure, April 4, 2022, document available at https://www.whitehouse.gov/briefing-room/statements-releases/2022/04/04/fact-sheet-the-biden-harris-action-plan-for-building-better-school-infrastructure/ (accessed January 28, 2023).

[172] United States Environmental Protection Agency, Through Public-Private Partnerships, EPA Helps to Advance Efficiency and Reduce Emissions of American Homes and Buildings, May 17, 2021, document available at: https://www.epa.gov/newsreleases/through-public-private-partnerships-epa-helps-advance-efficiency-and-reduce-emissions (accessed January 28, 2023)

[173] Fact Sheet: Biden-Harris Administration Advances Cleaner Industrial Sector to Reduce Emissions and Reinvigorate American Manufacturing, February 15, 2022, document available at: https://www.whitehouse.gov/briefing-room/statements-releases/2022/02/15/fact-sheet-biden-harris-administration-advances-cleaner-industrial-sector-to-reduce-emissions-and-reinvigorate-american-manufacturing/ (accessed January 28, 2023).

purchasing of low-carbon construction materials, $9.5 billion from the Bipartisan Infrastructure Law for clean hydrogen, and more, and the first comprehensive US government plan[174] *to build an Energy Sector Industrial Base.*

- *Issued the US Methane Emissions Reduction Action Plan with more than 40 actions*[175] *across multiple agencies to cut methane emissions from the oil and gas sector, abandoned coal mines, landfills, agriculture, buildings, and more, while protecting public health, promoting US innovation in new technologies, and helping employ thousands of skilled workers across the country.*
- *Launched the phase-down of super-polluting hydrofluorocarbons found in refrigerators, air conditioners, and other equipment, with actions*[176] *from six agencies to reduce HFC emissions by 85% over 15 years while strengthening domestic manufacturing of alternatives.*
- *Promoted responsible deployment of Carbon Capture, Utilization, and Sequestration (CCUS) technologies, with guidance*[177] *to help agencies ensure projects are environmentally sound, create union jobs, and reduce cumulative pollution in nearby communities.*

---

[174] Department of Energy, Office of Policy, Securing America's Clear Energy Supply Chain, document available at: https://www.energy.gov/policy/securing-americas-clean-energy-supply-chain (accessed January 28, 2023).

[175] Fact Sheet: Biden Administration Tackles Super-Polluting Methane Emissions, January 31, 2022, document available at: https://www.whitehouse.gov/briefing-room/statements-releases/2022/01/31/fact-sheet-biden-administration-tackles-super-polluting-methane-emissions/ (accessed January 28, 2023).

[176] Fact Sheet: Biden Administration Combats Super-Pollutants and Bolsters Domestic Manufacturing with New Programs and Historic Commitments, September 23, 2021, document available at: https://www.whitehouse.gov/briefing-room/statements-releases/2021/09/23/fact-sheet-biden-administration-combats-super-pollutants-and-bolsters-domestic-manufacturing-with-new-programs-and-historic-commitments/ (accessed January 28, 2023).

[177] White House: CEQ Issues New Guidance to Responsibly Develop Carbon Capture, Utilization, and Sequestration, February 15, 2022, available at: https://www.whitehouse.gov/ceq/news-updates/2022/02/15/ceq-issues-new-guidance-to-responsibly-develop-carbon-capture-utilization-and-sequestration/ (accessed January 28, 2023).

- *Expanded partnerships to reduce industrial emissions, with DOE's Better Buildings, Better Plants program*[178] *now covering 3,500 facilities representing almost 14% of the US manufacturing footprint, and launched the Low Carbon Pilot*[179] *to support even greater ambition.*"

Lands and Waters Sector

- "*Launched the America the Beautiful challenge to conserve 30 percent of US lands and waters by 2030*[180] *by accelerating locally led conservation, leveraging $1 Billion in public and private investments,*[181] *and putting natural solutions to work in our fight against climate change while strengthening local economies.*
- *Restored and strengthened protections for cherished places, including Bears Ears, Grand Staircase-Escalante, and Northeast Canyons and Seamounts National Monuments,*[182] *as well as the Tongass National*

---

[178] Department of Energy, DOE's Better Plants Industry Partners Save $9 Billion in Energy Costs, October 14, 2021, https://www.energy.gov/articles/does-better-plants-industry-partners-save-9-billion-energy-costs (accessed January 28, 2023).

[179] Better Buildings, US Department of Energy, visit: https://betterbuildingssolutioncenter.energy.gov/challenge/special-initiatives/low-carbon-pilot (accessed January 28, 2023).

[180] US Department of Interior, America the Beautiful, as directed by President Biden's Executive Order 14008, *Tackling the Climate Crisis at Home and Abroad*; the Department of the Interior has partnered with the Departments of Agriculture and Commerce, National Ocean and Atmospheric Administration, and the White House's Council on Environmental Quality to develop initial recommendations on how to advance an inclusive and collaborative conservation vision, document available at: https://www.doi.gov/priorities/america-the-beautiful (accessed January 28, 2023).

[181] Biden–Harris Administration Launches $1 Billion America the Beautiful Challenge to Support and Accelerate Locally Led Conservation and Restoration Projects, April 11, 2022, document available at: https://www.whitehouse.gov/ceq/news-updates/2022/04/11/biden-harris-administration-launches-1-billion-america-the-beautiful-challenge-to-support-and-accelerate-locally-led-conservation-and-restoration-projects/ (accessed January 28, 2023).

[182] Fact Sheet: President Biden Restores Protections for Three National Monuments and Renews America Leadership to Steward Lands, Waters, and Cultural Resources,

Forest[183] *and Bristol Bay*[184] *in Alaska — all of special importance to Tribal Nations.*

- *Protected sensitive areas from oil, gas, and hardrock mineral leasing, including the Arctic National Wildlife Refuge,*[185] *Chaco Canyon,*[186] *and Boundary Waters,*[187] *and ensured thorough and science-based review*[188] *of all fossil fuel projects on public lands.*
- *Accelerated the restoration of the Great Lakes with a $1 Billion investment from the Bipartisan Infrastructure Law*[189] *to provide clean*

October 7, 2021, document available at https://www.whitehouse.gov/briefing-room/statements-releases/2021/10/07/fact-sheet-president-biden-restores-protections-for-three-national-monuments-and-renews-american-leadership-to-steward-lands-waters-and-cultural-resources/ (accessed January 28, 2023).

[183] US Department of Agriculture, USDA Announces Steps to Restore Roadless Protections on Tongass National Forest, November, 2021, available at: https://www.usda.gov/media/press-releases/2021/11/19/usda-announces-steps-restore-roadless-protections-tongass-national (accessed January 28, 2023).

[184] United States Environmental Protection Agency, EPA Announces New Steps in Process to Protect Bristol Bay Watershed Under Clean Water Act Authority, September 9, 2021, document available at: https://www.epa.gov/newsreleases/epa-announces-new-steps-process-protect-bristol-bay-watershed-under-clean-water-act (accessed January 28, 2023).

[185] US Department of Interior, Interior Department Suspends Oil and Gas Leases in Arctic National Wildlife Refuge, January 6, 2021, available at: https://www.doi.gov/pressreleases/interior-department-suspends-oil-and-gas-leases-arctic-national-wildlife-refuge (accessed January 28, 2023).

[186] US Department of Interior, Secretary Haaland Announces Steps to Establish Protections for Culturally Significant Chaco Canyon Landscape, November 15, 2021, available at: https://www.doi.gov/pressreleases/secretary-haaland-announces-steps-establish-protections-culturally-significant-chaco (accessed January 28, 2023).

[187] US Department of Interior, Interior Department Takes Action on Mineral Leases Improperly Renewed in the Watershed of the Boundary Waters Wilderness, January 26, 2022, available at: https://www.doi.gov/pressreleases/interior-department-takes-action-mineral-leases-improperly-renewed-watershed-boundary (accessed January 28, 2023).

[188] US Department of Interior, Interior Department Suspends Oil and Gas Leases in Arctic National Wildlife Refuge, June 1, 2021, available at: https://www.doi.gov/pressreleases/interior-department-suspends-oil-and-gas-leases-arctic-national-wildlife-refuge (accessed January 28, 2023).

[189] United States Environmental Protection Agency, President Biden, EPA Announce $1 Billion Investment from the Bipartisan Infrastructure Law Will Significantly Accelerate Cleanup and Restoration of Great Lakes, February 17, 2022, document available at:

drinking water, economic opportunities and environmental benefits for communities in the region.

- *Announced a $1 Billion-dollar investment in Climate-Smart Agriculture through a partnership initiative*[190] *that will create new market opportunities for commodities produced using climate-smart practices.*
- *Expanded access to outdoor recreation spaces in urban areas with $150 million in grants through the Land and Water Conservation Fund's Outdoor Recreation Legacy Partnership*[191] *prioritizing communities that lack in outdoor recreation opportunities.*
- *Re-established regulations to protect America's waterways to ensure environmental protections for water bodies*[192] *that are critical to the health, safety and economic vitality of communities.*"

These sectored legal frameworks are intended to accompany the US economy toward a more sustainable mode, but sustaining a clean energy economy, and whether President Biden and his Administration will be able to transition the country to a greener future, will depend on many factors: (i) the political will and thus the ability of the Biden Administration to convince the opposition on the necessity to take adequate measures to tackle the climate crisis; (ii) science, which is fundamental to understanding how grave the situation is and developing new technologies that are able to contribute to reducing greenhouse emissions and ameliorating efficiency of alternative green sources of energy; and (iii) money. Green finance will play a fundamental role in providing the necessary resources to contribute to building a green economy; however, it will be necessary

---

https://www.epa.gov/newsreleases/president-biden-epa-announce-1-billion-investment-bipartisan-infrastructure-law-will (accessed January 28, 2023).

[190] US Department of Agriculture, USDA to Invest $1 Billion in Climate Smart Commodities, Expanding Markets, Strengthening Rural America, February 7, 2022, available at https://www.usda.gov/media/press-releases/2022/02/07/usda-invest-1-billion-climate-smart-commodities-expanding-markets (accessed January 28, 2023).

[191] US Department of Interior, Secretary Haaland Announces $150 Million to Create Public Parks, Expand Recreation Opportunities in Urban Areas, October 5, 2021, available at: https://www.doi.gov/pressreleases/secretary-haaland-announces-150-million-create-public-parks-expand-recreation (accessed January 28, 2023).

[192] United States Environmental Protection Agency, EPA and Army Take Action to Provide Certainty for the Definition of WOTUS, November 18, 2021, document available at: https://www.epa.gov/newsreleases/epa-and-army-take-action-provide-certainty-definition-wotus (accessed January 28, 2023).

to further cooperate at the international level to harmonize standards and render more fluid the use of these new green investment instruments.

4.1.3. *The US green transition and the importance of clean energy*

The green transition in the US is evident, and it is now pushed by a mix of elements such as policy, technology, business, and of course a reinvigorated awareness that only through sustainable development will it be possible to grant a future to future generations. All these elements have contributed to shaping the US Climate Change policy and achieving advancements in technology which have lowered the cost of clean energy and speeded up humanity's ability to decarbonize.

The energy sector is of paramount importance because it determines the development of the entire economy, not just of the US economy. Thus, it appears appropriate to invest more in renewables because not only will green and clean energy help fix climate change but also because investing in this sector helps in lowering the dependency on energy (e.g., oil and gas) from countries, like Russia, causing global destabilization with deplorable actions (the Invasion of Ukraine), putting at risk the fluid development of relations among nations. In order to shape a carbon-neutral economy more rapidly, it is also necessary to involve the industrial sector and make it profitable for companies to fight climate change, for example, by introducing tax incentives for investing in green technologies and green sources of energy. Our planet will benefit from this green transition, and so will the global economy, if all the parties making up this global community will be able to cooperate in transitioning toward a clean energy economy and phasing out fossil fuels to generate energy.

The question of how rapidly we can shift to 100 percent clean energy by 2050 depends on how fast the costs for renewable and its components, i.e., wind turbine, solar panels, and in general new technologies and applications necessary to generate green power, will further diminish rendering the production of clean energy more attractive for our economies. As reported by US research, "*Plummeting costs for wind and solar energy have dramatically changed the prospects for rapid, cost-effective expansion of renewable energy. At the same time, battery energy storage has become a viable option for cost- effectively integrating high levels of wind and solar generation into electricity grids.*"[193] This is good news for the entire global community and not only for the US, because it is evident that transitioning to clean energy, especially these two sources, is becoming more convenient.[194] If the rest of the global community follows the same path of the three major economies by increasing the use of renewables, it is more likely that we can meet the decarbonization targets by 2050 to limit the impacts of climate change on our planet. However, it is clear that in order to reach this goal major, economies need to cooperate and strictly adhere to their commitments to reduce emissions while accelerating on renewables.

Science and technology play a fundamental role in achieving net-zero emissions especially if we consider the recent success of the USA in generating energy from the fusion.[195] However, as it will be necessary to wait a few decades to have the needed technology in place, the use of renewable sources in the meantime becomes of extreme importance.

4.2. *EU, China, and the US cooperation on climate and energy*

As stated by President Biden, "*Achieving the goal of keeping the increase in global average temperature below 1.5°C to avoid the most severe*

---

[193] *Source*: Goldman School of Public Policy 2035 Report, June 2020, document available at: https://www.2035report.com/electricity/ (accessed January 28, 2023).

[194] Over the past decade, the cost of renewable energy has fallen sharply outpacing expert projections. From 2009 to 2019, the cost of wind power fell 70 percent, while the cost of large-scale solar fell close to 90 percent, according to Lazard. *Source*: https://www.lazard.com/perspective/lcoe2019?utm_medium=syndication&utm_source=newscred From 2010 to 2019, the cost of batteries also dropped close to 90 percent, according to Bloomberg New Energy Finance, see https://about.bnef.com/blog/battery-pack-prices-fall-as-market-ramps-up-with-market-average-at-156-kwh-in-2019/?utm_medium=syndication&utm_source=newscred (accessed January 28, 2023). The falling cost of batteries is a game changer, because batteries can store power for when the sky is dark and the wind is idle.

[195] See *US official announce nuclear fusion breakthrough*: *Scientists at Lawrence Livermore National Laboratory's National Ignition Facility have made history by successfully producing a nuclear fusion reaction resulting in a net energy gain, a breakthrough hailed by US officials as a "landmark achievement" and a "milestone for the future of clean energy.*" Article available at: https://edition.cnn.com/us/live-news/nuclear-fusion-reaction-us-announcement-12-13-22/index.html (accessed January 28, 2023).

consequences of climate change will depend crucially on the United States and other countries taking decisive action today to decarbonise the global economy and achieve net-zero emissions by 2050."[196]

Given the fact that the climate crisis now has the attention of the entire global community which is taking actions in the ambit of the Paris Agreement, major economies are also cooperating at bilateral levels (as seen with the EU–China Energy cooperation platform) to catalyze their efforts on specific areas and maximize the results. It is in fact normal that like all global policy issues, approaches to climate change may differ and are always influenced by domestic politics, including its relative prioritization and the nature of international relationships. It is clear that the crisis in Ukraine has attracted global attention and taken the center international stage, but it is also clear that environmental protection and climate change remain important global issues. And in this context, the US has established stronger bilateral relations, for example, with the EU in the energy sector following the energy crisis caused by Russia. The US is also reinforcing cooperation with China, at least in the ambit of climate change due to common concerns regarding the consequences of climate change if it is not tackled with appropriate action. Cooperation among nations is of utmost importance because climate change is the main challenge of the century threatening political and economic equilibriums and it should therefore be tackled united, regardless of geopolitical events, international tensions, and different positions on other issues.

Another element which must be considered is that only with a united front and demonstrable examples of cooperation will be possible to convince other parties of the necessity to act now and in the most effective manner to meet the objectives of the climate convention. Major emitters may prioritize different approaches including using the market, subsidies, green stimulus packages, and legislation, or regulation to accelerate the transition to a low-carbon society, but certainly they need to work together, in a bilateral modality, to reach climate goals.

---

[196]*Source*: Fact Sheet: President Biden Sets 2030 Greenhouse Gas Pollution Reduction Target Aimed at Creating Good-Paying Union Jobs and Securing US Leadership on Clean Energy Technologies, document available at: https://www.whitehouse.gov/briefing-room/statements-releases/2021/04/22/fact-sheet-president-biden-sets-2030-greenhouse-gas-pollution-reduction-target-aimed-at-creating-good-paying-union-jobs-and-securing-u-s-leadership-on-clean-energy-technologies/ (accessed January 28, 2023).

4.2.1. *US–China Joint Glasgow Declaration in enhancing climate action*

It is clear that the future sustainability of the earth depends on international cooperation in achieving the objectives of the Paris Agreement, but it cannot be achieved without the coordinated actions of its two largest carbon polluters — the United States and China.

These two blocks need to work together and be an example for the rest of the global community in relation to the climate crisis. But they also needs to find smart solutions for other critical issues such as the Ukraine crisis, Taiwan, and human rights, all questions which can impact the further evolution of their relations and the shaping of a new multilateralism. Hopefully, the two parties, as it appears, have come to understand that climate change has become a vital priority to be dealt with. The current situation urges the two blocks to unite their efforts to reduce emissions and take the lead in initiatives to tackle climate change for sustainable development because there is no other way to avoid catastrophic consequences. Therefore, it is not surprising that they were able to adopt the so-called *US–China Joint Glasgow Declaration on Enhancing Climate Action in the 2020s*[197] at the UN climate change conference COP26 in November 2021. First, it must be underlined that the joint statement truly evidenced the concerns of the two parties about the worsening climate change issues, expressed during one of the most turbulent times in US–China relations, a manifestation of their renewed commitments to tackling climate change through their respective accelerated actions in the critical decade of 2020s; it was both surprising and valued by the entire global community. Second, the declaration calls for "*concrete actions in the 2020s to reduce emissions aimed at keeping the Paris Agreement-aligned temperature limit within reach,*" including in the areas of methane reduction, decarbonization, and forest protection. While the declaration represents a promising step forward and offers reassurances about new

[197]At COP26, the United States and China issued a joint declaration committing to cooperate on a variety of climate change issues, including developing regulatory frameworks and environmental standards to reduce greenhouse gases emissions, encouraging decarbonization and electrification of end-use sectors, and fostering the circular economy. The "US–China Joint Glasgow Declaration on Enhancing Climate Action in the 2020s" is available at: https://www.state.gov/u-s-china-joint-glasgow-declaration-on-enhancing-climate-action-in-the-2020s/ (accessed January 28, 2023).

momentum for sustained future cooperation, it offers few details regarding concrete plans or the opportunities and challenges to enact and implement those plans.[198]

4.2.2. *The need for open science research and development cooperation*

It is evident that reaching climate goals is a complex task which needs open science research and development (R&D) collaboration regardless of the politicized environment surrounding US–China relations. There is no doubt that R&D is the foundation of innovative technologies, which can greatly accelerate the energy transition and green development. However, US–China cooperation on R&D has been thwarted due to Chinese companies' unrightful use of proprietary US intellectual property according to the Office of the United States Trade Representative.[199] This situation is limiting cooperation and the two parties need to work on this front too, because piracy of intellectual property is of grave concern for both parties and needs to be curbed. "*The two countries need to realize the crucial difference between fundamental research and proprietary research. Proprietary research, by definition, is owned and must receive its due protection. By contrast, fundamental or basic research is intended to be "out there" for all to learn and build on in advancing the understanding or prediction of phenomena. Therefore, fundamental research should be pursued under terms of academic freedom, especially within universities.*"[200] US–China scientific collaboration can be an invaluable tool to build both nations' capacity in addressing climate change, including protecting supply chains essential for meeting pledged goals, amid rising geopolitical tensions, and finding innovative solutions which can be

[198] In particular, refer to points 7, 8, and 9 of the Joint Declaration.

[199] *Source*: FINDINGS OF THE INVESTIGATION INTO CHINA'S ACTS, POLICIES, AND PRACTICES RELATED TO TECHNOLOGY TRANSFER, INTELLECTUAL PROPERTY, AND INNOVATION UNDER SECTION 301 OF THE TRADE ACT OF 1974, document available at: https://ustr.gov/sites/default/files/Section%20301%20FINAL.PDF (accessed January 28, 2023).

[200] *Source*: *Next steps in US–China climate contribution,* by **SHIRAN VICTORIA SHEN, JEAN C. OI, YI CUI AND LIANG MIN, THE HILL**, document available at: https://thehill.com/opinion/energy-environment/3464062-next-steps-in-us-china-climate-cooperation/ (accessed January 28, 2023).

exported to other countries. It is thus imperative that the two major emitters find solutions to their divergences and strengthen their cooperation in these areas to concretely contribute to addressing climate change.

Document: COP26 — US–China Climate Declaration Official Text

USs–China Joint Glasgow Declaration on Enhancing Climate Action in the 2020s

1. "*The United States and China recall their Joint Statement Addressing the Climate Crisis of April 17th, 2021. They are committed to its effective implementation and appreciate the intensive work that has taken place to date and the value of continued discussion.*
2. *The United States and China, alarmed by reports including the Working Group I Contribution to the IPCC Sixth Assessment Report released on August 9th, 2021, further recognize the seriousness and urgency of the climate crisis. They are committed to tackling it through their respective accelerated actions in the critical decade of the 2020s, as well as through cooperation in multilateral processes, including the UNFCCC process, to avoid catastrophic impacts.*
3. *The United States and China recall their firm commitment to work together and with other Parties to strengthen implementation of the Paris Agreement. The two sides also recall the Agreement's aim in accordance with Article 2 to hold the global average temperature increase to well below 2 degrees C and to pursue efforts to limit it to 1.5 degrees C. In that regard, they are committed to pursuing such efforts, including by taking enhanced climate actions that raise ambition in the 2020s in the context of the Paris Agreement, with the aim of keeping the above temperature limit within reach and cooperating to identify and address related challenges and opportunities.*
4. *Moving forward, the United States and China welcome the significant efforts being made around the world to address the climate crisis. They nevertheless recognize that there remains a significant gap between such efforts, including their aggregate effect, and those that need to be taken to achieve the goals of the Paris Agreement. The two sides stress the vital importance of closing that gap as soon as*

possible, particularly through stepped-up efforts. They declare their intention to work individually, jointly, and with other countries during this decisive decade, in accordance with different national circumstances, to strengthen and accelerate climate action and cooperation aimed at closing the gap, including accelerating the green and low-carbon transition and climate technology innovation.

5. *The two sides are intent on seizing this critical moment to engage in expanded individual and combined efforts to accelerate the transition to a global net zero economy.*
6. *The two sides recall their intention to continue discussing, both on the road to COP 26 and beyond, concrete actions in the 2020s to reduce emissions aimed at keeping the Paris Agreement-aligned temperature limit within reach. With that clear purpose, and anticipating that particular forms of cooperation will have the effect of significantly accelerating emission reductions and limitations, including in the form of specific goals, targets, policies, and measures, the two sides intend to engage in the actions and cooperative activities set forth below.*
7. *The two sides intend to cooperate on:*
   - *regulatory frameworks and environmental standards related to reducing emissions of greenhouse gases in the 2020s;*
   - *maximizing the societal benefits of the clean energy transition;*
   - *policies to encourage decarbonization and electrification of end-use sectors;*
   - *key areas related to the circular economy, such as green design and renewable resource utilization; and*
   - *deployment and application of technology such as CCUS and direct air capture.*
8. *Recognizing specifically the significant role that emissions of methane play in increasing temperatures, both countries consider increased action to control and reduce such emissions to be a matter of necessity in the 2020s. To this end:*
   - *The two countries intend to cooperate to enhance the measurement of methane emissions; to exchange information on their respective policies and programs for strengthening management and control of methane; and to foster joint research into methane emission reduction challenges and solutions.*
   - *The United States has announced the US Methane Emissions Reduction Action Plan.*

- *Taking into account the above cooperation, as appropriate, the two sides intend to do the following before COP 27:*
  - *They intend to develop additional measures to enhance methane emission control, at both the national and sub-national levels.*
  - *In addition to its recently communicated NDC, China intends to develop a comprehensive and ambitious National Action Plan on methane, aiming to achieve a significant effect on methane emissions control and reductions in the 2020s.*
- *The United States and China intend to convene a meeting in the first half of 2022 to focus on the specifics of enhancing measurement and mitigation of methane, including through standards to reduce methane from the fossil and waste sectors, as well as incentives and programs to reduce methane from the agricultural sector.*

9. *In order to reduce CO_2 emissions:*
   - *The two countries intend to cooperate on:*
     - *Policies that support the effective integration of high shares of low-cost intermittent renewable energy;*
     - *Transmission policies that encourage efficient balancing of electricity supply and demand across broad geographies;*
     - *Distributed generation policies that encourage integration of solar, storage, and other clean power solutions closer to electricity users; and*
     - *Energy efficiency policies and standards to reduce electricity waste.*
   - *The United States has set a goal to reach 100% carbon pollution-free electricity by 2035*
   - *China will phase down coal consumption during the 15th Five Year Plan and make best efforts to accelerate this work.*
10. *Recognizing that eliminating global illegal deforestation would contribute meaningfully to the effort to reach the Paris goals, the two countries welcome the Glasgow Leaders' Declaration on Forests and Land Use. The two sides intend to engage collaboratively in support of eliminating global illegal deforestation through effectively enforcing their respective laws on banning illegal imports.*
11. *The two sides recall their respective commitments regarding the elimination of support for unabated international thermal coal power generation.*

12. With respect to COP 26, both countries support an ambitious, balanced, and inclusive outcome on mitigation, adaptation, and support. It must send a clear signal that the Parties to the Paris Agreement:

- *Are committed to tackling the climate crisis by strengthening implementation of the Paris Agreement, reflecting common but differentiated responsibilities and respective capabilities, in the light of different national circumstances;*
- *Recall the Paris Agreement's aim to hold the global average temperature increase to well below 2 degrees C and pursue efforts to limit it to 1.5 degrees C and are committed to pursuing such efforts, including by taking ambitious action during this critical decade to keep the above temperature limit within reach, including as necessary communicating or updating 2030 NDCs and long-term strategies;*
- *Recognize the significance of adaptation in addressing the climate crisis, including further discussion on the global goal on adaptation and promoting its effective implementation, as well as the scaling up of financial and capacity-building support for adaptation in developing countries; and*
- *Resolve to ensure that their collective and individual efforts are informed by, inter alia, the best available science.*

13. Both countries recognize the importance of the commitment made by developed countries to the goal of mobilizing jointly \$100b per year by 2020 and annually through 2025 to address the needs of developing countries, in the context of meaningful mitigation actions and transparency on implementation, and stress the importance of meeting that goal as soon as possible.

14. Both countries will work cooperatively to complete at COP 26 the implementing arrangements ("rulebook") for Articles 6 and 13 of the Paris Agreement, as well as common time frames for NDCs.

15. Both countries intend to communicate 2035 NDCs in 2025.

16. The two sides intend to establish a "Working Group on Enhancing Climate Action in the 2020s," which will meet regularly to address the climate crisis and advance the multilateral process, focusing on enhancing concrete actions in this decade. This may include, inter alia, continued policy and technical exchanges, identification of programs and projects in areas of mutual interest, meetings of governmental and non-governmental experts, facilitating participation by local governments, enterprises, think tanks, academics, and other experts, exchanging updates on their respective national efforts, considering the need for additional efforts, and reviewing the implementation of the Joint Statement and this Joint Declaration."

4.3. *EU, China, and the US should focus their collaboration on green finance to foster green transition*

Reaching net-zero emissions in 2050 or 2060 and other climate-related and environmental goals will require significant investments to enable decarbonization across all sectors of the economy, implementing those needed technological innovations which will allow one to shape a truly green economy. Thus Shifting to a financial system which directs capital toward 'green objectives' and addresses climate-related and environmental financial risk, is determinant to making these investments a reality. This is happening in most advanced economies, but many countries are still at a nascent stage of greening their financial sector and they need to be supported by those economies which already are implementing their green financial markets.

4.3.1. *Networking for greening the financial system and the G20 Sustainable Finance Working Group*

There is a broad consensus concerning the utility of green finance to sustain the green transition. A concrete example is the *Network for Greening the Financial System*, NGFS,[201] which is a group of more than 116 members including central banks, supervisors, and observers committed to

[201] At the Paris "One Planet Summit' in December 2017, eight central banks and supervisors established the Network of Central Banks and Supervisors for Greening the Financial System — NGFS. Since then, the membership of the Network has grown dramatically, across the five continents. As of June 14, 2022, the NGFS consists of 116 members and 19 observers. The Central Banks and Supervisors Network for Greening the Financial System is a group of Central Banks and Supervisors willing, on a voluntary basis, to exchange experiences, share best practices, contribute to the development of environment and climate risk management in the financial sector, and to mobilize mainstream finance to support the transition toward a sustainable economy. Its purpose is to define and promote best practices to be implemented within and outside of the Membership of the NGFS and to conduct or commission analytical work on green finance. *Source*: https://www.ngfs.net/en (accessed January 28, 2023).

sharing best practices, contributing to the development of climate- and environment-related risk management in the financial sector and mobilizing mainstream finance to support the transition toward a sustainable economy.[202] This group includes the World Bank. Moreover, the G20 also formed its Sustainable Finance Working Group which was launched in 2016 during China's presidency.[203] G20 members have upgraded it to the G20 *Sustainable Finance Working Group* (SFWG), co-chaired by China and the United States, with secretariat support provided by the *United Nations Development Programme* (UNDP). Because of its purpose, and because green finance, also known as 'responsible finance,' incorporates environmental, social, and governance (ESG) principles into the decision-making processes of financial operators, green finance is now center stage in international affairs and all major operators want to participate in regulating it.

"*International Financial Institutions (IFIs), including Multilateral Development Banks (MDBs), play a critical role in supporting the goals of the Paris Agreement and 2030 Agenda: providing stable, long-term, and counter-cyclical lending at affordable rates and supporting climate action, such as the implementation of transition and low greenhouse gas emission development strategies, through the development of new financing instruments or frameworks. These instruments expand the pool of resources available for climate mitigation and adaptation efforts in accordance with countries Nationally Determined Contributions (NDC) and help catalyze investment from the private sector.*"[204]

Because this theme is of great importance for green transition and sustainable development, China and the EU are coordinating

---

[202] In this sense, see 'Network for Greening the Financial System' at: Network for Greening the Financial System — NGFS — IIASA (accessed January 28, 2023).

[203] During 2016–2018, the Group facilitated the formation of a global consensus on the need to scale up green finance and focused global attention on a range of key topics for the development of sustainable finance worldwide. Visit: G20 Sustainable Finance Working Group — G20SFWG. On April 7, 2021, under Italy's G20 Presidency, Finance Ministers and Central Bank Governors agreed to reestablish the Sustainable Finance Study Group (SFSG) and upgrade it to the 'G20 Sustainable Finance Working Group' (SFWG). Its agenda was anchored in the three G20 priorities: People, Planet, and Prosperity.

[204] *Source*: *2021 Synthesis Report — G20 Sustainable Finance Working Group*, document available at: https://g20sfwg.org/wp-content/uploads/2021/11/Synth_G20_Final.pdf (accessed January 28, 2023).

on taxonomies within the International Platform on Sustainable Finance (IPSF). The following section offers a brief introduction on this theme and on the Common Ground Taxonomy;[205] in fact, this instrument favors shared criteria for sustainable financial markets.

4.3.2. *The international platform on sustainable finance*

The ultimate objective of the *International Platform on Sustainable Finance* (IPSF) is to scale up the mobilization of private capital toward environmentally sustainable investments. The IPSF operates as a multilateral forum platform for policymakers that are in charge of developing sustainable finance regulatory measures to help investors identify and seize sustainable investment opportunities that truly contribute to climate and environmental objectives.[206] Together, the 18 members of the IPSF represent 55% of greenhouse gas emissions, 50% of the world population, and 55% of global GDP.[207] It is evident that their cooperation in shaping a standardized green finance system is of fundamental importance for the rest of the global community. In fact, through the IPSF, members can exchange and disseminate information to promote best practices, compare their different initiatives, and identify barriers and opportunities of sustainable finance, while respecting national and regional contexts.

All these global efforts aim to build a strong foundation for greening the financial sector, including through financial regulation, taxonomies,

---

[205] *Source*: *International Platform on Sustainable Finance — Common Ground Taxonomy — Climate Change Mitigation* Instruction report, IPSF Taxonomy Working Group Co-chaired by the EU and China. Part of this work focuses on deepening cooperation on the development of 'sustainable taxonomies' around the world and to help mitigate fragmentation of global green/sustainability definitions as far as possible. Over twenty jurisdictions around the world have developed or are in the process of developing national or regional sustainable taxonomies. Of these jurisdictions, China and the EU adopted their respective taxonomies into legislative frameworks, the entire document is available at: https://ec.europa.eu/info/sites/default/files/business_economy_euro/banking_and_finance/documents/211104-ipsf-common-ground-taxonomy-instruction-report-2021_en.pdf (accessed January 28, 2023).

[206] *Source*: European Commission, International Platform on Sustainable Finance, more information at: https://ec.europa.eu/info/business-economy-euro/banking-and-finance/sustainable-finance/international-platform-sustainable-finance_en (accessed January 28, 2023).

[207] *Ibid.*, see section 'Members.'

reporting and disclosure standards, and the development of green financial tools and instruments.

4.3.3. *Harmonization of green finance*

Naturally, to express its full potential and attract more capital, green finance needs to harmonize its standards and financial instruments to be more attractive for institutional and private investors, in order to let them play an effective role in the financial panorama. This is what the earlier mentioned network and institutions are working on. In fact, it is not only necessary to improve international coordination on sustainable finance standards, practices, and related policies critical to strengthen market integrity but also further scale up sustainable finance flows and of course facilitate cross-border green capital flows.

Sharing lessons and best practices on green finance will help countries move from ambition to large-scale action. Knowledge sharing and cooperation across countries will be instrumental in delivering an internationally harmonized approach to greening financial sectors globally and will help ensure that finance is flowing to where it is most urgently needed. China's central bank is cooperating with the European Union to converge green investment taxonomies across the two markets, aiming to implement a jointly recognized classification system for environmental credentials for businesses, which will certainly enhance the role of green finance and be an example for the rest of operators.

Yi Gang, governor of the People's Bank of China, stressing the importance of this theme and underlining the necessity to implement and standardize a green finance system in the country in coordination with global partners, affirmed that "*We will deepen the co-operation with Italy, US and other G20 members, to discuss and design an overall road map of sustainable finance, to further discussions with various parties about topics such as reporting and disclosure, as well as green taxonomy.*" The PBoC plans to set up a sustainable finance study group, with the US Treasury Department as a co-chair, to coordinate and build a road map to advance sustainable finance.

To achieve those objectives, the head of the central bank said China was working with the EU to push for greater convergence of taxonomies of green finance and investments. Noteworthily, the commitment from China to cooperation on establishing universal approaches to green investment came just days after the EU's Sustainable Finance Disclosure Regulation (SFDR) came into force on March 10, 2021[208] for fund houses operating or selling products in Europe. Notably, the SFDR requires financial market participants, including asset managers, private banks, venture capital funds, insurance companies, and credit institutions, to disclose on ESG[209] issues including any negative environmental and social impacts of their investments and categorize their products accordingly.

There is no doubt that harmonization efforts will continue and cooperation among all the platforms will increase to allow green finance to grow further and effectively contribute to the green economy.

[208]The Sustainable Finance Disclosure Regulation (SFDR) came into effect on March 10, 2021. It aims to trigger changes in behavioral patterns in the financial sector, discouraging greenwashing, and promoting responsible and sustainable investments. See European Commission, EU Sustainable Finance, April package, April 21, 2021, for more information visit: https://ec.europa.eu/info/sites/default/files/business_economy_euro/banking_and_finance/documents/sustainable-finance-communication-factsheet_en.pdf (accessed January 28, 2023).

[209]As ESG gains popularity against background of China's goal to achieve carbon neutrality by 2060, more Chinese investors show an interest in sustainable investing. In 2019, China's self-regulating body, the Asset Management Association of China, started to give emphasis to the ESG industry by asking asset managers to carry out a self-assessment on their green investing practices, in a move to further encourage responsible investing in the country.

Chapter 5

Understanding Green Finance and Its Role in the Transition to a Green Economy*

Green Finance will help achieve carbon neutrality, and this is a fact. Financial operators all around the globe are looking at green finance with great interest. Undoubtedly, green finance is gaining traction and popularity, and its importance will increase. However, investors sometimes do not completely grasp its meaning because this term has different facets and it refers to a broad category of activities, financial products, services, instruments, and mechanisms in the financial domain. All these elements are linked to investments in industrial activities with the aim of creating a positive impact on the society and on the environment in particular, including land, water, air, biodiversity resources, and people. With this term 'Green Finance,' we largely refer to investments needed to shape sustainable development and reach climate goals.

Green finance is an emerging specialized sector in the finance domain which combines concepts from traditional finance and the business world and deploys new technologies for a low-carbon economy which will help climate change management and thus in the preservation of nature.

---

*Part of the material contained in this chapter was extracted from the book titled *The Impact of COVID-19 on World Aviation Industry – Challenges and Opportunities*, World Scientific, 2022, Chapter 5 Toward a Green Aviation: Financial Investments in a Promising Sector by Mario Tettamanti.

This chapter is aimed at introducing the main concepts of green finance and its importance for the transition to a green economy.

1. Introduction: What is Sustainable or Green Finance?

'Green finance' has become a familiar term over the last decade due to its intensified use in relation to investment activities concerning the environment. This term is also frequently associated with related concepts, such as 'sustainable finance' and 'climate finance,' which have a slightly different meaning. A good description of what each term refers to is given by the *United Nation Environment Programme*.[1] In summary, we can affirm the following:

Sustainable Finance includes environmental, social, governance, and economic aspects.
Green Finance[2] includes climate finance but excludes social and economic aspects.
Climate Finance[3] is a subset of environmental (green) finance.

Sustainable finance is therefore the broadest term covering all financing activities that contribute to sustainable development.

---

[1] See: Definitions and Concepts – Background Note, UNEP, Inquiry Working Paper 16/13, September 2016, document available at: https://wedocs.unep.org/bitstream/handle/20.500.11822/10603/definitions_concept.pdf?sequence=1&isAllowed=y (accessed January 28, 2023).

[2] *'Green finance' is generally used to convey something broader than climate finance, in that it addresses other environmental objectives and risks. It tends to be understood with a greater focus on greening broad flows of private investment rather than mainly concerning public and public-leveraged financial flows. Source*: Definitions and Concepts – Background Note, UNEP, Inquiry Working Paper 16/13, September 2016.

[3] *'Climate finance' tends to be particularly associated with the United Nations Framework Convention on Climate Change (UNFCCC), which defines it as "local, national or transnational financing, which may be drawn from public, private and alternative sources of financing. Climate finance is critical to both reduce emissions and to allow countries to adapt to the adverse effects and reduce the impacts of climate change." Source*: Definitions and Concepts – Background Note, UNEP, Inquiry Working Paper 16/13, September 2016.

Sustainable finance has gained phenomenal momentum: In 2019, a record total of $257.7 billion in green bonds was issued globally, representing 51% growth from 2018. Despite the pandemic, this momentum has continued through 2020, with issuances of $69.4 billion in Q3, the highest ever recorded in any third quarter period. Equity markets have seen similar trends, with Morningstar[4] recording inflows of $54.6 billion into sustainable funds in Q2 2020.

What is important to remember is that 'sustainable finance,' also known as 'responsible finance' or 'ethical investment,' is closely related to impact investing which seeks to have a positive and tangible impact on the economy without damaging our environment. We can also put it in the following terms: Sustainable finance refers to any form of financial service integrating environmental, social, and governance (ESG)[5] criteria into the business or investment decisions for the lasting benefit of both clients and society at large. Sustainable finance consists in choosing

[4]*Source*: https://www.investopedia.com/terms/m/morningstarinc.asp (accessed June 14, 2022).

Morningstar is a Chicago-based investment research firm that compiles and analyzes fund, stock, and general market data. It also provides an extensive line of internet, software, and print-based products for individual investors, financial advisors, and institutional clients. The research reaches all corners of the world, including North America, Europe, Australia, and Asia. Among its many offerings, Morningstar's comprehensive, one-page mutual and exchange-traded fund (ETF) reports are widely used by investors to determine the investment quality of the more than 2,000 funds. The Motley Fool, for instance, uses them as a chief information source.

[5]*Businesses now recognize that environmental issues such as climate change produce materially significant impacts on their operations and the profitability of their ventures. Thus, deriving business insights, particularly risks in business from climate sciences is an important area today. Along with it, the impact of businesses on society is also a crucial metric now, particularly for the investors. Thus, evaluation of the materiality of climate related risks to business (which are further categorized as physical risks such as extreme weather events, natural disasters, etc and transition risks such as changing environmental laws, increasing carbon taxes, etc.) and the societal impacts of business are important components of corporate risk analysis today. Source*: Green finance for energy transition, climate action and sustainable development: Overview of concepts, applications, implementation and challenges, *Green Finance*, 2022, Volume 4, Issue 1, document available at: https://www.aimspress.com/article/doi/10.3934/GF.2022001 (accessed January 28, 2023).

which assets to operate on, not only on the basis of possible profits but also considering their social impact.[6]

Activities that fall under the heading of sustainable finance include the following: sustainable funds, green bonds, impact investing, microfinance, active ownership, and credits for sustainable projects. Sustainable finance encompasses all activities by financial service providers that aim to reduce harm to the environment and climate, to promote social engagement, and to encourage sustainable corporate governance. The Paris Agreement[7] and the EU Action Plan[8] set out concrete sustainability goals for the financial sector, thus evidencing the great importance of sustainable finance to reach not only climate goals but also sustainable development. Sustainable finance means that in the future capital will flow toward more sustainable investments, environmental risks will be taken into greater account, and transparency will be encouraged. In this way, the financial services sector is meant to support the transformation of the overall economy and guide the green transition.

---

[6]*Source*: https://www.lgt.ch/en/lp_investing-sustainably/ (accessed January 28, 20223. The criteria of the ESG sustainability rating (E stands for environment, S for social, and G for governance) have become established key assessment indicators and give you more transparency in your investment decisions.

[7]*Source*: https://unfccc.int/process-and-meetings/the-paris-agreement/the-paris-agreement (accessed January 28, 2023).

The Paris Agreement is a legally binding international treaty on climate change. It was adopted by 196 Parties at COP 21 in Paris, on 12 December 2015, and entered into force on 4 November 2016. Its goal is to limit global warming to well below 2, preferably to 1.5 degrees Celsius, compared to pre-industrial levels. To achieve this long-term temperature goal, countries aim to reach the global peak of greenhouse gas emissions as soon as possible to achieve a climate-neutral world by mid-century. The Paris Agreement is a landmark in the multilateral climate change process because, for the first time, a binding agreement brings all nations together in a common cause to undertake an ambitious effort to combat climate change and adapt to its effects.

[8]*Sources*: https://www.greenfinanceplatform.org/policies-and-regulations/european-commissions-action-plan-financing-sustainable-growth and https://www.pwc.de/en/sustainability/sustainable-finance.html (accessed January 28, 2023), PWC, A strategic advantage for the benefit of the environment, society and economy alike.

1.1. *The sustainable finance*

Sustainable finance refers to the process of taking ESG considerations into account when making investment decisions in the financial sector, leading to more long-term investments in sustainable economic activities and projects. Environmental considerations might include climate change mitigation and adaptation, as well as other environmental aspects, for instance, the preservation of biodiversity, pollution prevention, and circular economy. Social considerations could refer to issues of inequality, inclusiveness, labor relations, investment in human capital and communities, as well as human rights issues. The governance of public and private institutions – including management structures, employee relations, and executive remuneration – plays a fundamental role in ensuring the inclusion of social and environmental considerations in the decision-making process.

In the EU's policy context, sustainable finance is understood as finance to support economic growth while reducing pressures on the environment and taking into account social and governance aspects. Sustainable finance also encompasses transparency when it comes to risks related to ESG factors that may have an impact on the financial system and the mitigation of such risks through the appropriate governance of financial and corporate actors (Figure 1).

1.2. *The sustainable financial markets*

The sustainable financial markets represent an emerging opportunity for both private sector investment and project developers. Filling this gap to finance the preservation of the world's precious ecosystems will require billions of dollars in additional capital, and private investment capital may be the main source of such funds. This highlights the need for intelligent development finance that goes well beyond filling financial gaps and that can be used strategically to leverage private resources. The private sector is seeking new opportunities to invest capital in ways that could possibly generate market-rate financial returns and an environmental impact. Already, pioneering investors have put together financial solutions that combine real assets, like tropical forests, with cash flows from operations in fields, such as sustainable timber, agriculture, and eco-tourism. Scarce public funding can play a significant role in helping to unlock private sector investments required to fill the existing funding gaps.

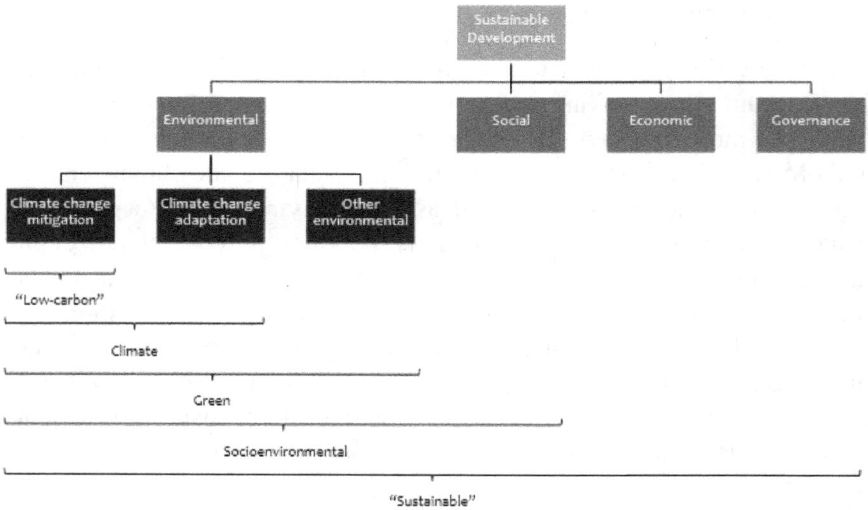

Figure 1: Sustainable Finance and Subdivisions

Source: UNEP – Definitions and Concepts, Background Note, UNEP, Inquiry Working Paper 16/13, September 2016.

Attracting investments in conservation is challenging because potential investors perceive high financial risks and low returns. Credit enhancements – whereby a company attempts to improve its debt or credit worthiness – can encourage the flow of capital to bankable projects by reducing risk or increasing returns. Impact investors – those interested in environmental and social impact – are using a broad range of tools for credit enhancements, one of which is catalytic first-loss capital.[9]

1.3. *Types of sustainable investments*[10]

Investing in sustainable companies and financial products seems to be a trend destined to grow and integrate into other investment processes and

---

[9]*Source*: https://thegiin.org/assets/documents/pub/CatalyticFirstLossCapital.pdf (accessed October 8, 2021). The Global Impact Investing Network (GIIN) is a nonprofit organization dedicated to increasing the scale and effectiveness of impact investing. The GIIN builds critical infrastructure and supports activities, education, and research that help accelerate the development of a coherent impact investing industry. For more information, see www.thegiin.org (accessed January 28, 2023).

[10]*Sources*: https://corporatefinanceinstitute.com/resources/knowledge/trading-investing/sustainable-investing/ (accessed January 28, 2023); https://www.sustainablefinance.ch/

products. What characterizes this type of investment is the conscious choice to invest in a company or fund considered attentive to social issues. Investors usually choose companies in the context of social justice, environmental sustainability, energy, and clean technologies. Sustainable finance also consists of avoiding those industries with a possible negative impact on society or harmful to the environment, such as those involved with alcohol, tobacco, oil and gas, fast food, or gambling.[11]

The new trend in finance is green. The need to adopt a sustainable footprint has, in fact, also extended to banks and investors who are showing a growing activism and interest in sustainable finance, a trend confirmed by the fact that the financial industry is moving toward an increasingly systematic integration of sustainable investing in investment processes and products.

The international debate has increasingly shifted attention to the crucial issue of environmental protection, focusing interest on the transition

---

upload/cms/user/201712_Handbook_on_Sustainable_Investments_CFA.pdf (accessed January 28, 2023). Handbook on sustainable investments. The CFA Institute Research Foundation is a not-for-profit organization established to promote the development and dissemination of relevant research for investment practitioners worldwide.

[11] *Source*: https://www.un.org/en/climatechange/paris-agreement (accessed January 28, 2023). Climate change is a global emergency that goes beyond national borders. It is an issue that requires coordinated solutions at all levels and international cooperation to help countries move toward a low-carbon economy. To tackle climate change and its negative impacts, 196 countries adopted the Paris Agreement at the COP21 in Paris on December 12, 2015. Entered into force less than a year later, the deal aims to substantially reduce global greenhouse gas emissions and to limit the global temperature increase in this century to 2 degrees Celsius while pursuing means to limit the increase even further to 1.5 degrees Celsius. Today, 189 countries have joined the Paris Agreement. The agreement includes commitments from all countries to reduce their emissions and work together to adapt to the impacts of climate change and calls on countries to strengthen their commitments over time. The Agreement provides a pathway for developed nations to assist developing nations in their climate mitigation and adaptation efforts while creating a framework for the transparent monitoring and reporting of countries' climate goals. The Paris Agreement provides a durable framework guiding the global effort for decades to come. The aim is to raise countries' climate ambition over time. To promote this, the agreement establishes two review processes, each on a five-year cycle. The Paris Agreement marks the beginning of a shift toward a low-carbon world – there is much more to do. Implementation of the Agreement is essential for the achievement of the Sustainable Development Goals as it provides a roadmap for climate actions that will reduce emissions and build climate resilience.

to a green economy. From the Sustainable Development Goals to COP21 in Paris, the path embarked upon in the past few years has been sealed toward an economic development model based on decarbonization.

In this context, finance has acquired an increasingly active role through the mobilization of capital directed toward sustainable projects. Initially, it was not easy for investors and financial markets to find the opportunities to conduct green business, considering the lack of available data on the climate risk of companies and on the returns of green investments.

Over the last decade, there has been an acceleration of the financial commitment toward sustainability, to the point where the term 'green finance' was coined to indicate a financial system focused on supporting investments and policies that aim to protect the environment and climate. This system not only includes the financing of specific projects of a public or private nature but also includes support for public policies for the benefit of the environment. Among the issues of interest to green investors are, as already evidenced, clean energy, the protection of biodiversity, energy efficiency, sustainable transport, water management, and adaptation to and mitigation of climate effects.

1.4. *The green financial instruments or products*

Generally speaking, instruments of green finance refer to the actual mechanisms by which capital is raised (or mobilized) to support the development of green projects, with expectations of earning a reasonable return on the amount invested. The issuers of these instruments could be banks, governments, or private investment institutions (Table 1).

1.4.1. *The green bonds*

The first green bond was launched in 2007,[12] similar in characteristic to the existing financial instruments in this category. The operation is similar

---

[12]The first green bond was issued in 2007 by the European Investment Bank, under the label Climate Awareness Bond, as a structured bond with proceeds dedicated to renewable energy and energy efficiency projects. See: https://openknowledge.worldbank.org/server/api/core/bitstreams/def24c02-c03b-54f0-b5ee-2c545d4df099/content (accessed January 28, 2023).

Table 1: Common Green and Sustainable Finance Products

Serial no.	Instrument	Salient features
1	Green bonds	Debt or fixed-income instrument labeled green by the issuer and used to raise capital for climate and environmentally beneficial projects, in line with the voluntary framework of Green Bonds Principles.
2	Green loans/ Concessional debt	Lending of capital dependent on the environmental and resource utilization criteria and characteristics of the projects.
3	Sustainability bonds	Bonds whose proceeds are used to finance or refinance a combination of both green and socially meaningful projects directed toward a specific population.
4	Climate bonds	Fixed income climate-aligned financial instruments that support endeavors with positive impact on climate, in line with Green Bonds Principles.
5	Social bonds	Financial instruments that aim to support ventures in education, health, and food security, toward creating positive social impact.
6	Carbon pricing	An economic cost applied to carbon emissions related to an industrial activity, generally in the form of a tax. The proceeds recovered by these mechanisms can be used to develop and deploy environment-friendly technologies. Current-day carbon markets operate via several mechanisms, described later.
7	Blended finance	Combination of development finance (from public and private sources) and voluntary, philanthropic contributions toward mobilizing additional financial flows for sustainable development in developing and emerging economies.
8	Grants	Financial assistance from the private industry (generally) toward environmentally and socially impactful projects.
9	Sustainability linked bonds	Bonds issued for general corporate uses but with specific sustainability-linked indicators incorporated in the financial characteristics of the instruments.

(Continued)

Table 1: (*Continued*)

Serial no.	Instrument	Salient features
10	Blue bonds	Debt finance instruments issued specifically to support measures for protecting the ocean and ocean-based communities, island nations, and preserving sustainable ocean economy.
11	Sovereign bonds	A debt security issued by a national government to meet part of its expenditures on various projects including those linked to sustainable development and environmental preservation.
12	Transition bonds	These instruments can be either green bonds or sustainability-linked bonds that are issued by the corporate sector looking to align its financing strategy to its climate transition and decarbonization strategies.
13	Green securitization	It indicates conversion of illiquid green assets (e.g., green buildings) into tradable financial instruments (debt). It is commonly used to refinance green loans and mortgages.
14	Green derivatives	It is a financial arrangement for mitigating and managing risk in some kinds of green investments by assigning a value to a green asset.
15	Green sukuk	It is an Islamic financial instrument that finances projects with environmentally positive impacts, in compliance with the Shariah principles.
16	Green/Eco-friendly insurance products	These include insurance products that invest a part of their proceeds into green projects or which help any damaged assets to be replaced by more sustainable and environmentally friendly assets.

Source: Larsen ML (2019) A growing toolbox of sustainable finance instruments. Available from: https://green-bri.org/a-growing-toolbox-of-sustainable-finance-instruments/?cookie-state-change=1622952055245.

to that of a normal debt security: The entity that issues the bond receives capital while the investors enjoy a fixed return in the form of interest. The difference is that green bonds explicitly provide for the allocation of proceeds for environmental purposes.[13]

[13] *Source*: https://www.sustainalytics.com/esg-research/resource/corporate-esg-blog/about-green-bond-principles (accessed January 28, 2023).

The green bond market has grown exponentially over the past few years. The demand for green, social, or sustainability bonds has also been triggered by more awareness among the investors looking for companies with an easier transition to the green economy and by end customers who are more willing to buy sustainable financial products. The green bond market has seen a surge in support from institutional investors, retail investors, governments, treasuries, and from central banks who are interested in buying green bonds. These investors are eager to invest in a credible green bond. The following is how a second-party opinion makes a green bond credible. While the large multilateral development banks have issued these financing mechanisms until 2012, other entities will enter the market in the following years. Green bonds can be corporate if issued by the private sector, municipal if issued by local governments, and city if issued by different cities. In recent years, the market has experienced constant growth and the need has emerged to adopt control and monitoring tools to protect investors regarding the green nature of the projects financed. In 2009, the Climate Bonds Initiative (CBI) was established, which monitors its size every year. Certification tools are also added that aim to standardize the characteristics of green bonds, such as the Climate Bonds Standard by the CBI and the Green Bond Principles (GBP), developed by the International Capital Markets Association (ICMA).

Though the market has evolved, green bonds remain the most popular form of green finance. *According to some estimates, the global green bond issuance has exceeded US $1 trillion by the end of 2020, with USA, Germany and France leading the list of issuing countries.*[14] *Most of the finances are deployed for renewable energy projects at the global level, since the clean energy transition is widely viewed as the backbone of all*

The green bond market aims to enable and mobilize debt markets to fund projects that contribute to environmental sustainability. Green bonds facilitates capital raising and investments for new and existing projects which have environmental benefits and can mitigate risks associated with climate change. With over 1,500 green bonds issued in 2018, valued at more than USD 175 billion, the green bond market is growing at a fast pace. It is estimated that by 2019, green bond issuance will surpass USD 210 billion.

[14]*Source*: Amundi Asset Management Company, International Finance Corporation (IFC) (2021) Emerging Market Green Bonds Report 2020: On the Road to Green Recovery, available at: https://www.ifc.org/wps/wcm/connect/0fab2dcd-25c9-48cd-b9a8-d6cc4901066e/IFC+Amundi+Emerging+Market+Green+Bonds+Report+2020+%2816April21%29.pdf?MOD=AJPERES&CVID=nzGuFTM (accessed January 28, 2023).

sustainable development and decarbonization efforts.[15] *Most green bonds are issued by the banking sector*[16] *but there are increasing numbers of non-banking firms which are joining the list of issuers today, in response to climate crisis and environmental degradation concerns of investors.*[17]

1.4.2. *The green mutual funds*[18]

In recent years, we have seen the development of green funds that aim to invest in the field of sustainability, with a strong exposure of pension funds and insurances; moreover, starting from 2014, various banks and rating companies launched benchmarks to assess the performance of green bonds (Bank of America Merrill Lynch Green Bond Index, Barclays MSCI Green Bond Index, S&P Green Bond Index, and Solactive Green Bond Index).

---

[15] *Source*: International Renewable Energy Agency (IRENA) (2020) Renewable Energy Finance: Green Bonds. Available from: https://committee.iso.org/sites/tc322/home/projects/ongoing/ongoing-1.html.

[16] *Source*: Hesary-Taghizadeh F, Yoshino N, Phoumin H (2021) Analyzing the Characteristics of Green Bond Markets to Facilitate Green Finance in the Post-COVID-19 World. *Sustainability*, 13, 5719. https://doi.org/10.3390/su13105719 (accessed January 28, 2023).

[17] *Source*: Green finance for energy transition, climate action and sustainable development: Overview of concepts, applications, implementation and challenges, *Green Finance*, 2022, Volume 4, Issue 1, document available at: https://www.aimspress.com/article/doi/10.3934/GF.2022001 (accessed January 28, 2023).

[18] https://economictimes.indiatimes.com/definition/mutual-fund (accessed January 28, 2023).

A mutual fund is a professionally managed investment scheme, usually run by an asset management company that brings together a group of people and invests their money in stocks, bonds, and other securities. As an investor, you can buy mutual fund 'units,' which basically represent your share of holdings in a particular scheme. These units can be purchased or redeemed as needed at the fund's current net asset value (NAV). These NAVs keep fluctuating, according to the fund's holdings. So, each investor participates proportionally in the gain or loss of the fund. All the mutual funds are registered with SEBI. They function within the provisions of strict regulation created to protect the interests of the investor. The biggest advantage of investing through a mutual fund is that it gives small investors access to professionally managed, diversified portfolios of equities, bonds, and other securities, which would be quite difficult to create with a small amount of capital.

1.4.3. *The stock market*

The stock exchanges, including London, Oslo, and Stockholm, have launched lists dedicated to green bonds; in 2016, the Luxembourg Stock Exchange established the Luxembourg Green Exchange (LGX), a platform reserved entirely for green products, with such success that the listing was then extended to stocks that support social and sustainable projects. The biggest challenge for green investments remains transparency – to allow investors to correctly assess the real impacts of each loan. Ultimately, green finance is increasingly active and can take on the role that everyone expects as an irreplaceable ally in achieving the climate objectives set out in Paris in 2015. However, several aspects still need to be improved, such as the uniformity of standards and certification criteria. The game is played on credibility: Investors need greater transparency on the allocation of funds to correctly assess the real impacts of each loan, thus avoiding the risk of greenwashing.

1.4.4. *The ETF: The so-called 'green exchange-traded funds'*

Today's investors have access to a growing number of green exchange-traded funds (ETFs), which allow them to incorporate environmentally friendly strategies into their investment decisions. ETFs are investment funds that trade on a stock exchange. Investors have a wide variety of ETFs from which to choose, from those that track a major market index to ETFs that track a basket of foreign currencies. Another type of ETF is the green ETF, which focuses on companies that support or are directly involved with environmentally responsible technologies, such as the development of alternative energy or the manufacture of green technology equipment and devices.[19,20]

---

[19] *Source*: https://www.investopedia.com/terms/e/etf.asp (accessed January 28, 2023).

An exchange-traded fund (ETF) is a type of security that tracks an index, sector, commodity, or other asset, but which can be purchased or sold on a stock exchange the same as a regular stock. An ETF can be structured to track anything from the price of an individual commodity to a large and diverse collection of securities. ETFs can even be structured to track specific investment strategies.

[20] *Source*: https://bussolafinanziaria.it/etf-energie-rinnovabili/ (accessed January 28, 2023).

Green economy/green energy ETFs are exchange-traded funds that invest mainly in shares of companies involved in the production of alternative energy, such as solar and

1.5. *The urgent need for improved regulation in the green financial sector*

The environmental value of green finance is only as robust as the classification, measurement, and transparency of the physical impacts. Without these, the use of green finance remains exposed to accusations of greenwashing, and efforts to improve the oversight mechanism will be crucial over the following years. The EU Taxonomy Regulation[21] is a classification system that has established a list of environmentally sustainable economic activities. The EU Platform on sustainable finance has laid out a set of global criteria to determine which financial products can be marketed as 'green' to investors. The Taxonomy Regulation establishes six environmental objectives: (1) Climate change mitigation; (2) Climate change adaptation; (3) The sustainable use and protection of water and marine resources; (4) The transition to a circular economy[22]; (5) Pollution prevention and control; (6) The protection and restoration of biodiversity and ecosystems (see Article 9 of the Regulation).[23]

---

wind. However, equity ETFs are not the only possible solution to invest in the green economy: Recently, so-called green bond ETFs, or funds that track the performance of an index composed of 'green' bonds (intended to finance projects from positive impact on the environment), have been prevalent.

[21] *Source*: https://ec.europa.eu/info/business-economy-euro/banking-and-finance/sustainable-finance/eu-taxonomy-sustainable-activities_en (accessed January 28, 2023).

[22] *Source*: Circular economy: solutions for a sustainable future (solarimpulse.com) (accessed June 14, 2021).

The circular economy refers to an economic model whose objective is to produce goods and services in a sustainable way, by limiting the consumption and waste of resources (raw materials, water, energy) as well as the production of waste. It is breaking away from the model of the linear economy, based on a take–make–consume–throw away pattern, by proposing to transform waste into recycled raw material.

[23] Member States, the European Union, and the relevant market actors will have to start complying with these requirements from December 2021 **in particular from January 1, 2022** for provisions in respect of: (i) climate change mitigation; and (ii) climate change adaptation. And from **January 1, 2023** for provisions in respect of: (iii) sustainable use and protection of water and marine resources; (iv) transition to a circular economy; (v) pollution prevention and control; and (vi) protection and restoration of biodiversity and ecosystems. Four requirements that economic activities need to comply with in order to qualify: (1) They provide a substantial contribution to at least one of the six environmental objectives above; (2) 'No significant harm' is caused to any of the other environmental

1.5.1. *Taxonomy in green finance: Examples of the EU regulation and China's catalogs*

The EU Taxonomy Regulation establishes a classification system which provides businesses with a common language to identify whether or not a given economic activity should be considered 'environmentally sustainable.' In fact, Green Finance taxonomy indicates a definition and classification framework related to the type and nature of the projects or activities which are eligible for financing under 'green finance.' It must be emphasized that there exist a number of taxonomies depending on the jurisdiction where these instruments are used, and they are often used to screen in or out certain projects for finance. It is important to underline that there is significant interest today in developing harmonized taxonomies for the international financial markets, cutting across borders and legal regimes. Harmonization is necessary to foster the use of these new financial instruments, and efforts are already in place to reach this objective. The most well-known of these taxonomies include the EU Sustainable Finance Taxonomy, ASEAN Capital Markets Forum guidelines, and the Green Bond Endorsed Projects Catalogue from China.[24,25]

It is noteworthy that the EU Taxonomy is seen as the most sophisticated initiative to define environmentally sustainable economic initiatives. This is because the attention to the environment has increased substantially, and financial markets, pushed by the political agenda of the

---

objectives; (3) Compliance with robust and science-based technical screening criteria; and, (4) Compliance with minimum social and governance safeguards "This system will not necessarily replace companies' existing sustainability policies. Rather, it will make it easier for companies with sustainability policies to raise funding for their projects, if they meet the criteria set out in the taxonomy."

[24]*Source*: *Developing A National Green Taxonomy* – A World Bank Guide, June 2020, document available at: https://documents1.worldbank.org/curated/en/953011593410423487/pdf/Developing-a-National-Green-Taxonomy-A-World-Bank-Guide.pdf (accessed January 28, 2023).

[25]*Source*: *Overview and Recommendations for Sustaianble Finance Taxonomies*, International Capital Market Association (ICMA), May 2021, document available at: https://www.icmagroup.org/assets/documents/Sustainable-finance/ICMA-Overview-and-Recommendations-for-Sustainable-Finance-Taxonomies-May-2021-180521.pdf?utm_source=ICMA%20Total%20Subscribes&utm_campaign=fa800ab3d8-EMAIL_CAMPAIGN_5_18_2021_12_18&utm_medium=email&utm_term=0_74a993020a-fa800ab3d8-75741622 (accessed January 28, 2023).

EU, were already shaping new instruments to accommodate the need for investments in the environment and climate spheres to meet the objectives of a carbon-neutral economy by 2050. It is possible to affirm that the EU taxonomy constitutes the main enabler of the 'European Green Deal' and illustrates the EU's intention to steer both private and public capital toward a sustainable economy.

The EU's Taxonomy Regulation was published in the Official Journal of the EU on 22 June 2021.[26] Given the range of interpretations by different Member States as to what counts as a 'sustainable' investment, the European Commission considered that a common taxonomy was needed. This EU Regulation substantially establishes a classification system which provides businesses with a common language to identify whether or not a given economic activity should be considered 'environmentally sustainable.' This, then, determines how far an investment is environmentally sustainable or 'green.'

As the European Commission put in evidence, "An EU-wide classification system will mean that we have a uniform and harmonized way of determining what economic activities can be regarded as sustainable. This is essential in order for the EU to become the first climate-neutral continent by 2050, as well as to urgently fight biodiversity loss and other environmental challenges."[27]

This political agreement, which is also an important achievement in the ambit of sustainable finance, is of great importance for the EU because (i) it gives Member States, market actors, and consumers a common understanding of what economic activities can unambiguously be considered as environmentally sustainable; (ii) it protects private investors and consumers by avoiding 'greenwashing' (i.e., preventing organizations from saying that their products, aims, or policies are environmentally friendly and resilient when they are in fact not); (iii) it facilitates cross-border investment and avoids market fragmentation by providing a single system of classification; and (iv) it provides a solid basis to help reorient

---

[26]Regulation on the establishment of a framework to facilitate sustainable investment, official document available at: https://eur-lex.europa.eu/legal-content/EN/TXT/PDF/?uri=CELEX:32020R0852&from=EN (accessed January 28, 2023).

[27]*Source*: European Commission, *Questions and Answers: Political agreement on an EU-wide classification system for sustainable investments (Taxonomy)*, visit: https://ec.europa.eu/commission/presscorner/detail/it/qanda_19_6804 (accessed January 28, 2023).

capital flows toward sustainable investment, manage financial risks stemming from climate change, environmental degradation, and social issues, and foster transparency and establish a long-term view of financial and economic activity, including standards, labels, and any future changes to prudential rules.[28]

The EU Regulation is a milestone not only for the EU but also for international financial operators and institutions which are free to refer to it.[29] It is possible to affirm that this Regulation will help efforts to unify taxonomy.

In China, 'Taxonomy' developed in two ways: The official sector guidelines on eligible projects for green bonds can be traced back to 2015 when two sets of standards prevailed in the market:

1. *The Green Bond Endorsed Projects Catalogue*[30] ('2015 Project Catalogue') was published by the China Green Finance Committee, an organization supported by the People's Bank of China (PBoC), applied to all types of green bonds in China, except green enterprise bonds which were regulated by the National Development and Reform Commission (NDRC)'s Guideline for Issuing Green Bonds ('2015 Guideline').[31]

   "Only in 2019, seven authorities – NDRC, the Ministry of Industry and Information Technology, the Ministry of Natural Resources, the Ministry of Ecology and Environment, the Ministry of Housing and Urban-Rural Development, PBoC, and the National Energy Administration – published a catalog of green industries."

---

[28] *Ibid.*

[29] This Regulation is also of particular relevance for financial market participants who offer financial products: Financial market participants, as defined in the Disclosure Regulation, will be required to disclose information on how and to what extent the investments that underlie their financial product support economic activities that meet all the criteria for environmental sustainability under the Taxonomy Regulation. For those products that do not invest in taxonomy-compliant activities, a statement will need to be made by the financial market participant, saying that the relevant investments do not take into account the EU Taxonomy Regulation. For more information: https://ec.europa.eu/commission/presscorner/detail/en/ip_21_1804 (accessed January 28, 2023).

[30] Only the Chinese version is available, visit: http://www.greenfinance.org.cn/displaynews.php?id=450 (accessed January 28, 2023).

[31] Only the Chinese version is available, visit: https://www.ndrc.gov.cn/xxgk/zcfb/tz/201601/t20160108_963561.html?code=&state=123 (accessed January 28, 2023).

2. *The Green Industry Guidance Catalogue* ("2019 Industry Catalogue")[32] is a remarkable consensus reached at the cross-ministerial level on what is green.[33]

   "The 2019 Industry Catalogue is intended to be used by various ministries, bureaus, and authorities in China for a wide range of policies not limited to those for the financial markets, including macro-economic policies, tax incentive policies, industry certifications, and standards for the financial sector. It allows the relevant authorities to develop further detailed catalogs or 'sub-catalogs' for the implementation for different policy purposes."[34]

As the name indicates, the 2019 Industry Catalogue identifies a concise list of industries considered green in China. It lists the categories in a three-level structure where:

- *Level 1 includes six broad categories: energy conservation and environmental protection sectors, clean manufacturing sectors, clean energy sectors, ecological environment sectors, green upgrade of infrastructures, and green services.*
- *Level 2 covers 30 categories.*
- *Level 3 lists out 211 categories.*

Based on the 2019 Industry Catalogue, PBoC, NDRC, and the China Securities Regulatory Commission (CSRC) published the *Green Bond Endorsed Project Catalogue* ('2021 Project Catalogue')[35] in April 2021."[36] "The new catalog replaces the two prevailing sets of guidelines, creating a unified national definition of 'green' for green bonds, while

[32] Only the Chinese version is available, visit: https://www.ndrc.gov.cn/fggz/hjyzy/stwmjs/201903/t20190305_1220625.html (accessed January 28, 2023).

[33] See in this sense, *Overview and Recommendation for Sustainable Finance Taxonomoes*, May 2021, ICMA, document available at: https://www.icmagroup.org/assets/documents/Sustainable-finance/ICMA-Overview-and-Recommendations-for-Sustainable-Finance-Taxonomies-May-2021-180521.pdf (accessed January 28, 2023).

[34] *Ibid.*

[35] Only the Chinese version is available, visit: http://www.pbc.gov.cn/goutongjiaoliu/113456/113469/4236341/index.html (accessed January 28, 2023).

[36] *Overview and Recommendation for Sustainable Finance Taxonomoes*, May 2021, ICMA, document available at: https://www.icmagroup.org/assets/documents/

making updates commensurate with technology developments, policy priorities and evolvement of technical standards. The 2021 Project Catalogue stipulates an exhaustive list of eligible projects for green bonds in China, envisioning green bonds' support in:

- *improving the environment;*
- *addressing climate change;*
- *saving and efficiently utilizing resources.*"[37]

1.5.2. *Green finance issuance framework, standards, certification, and other regulatory considerations: Essential elements*

Taxonomy standardization is an important step to instill greater confidence among investors in the use of green financial instruments. However, the issuance of such financial instruments needs to follow determinate principles to grant transparency and promote integrity in the development of the green bond market. It is worth noting that voluntary best practices guidelines called the '*Green Bond Principles*' (GBP or GBPs) were established in 2014 by a consortium of investment banks, namely, Bank of America Merrill Lynch, Citi, Crédit Agricole Corporate and Investment Bank, JPMorgan Chase, BNP Paribas, Daiwa, Deutsche Bank, Goldman Sachs, HSBC, Mizuho Securities, Morgan Stanley, Rabobank, and SEB.[38] The ongoing monitoring and development of guidelines has since moved to an independent secretariat hosted by the International Capital Market Association (ICMA).[39] It is also noteworthy the Green Bond Principles,

---

Sustainable-finance/ICMA-Overview-and-Recommendations-for-Sustainable-Finance-Taxonomies-May-2021-180521.pdf (accessed January 28, 2023).

[37] *Ibid.*

[38] *Source*: Green Bond Principles & Climate Bonds Standards, Initiative Climate Bonds, visit: https://www.climatebonds.net/market/best-practice-guidelines (accessed January 28, 2023).

[39] International Capital Market Association (ICMA) at: https://www.icmagroup.org/sustainable-finance/the-principles-guidelines-and-handbooks/green-bond-principles-gbp/ (accessed January 28, 2023).

Social Bond Principles (SBP),[40] Sustainability Bond Guidelines (SBG),[41] and Sustainability-Linked Bond Principles (SLBP)[42] (collectively the 'Principles') recommend that in connection with the issuance of a green, social, sustainability, or sustainability-linked bond or program, issuers appoint external review provider(s) to confirm the alignment of their bond or bond program with all the core components of the respective principles.

The GBPs emphasize the required transparency, accuracy, and integrity of the information that will be disclosed and reported by issuers to stakeholders through core components and key recommendations. The four core components for alignment with the GBP are (1) Use of Proceeds; (2) Process for Project Evaluation and Selection; (3) Management of Proceeds; and (4) Reporting.

In relation to the 'Use of proceeds,' the proceeds of the bond should be used for green projects including but not limited to the following:

- **Renewable energy:** Including production, transmission, appliances, and products.

[40]Social bonds are used to raise funds for new and existing projects with positive social outcome. The Social Bond Principles (SBP) seek to support issuers in financing socially sound and sustainable projects that achieve greater social benefits. Social Bond Principles, June 2021, document available at: https://www.icmagroup.org/assets/documents/Sustainable-finance/2022-updates/Social-Bond-Principles_June-2022-280622.pdf (accessed January 28, 2023).

[41]The Sustainability Bond Guidelines (SBG), updated as of **June 2021**, confirm the relevance of the Principles in this context and facilitate the application of their guidance on transparency and disclosure to the sustainability bond market. Sustainability Bond Guidelines are available at: https://www.icmagroup.org/assets/documents/Sustainable-finance/2021-updates/Sustainability-Bond-Guidelines-June-2021-140621.pdf (accessed January 28, 2023).

[42]The Sustainability-Linked Bond Principles provide guidelines that recommend structuring features, disclosure, and reporting. They are intended for use by market participants and are designed to drive the provision of information needed to increase capital allocation to such financial products. The SLBPs are applicable to all types of issuers and any type of financial capital market instruments. Sustainability-Linked Bond Principles, June 2020, document available at: https://www.icmagroup.org/assets/documents/Regulatory/Green-Bonds/June-2020/Sustainability-Linked-Bond-Principles-June-2020-171120.pdf (accessed January 28, 2023).

- **Energy efficiency:** For example, in new and refurbished buildings, energy storage, district heating, smart grids, appliances, and products.
- **Pollution prevention and control:** Including reduction of air emissions, greenhouse gas control, soil remediation, waste prevention, waste reduction, waste recycling, and turning energy/emission-efficient waste to energy.
- **Environmentally sustainable management of living natural resources and land use:** Including environmentally sustainable agriculture; environmentally sustainable animal husbandry; smart farm inputs related to climate such as biological crop protection or drip-irrigation; environmentally sustainable fishery and aquaculture; and environmentally sustainable forestry, including reforestation and preservation or restoration of natural landscapes.
- **Terrestrial and aquatic biodiversity conservation:** Including the protection of coastal, marine, and watershed environments.
- **Clean transportation:** Such as electric, hybrid, public, rail, non-motorized, multi-modal transportation, infrastructure for clean energy vehicles, and reduction of harmful emissions.
- **Sustainable water and wastewater management:** Including sustainable infrastructure for clean and/or drinking water, wastewater treatment, sustainable urban drainage systems, and river training and other forms of flood mitigation.
- **Climate change adaptation:** Including efforts to make infrastructure more resilient to impacts of climate change, as well as information support systems, such as climate observation and early warning systems.
- **Eco-efficient and/or circular economy-adapted products, production technologies, and processes:** Such as the design and introduction of reusable, recyclable, and refurbished materials, components, and products; circular tools and services.
- **Green buildings** that meet regional, national, or internationally recognized standards or certifications for environmental performance.[43]

[43] In this sense see: The Green Bond Principles, June 2021 (with June 2022 Appendix 1), ICMA, document available at: https://www.icmagroup.org/assets/documents/Sustainable-finance/2022-updates/Green-Bond-Principles_June-2022-280622.pdf (accessed January 28, 2023).

World Bank and IFC have their own criteria or definitions of eligible green projects.[44] *After a green finance instrument such as a green bond is issued, the objectives and use-of-proceeds stated by the issuer is often verified and certified by independent agencies by comparison with certain standards. The most widely known mechanisms for verification are the Climate Bonds Initiative Climate Bonds Standards, Green Bond Assessment and Verification Guidelines, European Union Green Bonds standards and ASEAN Green Bonds Standards.*[45]

As for the 'Process for project evaluation and selection,' the issuer should clearly communicate the following:

- *The environmental sustainability objective;*
- *The process by which the issuer determines how the project falls within the eligible green projects categories (examples are identified above); and*
- *Complementary information on processes by which the issuer identifies and manages perceived social and environmental risks associated with the relevant project(s).*[46]

In this context, issuers of green bond are also encouraged to do the following:

- *Position the information communicated above within the context of the issuer's overarching objectives, strategy, policy, and/or processes relating to environmental sustainability.*
- *Provide information, if relevant, on the alignment of projects with official or market-based taxonomies, related eligibility criteria, including if applicable exclusion criteria, and also disclose any green standards or certifications referenced in project selection.*

---

[44] https://www.worldbank.org/en/news/feature/2021/12/08/what-you-need-to-know-about-ifc-s-green-bonds (accessed January 28, 2023).

[45] Tolliver C, Fujii H, Keeley AR, *et al.* (2021) Green Innovation and Finance in Asia. *Asian Econ Policy Rev* 16: 67–87. https://doi.org/10.1111/aepr.12320 (accessed January 28, 2023).

[46] See: The Green Bond Principles, June 2021 (with June 2022 Appendix 1), ICMA, document available at: https://www.icmagroup.org/assets/documents/Sustainable-finance/2022-updates/Green-Bond-Principles_June-2022-280622.pdf (accessed January 28, 2023).

- *Have a process in place to identify mitigants to known material risks of negative social and/or environmental impacts from the relevant project(s). Such mitigants may include clear and relevant trade-off analysis undertaken and monitoring required where the issuer assesses the potential risks to be meaningful.*[47]

Regarding the **Management of proceeds**, it must be noted that the net proceeds should be credited to a sub-account or moved to a sub-portfolio or otherwise tracked by the issuer. So long as the Green Bond is outstanding, the balance of the tracked net proceeds should be periodically adjusted to match allocations to eligible green projects made during that period. The GBP recommends that an auditor or third party is used to verify the tracking and allocation of funds.[48]

Finally with regard to 'Reporting,' the issuer should make and keep readily available up-to-date information on the use of proceeds to be renewed annually until full allocation, and on a timely basis in case of material developments. The annual report should include a list of the projects to which Green Bond proceeds have been allocated, as well as a brief description of the projects, the amounts allocated, and their expected impact. The GBP recommends qualitative and quantitative performance indicators and, where feasible, quantitative performance measurement and disclosure of the key underlying methodology and/or assumptions used in the quantitative determination.[49] Issuers should refer to and adopt, where possible, the guidance and impact reporting templates provided in the Harmonized Framework for Impact Reporting.[50]

Substantially, all this summarizes the 'issuance and regulatory framework' for green bonds. Financial markets are witnessing an impressive growth of these instruments and investors are also looking with more interest toward these green financial opportunities. As exposed in the following section, Green Finance is gaining traction and it will play a key

---

[47] *Ibid.*

[48] *Ibid.*

[49] *Ibid.*

[50] *Source*: *Harmonized Framework for Impact Reporting*, June 2022, document available at: https://www.icmagroup.org/assets/documents/Sustainable-finance/2022-updates/Harmonised-Framework-for-Impact-Reporting-Green-Bonds_June-2022-280622.pdf (accessed January 28, 2023).

role in raising the necessary resources for green transition all over the globe.

2. The Green Finance Revolution is Gaining Traction

Green finance is blossoming: This is due to the fact that there is an increase of the issuers considering the environmental, social, and governance (ESG) impact of their actions. This is good news for the environment and naturally for operators in the financial sector helping those corporations which are 'going green' or, in other words, transforming themselves into economic entities more respectful toward the environment and adopting more sustainable production modalities. Moving to a decarbonized economy will require an unprecedented level of new capital investment, and the public sector money alone cannot cover this cost; thus, attracting capital from the private sector through green financial instruments is of paramount importance to reach climate goals.

2.1. *Green instrument issuance set to hit new records: The EU brings historic EUR 12 billion green bond to Luxembourg Stock Exchange*

According to the 'Climate Bonds Initiative,'[51] the world issued $106.86 billion in green bonds in the three months preceding March 31, 2021.

[51] *The Climate Bonds Initiative is an international organization working to mobilize global capital for climate change solutions. It promotes investment in projects and assets needed for a rapid transition to a low-carbon, climate resilient, and fair economy. Its mission is to help drive down the cost of capital for large-scale climate and infrastructure projects and to support governments seeking increased capital markets investment to meet climate and greenhouse gas emission reduction goals. Climate Bonds conducts market analysis and policy research; undertakes market development activities; advises governments and regulators; and administers a global green bond Standard and Certification scheme. Climate Bonds screens green finance instruments against its global Taxonomy to determine alignment, and shares information about the composition of this markets with partners. Source*: Sustainable Debt – Global State of the Market, 2021, document available at: https://www.climatebonds.net/files/reports/cbi_global_sotm_2021_02h_0.pdf (accessed January 28, 2023).

Amid the COVID-19 challenges, global green bond issuance reached a record high of $269.5 billion in 2020. The cumulative green bond issuance crossed over $1 trillion and stood at $1.05 trillion in 2020, registering an average annual growth rate of 60% since 2015. Globally, green bonds are expected to touch $2.36 trillion by the end of 2023.[52] These data indicate that we are already witnessing an unstoppable 'green finance revolution' which is gaining traction.

One of the reasons why green finance is gaining ground is because it is regarded as a way of meeting the needs of environmentalism and capitalism simultaneously, and of course the improved regulatory framework is also contributing to its success. "The G20 estimates that global investment of USD 90 trillion would be required over the next 15 years to achieve global sustainable development and climate objectives. According to the International Energy Agency, cumulative investment of USD 53 trillion is required by 2035 in the energy sector alone."[53] The record 2021 global sustainable debt issuance volume was reflected on the Luxembourg Green Exchange (LGX),[54] which became host to the largest green bond ever issued, a €12 billion inaugural green bond issued by the European Commission.[55] On the occasion, Mr. Johannes Hahn, the EU's

[52]*Source*: *Climate Bonds Initiative*. Reports available at: https://www.climatebonds.net/resources/reports/2020.

[53]*Source*: KPMG, *Green Financing: A necessary step towards a greener future – Climate change has become the defining political and economic issue and is likely to remain so for many years*, document available at: https://home.kpmg/th/en/home/media/press-releases/2022/04/green-financing.html (accessed January 28, 2023).

[54]The Luxembourg Green Exchange is the world's first and leading platform dedicated exclusively to sustainable finance. *LGX is a meeting place for issuers, asset managers and investors who wish to make their mark on sustainable finance by providing them with an environment for bonds, whether labelled or unlabelled, and funds with clear green, social, sustainable, or ESG characteristics. Entry is restricted to issuers and asset managers that provide full disclosure and fulfill their reporting obligations in the realm of labelled or unlabelled securities; in doing so, we ensure maximum transparency.* All bonds are verified as having clear green, social, sustainable characteristics, while all funds demonstrate a solid ESG, green or social investment policy. *Source*: https://www.bourse.lu/green (accessed January 28, 2023).

[55]In October 2021, the EU successfully brought a historic EUR 12 billion green bond emission to the Luxembourg Stock Exchange (LuxSe). In the presence of EU Commissioner in charge of Budget and Administration, Johannes Hahn, and Prime Minister of Luxembourg, Xavier Bettel, the Luxembourg Stock Exchange (LuxSE) marked the listing

budget and administration commissioner affirmed, "Our future is green and it is extremely important that we seize the opportunity to clearly show to investors that their funds will be used to finance a sustainable European recovery." In total, the EU plans to issue up to €250 billion in green bonds to finance the Next-Generation EU program[56] that aims to drive the block's recovery after the pandemic. According to the Commission, the total amount of the Next-Generation EU green bonds will make the EU the world's largest green bond issuer by far.

2.1.1. *Luxembourg Green Exchange lists half of the world's green bonds*

According to Capital Monitor, Luxembourg Stock Exchange (LuxSE) is the leading *bourse* for green, social, and sustainability (GSS) bonds, listing half the global total.[57]

As of May 31, 2022, the Luxembourg Green Exchange (LGX) encompassed a total of 2,800 sustainable securities, including 1,400 green, social, sustainability, and sustainability-linked bonds from 240 issuers in 50 countries, raising a total of EUR 736 billion for green and social investment and sustainable development across the world. The focus and dedication of the Luxembourg Stock Exchange (also indicated as 'LuxSE') on green instruments was noticed internationally, and in 2022 the LuxSE[58] was granted the 'Stock Exchange of the Year' award by Environmental

of the European Commission's inaugural green bond on Tuesday October 19, 2021. The EUR 12 billion bond is the world's largest green bond issued to date. The green bond is governed by Luxembourg law and displayed on the Luxembourg Green Exchange (LGX), the award-winning platform for sustainable securities. *Source*: https://www.bourse.lu/pr-EU-historic-green-bond-to-LuxSE (accessed January 28, 2023).

[56]The entire Next-Generation EU program amounts to €800 billion, most of which is allocated to the recovery and resilience facility (RRF). Under the rules of the RRF, every member state has to dedicate at least 37% of their national recovery plans to climate-relevant investments and reforms.

[57]See: Luxembourg exchange opposes mandatory green bond standards, Capital Market, article available at: https://capitalmonitor.ai/asset-class/fixed-income/luxembourg-exchange-opposes-mandatory-green-bond-standard/ (accessed January 28, 2023).

[58]To highlight the wider sustainable investment universe beyond labelled bonds and expand sustainable investment opportunities for impact-conscious investors while demand for green bonds exceeds the supply, LuxSE also added a new section featuring Climate-Aligned Issuers, showcasing companies that derive at least 75% of their revenues from

Finance[59] as part of the Sustainable Investment Awards 2022.[60] Julie Becker, CEO of LuxSE, commenting on the award affirmed that the following: "This award is an important recognition of the positive environmental and social impact that the Luxembourg Stock Exchange contributes to by facilitating sustainable investment towards the global goals. Every day, we strive to make sustainable investment more accessible not just to established players in developed markets but also in emerging markets, where the funding is needed the most. This recognition by Environmental Finance further strengthens our conviction that exchanges can and must drive the transition to a more sustainable and inclusive economy."

Since its creation in 2016, Luxembourg Green Exchange (LGX) has continuously grown in importance and has experienced a steep increase in GSS products. Luxembourg Green Exchange has always been at the forefront of sustainable finance and has played a pivotal role when it comes to green, social, and more recently, sustainability-linked bonds.[61]

---

environmentally friendly activities. https://www.bourse.lu/pr-luxse-named-stock-exchange-of-the-year-by-EF (accessed January 28, 2023).

[59]Environmental-Finance.com is an online news and analysis service established in 1999 to report on sustainable investment, green finance, and the people and companies active in environmental markets. https://www.environmental-finance.com/company/about-us.html (accessed January 28, 2023).

[60]The Environmental Finance Sustainable Investment Awards 2022 are global and recognize financial institutions and other companies which strive to incorporate ESG across all asset classes, contribute to making sustainability an integral part of investment decisions, and support projects that mitigate climate change or make a positive impact in the world. *Luxembourg Stock Exchange (LuxSE) and its Luxembourg Green Exchange (LGX) have prioritized sustainability-themed education, improvements in data and promoting gender-themed bonds in recent months. Source*: https://www.environmental-finance.com/content/awards/sustainable-investment-awards-2022/winners/stock-exchange-of-the-year-luxembourg-stock-exchange.html (accessed January 28, 2023).

[61]**Sustainability-Linked Bonds** (SLBs) are the latest addition to the universe of sustainable debt instruments and contribute to financing the issuer's strategy toward achieving predefined sustainability objectives within a set timeline. "Unlike Green, Social and Sustainability Bonds, which are 'Use-of-Proceeds' instruments, SLBs can be used to finance any corporate activity and their proceeds do not need to be allocated to specific projects. Yet, the issuer commits to reaching ambitious, science-based and measurable Sustainability Performance Targets (SPTs) around pre-determined Key Performance Indicators (KPIs), and to having these reviewed by an external party. A lot of the investor scrutiny around these products is placed at the level of the issuer's strategy, namely the

The issuances of these financial products over 2021 have increased dramatically, and this trend is expected to continue. In the following section, we briefly expose the products treated at LGX, highlighting the fact that their number has increased substantially, despite the fact that the debate concerning the European Green Bond Standards[62] – whether it should be mandatory or voluntary – is till animating experts and financial institutions as stated in Section 2.1.3.

2.1.2. *Bond classification and instruments listed at the Luxembourg Green Exchange*

The Luxembourg Green Exchange (LGX) was launched in 2016 as the world's first platform dedicated to green bonds and has since expanded to include social, sustainability, and sustainability-linked bonds, as well as Chinese domestic green bonds; it also includes climate-aligned issuers and Socially Responsible Investing (SRI) funds.[63] Now, LGX has become

---

level of ambition and materiality of its SPTs/KPIs. Another core feature of SLBs is that the financial and/or structural characteristics of the bond can vary depending on whether the issuer achieves the predefined sustainability objectives. SLBs represent a source of financing for companies from any sector that set clear and ambitious science-based targets to become more sustainable." *Source*: Luxembourg Stock Exchange at: https://www.bourse.lu/sustainability-linked-bonds (accessed January 28, 2023).

[62] The European green bond standard (EUGBS) is a voluntary standard to help scale up and raise the environmental ambitions of the green bond market. Establishing this standard was an action in the Commission's 2018 action plan on financing sustainable growth and is part of the European green deal. It is based on the recommendations of the Technical Expert Group on Sustainable Finance (accessed January 28, 2023).

[63] SRI Funds are specialized funds that have an eco-friendly or social responsible investing focus. There are many different SRI funds to choose from, and each has its own unique set of criteria. Some SRI funds only invest in companies that meet specific environmental standards while others only invest in companies that have good social and governance practices. When considering an SRI fund, it is important to research the fund's criteria and performance to make sure it is a good fit for your investment goals. A more precise definition of Socially responsible investing (SRI), also known as social investment, can be described as an investment that is considered socially responsible due to the nature of the business the company conducts. A common theme for socially responsible investments is socially conscious investing. Socially responsible investments can be made into individual companies with good social value, or through a socially conscious mutual fund or exchange-traded fund (ETF). https://www.investopedia.com/terms/s/sri.asp (accessed January 28, 2023).

the world's leading green exchange. Naturally, as a pioneer, having created a dedicated platform with all the necessary services to assist companies, governments, and investors around the world to meet their sustainable development targets has favored the rapid growth and success of the LGX.

Classification of Green Investment Products Listed at LGX

- **Green bonds:** *Green bonds are debt instruments issued to fund projects that have a positive environmental or climate impact. Proceeds from these bonds are typically earmarked for green projects and are backed by the issuer's entire balance sheet. Today, more than 660 green bonds list on our markets. Issuers range from sovereigns, Public International Bodies, agencies and development banks to financial institutions and corporates.*
- **Social bonds:** *A growing number of investors are incorporating ESG principles into their investment strategies. This new development has led to significant interest in social and sustainability bond issuance.*
- **Sustainability bonds:** *Although the sustainability bonds market is still in its infancy, the flexibility offered by these bonds, allowing for a much broader range of projects than just green to be financed, suggests a strong potential for the market to grow. The categories of eligibility for sustainability bonds are a blend of green and social projects, aligned with ICMA's Sustainability Bond Guidelines.*
- **Sustainability-linked bonds:** *The proceeds from this instrument contribute to financing the issuer's strategy towards achieving predefined sustainability objectives within a set timeline. As described in the ICMA's Sustainability-linked Bond Principles, the issuer commits to reaching ambitious science-based and measurable Sustainability Performance Targets (SPTs) around pre-determined KPIs, and to having these reviewed by an external party. Another core feature of SLBs is that the financial and/or structural characteristics of the bond can vary depending on whether the issuer achieves the predefined sustainability objectives. SLBs represent a source of financing for companies from any sector that set clear and ambitious science-based targets to become more sustainable.*

(*Continued*)

(*Continued*)

- **Chinese domestic green bonds:** *Chinese domestic green bonds are bonds traded on the China Interbank Bond Market (CIBM) or listed on one of the Chinese stock exchanges (SSE or SZSE). These bonds comply with national standards. China boasts one of the world's largest bond markets, valued at USD 11 trillion, with green bonds issuances amounting to more than RMB 250 billion. However, the market may appear off-limits to the international investor community due to the difficulties of accessing the right level of information on the traded bonds. By displaying information about Chinese domestic green bonds traded either on Chinese exchanges or on the Chinese Interbank Bond Market (CIBM), LGX is bridging the information gap between Chinese issuers and international investors. Green bonds listed on the Shanghai Stock Exchange can be traded via existing channels. The cooperation with LuxSE focuses on providing exhaustive information in English to offshore investors.*
- **Climate-aligned issuers:** *LGX also offers visibility to labeled or unlabeled debt instruments from climate-aligned-issuers, i.e., public or private companies that derive substantial revenues from climate-aligned activities:*
  - *Fully-aligned issuers: Derive more than 95% of their revenues from climate-aligned activities.*
  - *Strongly-aligned issuers: Derive more than 75% of their revenues from climate-aligned activities.*

  Due to their environmentally friendly lines of business, Climate-Aligned Issuers contribute directly to the global climate goals. Since February 2021, LGX offers such issuers the opportunity to apply for the CAI status and have their debt securities eligible within LGX's Climate-Aligned Issuers section. Screening of such issuers is made possible thanks to LGX partnership with Climate Bonds Initiative.

Source: Luxembourg Green Exchange. https://www.bourse.lu/documents/brochure-LGX-EN.pdf.

2.1.3. *The debate over green bond standard: The position of the CEO of Luxembourg Stock Exchange*

The green bond market has considerably furthered the debate on what is green by facilitating the emergence of both market-based and regulatory definitions of green eligibility and their transparent comparison.[64] The EU in order to foster sustainable finance, and in the ambit of the EU Green Deal and of the European Green Deal Investment Plan, has elaborated a series of reports on green bond standard (GBS) and recommendations for a bond to be classified as 'green.' Thus, to be classified as 'green bond,' issuers would have to apply the definitions as laid out in the GBS. However, the Technical Expert Group (TEG) on sustainable finance suggested that the EU GBS should be a voluntary standard proposed to issuers that wish to align with best practices in the market.[65] The CEO of Luxembourg Stock Exchange, Julie Becker, is also keen to retain the *status quo*, warning that mandating the standard would threaten Europe's leadership in sustainable finance and, by implication, LuxSE's commanding market position. Many issuers could not afford the cost of impact assessment reports and double verification by external bodies registered and supervised by ESMA,[66] she affirmed.[67] It is noteworthy that, speaking

[64]For a detailed analysis: China Green Finance Committee and EIB, White Paper on the Need for a Common Language in green Finance," November 2017. https://www.eib.org/attachments/fi/white-paper-green-finance-common-language-eib-green-finance-committee.pdf (accessed January 28, 2023).

[65]*Source*: Usability Guide – EU Green Bond Standard, EU Technical Expert Group on Sustainable Finance, Proposal for an EU Green Bond Standards, March 2020. This document also contains (Annex 1) the Draft Model of the EU Green Bond Standard, the entire document is available at: https://ec.europa.eu/info/sites/default/files/business_economy_euro/banking_and_finance/documents/200309-sustainable-finance-teg-green-bond-standard-usability-guide_en.pdf (accessed January 28, 2023).

[66]ESMA is the European Securities and Market Authority. ESMA identifies data reporting services providers to be supervised directly. The European Securities and Markets Authority (ESMA) is an independent European Union (EU) Authority that contributes to safeguarding the stability of the EU's financial system by enhancing the protection of investors and promoting stable and orderly financial markets. While ESMA is an independent Authority, it is accountable to European Institutions including the European Parliament, where it appears before the Economic and Monetary Affairs Committee (**ECON**) at their request for formal hearings, the Council of the European Union, and the European Commission. The Authority reports to the institutions on its activities regularly at meetings and also through its Annual Report. *Source*: https://www.esma.europa.eu/about-esma/esma-in-brief (accessed January 28, 2023).

[67]*Source*: *Luxembourg exchange opposes mandatory green bond standards*, CapitalMonitor, article avaiable at: https://capitalmonitor.ai/asset-class/fixed-income/luxembourg-exchange-opposes-mandatory-green-bond-standard/ (accessed January 28, 2023).

at the ICMA conference, Alexandra Jour-Schroeder, deputy director general of the European Commission, said, "This will remain voluntary... there is no obligation in it."[68] On this particular aspect, it is also necessary to evidence that in a November 2021 Opinion,[69] the European Central Bank said that "an immediate shift to a strictly mandatory standard might lead to divestment from non-taxonomy-aligned green bonds and a sudden drop in [EU-]based green bond issuance," but added that it should become mandatory for new issuances "within a reasonable time period."

According to the 'EU Technical Expert Group on Sustainable Finance' the EU GBS aims to represent the best practices of the current green bond market. "Green bonds already promote transparency especially on use of proceeds and through regular reporting on project impact. The EU GBS is designed to further promote this transparency and the market's integrity, especially with respect to concerns relating to possible misrepresentation of projects' green or sustainable aspects, objectives or impact (i.e., 'greenwashing')."[70] This ambition of the EU GBS is to achieve this objective by providing the green bond market stakeholders (issuers, investors, external reviewers/verifiers, public authorities, and civil society) with four key components as shown in Figure 2.

Green bonds play an increasingly important role in financing projects needed for the low-carbon transition, and this fact is evidenced by the booming of these financial instruments, regardless of whether the EU GBS is compulsory or not. In any case, to have in place GBS is useful for both the issuers and the investors of green bonds: (i) Issuers will have a robust tool to demonstrate that they are funding legitimate green projects

---

[68] ICMA Annual General Meeting and Conference 2022. Keynote address: The EU's twin transition agenda – what is in for capital markets? See the speech by **Alexandra Jour-Schroeder**, Deputy Director General, Directorate-General for Financial Stability, Financial Services, and Capital Markets Union, European Commission, available at: https://www.youtube.com/watch?v=D_1nhtnm-B8, see in particular minute 18:28.

[69] *Source*: Opinion of the European Central Bank of 5 November 2021 on a proposal for a regulation on European green bonds (CON/2021/30), Official Journal of the European Union, 19.1.2022, document available at: https://eur-lex.europa.eu/legal-content/EN/TXT/?home=ecb&uri=CELEX:52021AB0030 (accessed January 28, 2023).

[70] *Source*: EU Technical Expert Group on Sustainable Finance, Report on EU Green Bond Standard, Proposal for an EU Green Bond Standard, version June 2019, document available at: https://ec.europa.eu/info/sites/default/files/business_economy_euro/banking_and_finance/documents/190618-sustainable-finance-teg-report-green-bond-standard_en.pdf (accessed January 28, 2023).

Key Requirements under the Proposed Framework for EU Green Bond Standards (GBS)

- **Taxonomy alignment:** *The funds raised by the bond should be allocated fully to projects that are aligned with the EU taxonomy*
- **Transparency:** *Full transparency on how the bond proceeds are allocated through detailed reporting requirements*
- **External review:** *All European green bonds must be checked by an external reviewer to ensure compliance with the Regulation and taxonomy alignment of the funded projects*
- **Supervision by the European Securities Markets Authority (ESMA) of reviewers:** *External reviewers providing services to issuers of European green bonds must be registered with and supervised by the ESMA. This will ensure the quality of their services and the reliability of their reviews to protect investors and ensure market integrity*

Source: European Commission: European green bond standard, https://ec.europa.eu/info/business-economy-euro/banking-and-finance/sustainable-finance/european-green-bond-standard_en.

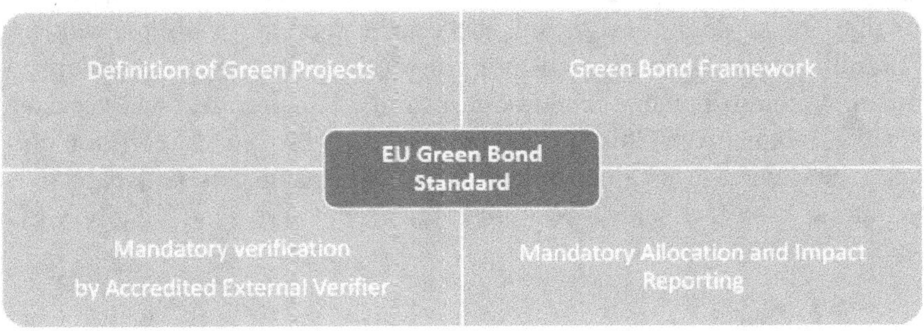

Figure 2: EU Green Bond: Elements of Transparency

Source: EU Technical Expert Group on Sustainable Finance, Report on EU Green Bond Standard.

aligned with the EU taxonomy. (ii) Investors buying the bonds will be able to more easily assess, compare, and trust that their investments are sustainable, thereby reducing the risks posed by greenwashing. Then, the EU GBS will be open to any issuer of green bonds, including companies, public authorities, and issuers located outside of the EU, and this will further foster their issuance favoring new records (see Section 2.2).

2.2. *Green bonds, sustainability-linked bonds, and social bonds increased to $1.2 trillion (March 2022) and the trend is set to continue*

The growth of green, social, and sustainability-linked (GSS) bonds is unstoppable: In the EU, the market for GSS debt stood at €1.2 trillion at the end of the first quarter (2022), which means an increase of 50% year on year, according to Verena Ross, chair of the European Securities Markets Authority (ESMA), at the International Capital Market Association (ICMA) conference in June 2022.[71] Moreover, the assets managed by EU-domiciled ESG funds grew by 20% over the same period, to €2.1 trillion.[72] These figures indicate significant market growth for these products. A report by the certification body Climate Bonds Initiative[73] revealed that overall issuance of sustainable debt, which includes green bonds, social bonds, and sustainability-linked bonds, rose nearly 60% to $1.1 trillion in 2021 – a record performance that Climate Bonds Initiative believes shows the sector is beginning to gain serious traction (Figure 3).

It is worth reporting that there was strong growth in green bond issuance from both financial and non-financial corporates, with these two issuer types together representing 44% of cumulative green bond volume. Among financial corporates, China Development Bank was responsible for the largest single deal during the year, valued at $6 billion, while a $2.5 billion green bond issued by Ford Motor Company was the largest issued by a non-financial institution. A third of total green bond issuance over 2021 came from China (17%) and Germany (16%). "The trillion dollars issued across sustainable markets in 2021 suggests that capital is beginning to shift at scale – but more is needed," says Sean Kidney, CEO

[71] ICMA Annual General Meeting and Conference 2022. Keynote address: Greening the financial markets: Challenges and opportunities at the current juncture. See the speech by **Verena Ross**, Chair, European Securities and Market Authority, see her speech at: https://www.youtube.com/watch?v=Ye3r6R4_ck0 (accessed January 28, 2023).

[72] ESMA calculation based on data provided by Climate Bonds Initiative, Refinitiv EIKON and Morningstar.

[73] Sustainable Debt – Global State of the Market 2021, by Climate Bonds Initiative, document available at: https://www.climatebonds.net/files/reports/cbi_global_sotm_2021_02h_0.pdf (accessed January 28, 2023).

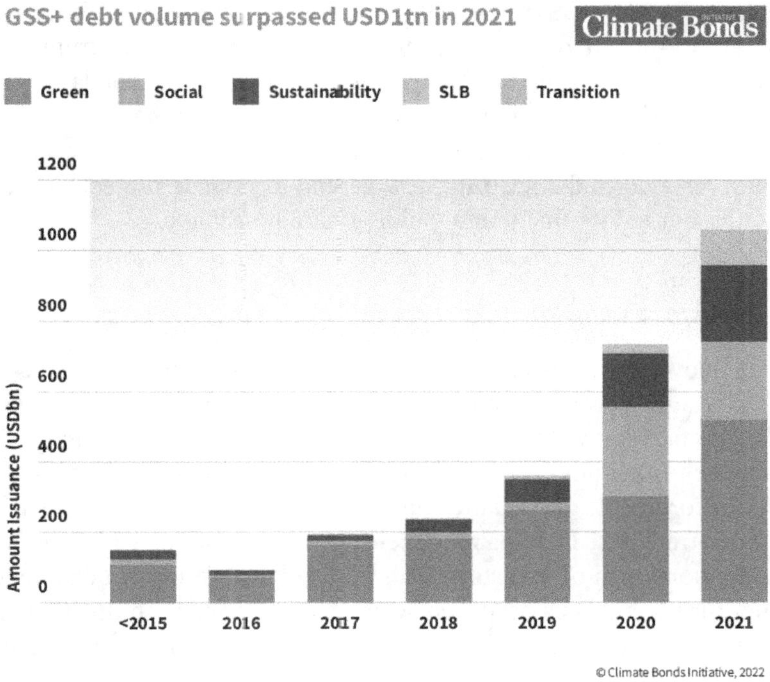

Figure 3: (Color online) Volume of Green Bonds and Other Products (2015–2021)
Source: Climate Bonds Initiative, Sustainable Debt – Global State of the Market 2021.

of Climate Bonds Initiative. "This year we hope to see a trillion raised in green bonds alone, rising to \$5trn by 2025."[74]

The certainty that this trend is set to continue resides in the fact that, beside green bonds, the market for social bonds and sustainability-linked bonds is at the embryonic stage, which is where green bonds were placed in 2007, as stated by **Leslie Maasdorp**, Vice President and Chief Financial Officer, New Development Bank, at the ICMA annual meeting.[75] Moreover, financial institutions and regulators can play a great role

[74] *Source*: The Global Treasurer, *Green bond issuance soars as sustainable debt tops \$1trn in 2021*, by Kam Patel, May 6, 2022, article available at: https://www.theglobaltreasurer.com/2022/05/06/green-bond-issuance-soars-as-sustainable-debt-tops-1trn-in-2021/ (accessed January 28, 2023).

[75] ICMA Annual General Meeting and Conference 2022. Keynote address: Key trends and challenges facing development finance on the road to Net Zero. See the speech by

in magnifying the scope and size of that new market (i.e., social and sustainability-linked bonds). It is foreseen that financial instruments in the sustainability space, including, for example, 'blue bonds' – is an instrument to finance marine and ocean-based projects that have positive environmental, economic, and climate benefits[76] – will surge in the near future to respond to the need for new capital to finance projects aimed at protecting our environment and tackling climate change.

2.3. *Investors seem to start responding to sustainability*

As data show, investors are keen to invest in 'sustainability'[77] given the impressive growth of green, social, and sustainability-linked (GSS) bonds. The fact that we cannot ignore transition and climate change favors investment in this ambit. It is evident that investors are now evaluating issuers according to the quality and clarity of their net-zero emissions transition strategies. This is a new scenario for institutions which are managing the portfolios of investors. This is also because institutions have to conduct further analysis on which securities will cope with this transition and which will not, and this is a challenging task for fund managers,

---

Leslie Maasdorp, Vice President and Chief Financial Officer, New Development Bank, see his speech at: https://www.youtube.com/watch?v=9NNjRaVKpvQ, see minute 7:32 (accessed January 28, 2023).

[76]The blue bond is inspired by the green bond concept, which people are more familiar with. The World Bank helped the government of Seychelles issue the world's first Blue Bond (2018). On October 29, 2018, the Government of Seychelles announced the issuance of the world's first sovereign Blue Bond.

The proceeds from the bond will help pay for marine protection, fishery management and other projects to safeguard the ocean economy that the country depends on. Grants and loans for the individual projects will be channeled through the Blue Grants Fund and Blue Investment Fund, managed respectively by the Seychelles' Conservation and Climate Adaptation Trust (SeyCCAT) and the Development Bank of Seychelles (DBS). https://thedocs.worldbank.org/en/doc/242151559930961454-0340022019/original/CasestudyBlueBondSeychellesfinal6.7.2019.pdf (accessed January 28, 2023).

[77]Sustainable investing, often also referred to as responsible investment, is an approach to investing that aims to incorporate environmental, social and governance (ESG) factors into investment decisions, so as to better manage risk and generate sustainable, long-term returns. Reading suggestion: Impact investments: A call for (re)orientation, article available at: https://link.springer.com/article/10.1007/s43546-020-00033-6 (accessed January 28, 2023).

wealth managers, and in general for professional operators considering the complexity of this environment, starting from taxonomy aspects (which is still fragmented) and standards though they already exist as they are not applied uniformly.

Undeniably, the number of companies now committed to net-zero impact on the environment is increasing and this offers the investors a growing number of opportunities; however, the issue of debt instruments that meet certain criteria is not always straightforward and sometimes lack of transparency could influence the issuance process. This is why financial institutions all around the world are working on these themes, trying to create a more comprehensive and inclusive framework (see taxonomy and GBS).

There is no doubt that investors and financial operators in general are more sensitive to the many emergencies of our time, and thus are channeling resources toward new instruments which can positively impact climate, environment, and society. This is the reason why the financial world (institutions, investors and operators) will inevitably favor standardization and further diversification (see, for example, the 'blue bonds') with the consequence of raising more capitals needed to finance the green transition. A new flow of capital is therefore inevitable and it will further foster green and sustainable finance. The real challenge is to work on standardization and agree on a common taxonomy to favor the use of all these new financial instruments. Due to its utility for the environment, climate, and society, sustainable and green finance will grow further toward the achievement of the SDGs.

As affirmed by **Christian Hyldahl**, Head of Continental Europe, BlackRock, at the ICMA annual meeting,[78] these themes are now becoming central to investor decisions, together with a particular attention to technology and those companies working on new solutions and applications to reduce carbon emissions, thus helping the green transition. However, as evidenced in his speech, "helping allocating resources and investing in these new instruments it is fundamental getting data and getting standardized and governments and institutions should contribute in instilling more confidence among investors improving these aspects."

[78]Annual General Meeting and Conference 2022. Keynote address: Asset owners: responding to sustainability and technology revolutions. See the speech by Christian Hyldahl, Head of Continental Europe, BlackRock, https://www.youtube.com/watch?v=sK--hi40wyE (accessed January 28, 2023).

3. Transition toward a Green Economy and the Role of Green Finance: Final Notes

Finance and sustainable economy have never been so interrelated. Transforming our economy into a carbon-neutral economy has become a priority, especially if we want to avoid catastrophic consequences for the entire world, but this transformation requires a large amount of investment especially to enable a green and low-carbon transition. However, tackling climate change is only one of the challenges; in fact, meeting the collective goals under the Paris Agreement and the 2030 Agenda of the United Nations will require an economy-wide transformation at the global level and a revision of our priorities with a new focus on the preservation of our environment. We are talking about a new version, 'an update' of our society, which can only be supported and achieved by significant financial flow from both the public and private sectors.

As shown in the previous sections, this transition has already begun, and in order to accompany this green transformation, institutions and financial markets have started drafting and adopting dedicated policies, shaping new regulatory frameworks, and creating new instruments which shall respond not only to the financial needs of a changing economy but also to the expectations of a growing number of investors focusing on real-world changes in terms of solving social challenges and/or mitigating ecological degradation. However, while the share of financial assets contributing to sustainability has increased, as data show, these investments still represent a tiny portion of global financial assets. Thus, there is the necessity to scale up sustainable and green finance and further align financial flows to the Sustainable Development Goals (SDGs) and the Paris Agreement targets; but in order to achieve this target, more work needs to be done, especially in the ambit of standardization and taxonomy, two areas of fundamental importance for this emerging green market, and thus for sustainable finance to gain further traction. This will further help mobilize financial resources to where they are most needed. A good example is the creation of *ad hoc* instruments such as the 'blue bonds'[79] used, in particular, to protect the oceans and marine species.

---

[79]According to the OECD, the blue economy will be worth US$3 trillion a year by 2030 globally, and therefore blue bond issuance is expected to grow in the coming years. https://www.oecd.org/sti/inno/the-ocean-economy-in-2030-9789264251724-en.htm (accessed January 28, 2023).

It is evident that with the evolving of European initiatives and the regulatory framework on sustainable finance, including the upcoming EU Green Bond Standard (EU GBS), Europe is the principal player in the ambit of sustainable finance worldwide, and it will serve as an example for other economies. According to EU inputs, leading international standards for green, social, sustainability, and sustainability-linked bonds recommend that issuers of such bonds undergo an external review of their bond framework and their allocation report. As evidenced, the EU GBS proposes to make the pre- and post-issuance external review mandatory, and furthermore introduces the idea of a market-based registration scheme for external verifiers. This should favor the expansion of these new financial instruments and increase investors' confidence; in fact, it will have more information about the use of proceeds of these products by the end users. There is no doubt about the necessity to raise more capital to tackle climate change and channel resources to transit our economy toward a more sustainable and green modality. As we have just entered the "make or break decade for climate action," as stated by European Commission President Ursula von der Leyen, we need to make finance part of the solution to our global challenges and contribute to making finance sustainable by default.[80]

[80] Speech by President Von Der Leyen at the High-level Conference "Investing in climate action: The Make-or-Break Decade," visit: https://www.pubaffairsbruxelles.eu/eu-institution-news/speech-by-president-von-der-leyen-at-the-high-level-conference-investing-in-climate-action-the-make-or-break-decade/ (accessed January 28, 2023).

Chapter 6

Investment Opportunities Deriving from the Transition toward a Green, Nature-Positive Economy

This chapter intends to explain the investment opportunities from the transition to a green, nature-positive economy, following the directions expressed in the Paris Convention and by the UN's Agenda for sustainable development. It is evident that this transition has become a priority for the entire global community, and its success depends on the development of green industries and the transformation, and reduced importance, of many traditional industries responsible for a majority of CO_2 emissions. Key priorities include an increase of clean energy and thus of the use of renewable sources, industrial energy conservation, improvement of energy efficiency, a further reduction of the impact of the transportation sector with an increase of bio/sustainable fuels, hydrogen usage and electrification of vehicles, and naturally more concrete actions to protect our environment and biodiversity. Nations need to work together in order to achieve these goals and promote a nature-positive transition to avoid catastrophic consequences linked to climate change. There is no doubt that international tensions are complicating the already dramatic situation; however, there is no other choice but to solve frictions and differences peacefully in order to tackle this global threat and shape a sustainable economy and a sharable future. Protection of our environment must become a priority. Only a world that is peaceful and widespread awareness of climate change will grant us a shared future with sustainable development.

This green transition will require enormous efforts in terms of new investments which will contribute to shaping a nature-positive economy paying particular attention to our environment and preserving our resources. Our future depends on how wisely the global community will be able to develop itself in harmony with nature. *While the estimates of the funding requirements differ, they are all in the trillions. The G20 estimates that global investment of USD 90 trillion would be required over the next 15 years to achieve global sustainable development and climate objectives. According to the International Energy Agency, cumulative investment of USD 53 trillion is required by 2035 in the energy sector alone. Also, it is now accepted that to enable a transition to a zero-carbon future, a mix of public and private sector capital will be required, and that public sector money alone cannot cover this cost.*[1] This evidences the fact that green finance will play a pivotal role in finding the necessary resources to accompany this green transition.

1. The Transition toward a Green, Nature-Positive Economy Offers Opportunities for Investment in Different Sectors

Climate change, while it is perceived as a major risk or threat for the entire global community, if not promptly and adequately addressed with coordinated actions, also represents a business opportunity. Going green for the global economy is a necessary path, and this low-carbon transition offers opportunities for innovation, efficiency, and growth which will accompany the shaping of sustainable development that extends beyond high-carbon industries, like energy and transportation, to all other sectors.

As we have seen in the previous chapter, the rapid growth in green lending and sustainable finance in general — where use of proceeds is tied to specific low-carbon projects — provides new opportunities to access resources needed for this green transition which can be used in a variety of sectors. As evidenced in this book, the 'final destination' is a zero-emission economy, and although the global community is not aligned on the year in which to reach this goal (2050 for the EU and USA and 2060 for China), this objective is inescapable. This is not only because climate change will stop only once net global emissions have reached zero but

---

[1] See https://home.kpmg/th/en/home/media/press-releases/2022/04/green-financing.html (accessed January 28, 2023).

also because it is necessary to change our development mode if we want to preserve this world for future generations. Green transition has a long way to go and a lot more value to create. In the following sections, we have indicated where opportunities are arising, and naturally the energy sector is one of the most important sectors. However, transiting toward a green economy and sustainable development means investing in nature and preserving resources.

1.1. *The energy sector: Opportunities created by renewables*

The energy sector needs to be completely revolutionized and its impact on the environment and climate change drastically reduced. Thus, the development and use of emerging technologies for exploiting renewable sources of energy, not only wind and solar but also all other forms of renewables, have a fundamental role to play in green transition. Moreover, all these clean sources will be the center of attention and will be inundated by new flows of capital. Also, battery storage, energy efficiency, and carbon capture and storage will absorb investments, thereby changing the structure of the energy sector and affecting the competitiveness of all the businesses involved. The production and distribution costs of energy derived from these sources are going to decrease, favoring their use and thus contributing to addressing this climate emergency. Reducing energy-related CO_2 emissions and rapidly shifting toward cleaner renewable forms of energy are critical to reaching climate goals as per the Paris Agreement. A variety of renewable sources are available, and their contribution is fundamental for this green transition. Implementing and further expanding the use of these resources will also create new investment opportunities as evidenced in the following sections.

1.1.1. *Solar energy: Falling costs unleash its potential and the policies of the three major economies (informative box)*

Scaling solar energy has become a priority to quickly and affordably meet the growing energy needs not only of developing countries but also of the most advanced economies which must become an example for the former by implementing and expanding the use of this renewable source. In particular, solar energy has become extremely attractive: photovoltaic technology costs have fallen dramatically, and solar PV can now deliver power less expensively and with more long-term price certainty than coal-fired power. These circumstances are creating opportunities for producers of PV panels to expand their production, and for final users. IRENA in one of its reports estimates that by 2050 solar PV would represent the second largest power generation source, just behind wind power, and lead the way for the transformation of the global electricity sector. According to its data, solar PV would generate 25% of the total electricity needs of the world, becoming one of the prominent sources by 2050.[2] According to IRENA, in annual growth terms, an almost threefold rise in yearly solar PV capacity additions is needed by 2030 and a fourfold rise by 2050, compared to current levels.[3]

It must be underlined that solar panels have improved substantially in their efficiency and power output over the last few decades. According to the report by IRENA (data refer to 2018), the efficiency of multi-crystalline PV reached 17%, while that of mono-crystalline PV reached 18%. This positive trend is expected to continue through to 2030. Thus, further investments in PV technology are expected to ameliorate performances and this will also contribute to improving the profitability for both producers and investors. Furthermore, "*the solar PV industry would employ more than 18 million people by 2050, five times more than the 2018 jobs total of 3.6 million. To maximize outcomes of the energy transition, however, a holistic policy framework is needed. Deployment policies will need to co-ordinate and harmonize with integration and enabling policies.*"[4] Major economies already have in place dedicated policies to favor renewables, and in particular solar energy seems to be at the center of their interests as evidenced in the following informative box.

---

[2]IRENA (2019), *Future of Solar Photovoltaic: Deployment, investment, technology, grid integration and socio-economic aspects*, IRENA — International Renewable Energy Agency, document available at: Future of Solar Photovoltaic — A Global Energy Transformation paper (irena.org) (accessed January 28, 2023).

[3]Thanks to its modular and distributed nature, solar PV technology is being adapted to a wide range of off-grid applications and to local conditions. In the last decade (2008–2018), the globally installed capacity of off-grid solar PV has grown more than tenfold, from roughly 0.25 GW in 2008, to almost 3 GW in 2018. Off-grid solar PV is a key technology for achieving full energy access and achieving the Sustainable Development Goals. *Ibid.*

[4]*Source*: IRENA (2019), *Future of Solar Photovoltaic: Deployment, Investment, Technology, Grid Integration and Socio-Economic Aspects*, IRENA.

Solar Energy: Policies of the Three Major Economies

The European Union and its solar energy strategy: *In May 2022 the EU Commission has adopted the 'EU Solar Energy Strategy'*[5] *which aims to bring online over 320 GW of solar photovoltaic by 2025 (more than doubling compared to 2020) and almost 600 GW by 2030.*

The strategy takes a comprehensive approach to the solar energy sector, covering all technologies and demand. It identifies the barriers that are still preventing solar energy from fully playing its role in the energy transition and proposes measures to lift them. In particular, the strategy proposes three initiatives:

- **A European Solar Rooftops Initiative** to accelerate the deployment of solar energy in buildings. The initiative includes a proposal to gradually introduce an obligation to install solar energy in different types of buildings over the next years.
- **An EU large-scale skills partnership** covering the renewable energy sector at large.
- **An EU Solar PV Industry Alliance**, a forum for the sector's stakeholders to collaborate towards increased production in the EU.

The EU has since long been a front-runner in the spread of solar energy. The accelerated deployment of solar energy contributes to reducing the EU's dependence on imported fossil fuels. The cost of solar power has decreased by 82% over the last decade, turning it into one of the most competitive source of electricity in the EU.

The EU Commission analysis indicates that additional investments in solar PVs under REPowerEU would amount to EUR 26 billion between now and 2027.

The US solar industrial strategy: *The United States has successfully deployed solar energy and the Biden Administration has made clean energy a priority and is investing heavily in solar research & development, however it does not exist a dedicated solar strategy. The Biden*

(*Continued*)

[5] *Source*: European Commission, *EU Solar Energy Strategy*, COM(2022) 221 final, document available at: EUR-Lex — 52022DC0221 — EN — EUR-Lex (europa.eu) The European Green Deal and the REPowerEU plan in May 2022 have turned solar energy into a building block of the EU's transition towards clean energy.

(*Continued*)

Administration see solar energy as a priority for meeting its ambitious climate targets.

The U.S. Department of Energy (DOE) released a Study on September 2021[6] *detailing the significant role solar will play in decarbonizing the nation's power grid. The study shows that United States can source 40% of the nation's electricity supply by 2035 and 45% by 2050 with solar energy, drive deep decarbonization of the grid, and employ as much as 1.5 million people — without raising electricity prices.*

The study lays out the blueprint for achieving this milestone, which requires strong decarbonization polices coupled with a massive deployment of renewable energy sources, large-scale electrification, and grid modernization. The study's key findings include:

- **A clean grid requires massive, equitable deployment of diverse, sustainable energy sources** — The U.S. must install an average of 30 GW of solar capacity per year between now and 2025 and 60 GW per year from 2025–2030. The study's modeling further shows the remainder of a carbon-free grid largely supplied by wind (36%), nuclear (11–13%), hydroelectric (5–6%) and biopower/geothermal (1%).
- **New tools that increase grid flexibility, like storage and advanced inverters, as well as transmission expansion, will help to move solar energy to all pockets of America** — Wind and solar combined will provide 75% of electricity by 2035 and 90% by 2050, transforming the electricity system. The deployment of storage enables more flexibility and resilience, growing from 30 GW to nearly 400 GW in 2035 and 1,700 GW in 2050. Advanced tools like grid-forming inverters, forecasting, and microgrids will play a role in maintaining the reliability and performance a renewable-dominant grid.
- **Supportive decarbonization policies and advanced technologies are needed to further reduce the cost of solar energy** — Without some combination of limits on carbon emissions and mechanisms to

[6]Solar Futures Study, U.S. Department of Energy — Office of Energy Efficiency & Renewable Energy, September 2021, document available at: https://www.energy.gov/sites/default/files/2021-09/Solar%20Futures%20Study.pdf (accessed January 28, 2023). The Solar Futures Study is the most comprehensive review to date of the potential role of solar in decarbonizing the U.S. electricity grid and broader energy system. The study was initiated by the U.S. Department of Energy's Solar Energy Technologies Office and led by the National Renewable Energy Laboratory.

(*Continued*)

incentivize clean energy, the U.S. cannot fully decarbonize the grid — models show that grid emissions fall only 60% without policy. Continued technological advances that lower the cost of solar energy are also necessary to enable widespread solar deployment.

China solar strategy: China released its 14th five-year plan (FYP) for renewable energy on 1 June 2021, outlining the country's renewable energy roadmap for the five years 2021–2025.

This is the first sub-sector plan issued since the 14FYP for a modern energy system, published earlier this year. Among all the documents that China has issued under the so-called ***"1+N" policy framework for enforcing its climate pledges****, the energy plan and its sub-sector plan on renewable energy might be the most fundamental to China's decarbonisation.*

The 14th FYP for renewable energy sticks with the previously announced vision of ***25% of China's energy coming from non-fossil sources by 2030****. In order to increase the share from 15.9% in 2020 to 20% by 2025, the plan lays out a framework with a series of targets and actions. Achieving these goals is expected to ensure China's carbon dioxide (CO_2) emissions peak before 2030.*[7]

Concerning solar power alone in June 2022 China reached 340 GW capacity up 25,8% compared to 2021 (affirmed Wang Bohua, Honorary Chairman of China Photovoltaic Industry association).[8]

China is aiming to bring total wind and solar capacity to 1,200 GW by the end of the decade, up from 635 GW at the end of last year, and is currently developing large-scale renewable energy bases in desert regions.

(*Continued*)

[7] *Source*: Energypost.eu, *Can China's 14th FYP for Renewable Energy Deliver an Early Emissions Peak before 2030?* Article available at: https://energypost.eu/can-chinas-14th-5-year-plan-for-renewable-energy-deliver-an-early-emissions-peak-before-2030/ (accessed January 28, 2023).

[8] *Source*: *The Economic Times*, China solar power installations more than double in first half, July 21, 2022, article available at: https://energy.economictimes.indiatimes.com/news/renewable/china-solar-power-installations-more-than-double-in-first-half/93020634?redirect=1 (accessed January 28, 2023).

(Continued)

***In 2021, China's investment in clean energy took up more than 30% of the total global investment**, according to the International Energy Agency, and this trend will continue.*[9]

***Renewable energy investment has been an important economic engine in China** and will play an even more significant role in boosting the economy than before, at a time when China faces the economic impact of COVID-19 and uncertainties caused by the Ukraine crisis.*

It is evident that solar power represents an important part of the energy strategies of major economies and it will be further expanded to meet the demand combined with other forms of renewables. China is the leading solar PV market, followed by the European Union and the USA, but other emerging economies in South America, Africa, Asia, and Oceania are now equipping themselves with more solar PV capabilities. The projections by IRENA confirm massive investments in the sector, including in the technologies enabling and enhancing solar power. Producers of PV panels and related products will surely experience a growth of business.

A variety of technologies are expected to continue to characterize the PV technology portfolio. First-generation technologies, which have been evolving along the whole PV value chain, still account for a majority of the global annual production, but advancements in research and technology will allow the appearance of new products in solar energy generation, catalyzing new investments (Figure 1).[10]

---

[9] *Source*: World Energy Investment 2022, document available at: https://iea.blob.core.windows.net/assets/db74ebb7-272f-4613-bdbd-a2e0922449e7/WorldEnergyInvestment2022.pdf (accessed January 28, 2023).

[10] *Tandem solar cells are stacks of individual cells, one on top of the other, that each selectively convert a specific band of light into electrical energy, leaving the remaining light to be absorbed and converted to electricity in the cell below. Emerging PV technologies comprise several types of tandem cells that can be grouped mainly depending on materials used (e.g., organic, inorganic, hybrid) as well as on the kind of connection used. The tandem cell approach has been used to fabricate the world's most efficient solar cells that can convert 46% of sunlight into electricity. Unfortunately, these devices use very expensive material and fabrication processes, and still cannot break through the market. Thin film technologies are often referred to as second-generation solar PV. The semiconducting*

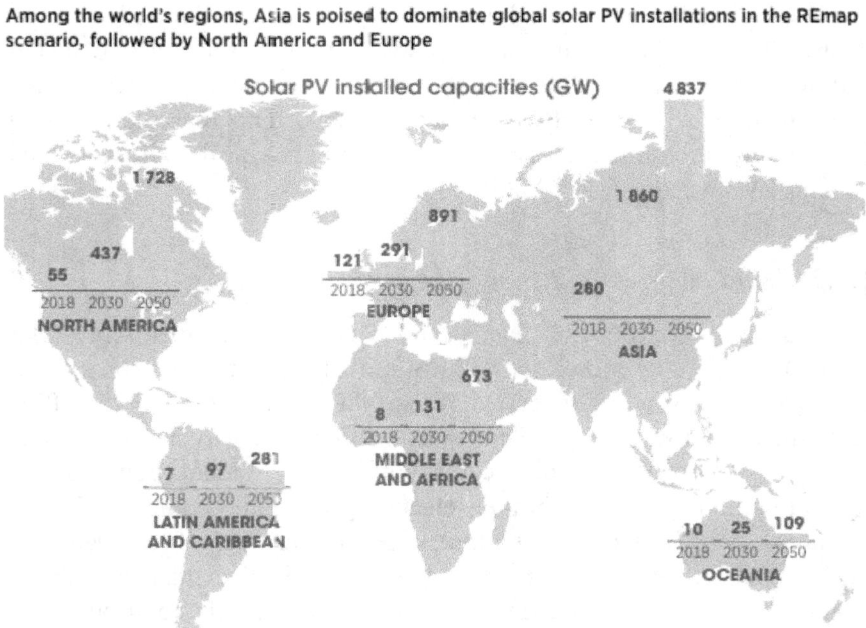

Figure 1: World-wide solar PV installed capacities

Source: IRENA.

---

materials used to produce thin-film cells are only a few micrometers thick (IRENA, 2016). These technologies generally include two main families: (1) silicon-based thin film (amorphous [a-Si] and micromorph silicon [a-Si/c-Si]; and (2) non-silicon based (perovskites, cadmium telluride [CdTe] and copper-indium-galliumdiselenide [CIGS]). These technologies can be cheaper to produce, as such they are being deployed on a commercial scale, but they have historically had lower efficiency levels. Non-silicon based thin-film technologies: Perovskites Currently most solar cells are made from silicon; however, an area to watch is the development of new materials for solar cells. In particular, one of the most promising material is perovskites, a type of mineral very good at absorbing light. The first perovskite PV devices in 2009 converted just 3.8% of the energy contained in sunlight into electricity. However, because crystals are very easy to make in the lab, their performance was quickly improved and by 2018 their efficiency had soared to 24.2%, set by researchers in the United States and the Republic of Korea — close to silicon's lab record of 26.7%. However, perovskite efficiency records have only been set on tiny samples. For more info, see Future of Solar Photovoltaic — Deployment, investment, technology, grid integration and socio-economic aspects by IRENA, pp. 42–43, document available at: *https://irena.org/-/media/Files/IRENA/Agency/Publication/2019/Nov/IRENA_Future_of_Solar_PV_2019.pdf* (accessed January 28, 2023).

Deploying a total installed capacity of more than 8,000 GW of solar PV by 2050 would necessitate a cumulative investment of nearly USD 6.4 trillion from now until 2050. This would translate into an annual average investment of USD 192 billion per year till 2050. This represents scaling up of annual investment by around 68% from now until 2050 compared to solar PV investment in 2018.[11]

1.1.2. *Wind energy and its growing importance*

Wind generation rose 14% last year (2021), and together with solar (+23%) it makes up more than 10% of global electricity generation. All clean electricity sources generated 38% of the world's electricity in 2021, more than coal (36%).[12] Wind and solar will lead the way in the transformation of the global electricity sector. With fifty individual countries now generating more than 10% of their electricity from these quick-to-deploy resources, and three countries already generating over 40%, (Denmark 52%, Luxembourg 43%, and Uruguay 47%), it is clear that these technologies are delivering and revealing their indispensable contribution to green transition. However, it is also necessary to state that "the Middle East and Africa had the fewest countries reach a landmark tenth of wind and solar. Saudi Arabia's electricity is still less than 1% wind and solar, and the next two hosts of UN climate summits — Egypt (2022) and the UAE — have only 3%. The countries which have transformed their electricity system the fastest since the pandemic were the Netherlands, Australia and Vietnam. From 2019 to 2021, they switched over 8% of their total electricity demand to wind and solar."[13]

---

[11] IRENA (2019), *Future of Solar Photovoltaic: Deployment, investment, technology, grid integration and socio-economic aspects*, IRENA. At the regional level, the major share of global investment would shift to Asia, with USD 113 billion per year from now until 2050, and China and India at the forefront accounting for approximately 57% and 18% of total annual investment, respectively. Asia is followed by North America at USD 37 billion per year and then Europe at USD 19 billion per year.

[12] *Source*: EMBER, Global Electricity Review 2022, March 2022, article available at: https://ember-climate.org/insights/research/global-electricity-review-2022/ (accessed January 28, 2023).

[13] See report by EMBER available at: https://ember-climate.org/app/uploads/2022/03/Report-GER22.pdf (accessed January 28, 2023).

It is worth noting that wind power is the second most important clean source of energy and is growing fast both in advanced economies and emerging markets. Projections by IRENA show that investments in this sector (both onshore and offshore) are destined to grow substantially (Figures 2 and 3).

Continued improvements in manufacturing and turbine design are improving the capacity of wind turbines of the new generation. Investments thus will be directed toward the deployment of new onshore and offshore wind farms. "*Developments in blade, drivetrain and control technologies, in particular, would enable the development of larger, more reliable turbines with higher capacity ratings. Turbine sizes have increased rapidly in recent decades. By 2018, offshore wind turbines with an average rated capacity of 5.5 MW with rotor diameters of around 150 meters were being deployed (IRENA, 2019). Offshore wind farms commissioned in Europe in 2018 used turbines of between 3.5 MW and 8.8 MW capacity (WindEurope, 2019). MHI Vestas' turbines of up to 10 MW capacity and 164-metre diameter blades have been commercially available since 2018 (MHI Vestas, 2018). These technology improvements are set to continue beyond 2022, with the largest turbine being developed by*

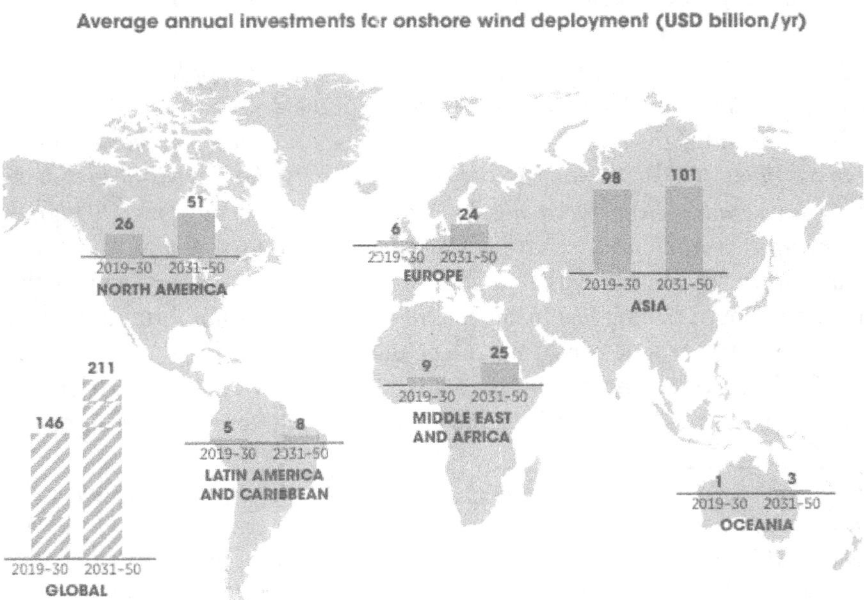

Figure 2: Average investments for onshore wind deployment

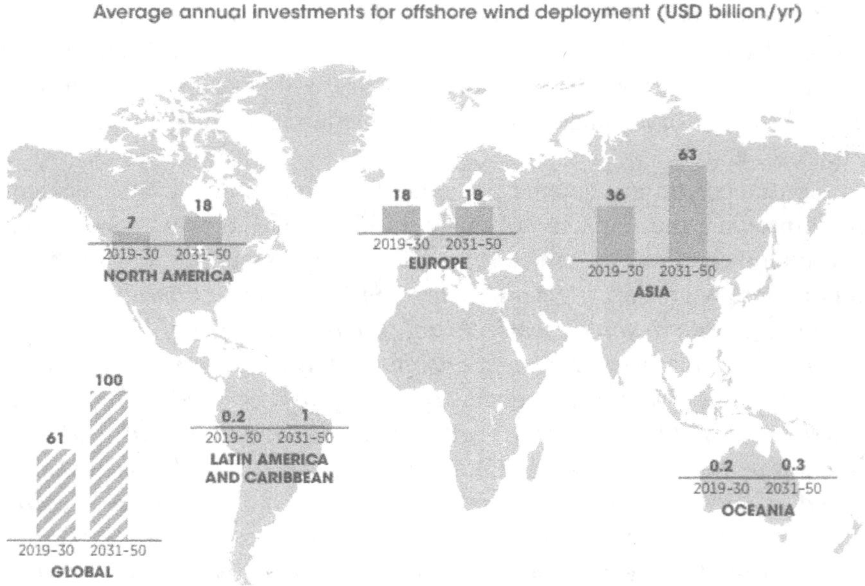

Figure 3: Average annual investments for offshore wind deployment

Source: *Future of Wind — Deployment, investment, technology, grid integration and socio-economic aspects*, report by International Renewable Energy Agency (IRENA), October 2019.

GE: the 12 MW Haliade-X turbine for offshore applications, with 107-metre-long blades resulting in blade diameters of over 200 meters (GE Renewable Energy, 2018). These turbines are likely to have higher capital costs (CAPEX) per MW of rated capacity than existing turbines, but they would allow for a much lower cost of energy through higher energy production and lower CAPEX per MW for the foundations and installation."[14] This proves that investments in wind energy and in the development of the biggest turbines will certainly continue, stimulating an increase in the production of this clean energy.

Globally, wind energy has generated 6.6% of the world's electricity in 2021, up from 3.5% in 2015, when the Paris Agreement was signed,[15]

[14]*Source*: *Future of Wind — Deployment, Investment, Technology, Grid Integration and Socio-Economic Aspects*, report by International Renewable Energy Agency (IRENA), October 2019, document available at: https://www.irena.org/-/media/files/irena/agency/publication/2019/oct/irena_future_of_wind_2019.pdf (accessed January 28, 2023).

[15]Report by EMBER available at: https://ember-climate.org/app/uploads/2022/03/Report-GER22.pdf (accessed October 28, 2022).

which is a substantial increase. However, wind generation needs to rise fourfold by 2030, taking it from 7% of global electricity in 2021 to 21% by 2030 to advance toward the goal of zero emissions. This means maintaining year-on-year growth of 18%, whereas growth in 2021 was 14% and averaged 15% over the last ten years. It is evident that the energy policies adopted by the major economies and emerging markets are of paramount importance in stimulating the implementation of both onshore and offshore wind farms. In the following text box, we have summarized the initiatives of the most important economies, which will be replicated by the rest of the emerging economies to meet the target of net-zero emissions by 2050, integrating wind energy into the mix of all the other renewables.

Wind Energy: Policies of the Three Major Economies

The European Union and its wind energy strategy: *The EU has helped develop wind power thanks to ambitious policies and investments. European companies have invaluable experience by being first movers — the first offshore wind farm was installed in Denmark in 1991. With already around 16 GW of grid-connected capacity, the EU is leading in offshore wind deployment, and it is currently a global leader in the manufacturing of key wind turbine components, as well as in the foundations and cables industry: almost half of the active companies in the wind sector (onshore and offshore) are headquartered in the EU.*

In November 2020, the Commission published a new ***'EU strategy on offshore renewable energy'*** *under the European Green Deal* (see Chapter 3). *The strategy aims to push for the step-change needed to have an installed capacity of at least 60 GW of offshore wind and at least 1 GW of ocean energy by 2030, with a view to reach 300 GW, 10 and 40 GW of installed capacity, respectively, by 2050. To maximize its impact the EU strategy goes beyond a narrow definition of the factors of energy production and addresses broader issues, such as: (i) Access to sea-space; (ii) Industrial and employment dimension; (iii) Regional and international cooperation; (iv) The technological transfer of research projects from the laboratory into practice.*

While reinforcing the role of offshore energy in the energy mix, the strategy underlines that sustainability and, more specifically, the

(*Continued*)

(Continued)

protection of the environment and biodiversity will be key principles for all dimensions concerned.

The EU **strategy on offshore renewable energy** *consists of many different clean sources and various technologies, which are at different stages of development and includes wind, wave and tidal.*[16] *These come with their own set of challenges and opportunities for European energy systems, sea-users, industrial actors and civil society.*

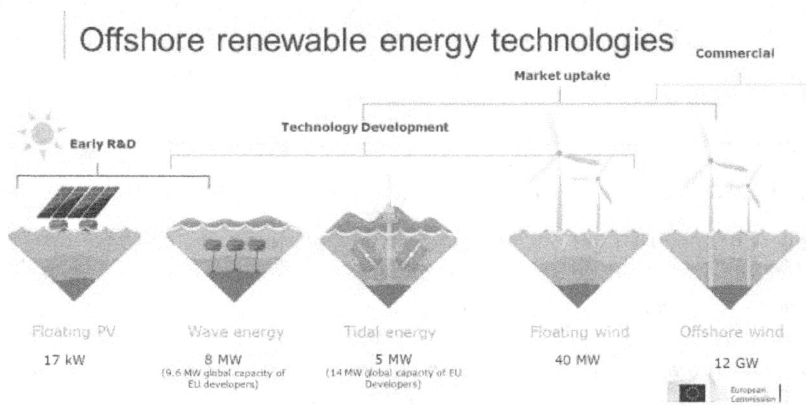

The US' wind energy policy. *The goal of the United States is to reach 100% carbon pollution-free electricity system by 2035, which can be*

---

[16]Floating offshore wind energy generation is strong in the EU in the ambit of renewable energy industries, but the EU is also the global leader for developing ocean energy technologies, mainly wave and tidal energy. EU companies hold 66% of patents in tidal and 44% of patents in wave energy, and 70% of the global ocean energy capacity has been developed by EU27-based companies. Currently, all projects worldwide use EU technology. Ocean energy technologies are relatively stable and predictable and can complement wind and solar PV. Currently, no specific ocean technology prevails and the sector still struggles to create an EU market despite progress in development and demonstration. *Source*: European Commission, 19.11.2020 COM(2020)741 final, *An EU Strategy to harness the potential of offshore renewable energy for a climate neutral future*, document available at: https://eur-lex.europa.eu/legal-content/EN/TXT/?uri=COM:2020:741:FIN&qid=1605792629666 (accessed January 28, 2023).

The EU is committed to becoming the global leader in renewables. Wind power has played an important part in this success and will be key to achieve the EU's renewable energy targets and make the EU carbon neutral by 2050.

(*Continued*)

achieved through multiple cost-effective technology and investment pathways. This transition has already been accelerating in recent years driven by plummeting costs of key technologies like solar, onshore wind, offshore wind as well as enhanced policies and increased consumer demand for clean, reliable and affordable power.[17]

The United States's vision for offshore wind is to build a strong industry with domestic supply chains and significant deployment of the technology off all the country's coasts.

Departments of Interior (DOI), Energy (DOE), and Commerce (DOC) in March 2021 announced a shared goal to deploy 30 gigawatts (GW) of offshore wind in the United States by 2030, while protecting biodiversity and promoting ocean co-use. Meeting this target will trigger more than $12 billion per year in capital investment in projects on both U.S. coasts, create tens of thousands of good-paying, union jobs, with more than 44,000 workers employed in offshore wind by 2030 and nearly 33,000 additional jobs in communities supported by offshore wind activity. It will also generate enough power to meet the demand of more than 10 million American homes for a year, and avoid 78 million metric tons of CO_2 *emissions.*[18]

The Biden Administration's goals of a carbon-free electricity system by 2035 and a net-zero emissions economy by 2050 are unlikely to be met without this further development of offshore wind energy in the United States. Achieving these goals, including 30 GW of offshore wind by 2030, will require major commitments by the Federal Government and partners to reduce risks and barriers to successful deployment of offshore wind energy. Despite risks and barriers, the future of offshore wind energy is promising, as eight Atlantic states have announced targets totaling 39 GW of offshore wind by 2040.[19]

(*Continued*)

---

[17] *Source*: U.S. Department of Energy — Offshore Wind Energy Strategies, January 2022, document available at: https://www.energy.gov/sites/default/files/2022-01/offshore-wind-energy-strategies-report-january-2022.pdf (accessed January 28, 2023).

[18] *Source*: Fact sheet: Biden Administration jumpstarts offshore wind energy projects to create jobs, March 29, 2021, document available at: https://www.whitehouse.gov/briefing-room/statements-releases/2021/03/29/fact-sheet-biden-administration-jumpstarts-offshore-wind-energy-projects-to-create-jobs/ (accessed January 28, 2023).

[19] *Source*: U.S. Department of Energy — Offshore Wind Energy Strategies, January 2022.

(*Continued*)

China's wind strategy: *The data, from the country's National Energy Administration, indicate that just under 17 gigawatts of offshore wind capacity were installed in 2021. The extraordinary expansion means that* ***China now operates almost half of the world's installed offshore wind, with 26 gigawatts of a total of 54 gigawatts worldwide****. China is now able to produce up to 26 GW of power annually through offshore wind capacity, which accounts for almost half of the world's offshore wind capacity of 54 GW.*[20]

Wind (and solar) power in China play a pivotal role in increasing the role of renewables to meet the targets of the government for 2030 and 2060.

On March 22, 2022, China released the 14th Five-Year Plan (FYP) for the energy sector, covering development plan through 2025. As the first energy-specific FYP released following China's carbon pledges, the policy pivots China's energy sector toward the long-term transition goals and the establishment of a modern energy system that addresses both sustainability and supply security issues. Although the policy does not include many new quantitative targets, it reaffirms the recent policy direction and provides more clarity on the short-term approach and measures. The plan was jointly published by the National Development and Reform Commission (NDRC), the state economic planner, and the National Energy Administration (NEA), the state energy regulator.

For Chinese companies, wind power is not just a growth market; it is a political project. China's cities are notoriously polluted. For years, Beijing has been comprehensively investing in wind power, and investments in this sector will further surge in the future.

1.1.3. *Other renewable sources (bioenergy, geothermal energy, and tides, wave, and ocean energy)*

Among renewables, we also have to mention bioenergy, geothermal energy, and tide, wave, and ocean energy. These renewables, with the exception of bioenergy, though playing a less prominent role among

[20]*Source*: China adds record offshore wind capacity as part of renewable energy drive, article available at: https://www.lexology.com/library/detail.aspx?g=e4216758-77f5-41e3-b0f8-8400a8bcc987.

renewable energy sources, are gaining attention and thus attracting new investments and they will certainly integrate into the mix of renewables.

Bioenergy is a form of renewable energy generated from biomass. **Biomass** is organic, non-fossil material of biological origin (plants and animals) used as raw material for the production of biofuels.[21] It can also be called biomass feedstock or energy crop. It includes a wide range of materials harvested from nature or the biological portion of waste.[22]

"*Many international bodies, including the European Union, recognize bioenergy as a low carbon renewable energy source. This is because, when burned, plants release the same amount of Carbon Dioxide (CO_2) as they have collected while growing. By comparison, fossil fuels release carbon that has been locked away in the ground for millions of years.*"[23]

It must be evidenced that the EU's 2021 renewable energy Directive[24] requires proof of significant reduction in greenhouse emissions in respect to

---

[21] ***Biofuels*** *are fuels derived directly or indirectly from biomass. Biofuels used for non-energy purposes are excluded from the scope of energy statistics (for example wood used for construction or as furniture, biolubricant for engine lubrication and biobitumen used for road surface). Biofuels can be split up into three categories: (i) Solid biofuels (for example: fuelwood, wood residues, wood pellets, animal waste, vegetal material); (ii) liquid biofuels (biogasoline, biodiesel, bio jet kerosene), (iii) biogases.* More info available at: https://ec.europa.eu/eurostat/statistics-explained/index.php?title=Glossary:Biofuels (accessed January 28, 2023).

[22] *The most typical example is wood (firewood, wood residues, wood waste, tree branches, stump, wood pellets,...), which is the largest biomass energy source. Other examples of biomass are grass, bamboo, corn, sugarcane, animal waste, sewage sludge and algae. Using biomass as a fuel is deemed carbon neutral as carbon was trapped from the atmosphere during the biomass life cycle (its grow). There are several sustainability concerns related to the use of biomass as fuel.* More information available at: *https://ec.europa.eu/eurostat/statistics-explained/index.php?title=Glossary:Biomass* (accessed January 28, 2023).

[23] In this sense, see Bioenergy and Greenhouse Gas Emission, Sustainable Energy Authority of Ireland (SEAI), at: https://www.seai.ie/technologies/bioenergy/bioenergy-and-greenhouse/ (accessed January 28, 2023).

[24] *The Renewable Energy Directive (2009/28/EC) was revised in 2018, but the Commission proposed another revision in 2021 to better align it with the increased climate ambitions. The directive sets a common target — currently set at 32% — for the amount of renewable energy in the EU's energy consumption by 2030. The proposed revision and the REPowerEU plan, presented in May 2022, suggest further evolution of the target to accelerate the take-up of renewables in the EU. The directive establishes common principles*

traditional fossil fuels. It also requires proof of sustainable land and forest management to reduce the risk of harmful land use change and carbon debt.

The bioenergy sector offers investors (banks, renewable funds, infrastructure funds, pension funds, and also private investors) valid and attractive opportunities for investments. In fact, bioenergy represents another piece of the renewables mix which will contribute to tackling climate change. A new flow of investments from both the private sector and the public sector is expected to further stimulate the bioenergy sector.

Bioenergy in the Three Major Economies

Bio-energy in the EU: *Bio-mass for energy (bio-energy) is the main source of renewable energy in the EU, with a share of almost 60%.*[25] *The EU has leadership in bio-energy technologies, but deployment remains limited. To count towards the renewables targets, or to be eligible for subsidies by EU countries, renewable energy sourced from biomass needs to fulfill sustainability criteria. The recast Renewable Energy Directive 2018/2001*[26] *extends sustainability criteria to cover also large-scale biomass for heat and power, in addition to bio-fuels and bio-liquids for transport.*

Bio-energy sector is one of the largest investors in R&D amongst Europe's renewables players, with bio-fuels attracting the third largest level of private R&D investment in the EU and with EU Member states investments in bio-energy R&D higher than in any other global competitors. Companies are actively investing in research and development to help Europe keep global leadership in deploying advanced bio-energy solutions, with such solutions also featured in the same European Commission

---

and rules to remove barriers, stimulate investments and drive cost reductions in renewable energy technologies, and empowers citizens, consumers and businesses to participate in the clean energy transformation. Further info available at: https://energy.ec.europa.eu/topics/renewable-energy/renewable-energy-directive-targets-and-rules/renewable-energy-directive_en (accessed January 28, 2023).

[25] *Source*: Brief on biomass for energy in the European Union, document available at: https://op.europa.eu/en/publication-detail/-/publication/7931acc2-1ec5-11e9-8d04-01aa75ed71a1/language-en/format-PDF/source-228478685 (accessed January 28, 2023).

[26] Directive (EU) 2018/2001 of the European Parliament and of the Council of 11 December 2018 on the promotion of the use of energy from renewable sources (Text with EEA relevance), document available at: https://eur-lex.europa.eu/legal-content/EN/TXT/?uri=uriserv:OJ.L_.2018.328.01.0082.01.ENG&toc=OJ:L:2018:328:TOC This act has

(*Continued*)

Communication as well as the most recent IEA and IPCC 2050 decarbonisation scenarios'.[27]

Challenges:

- *Improving the technology in terms of efficiency and cost reduction;*
- *Developing reliable, integrated bio-energy supply chains from feedstock cultivation, harvesting, transport, storage to conversion into heat, electricity and transport fuels;*
- *Integrating bio-energy in the overall energy system.*

Opportunities:

- *Bio-energy and bio-fuels are essential for both energy use and as energy carrier.*
- *The market for advanced bio-fuels is growing because of their large renewable energy density.*
- *Because they are compatible with existing engines, drop-in bio-fuels are the only deployable solution for replacing petroleum in transport in the mid-term, and in sectors like aviation and shipping in the long-term as well.*
- *Research*[28] *and innovation can improve the cost, performance, and sustainability needed to make bio-energy competitive.*

(*Continued*)

---

been changed. Current consolidated version: https://eur-lex.europa.eu/legal-content/EN/TXT/?uri=CELEX%3A02018L2001-20220607 (accessed January 28, 2023).

[27] *Source*: https://bioenergyeurope.org/index.php?option=com_content&view=article&id=279 (accessed January 28, 2023).

[28] Research focuses on (i) Technology improvement and diversification; (ii) Feedstock diversification; (iii) Modernizing and improving efficiency of biomass based heat and power co-generation; (iv) Market uptake measures for all technologies, in particular aviation, shipping, and heavy duty road; (v) breakthrough research and market-creating innovation (e.g., bionic leaf technology); (vi) coordinating EU research and innovation funding and risk financing to boost commercialization; (vii) integration of bioenergy in the overall energy system; and (viii) international cooperation to tackle global societal challenges. Visit: https://research-and-innovation.ec.europa.eu/research-area/energy/bioenergy_en.

(Continued)

The US and bioenergy. *Bioenergy in the US is gaining attention as it is an important portion of the renewable to achieve climate goals. The U.S. Department of Energy's (DOE) Biomass Program primarily works with industry, academic, and laboratory partners to develop advanced technologies and real-world solutions to reduce costs and spur market growth. Through a multitude of research, development, and demonstration (RD&D) projects, DOE is facilitating technology advancements that accelerate the sustainable production of clean, affordable energy. Unlocking the potential of diverse, non-food biomass resources — such as switchgrass, agricultural and forest residues, municipal waste, and algae — will yield advanced bio-fuels including cellulosic ethanol and renewable gasoline, aviation, and diesel fuels. These resources will also produce bio-power and bio-products.*[29]

President Biden on August 16, 2022 signed the 'Inflation Reduction Act' (IRA Act)[30] *into law calling the legislation the "biggest step forward in climate-ever" and stressing it will allow the US to boldly take addition steps towards meeting its climate goals. The IRA creates a manufacturing tax credit for eligible equipment, including PV cells, solar modules, wind energy components and battery cells, produced in the US and sold between December 31, 2022 and December 31, 2032. The law will raise $737 billion and authorize $369 billion in spending on energy and climate change.*

Of interest to the biofuel and bioenergy industries, the newly signed law establishes new tax credits for sustainable aviation fuel (SAF), clean

---

[29] *Source*: U.S. Department of Energy — Growing America's Energy Future, document available at: https://www.nrel.gov/docs/fy11osti/51241.pdf (accessed January 28, 2023).

[30] President Joe Biden signed into law the Inflation Reduction Act of 2022 (HR 5376) (the IRA or the Act), on August 16, 2022. Act available at: https://www.congress.gov/bill/117th-congress/house-bill/5376?q=%7B%22search%22%3A%5B%22inflation+reduction+act%22%2C%22inflation%22%2C%22reduction%22%2C%22act%22%5D%7D&r=1&s=1. U.S. Department of Energy — Growing America's Energy Future, document available at: https://www.nrel.gov/docs/fy11osti/51241.pdf (accessed January 28, 2023). The expansive legislative package addresses a wide range of issues, including inflation reduction, domestic energy production and manufacturing, carbon emissions reductions, Medicare and healthcare costs, and tax loopholes. Analysts affirmed the IRA Act's potential to achieve up to a 50-percent reduction in US GHG emissions by 2030. See Inside the Inflation Reduction Act, article available at: https://www.dlapiper.com/it/italy/insights/publications/2022/08/inside-the-inflation-reduction-act/.

(*Continued*)

transportation fuels and clean hydrogen. It also extends several existing tax credits that benefit transportation biofuels, such as renewable diesel and biodiesel, and includes funding for biofuel infrastructure development. Other provisions of the bill support the production of biogas- and biomass-based electricity and offer tax incentives for homeowners to install biomass-fired residential heating appliances. The bill also extends and expands the Section 45Q tax credit for carbon capture and storage (CCS).[31]

Bioenergy in China: Also in China Bio-energy represents an important component in the renewable panorama. Article 9 of the 14th FYP emphasises the need to seize opportunities for ecosystem driven development and includes provisions on bio-energy. China has pledged to further boost the high-quality development of the biomass power generation sector in 2021, as part of the government's ongoing efforts to peak carbon emissions by 2030 and achieve carbon neutrality by 2060.

The new plan, released by the National Development and Reform Commission, the Ministry of Finance and the National Energy Administration, targets practices such as adding funds for biomass power generation, clarifies rules for the allocation of subsidy funds between central and local governments and promotes technological advances in the biomass power generation sector. Under the new document, the country plans to earmark 2.5 billion yuan ($385 million) for the subsidy of biomass power generation. More efforts will also be made to increase financial support for biomass power generation projects, boosting the application of biomass energy and encouraging localities to establish a system for collection, storage, transportation and treatment of agricultural and forestry waste as well as household waste.

China's biomass energy resources mainly include straw and other agricultural wastes, such as waste from forestry and forest product processing, animal manure, energy crops and plantations, organic effluents from industry and household waste, which can be burned directly for heat or converted to renewable gaseous and liquid fuels through chemical,

(*Continued*)

[31] *Source*: *Biomass Magazine*, article available at: https://biomassmagazine.com/articles/19261/biden-signs-new-saf-hydrogen-clean-fuel-tax-credits-into-law (accessed January 28, 2023).

(*Continued*)

thermal and biochemical processes. Looking ahead, central funding subsidies for biomass power generation will gradually phase out annually in an orderly manner, and the funding scale for competitive allocation of biomass power generation projects is set to be increased yearly, the plan said.[32]

Another source of renewable is **geothermal energy**, namely, 'the energy available as heat from within the earth's crust, usually in the form of hot water or steam.' This form of energy, usually available close to tectonically active regions, covers a significant share of the electricity demand in countries like Iceland, El Salvador, New Zealand, Kenya, and Philippines and more than 90% of the heating demand in Iceland. According to a report by IRENA, "there are different geothermal technologies with distinct levels of maturity. Technologies for direct uses like district heating, geothermal heat pumps, greenhouses, and for other applications are widely used and can be considered mature. The technology for electricity generation from hydrothermal reservoirs with naturally high permeability is also mature and reliable, but its use is limited to determined regions. To promote wider geothermal energy development, IRENA coordinates and facilitates the work of the Global Geothermal Alliance (GGA)[33] — a platform for enhanced dialogue and knowledge sharing for coordinated action to increase the share of installed geothermal electricity and heat generation worldwide."[34]

The role of geothermal energy in respect to the other renewables is still limited; however, China, the USA, and the European Union are increasing their interest in this form of clean energy.

[32]*Source*: Global China Daily, China announces plans to boost biomass energy sector, August 2021, article available at: https://global.chinadaily.com.cn/a/202108/19/WS611e296ba310efa1bd669e3d.html (accessed January 28, 2023).

[33]To promote wider geothermal energy development, IRENA coordinates and facilitates the work of the **Global Geothermal Alliance (GGA)** — a platform for enhanced dialogue and knowledge sharing for coordinated action to increase the share of installed geothermal electricity and heat generation worldwide. For more info visit: http://www.globalgeothermalalliance.org/ (accessed January 28, 2023).

[34]*Source*: IRENA, Geothermal energy at: https://www.irena.org/geothermal (accessed January 28, 2023).

Geothermal green heating is part of China's decarbonization plans. Since early 2021, the Chinese government issued a series of notices and guidelines promoting the use of geothermal energy. Various levels of government are adopting low-carbon policies tailored to local conditions, and industries are exploring their own green development paths, making concerted efforts to achieve the ambitious goals of peaking carbon emissions by 2030 and achieving carbon neutrality by 2060. This includes green heating, green power, and green logistics. As an example, it is worth reporting that "*statistics from the Shaanxi provincial government show that more than 100,000 households in its central plain area have enjoyed green and clean heating services, and the number is expected to reach at least 600,000 over the next few years, reducing the annual emission of carbon dioxide by 3.6 million tonnes than heating by burning coal.*"[35]

In the US, geothermal resources are present but underexploited. The U.S. Department of Energy (DOE) 2019 GeoVision report[36] found that geothermal energy could account for 8.5% of electricity generation (up to 16% with technological improvements) and 11,500 district heating installations by 2050. This has led to renewed interest: The US Department of Energy (DOE) in July 2022 announced up to $165 million[37] to expand US

[35] *Source*: *Geothermal green heating part of China's decarbonization plans*, article available at: https://mronline.org/2022/01/28/geothermal-green-heating-part-of-chinas-decarbonization-plans/#:~:text=China%20is%20adopting%20geothermal%20because,neutrality%20and%20combating%20air%20pollution. *The geothermal district heating in the province has been developed with Icelandic support as part of Icelandic-Chinese joint venture Sinopec Green Energy Geothermal with the Icelandic partner Arctic Green Energy. Reykjavik-based Arctic Green Energy is the leading exporter of the Icelandic success and leadership in geothermal to markets around the globe. Learning from Iceland's expertise and experience has helped Sinopec Green Energy Geothermal Development, become the world's largest developer of projects that use underground geothermal energy to heat buildings. Sinopec Green Energy Geothermal Development is a joint venture between Arctic Green Energy, which owns 46 per cent, and state-owned oil and gas giant China Petrochemical Corporation (Sinopec Group), which owns the remaining 54 per cent.*

[36] GeoVision — *Harnessing the Heat Beneath Our Feet,* May 29, 2019, US Department of Energy, document available at: https://www.energy.gov/sites/default/files/2019/06/f63/GeoVision-full-report-opt.pdf (accessed January 8, 2023). The report summarizes the analyses and discusses the many opportunities that geothermal energy offers in both electric and non-electric uses.

[37] The Geothermal Energy from Oil and Gas Demonstrated Engineering (GEODE) initiative will provide $10 million to form a consortium of experts to develop a roadmap for addressing technology and knowledge gaps in geothermal energy, based on best practices

geothermal energy deployment following President Biden's priorities to deploy clean energy sources to combat climate change and reach zero net emission by 2050. "*The US has incredible, untapped geothermal potential beneath our very feet, which can be harnessed to meet our energy demands with a round-the-clock, clean renewable resource,*" said US Secretary of Energy Jennifer M. Granholm. "*Leveraging the extensive knowledge, technology, skill, and experience of the oil and gas sector is the perfect way to tackle barriers to geothermal deployment while also giving fossil-fuel-based communities and workers a role in the transition to clean energy.*" Through industry collaboration, geothermal deployment can expand to at least 60 gigawatts of clean, reliable electricity-generating capacity — enough to power more than 40 million American homes.[38]

In the ambit of bioenergy, and thus of the European Green Deal, the EU Commission's proposal (2021) to revise the Renewable Energy Directive[39] promotes a gradual shift away from conventional biofuels to advanced biofuels (mainly produced from non-recyclable waste and

---

used within the oil and gas industry. DOE will then use that roadmap to fund up to an additional $155 million in research to address those gaps. *Source*: https://www.energy.gov/articles/doe-invest-165-million-advance-domestic-geothermal-energy-deployment (accessed January 28, 2023).

[38]*Source*: Department of Energy, *DOE to Build a Consortium of Experts to Expand Geothermal Deployment by Leveraging Knowledge, Technologies, and Skills from the Oil and Gas Industry*, article available at: https://www.energy.gov/articles/doe-invest-165-million-advance-domestic-geothermal-energy-deployment (accessed January 28, 2023).

[39]The Renewable Energy Directive (2009/28/EC) was revised in 2018, but the Commission proposed another revision in 2021 to better align it with the increased climate ambitions. The EU wants to accelerate the take-up of renewable to contribute and reach the goal of reducing net greenhouse gas emission by at least 55% by 2030. *With bioenergy providing 60% of renewables in the EU, the proposal seeks to tighten the sustainability criteria for forest biomass to close a number of loopholes that might contradict the EU's biodiversity strategy. The first step is to prohibit the use of all biomass from primary and highly biodiverse forests (rather than just agricultural biomass, as under current rules) and the use of stumps and roots. GHG emissions-saving criteria should also apply to existing biomass-based installations (not just new ones) and the threshold for applying sustainability criteria for small-scale installations is lowered to 5 MW, rather than the current 20MW level. In order to minimise the use of round wood, the new rules also introduce an obligation on Member States to design support schemes in accordance with the* ***biomass cascading principle*** *whereby woody biomass is used according to its highest economic and environmental added-value and to phase out support for electricity installations using woody biomass. Source*: https://energy.ec.europa.eu/topics/renewable-energy/bioenergy/biomass_en (accessed January 28, 2023).

residues) and other alternative renewable fuels (e-fuels). The EU's Biodiversity Strategy for 2030[40] considers that this approach should continue for all forms of bioenergy, and the use of whole trees and food and feed crops for energy production — whether produced in the EU or imported — should be minimized.

Another form of renewable energy that deserves particular attention is **Global Ocean Energy**.[41] This form of energy is still underdeveloped but is now attracting a lot of interest because of its potential. Global Ocean Energy includes tidal streams and waves.

Ocean energy has been recognized by the Intergovernmental Panel on Climate Change (IPCC) as a means of mitigating climate change (IPCC, 2019). Ocean energy can also be an important key to advancing numerous United Nations Sustainable Development Goals (SDGs) beyond SDG 7 (affordable and clean energy) and SDG 13 (climate action) and could impact a wide array of SDGs including SDG 1 (no poverty), SDG 2 (zero hunger), SDG 5 (gender equality), SDG 6 (clean water and sanitation), SDG 8 (decent work and economic growth), SDG 9 (industry innovation and infrastructure), SDG 14 (life below water), and SDG 17 (partnership for the goals).[42]

The global market for Ocean Energy (Tidal Stream and Wave), estimated at 58.7 Thousand Kilowatts in the year 2020, is projected to reach a revised size of 348.1 Thousand Kilowatts by 2026, growing at a CAGR of 35.4% over the analysis period.[43]

---

[40] The EU's biodiversity strategy for 2030 is a comprehensive, ambitious, and long-term plan to protect nature and reverse the degradation of ecosystems. The strategy aims to put Europe's biodiversity on a path to recovery by 2030, and contains specific actions and commitments. https://environment.ec.europa.eu/strategy/biodiversity-strategy-2030_en (accessed January 28, 2023).

[41] Ocean energy, also called marine energy, marine power, and marine renewable energy, relates to energy that is harnessed from ocean waves, tidal streams, tidal range, ocean currents, salinity gradients, and temperature gradients without the emission of harmful greenhouse gases.

[42] *Source*: IRENA, *Innovation Outlook — Ocean Energy Technologies*, 2020, document available at: https://www.irena.org/-/media/Files/IRENA/Agency/Publication/2020/Dec/IRENA_Innovation_Outlook_Ocean_Energy_2020.pdf (accessed January 28, 2023).

[43] *Source*: PR Newswire, *Global Ocean Energy (Tidal Stream and Wave) Markets, 2022–2026: Despite Dominance of Tidal Energy, wave Energy Garner Growing Attention and*

The growing global focus on energy efficiency against a backdrop of rising energy costs and environmental pollution is poised to benefit the market for ocean energy. The market is also expected to gain from the efficient monitoring and smart architecture of technologies.[44] Thus, investments in *ocean energy* will certainly increase considering its potential, especially in technologies enabling the harnessing of this energy.

The European Union is particularly focused on this source of energy with various policy systems and initiatives being implemented in the EU (see previous paragraph and Box) to enable ocean energy technologies to become cost effective. The region remains the leader in tidal and wave technologies, and has investments to the tune of over EUR 100 million in ocean energy systems. According to Ocean Energy Europe, "ocean energy deployments are back to pre-pandemic levels, with Europe installing over ten times as much tidal energy capacity and three times as much wave energy compared to 2020. Investment interest in the sector also rose, with a slew of announcements by large industrial players and public authorities *Statistic published by Ocean Energy Europe*[45] show that ocean energy is back on track, despite COVID-19 restrictions still affecting activity last year."[46] According to Ocean Energy Europe, "both the wave and tidal energy sectors installed significantly more capacity in 2021 than the previous year, adding 1.39 MW and 3.12 MW respectively worldwide. While Europe still dominates global tidal stream activity, more and more wave capacity is being installed outside Europe, often driven by significant government support."[47] Among the other noteworthy geographic markets are Japan and Canada, each forecast to grow at 34.6% and 33.5%,

---

Investment, article available at: https://www.prnewswire.com/news-releases/global-ocean-energy-tidal-stream-and-wave-markets-2022-2026-despite-dominance-of-tidal-energy-wave-energy-garner-growing-attention-and-investments-301545004.html and Ocean Energy (Tidal Stream and Wave) — Global Market Trajectory & Analytics (researchandmarkets.com).

[44] *Ibid.*

[45] Ocean Energy — Key trends and statistics 2021, March 2022, document available at: https://www.oceanenergy-europe.eu/wp-content/uploads/2022/03/OEE_Stats_2021_web.pdf (accessed January 28, 2023).

[46] *Source*: Ocean Energy Europe, *Ocean energy bounces back with increased investment and installation in 2021*, article available at: https://www.oceanenergy-europe.eu/ocean-energy-bounces-back-with-increased-investment-and-installations-in-2021/ (accessed January 28, 2023).

[47] *Ibid.*

respectively. This clearly is an indicator of the future trends in ocean energy. Ocean energy will also increase in other countries, especially in the US and China where this source of energy is seen as an important part of the renewables mix. This source will play a substantial role if adequately funded and developed. The US Market was estimated at 6 thousand kilowatts in 2022, while China is forecast to reach 32.8 thousand kilowatts by 2026.

The US is only recently placing particular emphasis on marine sources.[48] On January 2022, the Department of Energy (DOE) announced $25 million in funding to support increased research, development, and demonstration of technologies that harness wave power to create electricity.[49] Furthermore, on July 2022, the DOE announced an additional $27 million to accelerate ocean wave energy technology to market.[50]

---

[48] *Marine energy resources are distributed throughout the United States and provide unique opportunities to different states and regions. Massive quantities of wave energy arrive at our coastlines every year, and this resource is particularly energetic along the nation's Pacific shorelines (California, Oregon, Washington, Alaska, and Hawaii). Tidal energy, perhaps the most predictable renewable energy resource, could play a major role in Alaska's electricity generation and could realistically contribute sizable quantities of power in Washington state and several Atlantic states. Ocean current energy, which is primarily contained in the Gulf Stream, has the potential to provide steady, reliable power to homes in North Carolina, South Carolina, Georgia, and Florida. Ocean thermal energy is another significant opportunity for parts of the Atlantic coast as well as the Gulf Coast states, Hawaii, and U.S. Pacific territories and freely associated states. Finally, the nation's riverine resource can be harnessed without the need for dams or river diversion to provide reliable power throughout the country.* Marine energy is defined in the Energy Act of 2020 as energy from waves, tides, ocean currents, free-flowing rivers, and man-made channels, as well as from differentials in salinity, temperature, and pressure (116th U.S. Congress 2020). Before this bill was enacted, marine energy had often been known as marine and hydrokinetic energy (MHK). *Source*: Kilcher, Levi, Michelle Fogarty, and Michael Lawson. 2021. Marine Energy in the United States: An Overview of Opportunities. Golden, CO: National Renewable Energy Laboratory. NREL/TP-5700-78773, document available at: https://www.energy.gov/sites/default/files/2021/02/f82/78773_3.pdf (accessed January 28, 2023).

[49] Department of Energy (DOE) Announces $25 Million for Cutting-Edge Wave Energy Research, January 2022, available at: https://www.energy.gov/articles/doe-announces-25-million-cutting-edge-wave-energy-research (accessed January 28, 2023).

[50] *Source*: DOE, Funding will support marine energy R&D projects that will diversify America's renewable power sources, boost carbon-free electricity, available at:

This further funding is aimed at advancing wave energy technologies toward commercial viability and supports the Biden–Harris Administration's efforts to build a clean energy economy that will create good-paying jobs and reach net-zero carbon emissions by 2050:

> "*Harnessing the unrelenting power of the ocean is a clean, innovative, and sustainable way to curtail carbon pollution — benefiting American businesses and families, especially coastal communities hit hardest by the impacts of climate change*," said US Secretary of Energy Jennifer M. Granholm. "*Diversifying and expanding our clean energy sources will usher in a new era of energy independence that makes the grid more resilient, curbs the climate crisis, and saves Americans money on their energy bills*."[51]

It must be evidenced that promoting large-scale development of ocean energy in China in 2021 has been set out in the "*The Outline of the 14th Five-Years Plan (2021–2025) for National and Social Development and the Long-Range Objectives Through the Year 2035*." This is in line with the plans China implemented in 2021 for a series of climate change strategies, measures, and actions to support the development of renewable energy,[52] including, of course, ocean energy. China will release implementation plans and supporting measures in relevant sectors and industries in the next stage, with a view to build and strengthen the already introduced '1+N' policy system (see Chapter 3, paragraph 2) of carbon peak and carbon neutrality by 2060.[53]

It is noteworthy that though ocean energy in China is still in its early stage, the development of this form of energy will contribute to the mix

---

https://www.energy.gov/articles/doe-announces-27-million-accelerate-ocean-wave-energy-technology-market (accessed January 28, 2023).

[51] *Source*: Department of Energy, available at: https://www.energy.gov/articles/doe-announces-25-million-cutting-edge-wave-energy-research (accessed January 8, 2023).

[52] According to the International Energy Agency in 2021, China's investment in clean energy took up more than 30% of the total global investment, and this trend will continue including all the other renewables. The complete report by the IEA titled *World Energy Investment 2022*, available at: https://iea.blob.core.windows.net/assets/db74ebb7-272f-4613-bdbd-a2e0922449e7/WorldEnergyInvestment2022.pdf (accessed January 28, 2023).

[53] *Source*: Ocean Energy System, (China) Supporting Policies for Ocean Energy, further info available at: https://www.ocean-energy-systems.org/ocean-energy-in-the-world/china/ (accessed January 28, 2023).

of renewables to reach China's climate goals. In consideration of its potential and the sustainable path China is taking, investments in this form of energy will increase, helping the commercialization of most of its ocean energy power generation devices which are still in the design and test phase.[54]

Finally, to conclude this section on ocean energy, it is worth reporting that "*an increase in private investment and the entrance of important industrial players into the sector reflect the growing appeal of ocean energy to investors, power producers and manufacturers. In 2021, the sector signed deals with GE Renewable Energy, Kawasaki Kisen Kaisha (K-Line), Chubu Electric Power, TechnipFMC and Schneider Electric. Governments in the UK, Italy, Spain and the USA also committed significant new funding to ocean energy and innovative renewables.*"[55]

1.1.4. *Conservation of energy and improvement of energy efficiency*

Energy Conservation and Energy Storage (ES) play a key role in the transition toward a carbon-neutral economy. The development, implementation, and integration of energy storage technologies to optimize the energy efficiency (of all kinds of energy systems) and enable the increased use of renewable energy instead of fossil fuels are very important to enhance energy security, especially now with the rising costs of energy. Thus, it is not surprising that investments in this sector are literally surging. According to the International Energy Agency, "*investment in battery energy storage is currently experiencing the biggest momentum in the power sector, with capital spending expected to nearly triple in just two years. It is led by grid-scale deployment, which represented more than 70% of total spending in 2021 and by lithium ion batteries, which took*

[54]A more precise description of the ocean energy devices China is using and of the ones which are in a development stage is available and of the policy favoring this form of energy is contained in the article "*Ocean Energy Management Policy in China*," by Chang Lei Ma, National Ocean Technology Center, Tianjin, 2019. https://www.sciencedirect.com/science/article/pii/S1877050919308440 (accessed January 28, 2023).

[55]*Source*: Ocean Energy Europe, see https://www.oceanenergy-europe.eu/ocean-energy-bounces-back-with-increased-investment-and-installations-in-2021/ (accessed January 28, 2023).

more than 90% of total deployments in 2020 and 2021."[56] Though this sector is certainly destined to growth and to attract a new flow of investments, it is necessary to keep in mind that "*batteries are, among energy assets, one of the most sensitive to critical mineral supply chains. Depending on the chemistry, they require lithium, cobalt, nickel, graphite, copper and manganese, supplies of which are under high stress and majorly controlled by Chinese actors. The supply chain bottlenecks and price spikes affecting these minerals could limit growth in the sector, and capital costs for batteries are expected to rise by between 5% and 10% in 2022, the first time in a decade, leading to possible delays and rescheduling in project deployment.*"[57]

Given its importance and the role it plays in the ambit of energy security, it is not surprising that all the three major economies have in place specific policies to foster energy storage. Starting from China, "energy storage is crucial for the Middle Kingdom's green transition, as the country needs an advanced, efficient, and affordable energy storage system to respond to the challenge in power generation"[58] and meet its climate goals. Energy storage and improvement of energy efficiency are to be seen an integral part of China's plans for reaching its peak carbon target by 2030 and net-zero target by 2060 in the ambit of the '1+N'

---

[56] In this sense see the report by the IEA titled *World Energy Investment 2022* is available at: https://iea.blob.core.windows.net/assets/db74ebb7-272f-4613-bdbd-a2e0922449e7/WorldEnergyInvestment2022.pdf (accessed January 28, 2023).

[57] *Ibid.*

[58] *Source*: China Briefing, *China's Energy Storage Sector: Policies and Investment Opportunities*, article available at: https://www.china-briefing.com/news/chinas-energy-storage-sector-policies-and-investment-opportunities/ in the article it is also stated that: *While China's renewable energy sector presents vast potential, the blistering pace of plant installation is not matched with their usage capacity, leading more and more clean energy to be wasted. Some provinces in the northwest region with rich wind and solar resources generally have an oversupply of electricity. Analysis* (see "China's Renewable Energy Fleet is growing too fast for its grid," available at: https://www.bloomberg.com/news/articles/2022-06-06/china-s-renewable-energy-fleet-is-growing-too-fast-for-its-grid-l425v47z) *shows that nearly 12 percent of power generated by wind turbines in Inner Mongolia and 10 percent of solar power in Qinghai this year has been wasted. In Gansu, due to low consumption capacity, the overall utilization rate of energy may drop below 90 percent, compared with 96.83 percent in 2021.* See https://www.solarpaces.org/chinas-curtailments-go-up-as-renewables-growth-explodes/ (accessed January 28, 2023).

framework.[59] It is worth reporting that China's energy storage market is expected to break through 100 gigawatt hours (GWh) by 2025. China is set to become the world's fastest-growing energy storage market, overtaking Europe and the United States.[60] It is also worth evidencing that China is planning to further develop the energy storage sector. "On March 21, 2022, the National Development and Reform Commission (NDRC) and the National Energy Administration (NEA) jointly released the Implementation Plan for the Development of New Energy Storage Technologies during the 14th Five-Year Plan Period[61] (the 14th FYP for Energy Storage), which calls for a wider ecosystem of government and private entities to build the energy storage sector and emphasizes the role of market forces, including generation utilities and independent service providers, in investing in storage projects."[62] It is evident that investments in energy storage technologies will increase after China's recent signals to boost capital spending to help stimulate the economy. In this scenario, storage service providers will then become key business players.

Energy storage in the EU is considered a key element of the energy transition, supporting several key priorities of the European Green Deal, such as the following:

- *Achieving ambitious 2050 and 2030 decarbonization targets requires increased deployment of energy storage solutions, which can support a cost-effective transition by facilitating integration of high shares of variable renewables (vRES).*

---

[59] Energy storage and China's plans for reaching its carbon targets are strictly linked: By saving surplus energy and releasing when the demand is higher, the energy storage sector will balance out the variability in power generation from renewables. In doing so, it will integrate more renewable sources into China's energy systems and further facilitate the transition towards a carbon-neutral economy.

[60] *Source*: China Briefing, *China's Energy Storage Sector: Policies and Investment Opportunities*, article available at: https://www.china-briefing.com/news/chinas-energy-storage-sector-policies-and-investment-opportunities/ (accessed January 28, 2023).

[61] Only the Chinese version of this document is available at the following website: https://www.ndrc.gov.cn/xwdt/tzgg/202203/P020220321550104020921.pdf (accessed January 28, 2023).

[62] China Briefing, *China's Energy Storage Sector: Policies and Investment Opportunities*, article available at: https://www.china-briefing.com/news/chinas-energy-storage-sector-policies-and-investment-opportunities/ (accessed October 28, 022).

- *Investing in energy storage research, demonstration, and deployment is essential to support the EU's global leadership in clean energy technologies.*
- *Energy storage will support the energy transition across the entire EU and in particular, has the potential to facilitate the transition of industrial, coal, and energy intensive regions (since existing infrastructure can be upgraded or complemented with energy storage solutions), and islands (where energy storage allows reducing the use of costly imported fossil fuels).*[63]

According to the European Commission, 'energy storage' can help increase the EU's security for supply[64] and decarbonization. Energy storage therefore in the EU has a key role to play in the transition toward a carbon-neutral economy by balancing power grids and saving surplus energy. It thus represents a concrete means of improving energy efficiency and integrating more renewable energy sources into electricity systems. With electrification set to be one of the main pathways to decarbonization, batteries as electricity storage devices will become one of the key enablers of a low-carbon economy. The EU Commission in May 2020 published the "*Study on energy storage — Contribution to the security of the electricity supply in Europe*"[65] which evidences the importance of energy storage for the European Union, and it reported the following:

[63] *Source*: European Association for Storage of Energy, *Energy Storage for a Decarbonised Europe by 2050*, article available at: https://ease-storage.eu/publication/decarbonised-europe-2050/ (accessed January 28, 2023).

[64] At any moment in time, the consumption of electricity has to be perfectly matched with the generation of electricity. This balance is necessary in all electricity grids to maintain a stable and safe supply. More info available at: https://energy.ec.europa.eu/topics/research-and-technology/energy-storage_en (accessed January 28, 2023).

[65] *Study on energy storage — Contribution to the security of the electricity supply in Europe*, document available at: https://op.europa.eu/en/publication-detail/-/publication/a6eba083-932e-11ea-aac4-01aa75ed71a1/language-en?WT.mc_id=Searchresult&WT.ria_c=37085&WT.ria_f=3608&WT.ria_ev=search (accessed January 28, 2023). "This study is organised in three main parts: we begin by presenting the current state of play of storage technologies (deployment in Member States and key characteristics), then proceed to identify the need for various types of flexibility solutions at the 2030 and 2050 horizons, and finally examine the regulatory conditions that should be put in place to enable the market to deliver the appropriate level of energy storage technologies."

- "*The main energy storage reservoir in the EU is currently, and by, far Pumped Hydro Storage. As their prices plummet, new batteries projects are rising.*
- *Lithium-ion batteries represent most of electrochemical storage projects. The recycling of such systems should be strongly taken into consideration, as well as their effective lifetime: such theoretical specifications submitted to grids may be relatively optimistic compared with their use at nominal conditions.*
- *In the EU, the segment of operational electrochemical facilities is led by UK and Germany.*
- *Behind-the-meter storage is still growing. It is quite heterogeneous, depending on local markets and countries: as a new market, it is still driven by political aspects and/or subsidies.*"[66]

The report contains detailed information which evidences the growing importance of energy storage for the EU. Noteworthily, several instruments have been deployed by the EU to sustain energy storage, including the following:

The Just Transition Fund

The Just Transition Fund will play an important role in fostering research and development in the storage sector. It will dedicate €40 billion to support the energy transition in fossil fuel-dependent regions, including islands and isolated systems. It foresees productive investments in Small and Medium-sized Enterprises, up- and reskilling of workers, as well as the transformation of existing carbon-intensive installations. The Fund recognises energy storage as a solution for the economic transition from an energy production dominated by fossil fuels to a model with high shares of renewables.

The Recovery and Resilience Facility

Another promising source of funding for energy storage is the Recovery and Resilience Facility that will be launched under the 'Next Generation

(*Continued*)

[66] Study on energy storage, available at: Study on energy storage — Publications Office of the EU (europa.eu) (accessed January 28, 2023).

(*Continued*)

EU' recovery programme. The Recovery and Resilience Facility will unlock €672.5 billion in grants and loans to support Member States' recovery from the COVID-19 pandemic. 37% of this funding — nearly €250 billion — should be earmarked for climate spending, giving a significant amount of funding available in the coming years for energy storage projects around the EU.

Horizon Europe

Finally, 2020 also featured discussions and agreement on the follow-up to Horizon 2020, EU's flagship R&D programme. Horizon Europe will kick off in January 2021 with a budget of €95.5 billion for 2021–2027. Dedicated calls will be launched to support research in all different types of energy storage technologies.[67]

In the United States, energy storage has assumed a particular important role. Battery storage capacity in the United States more than tripled in 2021, growing from 1,438 MW in 2020 to 4,631 MW, according to the U.S. Energy Information Administration. More than 100 utility-scale projects were brought online in 2021.[68] To help commercialize emerging energy storage that can power the grid for at least 10 hours, the Department of Energy has launched a $505 million four-year initiative. It aims to lower barriers to grid energy storage, and support small-scale, behind-the-meter pilots as well as large utility-scale demonstrations. In particular, the Biden Administration, through the US Department of Energy (DOE), has issued a Request for Information (RFI) seeking public input on the structure of this $505 Million long-duration energy storage initiative to increase the availability of electricity and deliver affordable, reliable clean energy. The new **Long-Duration Energy Storage for Everyone, Everywhere Initiative**, created by President

[67]*Source*: European Association for Storage of Energy, *How the EU Funding Is Driving Energy storage Innovation,* article available at: https://ease-storage.eu/news/how-eu-funding-is-driving-energy-storage-innovation/ (accessed January 28, 2023).

[68]*Source*: Electricity Monthly Update — U.S. Energy Information Administration (EIA) (accessed January 28, 2023).

Biden's Bipartisan Infrastructure Law,[69] will advance energy storage systems toward widespread commercial deployment by lowering the costs and increasing the duration of energy storage resources. Cheaper, longer energy storage can increase local control of the power system, build resilience for communities, minimize power grid disruptions, and help reach President Biden's goal of 100% clean electricity by 2035.

To conclude this section, it is worth noting that 'Improved Energy Efficiency' according to the International Energy Agency is key to limiting climate change. Therefore, investment in new technologies and projects that help in reaching this goal will certainly surge, and operators in the energy storage sector will play their part in granting energy supply and decarbonization. To this extent, it is time to turn our attention to the transportation system; in fact, the electrification of transport and the use of sustainable fuels will also be part of this green transition, offering interesting opportunities for investors.

1.2. *The greening of the transport system*

The international community has come to understand that the key to fighting climate change is to decarbonizing the energy mix, and this includes our transportation system which represents approximately one-third of the greenhouse emissions.[70] The greening of this sector is of fundamental

[69] *Source*: Bipartisan Infrastructure Investment and Jobs Act (Summary) A road to Stronger Economic Growth, see p. 69 of this document available at: https://www.cantwell.senate.gov/imo/media/doc/Infrastructure%20Investment%20and%20Jobs%20Act%20-%20Section%20by%20Section%20Summary.pdf (accessed October 8, 2022). *Deployment of technologies to enhance grid flexibility. This section amends the Energy Independence and Security Act of 2007 to include Smart Grid investments that provide flexibility and help quickly rebalance the electrical system, facilitate the aggregation or integration of distributed energy resources, provide energy storage to meet fluctuating, provide voltage support, integrate intermittent generation sources, increase the network's operational transfer capacity, and anticipate and mitigate impacts of extreme weather events or natural disasters on grid resilience. The section authorizes $3,000,000,000 for the Smart Grid Investment Matching Grant Program.*

[70] *At the heart of the* ***transition to renewable energy systems*** *is the need to reduce energy-related CO_2 emissions to limit climate change and mitigate its impacts. An energy transition that is grounded in renewables is important because it delivers jobs and economic*

importance to reach a carbon-neutral society by 2050. Naturally, to reach this goal, the key is energy transition to more sustainable forms of energy and electrification powered by renewables. Examples of electrification include switching to electric cars and buses and the use of sustainable fuel for the aviation sector as will be detailed in this section.

1.2.1. *Electrification of transportation: A necessary path to reach net-zero emissions*

The transport sector, both private and public, has recently seen progressive electrification which should further accelerate, but it is evident that legislation, financing, and technological innovation have a fundamental role to play in this transition.

As evidenced in the report *Long-Term Electric Vehicle Outlook,* "to get on track for a net-zero global fleet by 2050, zero-emission vehicles need to represent 61% of global new passenger vehicle sales by 2030, 93% by 2035, and the last internal combustion engine (ICE) vehicle of any segment needs to be sold by 2038."[71] According to the report, sales of internal combustion engine vehicles already peaked in 2017 and the same source expects the global fleet of ICE passenger vehicles to start to decline in 2024. The report also found that vehicle-to-grid (V2G) technology can play a role in driving down power sector emissions and generating value for consumers.[72] According to the report by *Bloomberg NEF,* "*developed countries and multilateral institutions should include electric*

---

growth, underpins ***sustainable development****, improves health by reducing pollution, and is among the most effective responses to climate change, according to IRENA.* For a more complete analysis on energy transition, refer to the many reports produced by IRENA, visit: https://www.irena.org/energytransition.

[71] *Source*: Electric Vehicle Outlook 2022, BloombergNEF, document available at: https://about.bnef.com/electric-vehicle-outlook/ (accessed October 8, 2022). This report is an executive summary of BloombergNEF's seventh annual Long-Term Electric Vehicle Outlook (EVO). There are now almost 20 million passenger EVs on the road and electrification has spread to other segments of road transport. There are over 1.3 million commercial EVs, including buses, delivery vans, and trucks, and there are over 280 million electric mopeds, scooters, motorcycles and three-wheelers on the road globally. Battery technology continues to improve, policy pressure toward "net zero" is rising in many countries, and automakers are ramping up manufacturing of compelling new EV models.

[72] *Source*: Extract of the report by BloombergNEF, available at: https://about.bnef.com/blog/net-zero-road-transport-by-2050-still-possible-as-electric-vehicles-set-to-quintuple-by-2025/ (accessed January 28, 2023).

vehicle investments, incentives and charging infrastructure deployments in their international climate finance plans, making capital available to emerging economies that have credible plans to develop this sector. Concessional finance has been a key enabler for the development of renewable power generation in emerging economies and could play a similar role in the EV sector."

It must be noted that global EV sales more than doubled in 2021, with most of the growth in China and Europe where for the first time EVs surpassed diesel vehicle sales. All the net growth in global car sales in 2021 was from EVs. Renewed interest in EVs was also seen in the United States, where sales recovered the ground lost during the pandemic. Together, China and Europe accounted for more than 80% EV sales. The market grew more slowly in Japan as the automotive industry has taken a more cautious approach toward shifting to zero-emission vehicles (ZEVs) and has tended to focus on plug-in hybrid models.

Despite the rapid growth of EV sales, only a few countries are currently on track to reach net zero by 2050, and most will need additional policy interventions in the years ahead to favor the widespread use of EVs. As noted in the report by Bloomberg NEF, "*by 2025 there are 77 million passenger EVs on the road, representing 6% of the fleet. Some regions go faster, with EVs represent 13% of all vehicles on the road in China and 8% in Europe in that year.*" As of mid-2022, there have been just under 20 million passenger EVs on the road (including plug-in hybrids), representing 1.5% of the global fleet. It will take time for the change but the global fleet of new EVs will become predominant before 2050. In the abovementioned report, it is stated that EVs represent a \$9 trillion market opportunity between today and 2030, and \$53 trillion between today and 2050, but this figure might increase to \$82 trillion between today and 2050 depending on the trend of sales. The same source affirms that "the EV share of sales in some markets is much higher, with EVs reaching 39% of sales in 2025 in China and in Europe. Some of the major European car markets go even faster, with Germany, the UK and France all between 40–50% in 2025. China and Europe account for almost 80% of EV sales in 2025, with adoption running much slower elsewhere. The US market starts to pick up from 2023 but still only represents 15% of the global EV market in 2025." It is noteworthy that progress on municipal e-buses in the US is slower than in Europe and China, but there is a unique opportunity emerging to electrify the country's 500,000 school buses with $2.5 billion in new government support for this area. Thus, the adoption of more specific measures and incentives in the US could further push the sales of EVs. However, it must be underlined that "the market is shifting from being driven primarily by policy, to one where organic consumer demand is the most important factor."[73] Of course, EVs are needed to bring transport emissions under control, but using them alone is not the most efficient way to reach net zero by 2050. In fact, according to the *Outlook 2022 report*, governments should also encourage alternative modes of transport including cycling and walking and increase public transport while reducing car dependency: "Even a modest 10% reduction in kilometers traveled by car globally in 2050 yields major benefits and makes the journey to net zero much easier."[74]

Naturally, in this context, batteries play a fundamental role. "Direct electrification via batteries is still the most economically attractive and efficient approach to decarbonizing road transport and should be pursued wherever possible. Hydrogen fuel cell vehicles can help fill the small gaps left by electrification in some heavy vehicles, in regions or duty cycles where batteries struggle."[75] It is also necessary to put in evidence that EV battery demand is rising quickly, with 2021 shipments 94% higher than those of 2020. By 2030, EV battery demand will grow to 3,486GWh and manufacturers have announced plans totaling 4,151GWh of annual capacity due by 2025, regardless of the rising costs.[76] China still

---

[73] *Ibid.*

[74] *Ibid.*

[75] *Ibid.*

[76] The timing for achieving battery pack prices below $100/kWh on a volume-weighted average basis has become less certain, as raw material prices have significantly impacted costs over the last 12 months. If raw material prices remain elevated or climb further, this could delay the timeline by a couple of years, out from 2024 in most markets. Automakers have significantly grown their commitment to lithium iron phosphate (LFP)-based chemistries, which we now expect to account for 42% of battery demand by 2023, including through variations such as lithium iron manganese phosphate (LMFP), where the addition of manganese will further improve energy density. New EV battery chemistries will continue to be adopted in an effort to provide longer ranges or lighter packs. By the end of the decade, new chemistries using more manganese, such as NMCA and NMC (96Ni), will become prevalent to reduce pressure on nickel. However, introduction of new cell chemistries and manufacturing equipment and techniques will help to continue to bring costs

dominates this market, but capacity is growing in other regions. As batteries are becoming a strategic market, the European Parliament is working on new rules to tackle related environmental, ethical, and social issues. At least 30 million zero-emission electric vehicles[77] are forecast to be on EU roads by 2030. While electric cars are expected to significantly decrease greenhouse gas emissions, they have an environmentally damaging downside — their batteries. This is why it is necessary to introduce new rules for more sustainable and ethical batteries.[78] It is likely that all the other major economies and emerging economies will follow the same path.

Another critical aspect to favor the acceleration of the deployment of EVs is the prevalence of charging spots. Concerning this aspect, the report by Bloomberg states that "between today and 2040, the cumulative investment in charging infrastructure will exceed $1 trillion globally in the Economic Transition Scenario, and $1.4 trillion in the Net-Zero Scenario.

---

down. Simplified pack designs for battery-electric vehicle platforms also contribute. *Source*: Outlook 2022 report, (BloombergNEF).

[77] *Source*: European Commission: *Sustainable and Smart Mobility Strategy — putting European transport on track for the future*, COM(2020)789 final, document available at: https://eur-lex.europa.eu/legal-content/EN/TXT/?uri=CELEX%3A52020DC0789 (accessed January 8, 2023). In relation to transport systems, the European Commission's Sustainable and smart mobility strategy aims at delivering a 90 percent reduction in transport-related emissions by 2050. Battery electric vehicles will play a strategic role in the decarbonization of the European transport sector. There is support for increased European battery manufacturing capacity, with the European Investment Bank increasing its financing for the sector in 2020 to €1bn. Electric vehicle sales remain strong despite the present economic downturn and, with a growing number of commitments by manufacturers and governments to phase out internal combustion engines, proposals for gigafactories in Europe are multiplying as a result. In this sense: Energy storage and the EU Green Deal | Italy | Global law firm | Norton Rose Fulbright (accessed January 28, 2023).

[78] The European Parliament is working on an update of the EU's battery directive to ensure that batteries can be repurposed, remanufactured, or recycled at the end of their life. Battery Directive available at: https://eur-lex.europa.eu/legal-content/EN/TXT/?uri=celex%3A32006L0066 (accessed January 28, 2023). The EU Parliament on 10 March 2022 adopted a report that aims to govern the entire product life cycle, from design to consumption and all the way to recycling into new products. Document available at: https://www.europarl.europa.eu/doceo/document/ENVI-PR-696435_EN.html (accessed January 28, 2023). The proposal is linked to the EU's circular economy action plan and the EU's industrial strategy.

By this time between 340 and 490 million chargers are needed across all locations globally, with the total dominated by home chargers. Chargers outside the home account for between 42 and 59 million chargers by 2040, depending on scenario."

> "*EV charging infrastructure is a trillion dollar market opportunity over the next 20 years, but the pace of installations needs to accelerate rapidly.*"
>
> ***Source*: Electric Vehicle Outlook 2022, BloombergNEF.**

A big push is needed to scale up the industry quickly enough so that charging infrastructure is installed in time to support the expected electric vehicle fleet. The US faces one of the most difficult challenges, requiring a sixfold increase in average annual public charging installations over the next four years from those in 2021 to meet the numbers forecasted in the report by Bloomberg. The US however is acting quickly and, on June 9, 2022, the Biden–Harris Administration announced new steps to meet President Biden's goal to build the first ever national network of 500,000 electric vehicle chargers along America's highways and in communities, which is a key piece of the Bipartisan Infrastructure Law.[79] As an example, at the end of 2021, President Joe Biden signed an executive order directing the federal government to acquire 100% zero-emission vehicles (ZEVs) by 2035, including 100% zero-emission light-duty vehicle acquisitions by 2027, among other commitments to achieve zero emissions by 2050.[80]

[79] The Department of Transportation, in partnership with the Department of Energy, is proposing new standards (visit: https://www.transportation.gov/briefing-room/biden-harris-administration-takes-key-step-forward-building-national-network-user) to make charging electric vehicles (EVs) convenient, reliable, and affordable for all Americans, including when driving long distances. Without strong standards, chargers would be less reliable, may not work for all cars, or lack common payment methods. The new standards will ensure everyone can use the network — no matter what car you drive or which state you charge in. The proposed standards, along with new coordinated federal actions on EVs, support President's Biden's priorities to lower costs for families, create good-paying jobs, and combat climate change. For more info visit: https://www.whitehouse.gov/briefing-room/statements-releases/2022/06/09/fact-sheet-biden-harris-administration-proposes-new-standards-for-national-electric-vehicle-charging-network/ (accessed January 28, 2023).

[80] *Source*: Biden Calls for All Federal Fleet Purchases to be zero emission vehicle (ZEVs) by 2035, December 8, 2021, article available at: https://www.government-fleet.

As for China, driven by government support, EV sales increased to 3.52 million units in 2021, and this trend is expected to continue,[81] with China striving to cut carbon emissions in all fields. The Chinese government's goal is to reach 40 percent EVs in China out of all vehicles by 2030. In order to achieve this target, the government is negotiating with manufacturers about extending costly electric vehicle (EV) subsidies that were originally set to expire in 2022.[82] The new attitude of the Chinese government toward this sector is not surprising; in fact, China's transition to a green, low-carbon, and circular economy, which will have a far-reaching socioeconomic, industrial, and business impact, also touches the mobility sector. In the ambit of China's decarbonization commitments and climate policy framework, consumption behavior will be directly related to the country's progress in tackling climate change and environmental degradation. Thus, the Chinese government is trying to direct the choices of consumers by offering incentives on products which positively impact greenhouse gas emissions.

As evidenced, the EV sector is set to grow globally, offering a variety of investment opportunities ranging from batteries to charging stations, but in order to fight greenhouse emissions of the transport system, it is also necessary to decarbonize the aviation and maritime sectors. Thus, opportunities for investment will spread to these sectors too, requiring technological progress to develop affordable and technologically feasible solutions (including biofuels and synthetic fuels) to reach net-zero emissions by 2050.

1.2.2. *Biofuel/sustainable fuels: A necessary path for maritime and air transportation*

The transport system includes the maritime (or shipping) industry and the aviation sector. The maritime sector is a small contributor (about 3%) to the total volume of greenhouse emissions compared to road vehicles and

---

com/10157528/biden-calls-for-federal-fleet-to-purchase-all-zevs-by-2035 (accessed January 28, 2023).

[81]According to the China Association of Automobile Manufacturers, EV sales in China will increase by 47 percent to five million by 2022.

[82]*Source*: *China Considers Extending its EV Subsidies to 2023*, article available at: https://www.china-briefing.com/news/china-considers-extending-its-ev-subsidies-to-2023/ (accessed January 28, 2023).

air transport; however, the enormous scale of the industry caused a rise of 4.9% in emissions in 2021.[83] On the other hand, the global aviation industry produces around 2.1% of all human-induced CO_2 emissions. Aviation is responsible for 12% of CO_2 emissions from all transport sources, compared to 74% from road transport.[84]

Given the harmful effects of global warming, the shipping industry and the aviation sector need to act urgently, collaboratively, and comprehensively across multiple dimensions to put the respective industries on a path to zero emissions. Several decarbonization enablers have emerged including energy technologies (like alternative fuels and improved energy efficiency onboard ships), regulatory measures, and financial measures (such as carbon pricing).[85]

As for the shipping industry, setting it on a zero-emission trajectory will require the introduction of zero-emission ocean-going vessels in the global fleet by 2030. "Getting to zero emission vessels at sea involves the entire maritime value chain, from ship owners to fuel producers to port and terminal operators. In addition, given the international nature of the maritime industry, international collaboration is required amongst states, companies, and non-state actors to reach the international climate goals set in the Paris Agreement and in the International Maritime Organization's[86]

---

[83] *Source*: Lloyd's List, *Shipping emissions rise 4.9% in 2021*, article available at: https://lloydslist.maritimeintelligence.informa.com/LL1139627/Shipping-emissions-rise-49-in-2021.

[84] *Source*: ATAG, visit: https://www.atag.org/facts-figures.html (accessed January 28, 2023).

[85] *Source*: UNCTAD, see *Decarbonizing the maritime sector: Mobilizing coordinated action in the industry using an ecosystem approach*, article available at: https://unctad.org/news/decarbonizing-maritime-sector-mobilizing-coordinated-action-industry-using-ecosystems-approach (accessed January 28, 2023).

[86] The *International Maritime Organization* (IMO) is the United Nations' specialized agency with responsibility for the safety and security of shipping and the prevention of marine and atmospheric pollution by ships. IMO's work supports the UN sustainable development goals. *The IMO is not new to the idea of reducing GHG emissions from shipping: it adopted its initial strategy in this regard in 2018, setting itself the goal to reduce average carbon intensity (CO_2 per tonne-mile) by at least 40% by 2030 and by 70% in 2050, as well as to cut total emissions by at least 50% by 2050 (compared to 2008) and phase them out as soon as possible. While the IMO is to review its initial strategy in 2023, international pressure has been mounting on it to act faster*. *Source*: Sustainable maritime fuels, document available at: https://www.europarl.europa.eu/RegData/etudes/BRIE/2021/698808/EPRS_BRI(2021)698808_EN.pdf (accessed January 28, 2023).

Initial GHG strategy."[87] It is worth noting that on 5 October 2021, in order to advance the decarbonization of the industry, the International Chamber of Shipping (ICS),[88] the global trade association of shipowners and operators, submitted plans[89] to the IMO proposing measures to be taken by governments to help the industry achieve net-zero CO_2 emissions by 2050, thus doubling initial IMO ambitions. To them, meeting the net-zero target with a typical 25-year life of new ocean-going ships means that thousands of zero-emission ships will need to be in the water by 2030. The ICS proposes introducing a carbon levy on shipping to speed up the switch to more expensive zero-carbon fuels and setting up a compulsory R&D fund to support the development of zero-carbon technologies.[90]

In the aviation sector, 'Sustainable Aviation Fuels' (SAFs) are one element of the ICAO basket of measures to reduce emissions, which also includes technology and standards, operational improvements, and the 'Carbon Offsetting and Reduction Scheme for International Aviation' (CORSIA).[91] "In its Resolution A40-18 (see previous footnote), the ICAO

---

[87] For greenhouse gas emissions to peak as soon as possible and to reduce shipping's total annual GHG emissions by at least 50% by 2050 compared to 2008, see Industry Roadmap for Zero-Emissions Shipping, April 2022 1st Edition, available at: ZESM Roadmap.pdf. Read more: http://mission-innovation.net/missions/shipping.

[88] Visit International Chamber of Shipping, website at: https://www.ics-shipping.org/about-ics/ (accessed January 28, 2023).

[89] International Chamber of Shipping, *Shipping industry sets out bold plan to global regulator to deliver net zero by 2050*, article available at: https://www.ics-shipping.org/press-release/shipping-industry-sets-out-bold-plan-to-global-regulator-to-deliver-net-zero-by-2050/ (accessed January 28, 2023).

[90] For more information on this theme, refer to the following document: https://www.europarl.europa.eu/RegData/etudes/BRIE/2021/698808/EPRS_BRI(2021)698808_EN.pdf (accessed January 28, 2023).

[91] In 2016, ICAO adopted CORSIA, a global carbon offsetting scheme to address CO_2 emission from the international aviation which consists of a market-based measure that sets a target of net CO_2 emissions of international aviation at the average of 2019–2020 levels for the years 2021–2035 (before the impact of COVID-19). CORSIA requires individual aero plane operators to compensate for their calculated share of emissions above their 2020 baselines using eligible emissions units and sustainable alternative fuels with demonstrably lower life-cycle emissions. While CORSIA is anticipated to address up to 2.5 Gt of CO_2 emissions between 2021 and 2035, this is not enough to ensure that this rapidly growing industry decarbonizes at levels and timeframes required to meet the 1.5C temperature goal of the Paris Agreement. After the adoption of these measures in 2016, it

Assembly acknowledged the need for SAF to be developed and deployed in an economically feasible, socially and environmentally acceptable manner and requested States to recognize existing approaches to assess the sustainability of all alternative fuels in general, including those for use in aviation which should (i) achieve net Green House Gas (GHG) emissions reduction on a life cycle basis; (ii) respect the areas of high importance for biodiversity, conservation and benefits for people from ecosystems, in accordance with international and national regulations; and contribute to local social and economic development, and competition with food and water should be avoided."[92]

In the EU, this theme is of particular interest, and initiatives have been introduced to gradually switch the EU aviation sector to sustainable fuels, such as synthetic fuel, used cooking oil, or even hydrogen. This will help the EU become climate neutral by 2050. EU-level action on SAFs would contribute to achieving the increased climate ambition as set out in the European Climate Law. The 2030 Climate Target Plan establishes that SAFs have a major role to play to reduce emissions from aviation by 2030 and 2050 and attain EU climate goals.[93] In particular, the Members of the EU Parliament (MEPs) on the Transport and Tourism Committee adopted

---

must also be remembered that the ICAO Assembly at its 40th Session in 2019 adopted Resolution A40-18: *Consolidated statement of continuing ICAO policies and practices related to environmental protection — Climate change.* In this sense *Impact of COVID-19 on World Aviation Industry — Challenges and Opportunities*, Paolo Rizzi, Cristiano Rizzi, Mario Tettamanti, see Chapter 2 paragraph 2.3 "CORSIA — The ICAO global market-based measures, World Scientific, March 2022).

[92]More info on this theme is available at: https://www.icao.int/environmental-protection/pages/SAF.aspx (accessed January 8, 2023). *Source*: *Impact of COVID-19 on World Aviation Industry — Challenges and Opportunities*, Paolo Rizzi, Cristiano Rizzi, Mario Tettamanti.

[93]*Source*: European Commission, Proposal for a Regulation of the European Parliament and the Council on ensuring a level playing field for sustainable air transport, COM(2021) final, document available at: EUR-Lex — 52021PC0561 — EN — EUR-Lex (europa.eu) On July 14, 2021, the European Commission presented a package of proposals to make the EU's climate, energy, land use, transport and taxation policies fit for reducing net greenhouse gas emissions by at least 55 % by 2030, compared with 1990 levels — the 'fit for 55' package. The package includes a proposal to ensure a level playing field for sustainable air transport, also known as the ReFuelEU Aviation initiative. In the draft regulation, the Commission proposes obligations on fuel suppliers to distribute sustainable aviation fuels (SAF), with an increasing share of SAF (including synthetic aviation fuels,

a draft negotiating mandate on the ReFuelEU[94] aviation rules on June 27, 2022. The adopted text aims to increase the uptake of sustainable fuels by aircraft operators and EU airports to cut emissions from aviation and ensure that Europe becomes climate neutral by 2050. MEPs amended the proposed definition of sustainable aviation fuel, a term that covers synthetic fuels or certain biofuels, produced from agricultural or forestry residues, algae, bio-waste, or used cooking oil. They included under their definition recyclable carbon fuels produced from waste processing gas and exhaust gas derived from production processes in industrial installations. They also suggested some biofuels, produced from animal fats or distillates, to be used in the aviation fuel mix for a limited time (until 2034). However, MEPs excluded feed and food crop-based fuels, and those derived from palm oil, because they do not align with the sustainability criteria. The Transport Committee also included renewable electricity and hydrogen as part of a sustainable fuel mix, as both are promising technologies that could progressively contribute to the decarbonization of air transport. According to the draft rules, EU airports should facilitate the access of aircraft operators to sustainable aviation fuels, including with infrastructures for hydrogen refueling and electric recharging.[95] It is noteworthy that transport MEPs proposed the creation of a Sustainable Aviation Fund from 2023 to 2050 to accelerate the decarbonization of the aviation sector and support investment in sustainable aviation fuels, innovative aircraft propulsion technologies, or research for new engines. The fund would be boosted by the penalties generated by the enforcement of these rules and from 50% of the revenues of the auctioning of aviation emission allowances under the EU Emission Trading System.[96]

---

commonly known as e-fuels) over time, in order to increase the uptake of SAF by airlines and thereby reduce emissions from aviation.

[94]A summary of the ReFuelEU Aviation Initiative is available at: https://www.europarl.europa.eu/RegData/etudes/BRIE/2022/729457/EPRS_BRI(2022)729457_EN.pdf (accessed January 28, 2023).

[95]https://www.europarl.europa.eu/news/it/press-room/20220627IPR33913/fit-for-55-transport-meps-set-ambitious-targets-for-greener-aviation-fuel (accessed January 28, 2023).

[96]EU Emission Trading System (EU ETS), see Chapter 3, Section 1.1.2. for more detailed information also visit: https://ec.europa.eu/clima/eu-action/eu-emissions-trading-system-eu-ets_en (accessed January 28, 2023).

Fit for 55: Transport MEPs Set Ambitious Targets for Greener Aviation Fuels

- *85% of aviation fuel should be sustainable by 2050*
- *Leave space for electricity and hydrogen to be part of new fuel mix*
- *Create a Sustainable Aviation Fund*

In the US, the theme of sustainable fuels is also of extreme interest for the Biden Administration Climate Agenda. On September 9, 2021, President Biden took steps to coordinate leadership and innovation across the federal government, aircraft manufacturers, airlines, fuel producers, airports, and non-governmental organizations to advance the use of cleaner and more sustainable fuels in American aviation. These steps will help make progress toward our climate goals for 2030 and are essential to unlocking the potential for a fully zero-carbon aviation sector by 2050.[97] The Biden administration said that cuts in aviation emissions would be essential if the US transport sector is to deliver its required share of carbon reductions as part of wider climate commitments. It is worth reporting that the White House has also proposed a 'memorandum of understanding' for an SAF 'grand challenge' to draw on the resources of the Departments of Energy, Transport and Agriculture to encourage greater investment, research, and development in SAF. This move shows the great interest of the government in sustainable fuels. "Through what the White House called a 'whole of government' approach, these three federal government departments would be required to set up an executive team to co-ordinate with the Environmental Protection Agency and other agencies to deliver aims such as higher investments in SAF, the use of novel feedstocks, scaled-up testing of SAF and enhanced efforts at commercializing bio-jet. In the intention of the White House this initiative will enable aviation emissions to drop 20% by 2030 when compared to business as usual. Furthermore, the Biden Administration underlined that without increased action, aviation's share of emissions is likely to increase as more people and goods fly. Thus, innovation in this sector is essential to put the

[97]Biden Administration Advances the Future of Sustainable Fuel in America Aviation, see https://www.whitehouse.gov/briefing-room/statements-releases/2021/09/09/fact-sheet-biden-administration-advances-the-future-of-sustainable-fuels-in-american-aviation/ (accessed January 28, 2023).

aviation industry, and the US economy, on track to achieve net-zero greenhouse gas emissions by 2050," affirmed the White House.[98] "In the future, electric and hydrogen-powered aviation may unlock affordable and convenient local and regional travel. But for today's long-distance travel, we need bold partnerships to spur the deployment of billions of gallons of sustainable aviation fuels quickly." That is why President Biden proposed a Sustainable Aviation Fuel tax credit as part of the Build Back Better Agenda. This credit will help cut costs and rapidly scale domestic production of sustainable fuels for aviation. The proposed tax credit requires at least a 50% reduction in life cycle greenhouse gas emissions and offers increased incentive for greater reductions

As for China, it is necessary to stress that China's aviation sector is one of the most promising in the world, notwithstanding the impact of COVID-19, and it is set to become one of the most important markets in the near future due to its internal dimension.[99] This poses a serious threat to China's plans to reduce its emissions, and thus China has introduced energy intensity and carbon emissions-related targets for the aviation segment in the 14th Five-Year Plan,[100] paving the way for the inclusion of a

---

[98] *Ibid.*

[99] *Source*: *Impact of COVID-19 on World Aviation Industry — Challenges and Opportunities*, Paolo Rizzi, Cristiano Rizzi, Mario Tettamanti, refer to Chapter 6 and in particular Section 3.

[100] The five-year economic plan is one of China's most important policy documents that maps out development strategies and sets growth targets. The 14th Five-Year Plan for 2021–2025, in particular, is expected to lay the groundwork for China's long-term decarbonization after its COP26 pledges. *By 2025, China's aviation sector aims to reduce carbon emissions per ton-km by 4.5%, and energy consumption per person-time in the airport by 10% from 2020 levels. It aims to increase total turnover by 17% annually, and total passengers by 17.2% annually. The five-year plan highlighted the possibility of pilot airports in China with near-zero emissions and demonstrated projects for sustainable jet fuels. These will be necessary as China will build more airports and open new routes in the coming years. China's jet fuel demand registered year-on-year declines both in 2020 and 2021, and demand growth in 2022 will be limited to single-digits due to Beijing's zero-COVID-19 policy. However, China's future jet fuel demand is expected to grow exponentially. Analysts said jet fuel is expected to be China's last transportation fuel to reach demand peak around 2030, and COVID-19 has slowed investment in sustainable fuel development, adding that, while China tested on bio-jet fuel in domestic flights, it is far from commercial adoption. Source*: https://www.spglobal.com/commodityinsights/en/market-insights/podcasts/oil/082522-china-inspection-crude-oil-refineries-gasoline-gasoil (accessed January 28, 2023).

key transportation sector in the country's carbon market. It is noteworthy that the Civil Aviation Administration of China under the Ministry of Transport set carbon and energy intensity targets for Chinese airlines during the 2021–2025 period. Based on these new directives, China's aviation sector aims to cut fuel consumption per mt-km to 0.293 kg by 2025 from 0.295 kg in 2020, and CO_2 emissions per mt/km to 0.886 kg from 0.928 kg. The government agency also established a target for SAF consumption of 50,000 mt at the aggregate level in the five years, and 20,000 mt on a single-year basis in 2025.[101] Given its importance, China's environment ministry plans to enroll the aviation sector into the national carbon market by 2025, as one of its eight targeted sectors. The five-year plan expects to prepare the sector with concrete roadmaps for carbon peaking by 2030 and carbon neutrality by 2060, and aims to measure and report emissions statistics for carbon trading.[102]

Sustainable fuels represent the future for the aviation industry while awaiting the introduction of electric aircrafts and utilizing hydrogen as a reliable and cost-effective propellant. Thus, investment in research and technologies to produce SAF and synthetic fuels is expected to intensify to help the aviation industry reaching its goal to decarbonize the sector by 2050.[103]

---

[101] *Source*: *Sinopec ushers in new era for China's sustainable aviation fuel industry*, July 11, 2022, article available at: https://cleanenergynews.ihsmarkit.com/research-analysis/sinopec-ushers-in-new-era-for-chinas-sustainable-aviation-fuel.html (accessed January 28, 2023).

[102] The registration for China's domestically certified voluntary carbon credits — China Certified Emission Reductions, or CCERs — is expected to restart this year, and a national CCER trading platform will be launched, hosted by the Beijing Green Exchange. CCERs are eligible for offsetting carbon emissions under CORSIA, the well-established UN-led global carbon scheme for aviation. The inclusion of China's aviation sector in carbon trading and CCERs could potentially open opportunities for a more hybrid carbon market with international participants and cross-border trading. According to the five-year plan, China will work with ICAO to develop standards for decarbonization technologies in aviation and emphasized the principle of common but differentiated responsibilities between developed and developing countries.

[103] For a more detailed analysis concerning the impact of new technologies on the evolution of a greener aviation industry, see; *Impact of COVID-19 on World Aviation Industry — Challenges and Opportunities*, Paolo Rizzi, Cristiano Rizzi, Mario Tettamanti, refer to Chapter 2, Section 2 "Policies of ICAO and IATA regarding the emissions of CO_2," and Chapter 3 where electrical propulsion and hydrogen are considered.

1.3. *Building sector: Smart solutions shall contribute to decarbonization*

As a matter of fact, at every phase of its existence, a building has an impact on our climate. It is estimated that the **construction sector** generates nearly 50% of annual global CO_2 emissions. Of those total emissions, building operations are responsible for approximately 27% annually, while building materials and construction (typically referred to as embodied carbon) are responsible for an additional 20% annually.[104] It is also estimated that "*in 2040 approximately 2/3 of the global building stock will be buildings that exist today. Thus it is evident that without widespread existing building decarbonization across the globe, these buildings will still be emitting CO_2 emissions in 2040 and we will not achieve the Paris Agreement's 1.5°C target. Achieving zero emissions from the existing building stock will require leveraging building intervention points to accelerate the rate of energy upgrades (increasing energy efficiency, eliminating on-site fossil fuels, and generating and/or procuring 100% renewable energy).*"[105] It is evident that policy enablers are needed in driving building electrification and efficient renovation of buildings, which can contribute to reducing emissions from this sector. A forward-looking policy framework in the building sector should prioritize the following: (1) well-targeted renovation objectives for the building stock; (2) updated building codes requiring electrification technologies and energy management systems to be present in new and renovated buildings; (3) simplification of administrative procedures for building renovations; (4) mandatory energy efficiency audits and inspection schemes linked to energy performance certificates and building renovation passports; (5) tax reductions and deductions for building renovations; and (6) funding incentives to install PV panels where it is possible to use them.

The building sector thus offers several opportunities for investments especially for material and energy suppliers considering urbanization will further expand. Technology and smart solutions will help in saving energy and limit emissions so that this sector also will contribute to reaching climate targets.

---

[104] *Source*: The Build Environment, Architecture 2030, visit: https://architecture2030.org/why-the-building-sector/ (accessed January 28, 2023).

[105] *Ibid.*

1.4. *Investment in conservation of nature and biodiversity*

Conservation of nature and of biodiversity is essential for the processes that support all life on earth, including humans. Biodiversity refers not just to species but also to ecosystems. Everywhere on the planet, species live together and depend on one another. Every living thing, including man, is involved in these complex networks of interdependent relationships, which are called *ecosystems*. Healthy ecosystems are of paramount importance because they clean our water, purify our air, maintain our soil, regulate the climate, recycle nutrients, and provide us with food. The United Nations has made it clear that without effective measures to conserve biodiversity and use its components in a sustainable manner, the 2030 Agenda will not be achievable. "There are critical biodiversity dependencies for SDG 2 on zero hunger,[106] including Target 2.4 relating to maintaining ecosystems and improvement of land and soil quality, and Target 2.5 on maintaining the genetic diversity of seeds, cultivated plants and farmed and domesticated animals and their wild species. Similarly, for SDG 8 on decent work and economic growth,[107] biodiversity and healthy ecosystems are reflected in Target 8.4 on decoupling economic growth from environmental degradation and Target 8.9 relating to sustainable tourism."[108] Scientists have put in evidence that the destruction of natural habitats caused by human activities leads to ecological imbalance, with some viruses present in wild animals spreading directly to human beings.[109] Emerging infectious disease (EID) events are dominated by zoonoses (60% of EIDs), of which over 70% originate in

[106]For more info on Sustainable Development Goal 2, visit: https://sdgs.un.org/goals/goal2.

[107]*Ibid.*

[108]*Source*: Convention on Biological Diversity, available at UN Sustainable Development Goals https://sustainabledevelopment.un.org/index.php?page=view&type=30022&nr=1734&menu=3170 (accessed January 28, 2023).

[109]Cunningham, Andrew A., Daszak, Peter and Wood, James L. N., "One Health, emerging infectious diseases and wildlife: two decades of progress?," The Royal Society, June 5, 2017, https://royalsocietypublishing.org/doi/10.1098/rstb.2016.0167.

wildlife, such as the Ebola virus and SARS-CoV-2 (the virus causing COVID-19).[110]

It is therefore evident that protecting nature, its ecosystems, and biodiversity is essential for sustainable development. The Sustainable Development Goal 15[111] of the 2030 Agenda for Sustainable Development requires us to "*protect, restore and promote sustainable use of terrestrial ecosystems, sustainably manage forests, combat desertification, and halt and reverse land degradation and halt biodiversity loss*." Large-scale loss of natural resources has the potential to affect our economies and impact our society.

> ***Biodiversity loss and ecosystem collapse are one of the biggest threats facing humanity in the next decade.[112] They also threaten the foundations of our economy and the costs of inaction are high and are anticipated to increase.[113]***

1.4.1. *Initiatives by the three major economies to preserve nature and biodiversity*

Since conservation of nature and biodiversity is an important part of the UN's Agenda for Sustainable Development and two fundamental aspects of our existence, it is comforting that initiatives by the global community have been put in place to help restore them.

---

[110]"How WHO is working to track down the animal reservoir of the SARS-CoV-2 virus," World Health Organization, November 6, 2020, https://www.who.int/news-room/feature-stories/detail/how-who-is-working-to-track-down-theanimal-reservoir-of-the-sars-cov-2-virus.

[111]United Nations, Department of Economic and Social Affairs, Goal 15, see https://sdgs.un.org/goals/goal15.

[112]World Economic Forum (2020), The global risks report 2020 (accessed January 8, 2023).

[113]Organization for Economic Co-operation and Development (OECD) (2019), Biodiversity: Finance and the economic and business case for action (accessed January 28, 2023).

In particular, if we look at the three major economies, it is worth noting that many important policies for nature restoration and protection have been issued and adopted:

- On this particular theme, the European Union adopted the "*EU Biodiversity Strategy for 2030 and an associated Action Plan (annex)*"[114] which is a comprehensive, ambitious, long-term plan for protecting nature and reversing the degradation of ecosystems. It was adopted by the European Commission on May 20, 2020, and aims to put Europe's biodiversity on a path to recovery by 2030 with benefits for people, the climate, and the planet.

Informative Box: Extract from the EU Biodiversity Strategy

Investing in nature protection and restoration will also be critical for Europe's economic recovery from the COVID-19 crisis. When restarting the economy, it is crucial to avoid falling back and locking ourselves into damaging old habits. The European Green Deal — the EU's growth strategy — will be the compass for our recovery, ensuring that the economy serves people and society and gives back to nature more than it takes away. The business case for biodiversity is compelling. Industry and companies rely on genes, species, and ecosystem services as critical inputs for production, notably for medicines. Over half of global GDP depends on nature and the services it provides, with three key economic sectors — construction, agriculture, and food and drink — all highly dependent on it.[115]

Biodiversity conservation has potential direct economic benefits for many sectors of the economy. For example, conserving marine stocks could increase annual profits of the seafood industry by more than €49 billion, while protecting coastal wetlands could save the insurance industry around €50 billion annually through reducing flood damage losses.[116] *The overall benefit/cost ratio of an effective global programme for the conservation of remaining wild nature worldwide is estimated to be at least*

[114] European Commission, EU Biodiversity Strategy, document available at: https://eur-lex.europa.eu/legal-content/EN/TXT/?qid=1590574123338&uri=CELEX:52020DC0380 (accessed January 28, 2023).

[115] World Economic Forum (2020), Nature risk rising: Why the crisis engulfing nature matters for business and the economy (accessed January 28, 2023).

[116] Barbier *et al.* (2018), How to pay for saving biodiversity (accessed January 8, 2023).

(*Continued*)

100 to 1.[117] *Natural capital investment, including restoration of carbon-rich habitats and climate-friendly agriculture, is recognised to be among the five most important fiscal recovery policies, which offer high economic multipliers and positive climate impact 5 . It will be important for the EU to tap into this potential to ensure prosperity, sustainability and resilience in the recovery.*

Source: European Commission, EU Biodiversity Strategy.

Through concrete commitments and actions, the plan is for EU countries to put in place effective restoration measures to restore degraded ecosystems, in particular those with the most potential to capture and store carbon and to prevent and reduce the impact of natural disasters. As part of this plan, the Commission proposed the EU's first ever *Nature Restoration Law*[118] which includes an overarching restoration objective for the long-term recovery of nature in the EU's land and sea areas, with binding restoration targets for specific habitats and species (Figure 4).

[117]Balmford *et al.* (2002), Economic reasons for conserving wild nature (accessed January 8, 2023).

[118]The European Commission's proposal for a Nature Restoration Law is the first continent-wide, comprehensive law of its kind. It is a key element of the EU Biodiversity Strategy, which calls for binding targets to restore degraded ecosystems, in particular those with the most potential to capture and store carbon and to prevent and reduce the impact of natural disasters. Europe's nature is in alarming decline, with more than 80% of habitats in poor condition. Restoring wetlands, rivers, forests, grasslands, marine ecosystems, and the species they host will help (i) increase biodiversity; (ii) secure the things nature does for free, like cleaning our water and air, pollinating crops, and protecting us from floods; (iii) limit global warming to 1.5°C; and (iv) build up Europe's resilience and strategic autonomy, preventing natural disasters and reducing risks to food security. The proposal combines an overarching restoration objective for the long-term recovery of nature in the EU's land and sea areas with binding restoration targets for specific habitats and species. These measures should cover at least 20% of the EU's land and sea areas by 2030, and ultimately all ecosystems in need of restoration by 2050. Proposal for a Regulation of the European Parliament and of the Council On Nature restoration, Bruxelles, June 22, 2022, COM(2022) 304 final, document available at: https://environment.ec.europa.eu/publications/nature-restoration-law_en (accessed January 8, 2023).

Figure 4: Environment protection in the EU

Source: European Commission at: https://environment.ec.europa.eu/topics/nature-and-biodiversity/nature-restoration-law_en#documents.

As for the US, it must be noted that even though President Biden has not made biodiversity a top priority of his agenda, in the same manner that he has done for the climate, he has expressed his unequivocal support for one significant biodiversity initiative, namely, the '30 by 30' which aims "*to achieve the goal of conserving at least 30 percent of our lands and waters by 2030.*"[119] This initiative was outlined in a report titled *Conserving and Restoring America the Beautiful* 2021, released on May 6, 2021.[120] It is worth noting that the report is supported by four agencies, namely, (1) the US Department of the Interior, (2) the US Department of Agriculture, (3) the US Department of Commerce, and (4) the Council on Environmental Quality. This signals the extreme importance the US is placing on the protection and restoration of biodiversity, considering the importance it has for the US economy.

The report calls for a decade-long effort to support locally led and voluntary conservation and restoration efforts across public, private, and tribal lands and waters in order to create jobs and strengthen the economy's foundation, tackle climate and nature crises, and address inequitable access to the outdoors.

As evidenced by the report, nature is essential to the health, well-being, and prosperity of every family and every community in America.

---

[119]These words are contained in the Executive Order 14008 on 'Tackling the Climate Crisis at Home And Abroad,' January 27, 2021, see Part II — Taking a Government-Wide Approach to the Climate Crisis, Sec. 216, document available at: https://www.whitehouse.gov/briefing-room/presidential-actions/2021/01/27/executive-order-on-tackling-the-climate-crisis-at-home-and-abroad/ (accessed January 28, 2023).

[120]The report titled 'Conserving and Restoring America the Beautiful' is available at: https://www.doi.gov/sites/doi.gov/files/report-conserving-and-restoring-america-the-beautiful-2021.pdf (accessed January 28, 2023).

Thus, it is time to pay more attention to it and act to preserve and restore biodiversity. It is worth reporting three passages of the report because they highlight the current status and urgency to act without any further delay to avoid more costly consequence.

- **The disappearance of nature:** *Both globally and nationally, scientists are sounding the alarm about a catastrophic extinction crisis that threatens the biodiversity of our planet and the health of the natural systems that supply our food, water, and other resources.*[121] *In the U.S., approximately 12,000 wildlife species need conservation assistance to avoid the threat of extinction.*[122] *The disappearance of bees and other pollinators is reducing crop yields and threatens food security.*[123] *Already, there are three billion fewer birds in North America than there were 50 years ago.*[124] *Critical ocean habitats are declining, including an estimated 90 percent loss of live corals in the Florida Keys over the past 40 years and up to a 90 percent loss of bull kelp off of the northern coast of California in less than 10 years.*[125] *Roughly half of the riparian ecosystems and*

(*Continued*)

[121] Intergovernmental Science-Policy Platform on Biodiversity and Ecosystem Services, "The global assessment report on biodiversity and ecosystem services," 2019, available at https://ipbes.net/sites/default/files/2020-02/ipbes_global_assessment_report_summary_for_policymakers_en.pdf; G Ceballos and others, "Vertebrates on the brink as indicators of biological annihilation and the sixth mass extinction," *Proceedings on the National Academy of Sciences*, 2020, available at https://www.pnas.org/content/pnas/117/24/13596.full.pdf (accessed January 28, 2023).

[122] B. Stein and others, "Reversing America's wildlife crisis: Securing the future of our fish and wildlife," 2018, available at https://www.nwf.org/-/media/Documents/PDFs/NWF-Reports/2018/Reversing-Americas-Wildlife-Crisis_2018.ash (accessed January 28, 2023).

[123] Reilly and others, "Crop production in the USA is frequently limited by a lack of pollinators," *Proceedings of the Royal Society*, 2020, available at https://royalsocietypublishing.org/doi/10.1098/rspb.2020.0922 (accessed January 28, 2023).

[124] K. Rosenberg and others, "Decline of the North American avifauna," Science, 2019, available at https://science.sciencemag org/content/366/6461/120 (accessed January 28, 2023).

[125] National Oceanic and Atmospheric Administration, "Restoring seven iconic reefs: A mission to recover the coral reefs of the florida keys," accessed October 2021, available at: https://www.fisheries.noaa.gov/southeast/habitatconservation/restoring-seven-iconic-reefs-mission-recover-coral-reefs-florida-keys; L. Rogers-Bennett and C.A. Catton,

(*Continued*)

wetlands in the lower 48 States have already been lost, while more than 17,000 square miles of ranchland and farmland were lost to development or fragmented in the last two decades.[126]

- **Climate change:** *The nature crisis is exacerbated by climate change, which is rapidly altering ecosystems on land and water. Ocean waters are warming, causing sea level rise, species migration, and altering circulation patterns.*[127] *Ocean acidification and deoxygenation due to climate change pose significant threats to many marine species that sustain ocean life as we know it, such as seagrasses, krill, and corals.*[128] *Climate change is contributing to historic droughts and floods, more frequent and intense wildfires and natural disasters, and the spread of invasive species.*[129] *The impacts of climate change on habitat are forcing some wildlife to new areas to survive, while squeezing other species closer to extinction.*[130] *These trends are predicted to continue, disrupting the balance of nature across the country.*
- **Inequitable access to the outdoors:** *As a result of discrimination and segregation in housing, transportation, conservation, and natural resource policy, communities of color and low-income communities have disproportionately less access to nature's benefits, such as clean water, clean air, and access to nature.*[131] *These same communities, meanwhile, shoulder a*

"Marine heat waves and multiple stressors tip bull kelp forest to sea urchin barrens," *Scientific Reports*, 2019, available at: https://www.nature.com/articles/s41598-019-51114-y (accessed January 28, 2023).

[126] J. Freedgood and others, 'Farms under threat: The state of the states,' 2020, available at: https://s30428.pcdn.co/wp-content/uploads/sites/2/2020/09/AFT_FUT_StateoftheStates_rev.pdf (accessed January 28, 2023).

[127] Fourth National Climate Assessment, "Oceans," 2018, available at: https://nca2018.globalchange.gov/chapter/8/ (accessed January 28, 2023).

[128] *Ibid.*

[129] Fourth National Climate Assessment, "Land," 2018, available at https://nca2018.globalchange.gov/chapter/5/; Fourth National Climate Assessment, "Forests," 2018, available at: https://nca2018.globalchange.gov/chapter/6/.

[130] Fourth National Climate Assessment, "Ecosystems, Ecosystem Services, and Biodiversity," 2018, available at: https://nca2018.globalchange.gov/chapter/7/ (accessed January 28, 2023).

[131] D. Theobald and others, "Summary and metadata for an environmental justice analysis using data from The Disappearing West," 2016, available at: https://www.csp-inc.org/public/CSP-CAP_Env_Justice_Report_20160727.pdf (accessed January 28, 2023).

(*Continued*)

disproportionate share of the costs of nature's decline, including more pollution nearby, loss of subsistence fishing and hunting, and encroaching industrial development.[132] *An estimated 100 million Americans do not have a park within a ten-minute walk of their home.*[133] *In too many neighborhoods and communities across America, families are finding too few close-to-home opportunities to safely enjoy the outdoors.*

Source: '*Conserving and Restoring America the Beautiful.*'

The Biden Administration's goal of conserving 30 percent of lands and waters by 2030 echoes the recommendations of scientists who encourage world leaders to work together to conserve or restore a substantial portion of our planet to stem the extinction crisis, safeguard water and food supplies, absorb carbon pollution, and reduce the risks of future pandemics and other global health emergencies.[134]

As for China, we have seen that it is implementing a framework dedicated to the transition toward a new nature-positive, net-zero economy and this naturally includes biodiversity. The country has issued and implemented many important policies for nature restoration and protection and enshrined the concept of ecological civilization in its constitution, though in order to reach its goals, it is also necessary to ensure the participation of citizens and the government. In particular, the government is updating the China National Biodiversity Conservation Strategy and Action Plan[135]

---

[132] J. Larsen and others, "A just green recovery," 2020, available at: https://rhg.com/research/a-just-green-recovery/ (accessed January 28, 2023).

[133] The Trust for Public Land, "10-minute walk," last accessed April 2021, available at: https://www.tpl.org/parkscore (accessed January 28, 2023).

[134] Intergovernmental Science-Policy Platform on Biodiversity and Ecosystem Services, "The Global Assessment Report on Biodiversity and Ecosystem Services," 2019, available at: https://ipbes.net/sites/default/files/2020-02/ipbes_global_assessment_report_summary_for_policymakers_en.pdf; E. Dinerstein and others, "A global deal for nature: Guiding principles, milestones, and targets," *Science Advances*, 2019, available at: https://advances.sciencemag.org/content/5/4/eaaw2869; E. Dinerstein and others, "A 'global safety net' to reverse biodiversity loss and stabilize Earth's climate," *Science Advances*, 2020, available at: https://advances.sciencemag.org/content/6/36/eabb2824 (accessed January 28, 2023).

[135] Document available at: https://www.cbd.int/doc/world/cn/cn-nbsap-v2-en.pdf (accessed January 28, 2023).

(2011–2030) to build a system of protected areas, with a focus on national parks. Currently, China has established over 10,000 protected areas of all types, including national parks and other categories of protected areas, accounting for about 18% of its total land area.[136] It is also worth noting that in 2020, the government released the *Master Plan for National Key Ecosystem Protection and Restoration Major Projects* (2021–2035),[137] specifying conservation programs for three eco-zones and four eco-belts.[138] "*Highlighted as China's far-reaching guideline on ecosystem protection and restoration in the upcoming period, the Master Plan stipulates a set of time-bound ecosystem quality improvement targets by 2035, while rolling out nine major ecosystem protection and restoration projects across the country to put it on this envisioned path. The Master Plan characterizes the prescribed period as a pivotal time window for pursuing an 'Ecological Civilization,' while paving the way towards the long-term strategic goals of realizing 'Socialist Modernization' and achieving a 'Beautiful China' by 2035.*[139] The master plan's goals for 2035 include the following: *(i) Expand forest coverage to 26% of China's terrestrial area,*

---

[136]"Biodiversity conservation in China," State Council Information Office of the People's Republic of China, 8 October 2021, http://www.gov.cn/zhengce/2021-10/08/content_5641289.htm (accessed January 28, 2023).

[137]*Amid concerns on how "green" China can remain under enormous recovery pressure due to the mounting economic fallout of the coronavirus outbreak, China's National Development and Reform Commission (NDRC) and the Ministry of Natural Resources (MNR) jointly released the "Master Plan for National Key Ecosystem Protection and Restoration Major Protects (2021-2035)" (herein referred to as the "Master Plan") on June 11, 2020. This key overarching policy framework was issued as both a continuation of the long-term national strategy and as a strong signal to reassure the world that China remains firmly committed to its environmental protection agendas.* For more info, visit: https://climatecooperation.cn/environment/policy-summary-on-the-master-plan-for-national-key-ecosystem-protection-and-restoration-major-projects-2021-2035/ (accessed January 8, 2023).

[138]Three Eco-zones and Four Eco-belts refer to the Qinghai-Tibet Plateau Ecological Barrier Zone, Yellow River Key Ecological Zone, Yangtze River Key Ecological Zone, Northeast Forest Eco-Belt, Northern Sand Control Eco-Belt, Southern Hills and Mountains Eco-Belt, and the Coastal Eco-Belt.

[139]*Source*: Policy Summary on the "Master Plan for National Key Ecosystem Protection and Restoration Major Projects (2021-2035)" — Sino-German Cooperation on Climate Change, Environment, and Natural Resources (climatecooperation.cn) (accessed January 28, 2023).

increase its growing stock volume to 21 billion cubic metres, and maintain the area of natural forest at 200 million hectares; (ii) Cover 60% of grassland with vegetation — Ensure no further loss of wetlands and protect 60% of wetlands; (iii) Increase the total integrated management area for soil and water erosion control to 56.4 million hectares; (iv) Ensure 75% of recoverable desertified area is under treatment; (v) Safeguard at least 35% of the country's natural coastlines and prevent the marine ecological condition from worsening; (vi) Ensure the National Park-centred protected areas system accounts for over 18% of national terrestrial areas; vii) Fully protect endangered species and their habitats."

China has given particular attention to biodiversity and restoration of nature because it is well aware that these two elements are an integral part of our economies and only with a healthy planet and nature we can advance toward sustainable development. China, following its new ecological civilization concept, has extensively engaged in international exchanges and cooperation related to biodiversity and climate change. China hosted the UN Convention on Biodiversity (CBD) COP15, and also successfully organized the first phase of the Biodiversity Conference in October 2021 with the adoption of the Kunming Declaration, in which more than 100 countries committed to living in harmony with nature. Furthermore, in 2019, China launched the Belt and Road Initiative International Green Development Coalition (BRIGC).[140] At the Glasgow COP26 Climate Change Conference

[140] Visit: The Belt and Road Initiative International Green Development Coalition (BRIGC) | Asia and the Pacific | UNEP — UN Environment Programme, more information available at: https://www.unep.org/regions/asia-and-pacific/regional-initiatives/belt-and-road-initiative-international-green (accessed January 28, 2023). For a complete analysis, the following must be referenced: *Belt and Road Initiative — And Its Financial Focus*, Yu Xugang, Cristiano Rizzi, Mario Tettamanti, Fabio E. Ziccardi, Guo Li, World Scientific, 2018. The Belt and Road Initiative is a China-led effort to promote economic development and interregional connectivity in the Eurasian continent, and is arguably the largest single investment in infrastructure up to date. This undertaking will involve trillions of dollars of investments, largely in transportation, energy, telecommunications infrastructure, industrial capacity, and technical capacity building. However, such large-scale development might create negative environmental consequences. For this reason, where BRI investments could undermine the ability of many countries to meet their targets under the 2030 Agenda for Sustainable Development, particular care must be taken to ensure that decisions are based on sound knowledge and solid science. Social and environmental safeguards must be put in place so that projects include effective stakeholder engagement and that benefits are equitably shared.

in November 2021, 141 states including China signed a declaration committing to halt and reverse deforestation by 2030.

In consideration of the initiatives of the major economies to preserve nature and restore biodiversity, it is not surprising that investments in this sector are attracting growing interest. The next section is aimed at introducing approaches to investment in biodiversity and nature-related risks and opportunities, highlighting current biodiversity finance practices.

1.4.2. *Investing in preserving biodiversity and the necessity to create innovative financial instruments*

We have already analyzed the financial instruments at the disposal of investors to contribute to the green transition. While there is a full range of instruments which can be utilized by investors (see Chapter 5), in this short paragraph, we want to highlight the fact that the theme of biodiversity has gained ground in the financial services panorama, and more frequently asset managers offer this kind of investment opportunity to their clients/investors, though the offer is still not so extensive because biodiversity adds an additional layer of complexity. In fact, while carbon emissions and greenhouse gasses are good alternatives for measuring climate, biodiversity is too complex to measure and conceptualizing a single instrument for investment is quite complicated.[141] In any case, biodiversity concerns are part of ecosystems which are location specific, varying widely depending on weather, soil, water, and type of ecosystem, like a forest, wetland, dry land, grassland, or coral reefs in oceans, and this can help in shaping dedicated instruments, e.g., 'blue bonds,' for specific projects. However, this requires innovative real asset investments (to be included in the nascent landscape of climate finance, green finance, and blue finance) for nature-based solutions to climate, ecosystem, and biodiversity issues, which leads us to the necessity to develop innovative instruments dedicated to specific themes.

As reported in the *White Paper* of the World Economic Forum (see previous footnote), "*biodiversity loss could pose risks for investors that*

---

[141] In June 2022, the World Economic Forum released a White Paper titled Investing in a Biodiversity-Integrated Manner, which analyzes the opportunities arising from this sector and the necessity also to shape new investment instruments to better cover this delicate theme of biodiversity; document available at: https://www3.weforum.org/docs/WEF_Investing_in_a_Biodiversity_Integrated_Manner_2022.pdf (accessed January 28, 2023).

could manifest in the form of transition, physical and litigation risks for assets where they are invested.[142] *Whatever the risk form, biodiversity risks are 'green swans.'*"[143] Investors are increasingly aware that the preservation of their capital is, at the very least, a function of biodiversity, which is essential to the success of the underlying portfolio of invested assets.

Given that the investor community is at various stages of integrating ESG (Environment, Social, and Government) factors (refer to Chapter 5) "in their decision making, considering biodiversity factors within the E of ESG will make investments more downside resilient and future ready. Biodiversity issues also need to be accounted for under social issues because people and communities need to believe that protecting biodiversity makes more economic sense than ecosystem destruction does."[144]

Though biodiversity represents an essential part in the ambit of nature preservation, there is still a lack of available instrumentation with respect to the existing listed green bonds to be used to finance projects aimed at protecting nature. While considering biodiversity risks and impact, asset managers can leverage emerging investment opportunities in nature-positive avenues. More specifically, there is increasing reference to nature as an asset class. However, clearly, the necessity to create new instruments more specifically dedicated to biodiversity emerges. There is no doubt that new tools calibrated on the risks and characteristics of biodiversity will be defined and refined as new financial instruments to serve the necessities of both investors and promoters of initiatives to protect and restore biodiversity. According to the White Paper by the World Economic Forum, "*the investment community feels that biodiversity related reporting has to improve. Unless an international standard is adopted, there will always be scope for conflicting interpretations. Current ESG data and metrics do not cover biodiversity adequately. There is a gap in ESG measurement and reporting specifically for*

---

[142]The central bank of the Netherlands in its Indebted to Nature report recommends that financial institutions identify nature-related risks as systemic. DNB, Indebted to nature: Exploring biodiversity risks for the Dutch financial sector, June 2020, https://www.dnb.nl/media/4c3fqawd/indebted-to-nature.pdf. (accessed January 28, 2023).

[143]Environmental black swans are unusual, hard-to-predict biosphere-related risks that can have a massive impact on the economy. They are quite certain to occur but their timing or form of occurrence is uncertain. Green swans are events caused by climate change and biodiversity loss. They are more predictable than black swans.

[144]*Source*: White Paper by the World Economic Forum.

biodiversity impact. Further, financial innovations will have to set clear expectations for risk and return considerations in order to entice mainstream investors. Biodiversity integrated investing is following a similar path as that of impact investing, which has, over the years, graduated to mainstream investing as risk and return characteristics, expectations and impact measurement metrics have become standardized."

It is likely, given the growing interest in biodiversity, that we will witness further financial innovations in nature-related investment opportunities, which are expected to deepen suitably for interested investors seeking not only to contribute to the green transition but also to secure a reasonable return of investment. Meanwhile, for investors seeking responsible investment opportunities, they can turn their attention to financial tools shaped to address specific environmental issues, for example, the conservation of marine and aquatic ecosystems, including the development of sustainable seafood supply chains.

1.4.3. *Oceans: Blue bonds and the conservation of marine ecosystems*

Blue bonds for ocean conservation represent a meaningful example of investment opportunity for preserving the marine ecosystem and biodiversity.

The issuance of blue bonds[145] creates a financial flow that supports concerned governments reach their protection targets for their ocean areas, including coral reefs and other important habitats, and engage in ongoing conservation work, such as improving fisheries management and addressing climate change adaptation. Aligned with the ICMA's

[145]Blue bonds are defined as "Debt finance instruments issued specifically to support measures for protecting the ocean and ocean-based communities, island nations and preserving sustainable ocean economy." *Source*: Larsen ML (2019) A growing toolbox of sustainable finance instruments. Available from: https://green-bri.org/a-growing-toolbox-of-sustainable-finance-instruments/?cookie-state-change=1622952055245 (accessed January 28, 2023). The Seychelles government launched the world's first sovereign blue bond: The Seychelles' blue bond was partially guaranteed by the World Bank (International Bank for Reconstruction and Development). The ten-year, privately placed bond raised USD15 million from three US international investors. https://www.worldbank.org/en/news/press-release/2018/10/29/seychelles-launches-worlds-first-sovereign-blue-bond (accessed January 28, 2023).

Green Bond Principles,[146] '*Blue Bond*' proceeds are also used to boost the expansion of sustainable blue economy through marine-related green projects across various domestic and overseas markets including but not limited to offshore renewable energy and wastewater treatment.

Blue bonds are a relatively new type of sustainability bond, and they gained attention in October 2018 after the World Bank facilitated a bond agreement to offload a small portion of the Republic of Seychelles' debt in exchange for marine protection (see footnote 432). This blue bond served the dual purpose of stabilizing the country's credit rating and investing in its economy, which is closely tied to the ocean. As the Seychelles' *blue bond* demonstrated, this is not purely an environmental issue, it is an economic one.[147] All activities aimed at preserving our environment generating some kind of business, but we can include all business practices, need to align themselves with the United Nations' Sustainable Development Goals.[148] In particular when it comes to protect oceans 'Blue bonds are emerging as a viable instrument to finance solutions at scale. *Blue bonds* are emerging as a viable instrument to finance solutions at scale. Another example is as follows: As concerns grow about the millions of tons of plastic waste added annually to the oceans, *blue bonds* could serve as an instrument to raise the capitals needed to solve the problem with projects aimed at reducing plastic waste, in this case marine plastic waste.

Now that we have explained the many investment opportunities green transition offers in different areas, it is time to turn our attention to the

---

[146] Visit: International Capital Market Association (ICMA) at: https://www.icmagroup.org/sustainable-finance/the-principles-guidelines-and-handbooks/green-bond-principles-gbp/ (accessed January 28, 2023).

[147] In this sense: Out of the Blue, International Financial Law Review, February 2019, document available at: https://www.lw.com/admin/upload/SiteAttachments/Latham%20-%20IFLR%20-%20Out%20of%20the%20Blue%20-%20Reprint.pdf (accessed January 28, 2023).

[148] "About the Sustainable Development Goals." The United Nations, visit: https://www.un.org/sustainabledevelopment/sustainable-development-goals/ (accessed January 28, 2023). The United Nations Sustainable Development Goals (SDGs) are increasingly gaining traction as an organizing framework for many investors, particularly those looking for a thematic investment approach. The SDGs are a set of 17 global goals focused on sustainable development themes such as poverty, equality, education, climate change, infrastructure, land and water, and production/ consumption, with a target of 2030. Within the context of thematic investing, the SDGs are a framework for thinking about and pursuing impact. A number of companies, organizations, and government entities have committed to addressing SDG 6 (Clean Water and Sanitation) and SDG 14 (Life Below Water).

necessity to enhance international cooperation to secure this transition. As green and social values are at the core of this ecological revolution, it is appropriate to expound on this important theme.

2. The Necessity to Enhance International Cooperation for Green Transition in Line with the Sustainable Development Goals (SDGs)

Green transition is a necessary path if we want to preserve our future. At the international level, the global community has come to understand that economies worldwide can only grow 'sustainably,' but it is necessary to simultaneously manage the growing urgency of environmental degradation and climate change. This target can only be reached by coordinated actions and a common roadmap which has been substantially delineated by the UN and its 2030 Agenda for sustainable development. Following COP26 in Glasgow, many countries raised their ambitions and pledges to contribute to the decarbonization of our society. But according to the International Energy Agency (IEA), the latest pledges still leave a significant gap in the emissions reductions needed by 2030 to keep the 1.5°C goal within reach. This poses serious threats to the entire planet and to the global community if adequate actions and initiatives are not taken immediately to reverse the damage caused by development driven by fossil fuels and an unsustainable use of natural resources.

As experts affirmed, "*the scale of action required cannot be underestimated. It requires a fundamental transformation of all sectors, including energy, manufacturing, transport, infrastructure, agriculture, forestry and land use. Humans must also radically rethink how we produce and consume food and fuel and manage waste.*"[149] As we have evidenced in the development of this book, the major world economies have elaborated on plans and initiatives to tackle climate change and advance toward a carbon-neutral economy. This is an important step to shaping sustainable development, but this new sustainable development modality requires enormous effort from the financial point of view, and it needs to be pursued incorporating the goals indicated by the UN.

---

[149] *Source*: EY, Six ways that governments can drive the green transition, document available at: https://www.ey.com/en_gr/government-public-sector/six-ways-that-governments-can-drive-the-green-transition (accessed January 28, 2023).

It is evident that the major economies have to take the lead and, as has emerged, many governments all around the globe have set targets — some enshrined in law — to achieve net-zero carbon emissions by specified dates (from as early as 2030 in Uruguay and 2035 in Finland to 2050 for most other countries. It is worth remembering that China choose 2060 to become a carbon-neutral economy).[150] The fact that the world's two biggest emitters, the US and China, have both committed to carbon neutrality by 2050 and 2060, respectively, is good news, but the more rapid changes in climate patterns have alarmed scientists. Thus, measures and new initiatives should be implemented even faster. It must be noted that the EU is 'setting the pace' with a new set of policies to achieve its sustainability goals: **EU Green Deal** and **Climate Law** set binding targets to cut emissions by 55% by 2030 (from 1990 levels) and reach climate neutrality by 2050. This is not only an ambitious target (but absolutely achievable with the push of renewables) but also represents an example for the rest of the global community.

2.1. *The role of the UN Agenda 2030*

The implementation of the 2030 Agenda for a Sustainable Development in all countries, through public and private, domestic, and international resources, is a '*conditio sine qua non*' for reaching green transition which will lead to a carbon-neutral society needed to preserve nature and our environment which represent our 'life support system.' To achieve the *Sustainable Development Goals* indicated by the UN, partnerships are necessary between governments, the private sector, civil society, and other parties composed of every facet of this global community.

The Sustainable Development Goals are a universal call to action to improve the lives and prospects of everyone, everywhere, to end poverty, and to protect the planet. The UN Agenda and its 17 goals adopted by **all** UN Member States in 2015 are to be read as a component of green transition. If we do not protect nature and do not adopt more sustainable development, phasing our fossil fuels and favoring the passage to renewables, the whole of humanity is at risk. Thus, increasing international cooperation is a necessary path to shape a zero-emission society, a legacy the current governments and leaders have the obligation to leave to future generations, as future generations have the right to inherit a healthy planet.

---

[150] Visit: Net Zero Tracker | Energy & Climate Intelligence Unit (eciu.net) at: https://eciu.net/netzerotracker (accessed January 23, 2023).

On July 7, 2022, the UN released *The Sustainable Development Goals Report 2022*[151] which provides a global overview of progress on the implementation of the 2030 Agenda for Sustainable Development using the latest available data and estimates. It tracks the global and regional progress toward the 17 Goals with in-depth analyses of selected indicators for each Goal.

According to the report, "*cascading and interlinked crises are putting the 2030 Agenda for Sustainable Development in grave danger, along with humanity's very own survival. The Report highlights the severity and magnitude of the challenges before us. The confluence of crises, dominated by COVID-19, climate change, and conflicts, are creating spin-off impacts on food and nutrition, health, education, the environment, and peace and security, and affecting all the Sustainable Development Goals (SDGs).*"[152] The report details the reversal of years of progress in eradicating poverty and hunger, improving health and education, providing basic services, and much more. It also points out areas that need urgent action in order to secure the SDGs and deliver meaningful progress for people and the planet by 2030.

Given the importance of enhancing international cooperation to reach these goals and achieve green transition, it appears appropriate to introduce SDG 17 which is the one goal that emphasizes the paramount importance of shaping an inclusive partnership at a global level to achieve these goals and therefore a sustainable future for the whole of humanity.

2.2. *SDG 17: The goal to link the World*

> "*A successful development of the UN Agenda 2030 requires inclusive partnerships — at the global, regional, national and local levels — built upon principles and values, and upon a shared vision and shared goals placing people and the planet at the centre.*"[153]

[151] The Sustainable Development Goals Report, by the UN, document available at: https://unstats.un.org/sdgs/report/2022/. EY, Six ways that governments can drive the green transition, document available at: https://www.ey.com/en_gr/government-public-sector/six-ways-that-governments-can-drive-the-green-transition (accessed January 28, 2023).

[152] *Ibid.*

[153] See SGS 17, available at: https://www.un.org/sustainabledevelopment/globalpartnerships/.

The huge and complex challenge of climate change, which is strictly linked to the green transition and to the UN's Goals for a Sustainable Development, inevitably demands collaboration not only from every individual and organization across society but also a more stringent collaboration among nations. Strong international cooperation is needed now more than ever to ensure that countries have the means to completely recover from the COVID-19 pandemic, a recession caused by the conflict in Ukraine, and more importantly from a climatic crisis which affects the entire global community, and thus build back better and achieve the Sustainable Development Goals.

Tackling the environmental, economic, and social impacts of climate change, which inevitably influence relations among nations, requires a major transformation across all sectors which will necessarily lead to a greener economy. Meeting ambitious sustainability targets requires a bold, whole-of-society approach sustained by long-term government commitments to be aligned with the SDGs and also transform our society into a carbon-neutral society possibly before 2050. Because this is not an easy task, governments can also do more to educate people on the impact of their lifestyle choices, nudging them toward more sustainable consumption and behavior, for example, favoring the use of electric vehicles, also raise awareness about the necessity of protecting nature. Governments should also advice people to favor ethical investments, informing them about the novelty and convenience of green and sustainable finance. In fact, the public sector alone can likely not supply all the needed resources to accomplish this green transition. Wealthier economies can support the green transition in other countries and promote the development of renewables as clean energy plays a fundamental role in decarbonizing our economies. Transiting toward more sustainable development also includes the implementation of the other SDGs which can only be realized with strong global partnerships and cooperation.

2.3. *The global community has no choice but to act in a concerted manner*

If we do not act immediately to stop climate change by finding adequate solutions to reverse the degradation of nature, and if we fail to implement the SDGs and green transition, aside from the catastrophic impact on the lived environment — such as depletion of natural resources, frequent and intense drought, and extreme weather events — we will severely impact our lives, heighten health and social inequalities, and push millions of people into extreme poverty. Not acting or delaying putting in place adequate measures will also undermine countries' resilience to future shocks.

It must be stressed that while the 'Green Deal' is an EU-focused initiative, it nonetheless recognizes that green transition cannot be understood only as a European challenge but as a global one that requires a worldwide effort and response. "This is why the Deal sets the EU to be a global leader in the climate and environmental transition, and commits the European Union to continuing to promote and implement ambitious environment, climate and energy policies around the world, while ensuring support and opportunities to those people who are most affected by and vulnerable to the consequences of this transition."[154] The EU is actively promoting international cooperation and reinforcing its partnership with both the US (reinforcing the transatlantic relationship) and China though the new Comprehensive Agreement on Investment (though still frozen) and the Green Partnership (see Chapter 3). Furthermore, the EU and the African Union have also established an Africa–EU Energy Partnership (AEEP)[155] that will be one of the pillars of the new Joint Africa–EU Strategy (JAES).[156] This will constitute a long-term framework for

[154] See in this sense: 'The EU Green Agenda & International Partnership,' included in The EU Green Deal In International Partnerships: An example guide of EU and SOLAR members' work; the entire document is available at: https://www.arcsculturesolidali.org/wp-content/uploads/2021/06/Solidar-Briefing-paper-v07.pdf (accessed January 28, 2023).

[155] AEEP | Africa-EU Energy Partnership: *The Africa-EU Energy Partnership was launched by African and European Heads of State in 2007 at the AU-EU Summit in Lisbon, Portugal. A central partnership of the Joint Africa-EU Strategy, the AEEP is the key political platform through which both continents work together on energy. The overall aim of the AEEP is to facilitate the achievement of universal access to affordable, sustainable and modern energy services in Africa, including in rural areas, as a necessity and as a pre-requisite to generating inclusive development and jobs.* Visit: https://africa-eu-energy-partnership.org For more information concerning Africa–EU Partnership, see also the European Commission webpage "Africa–EU Partnership" at: https://international-partnerships.ec.europa.eu/policies/africa-eu-partnership_en (accessed January 28, 2023).

[156] A Joint Africa–EU Strategy: *In 2007, the Joint Africa-EU Strategy (JAES) was adopted at the Lisbon Summit, which brought together the Leaders of 27 European and 54 African States as well as the Presidents of the continental Institutions. The purpose of the Joint Strategy is to take the Africa-EU Partnership to a new strategic level with a strengthened political dialogue and enhanced cooperation at all levels. The JAES reflects the*

strategic dialogue between the two continents, aimed at sharing knowledge, setting political priorities, and developing joint programs on key energy issues. The overall objective of the AEEP will be to improve access to secure, affordable, and sustainable energy for both continents, with a special focus on increasing investment in energy infrastructure in Africa.

It must be noted that at the sub-regional and country levels, the EU will also reinforce its support to the green transition by funding tools such as the Neighbourhood, Development and International Cooperation Instrument (NDICI).[157] The funding allocation of the NDICI will depend on the elaboration of country and regional Multiannual Indicative Programs (MIPs).[158]

Euro-African consensus on values, joint interests and common strategic objectives, he Joint Africa-EU Strategy, which provides the overarching long-term framework for Africa-EU relations, is implemented through jointly identified priorities, which are of common interest to both the EU and Africa, and significantly impact on the daily lives of citizens on both continents. Within each area of cooperation, the focus is on actions at the global, continental or cross regional levels and in which participating actors have a collective capacity to deliver. More at https://knowledge4policy.ec.europa.eu/publication/joint-africa-eu-strategy_en (accessed January 28, 2023).

[157]Neighbourhood, Development and International Cooperation Instrument — Global Europe (NDICI — Global Europe). Global Europe instrument merges several former EU external financing instruments. It aims to support countries most in need to overcome long-term developmental challenges and will contribute to achieving the international commitments and objectives that the Union has agreed to, in particular the 2030 Agenda and its Sustainable Development Goals and the Paris Agreement. Overall allocation= €79.5 billion. More at: https://neighbourhood-enlargement.ec.europa.eu/funding-and-technical-assistance/neighbourhood-development-and-international-cooperation-instrument-global-europe-ndici-global-europe_en (accessed January 28, 2023).

In particular, the 'Global Challenges' program of the Neighbourhood, Development and International Cooperation Instrument — Global Europe (NDICI-Global Europe) covers the global and multilateral dimension of the EU's action to implement its political priorities. It aims to strengthen the EU as a global actor in the delivery of the United Nations' 2030 Agenda for Sustainable Development and the Paris Agreement to help eradicate poverty, reduce inequalities, and achieve sustainable development. Visit: https://international-partnerships.ec.europa.eu/system/files/2022-01/mip-2021-c2021-9157-global-challenges-annex_en.pdf (accessed January 28, 2023).

[158]The *National Indicative Programme* (NIP), together with the Single Support Framework (SSF) and Multi-Annual Indicative Programme (MIPs), represents an important step in the programming of EU aid, outlining areas where EU assistance will be directed. These instruments define the sectors where the EU funding will be focused to achieve maximum

In the international context, is evident that a new multilateralism is emerging, and the recent crisis in Ukraine is evidence that it will be more difficult to follow the same path for certain international issues, such as securing sources of energy (especially gas). However, it is also necessary to find common ground and reinforce international cooperation, at least to tackle global warming and reduce greenhouse emissions because this is the only path humanity has at its disposal to secure its survival while shaping sustainable development. The urgencies we need to face are numerous and are exacerbated by the pandemic, which has not ended yet, and the recent crisis and recession caused by the conflict in Ukraine. Only with reinforced international cooperation will it be possible to tackle climate change and find proper solutions to reverse it before it is too late and build a shared future for the entire global community.

---

impact and value for money of EU cooperation. Visit: https://europa.eu/capacity4dev/ (accessed January 28, 2023).

Conclusion

From the pages of this manuscript, the urgency of the radical transformation of our growth model has clearly emerged, and thus the necessity to embrace green transition, a transition to a more sustainable economy coupled with and the increased use of clean and renewable sources of energy if we want to preserve our own existence and society. Science leaves no doubt about the urgency of the situation. Research has proved the rapid degradation of our environment and global warming, and changes in climate patterns are putting at risk the existence of many species and ecosystems, elements of extreme importance for our very existence and prosperity. Protecting and restoring nature and biodiversity is the only way to preserve the quality and continuity of human life on earth. To achieve this objective, it is necessary to adopt a more sustainable development modality which includes a drastic reduction of fossil fuels responsible not only for the great majority of greenhouse gas emissions but also for the degradation of our environment and destruction of ecosystems when intrusive methodologies are used to extract resources. Transition to renewable sources of energy is a necessary path to contribute to the greening of our economies and green transition, which represents the only choice we have to ensure a shared future for mankind. Commitments from the most advanced economies and emerging economies have been translated into political initiatives to pave the way for ambitious and necessary changes — that will ensure the well-being and economic prosperity of present and future generations in a healthy environment. These initiatives will serve as an example for the rest of the global community. The boldness of these initiatives concerns the gradual decarbonization of industries and the substantial reduction of emissions from other sectors, in particular the energy sector, favoring the development of renewables and new technologies enabling and facilitating the achievement of a neutral carbon society by 2050 (2060 for China). But this represents only a part of the targets. We have the example of the UN's Agenda 2030 for Sustainable Development, which serves as a roadmap for the entire global community. The implementation of these commitments will contribute to shaping a sustainable future for all and in forging new partnerships needed not only to tackle climate change but also new challenges. The pandemic caused by COVID-19 has not ended, and from the experience of these last 3 years we should have learned that cooperation among nations is more than desirable to contain the devastating effects of unforeseen and unwanted events affecting the entire global community.

As evidenced, global warming and the consequences of climate change represent an existential threat for the whole of humanity far larger than any current or recent exigencies. But since the components of the global community are only affected indirectly or partially, and potential solutions require concerted alignment and common efforts, collaboration is not automatically materializing to the degree that is needed as the most recent data from the IPCC have shown. To act in a coordinated manner is now a necessity to avoid a climatic global disaster. It has been scientifically proved that if we do not stop climate change and converge toward a nature-positive economy, the costs to repair damage to our environment will be extremely high. Scientists have been able to make projections of what may await us if the world temperature increase hits 1.5°C, but the uncertainty around the impacts, vulnerabilities, and costs increases exponentially beyond this point. It is therefore evident that there is no time to waste and action is to be taken now, putting aside divergences and conflicts to address the many challenges to transition toward a carbon-neutral economy. However, to reach this target and shape sustainable development, it is necessary to invest more in nature, and indeed the finance sector will play a fundamental role, with the development of the green and sustainable finance, to provide for the necessary resources. Green bonds, blue bonds, and in general investment in sustainable projects not only represent an opportunity for investors to contribute to preserving or restoring ecosystems, and fighting climate change, but also have the potential to become a huge business opportunity because companies through innovation and technological improvements will support the transition to a lower-carbon and a more energy-efficient economic system, and this naturally can have a significant impact on businesses too if they are able to grasp this opportunity. At the same time, this will also stimulate and revolutionize the financial sector. New financial instruments will be created for specific exigencies, thus further favoring the developing of green finance which will support this green transition.

In the ambit of climate change, the EU continues to lead by example in its attempt to achieve climate neutrality by 2050 with the implementation of its 'Green Deal' which is not limited to preserving Nature *per se,* but to advance toward a carbon-neutral economy, valorizing our environment as a fundamental component of our economies, and naturally promoting the further deployment of alternative and renewable sources of energy that are needed to accompany this green transition. As noted in the pages of this manuscript, this is also the path followed by the US and China with their recent initiatives aimed at placing nature at the center of their attention and development Their decisions will have a significant external impact in a globalized and connected world. Though approaches to climate change are influenced by domestic politics, including relative prioritization, and the nature of international relationships, it is clear that environmental protection and climate change remain important global issues for maintaining common interest and addressing shared concerns. China has become a world leader in solar and wind energy and it plans to further expand its capacity, imitated by the other major economies which are emphasizing the role of renewables in this endeavor to phase out fossil fuels. Countries all around the world will inevitably follow these examples because it is the only path we have in order to accomplish the targets in line with the Paris Convention. Green globalization is the only way forward and the major economies are setting an example for the entire global community.

The EU with its 'Green Deal' has become a meaningful global actor, a model, and a driver for change, and it is actively encouraging its partners to advance toward sustainable development. It is worth emphasizing that no other major country has made so clear and so forceful a commitment to making the green transition and, if China and the US are genuinely involved, as it seems considering the adoption and the implementation of their new policies, the positive impact on the planet will be enormous and will prove that collaboration is still possible notwithstanding differences when the survival of the whole of humanity is at risk.

Bibliography

Textbooks

Paolo Rizzi, Cristiano Rizzi, Mario Tettamanti, Cristiano Rizzi, *The Impact of COVID-19 on World Aviation Industry — Challenges and Opportunities*, World Scientific, April 2022.

Xi Jinping, *The Governance of China*, Vol. II, Foreign Language Press, Beijing, 2017.

Yu Xugang, Cristiano Rizzi, Mario Tettamanti, Fabio E. Ziccardi, Guo Li, *China's Belt and Road: The Initiative and Its Financial Focus*, World Scientific, June 2018.

Yu Xugang, Mario Tettamanti, Cristiano Rizzi, *China–US Trade Frictions Shaping New Equilibriums with the EU and the US — Towards a New Multilateralism or Tripolarism*, World Scientific, February 2021.

Yu Xugang, Mario Tettamanti, Cristiano Rizzi, *China's Continued Reforms on a New Era — Their Impact on Chinese Foreign Direct Investments and RMB Internationalization*, World Scientific, March 2020.

Zhang Hong *et al.*, *China's 40 Years of Reform and Development 1978–2018*, ANU Press, The ANU Press Australian National University, 2018.

Other Sources

Official Documents, Pieces of Legislation, Reports and Articles (Main)

Of global relevance

Andréa Worden, "China at the UN Human Rights Council: Conjuring a 'Community of Shared Future for Humankind'?" and Malin Oud, "Harmonic Convergence: China and the Right to Development," in Nadège Rolland (ed.), *An Emerging China-Centric Order*, NBR Special Report 87, August 2020.

Electric Vehicle Outlook 2022, BloombergNEF, document available at: https://about.bnef.com/electric-vehicle-outlook/ (accessed January 28, 2023).

Energy Tracker Asia, *What the 2021 China Wind Power Boom Means for the World*, article available at: https://energytracker.asia/what-the-2021-china-wind-power-boom-means-for-the-world/ (accessed January 28, 2023).

EY, *Six Ways That Governments Can Drive the Green Transition*, document available at: https://www.ey.com/en_gr/government-public-sector/six-ways-that-governments-can-drive-the-green-transition (accessed January 28, 2023).

Global Electricity Review 2021, this is a report by Ember. This report showcases a global dataset for electricity generation and demand across 217 countries from 2000 to 2020. Data for 2020 contained in the report covers 90 percent of the world's electricity production, available at: https://ember-climate.org/insights/research/global-electricity-review-2021/ and "*G20 Profile — China — Global Electricity Review 2021*," document available at: https://ember-climate.org/app/uploads/2022/02/Global-Electricity-Review-2021-China.pdf (accessed January 28, 2023).

IEA (International Energy Agency), *Renewables 2021 — Analysis and Forecast to 2026*, document available at: https://iea.blob.core.windows.net/assets/5ae32253-7409-4f9a-a91d-1493ffb9777a/Renewables2021-Analysisandforecastto2026.pdf (accessed January 28, 2023).

IEA, *An Energy Sector Roadmap to Carbon Neutrality in China*, document available at: https://iea.blob.core.windows.net/assets/6689062e-43fc-40c8-9659-01cf96150318/AnenergysectorroadmaptocarbonneutralityinChina.pdf (accessed January 28, 2023).

IEA, *Hydropower Special Market Report — Analysis and Forecast to 2030*, revised version, July 2021, document available at: https://iea.blob.core.windows.net/assets/4d2d4365-08c6-4171-9ea2-8549fabd1c8d/HydropowerSpecialMarketReport_corr.pdf (accessed January 28, 2023).

International Chamber of Shipping, *Shipping Industry Sets Out Bold Plan to Global Regulator to Deliver Net Zero by 2050*, article available at: https://www.ics-shipping.org/press-release/shipping-industry-sets-out-bold-plan-to-global-regulator-to-deliver-net-zero-by-2050/ (accessed January 28, 2023).

IPCC, *The Evidence Is Clear: The Time for Action Is Now. We Can Halve Emissions by 2030*, April 4, 2022, available at: https://www.ipcc.ch/2022/04/04/ipcc-ar6-wgiii-pressrelease/ (accessed January 28, 2023).

IPCC: *AR5 Climate Change 2014: Mitigation of Climate Change*, Assessment Report, document available at: https://www.ipcc.ch/report/ar5/wg3/ (accessed January 28, 2023).

IRENA (International Renewable Energy Agency), *Green Hydrogen — A Guide to Policy Making*, November 2020, document available at: https://irena.org/publications/2020/Nov/Green-hydrogen (accessed January 28, 2023).

IRENA, *Energy Transformation 2050*, publication available at: https://irena.org/-/media/Files/IRENA/Agency/Publication/2020/Apr/IRENA_GRO_Summary_2020.pdf?la=en&hash=1F18E445B56228AF8C4893CAEF147ED0163A0E47 (accessed January 28, 2023).

IRENA, *Future of Solar Photovoltaic: Deployment, Investment, Technology, Grid Integration and Socio-Economic Aspects*, 2019, document available at: Future of Solar Photovoltaic — A Global Energy Transformation paper (irena.org) (accessed January 28, 2023).

IRENA, *Future of Wind — Deployment, Investment, Technology, Grid Integration and Socio-Economic Aspects*, October 2019, document available at: https://www.irena.org/-/media/files/irena/agency/publication/2019/oct/irena_future_of_wind_2019.pdf (accessed January 28, 2023).

IRENA, *Innovation Outlook — Ocean Energy Technologies*, 2020, document available at: https://www.irena.org/-/media/Files/IRENA/Agency/Publication/2020/Dec/IRENA_Innovation_Outlook_Ocean_Energy_2020.pdf.

Is the Global Climate Governance System Working? Jimera Leiva Roesch, Julia Almeida Nobre, and Eimer Curtin, IPI Global Observatory, November 23, 2021, article available at: https://theglobalobservatory.org/2021/11/is-the-global-climate-governance-system-working/ (accessed January 28, 2023).

Kunming Declaration, *Declaration from the High-Level Segment of the UN Biodiversity Conference 2020* (Part I) under the theme: "Ecological Civilization: Building a Shared Future for All Life on Earth" (final Draft), document available at: https://www.cbd.int/doc/c/df35/4b94/5e86e1ee09bc8c7d4b35aaf0/kunmingdeclaration-en.pdf (accessed January 28, 2023).

Net-Zero Carbon Emissions by 2050, IATA, Press Release No. 66, October 4, 2021, document available at: https://www.iata.org/en/pressroom/2021-releases/2021-10-04-03/ (accessed January 28, 2023).

Press release by IEA, *China has Clear Pathway to Build a More Sustainable, Secure and Inclusive Energy Future*, September 29, 2021, available at: https://www.iea.org/news/china-has-a-clear-pathway-to-build-a-more-sustainable-secure-and-inclusive-energy-future (accessed January 28, 2023).

"*Progress towards the Sustainable Development Goals*," Report of the Secretary-General, 2017, document available at: https://unstats.un.org/sdgs/files/report/2017/secretary-general-sdg-report-2017--Statistical-Annex.pdf, see also https://unstats.un.org/sdgs/indicators/database/?indicator=9.1.2 (accessed January 28, 2023).

Seizing Business Opportunities in China's Transition Towards a Nature-Positive Economy, World Economic Forum, 2022, available at: https://www3.weforum.org/docs/WEF_New_Nature_Economy_Report_China_2022.pdf (accessed January 28, 2023).

Sharm el-Sheiks Implementation Plan, Decision CP.27, The Conference of the Parties on Climate Change (COP27), document available at: https://unfccc.int/sites/default/files/resource/cop27_auv_2_cover%20decision.pdf (accessed January 28, 2023).

The Global Risks Report 2020 (15th Edition), *World Economic Forum*, document available at: https://www3.weforum.org/docs/WEF_Global_Risk_Report_2020.pdf (accessed January 28, 2023).

The Paris Agreement, The Paris Agreement is a legally binding international treaty on climate change. It was adopted by 196 Parties at COP 21 in Paris, on December 12, 2015 and entered into force on November 4, 2016, available at: https://unfccc.int/process-and-meetings/the-paris-agreement/the-paris-agreement (last accessed January 28, 2023).

Transforming Our World: 2030 Agenda for Sustainable Development, United Nations, document available at: https://sustainabledevelopment.un.org/post2015/transformingourworld (accessed January 28, 2023). The 17 Goals of the 2030 Agenda are available at: https://sdgs.un.org/2030agenda (accessed January 28, 2023).

UNCTAD, see: *Decarbonizing the Maritime Sector: Mobilizing Coordinated Action in the Industry using an Ecosystem Approach*, article available at: https://unctad.org/news/decarbonizing-maritime-sector-mobilizing-coordinated-action-industry-using-ecosystems-approach (accessed January 28, 2023).

World Economic Forum White Paper, *Investing in a Biodiversity-Integrated Manner*, document available at: https://www3.weforum.org/docs/WEF_Investing_in_a_Biodiversity_Integrated_Manner_2022.pdf (accessed January 28, 2023).

World Economic Forum, *Nature Risk Rising: Why the Crisis Engulfing Nature Matters for Business and the Economy,* 2020, document available at: https://www3.weforum.org/docs/WEF_New_Nature_Economy_Report_2020.pdf (accessed January 28, 2023).

EU, US, and China (Single Block, and Bilateral Relevance)

EU

A Framework Strategy for a Resilient Energy Union with a Forward-Looking Climate Change Policy/COM/2015/080 final, document available at: https://eur-lex.europa.eu/legal-content/EN/TXT/?uri=COM:2015:80:FIN (accessed October 28, 2022).

An EU Strategy to Harness the Potential of Offshore Renewable Energy for a Climate Neutral Future, COM(2020)741 final, document available at: https://eur-lex.europa.eu/legal-content/EN/TXT/?uri=COM:2020:741:FIN&qid=1605792629666 (accessed January 28, 2023).

"Communication from the Commission to the European Parliament, the Council, the European Economic and Social Committee and the Committee on the Regions — A hydrogen strategy for a climate-neutral Europe, COM, 2020, 301 final, document available at: https://ec.europa.eu/energy/sites/ener/files/hydrogen_strategy.pdf (accessed January 28, 2023).

COM(2020)21 final, *Sustainable Europe Investment Plan — European Green Deal Investment Plan,* This plan represents the pillar of the green deal, document available at: https://ec.europa.eu/commission/presscorner/api/files/attachment/860462/Commission%20Communication%20on%20the%20European%20Green%20Deal%20Investment%20Plan_EN.pdf (accessed January 28, 2023).

COM(2020)98 Final, Communication from The Commission to the European Parliament, The Council, The European Economic and Social Committee and The Committee of The Regions — *A New Circular Economy Action Plan for a Cleaner and More Competitive Europe*, document available at: https://eur-lex.europa.eu/resource.html?uri=cellar:9903b325-6388-11ea-b735-01aa75ed71a1.0017.02/DOC_1&format=PDF (accessed January 28, 2023).

COM(2020)318 final, A Farm to Fork Strategy for a fair, healthy and environmentally-friendly food system, document available at: https://eur-lex.europa.eu/legal-content/EN/TXT/?uri=CELEX:52020DC0381 (accessed January 28, 2023).

COM(2020)667 final, *Chemicals Strategy for Sustainability Towards a Toxic-Free Environment*, document available at: https://ec.europa.eu/environment/pdf/chemicals/2020/10/Strategy.pdf (accessed January 28, 2023).

COM(2020)789 Sustainable and Smart Mobility Strategy — Putting European transport on track for the future, document available at: https://eur-lex.europa.eu/legal-content/EN/TXT/?uri=CELEX%3A52020DC0789 (accessed January 28, 2023).

COM(2021)400 final, *Pathway to a Healthy Planet for All — EU Action Plan: Towards Zero Pollution for Air, Water, and Soil*, document available at: https://eur-lex.europa.eu/legal-content/EN/TXT/?uri=CELEX%3A52021DC0400&qid=1623311742827 (accessed January 28, 2023).

EU Biodiversity Strategy for 2030 — Bringing nature back into our lives, available at: https://ec.europa.eu/info/sites/default/files/communication-annex-eu-biodiversity-strategy-2030_en.pdf (accessed January 28, 2023).

EU Hydrogen Strategy: COM(2020)301 Final — A hydrogen strategy for a climate-neutral Europe. This strategy was designed with a phased approach and its goal is to increase hydrogen shares from less than 2 percent today up to 13–14 percent by 2050, document available at: https://eur-lex.europa.eu/legal-content/EN/TXT/?uri=CELEX:52020DC0301 (accessed January 28, 2023).

European Commission, COM(2021)558 final, Proposal for a Directive of the European Parliament and of the Council on Energy Efficiency, official document available at: https://eur-lex.europa.eu/resource.html?uri=cellar:a214c850-e574-11eb-a1a5-01aa75ed71a1.0001.02/DOC_1&format=PDF (accessed January 28, 2023).

European Commission, Communication from the Commission to the European Parliament, the European Council, the Council, the European Economic and Social Committee and the Committee of the Regions, REPowerEU Plan, Brussels, 18.5.2022, COM(2022)230 final, document available at: https://eur-lex.europa.eu/legal-content/EN/TXT/?uri=COM%253A2022%253A230%253AFIN&qid=1653033742483 (accessed January 28, 2023).

European Commission, Communication From the Commission to the European Parliament, the European Council, the Council, the European Economic and Social Committee and the Committee of the Regions, The European Deal, Brussels, 11.12.2019 COM, 2019, 640 final, document available at: https://ec.europa.eu/info/sites/default/files/european-green-deal-communication_en.pdf (accessed January 28, 2023).

EU Solar Strategy, COM(2022) 221, (18.05.2022), official document available at: https://eur-lex.europa.eu/legal-content/EN/TXT/?uri=COM%3A2022%3A221%3AFIN&qid=1653034500503 (accessed January 28, 2023).

Regulation (EU) 2021/1119 of the European Parliament and of the Council of 30 June 2021 establishing the framework for achieving climate neutrality and amending Regulations (EC) No 401/2009 and (EU) 2018/1999

('European Climate Law'), document available at: https://eur-lex.europa.eu/legal-content/EN/TXT/?uri=CELEX:32021R1119 (accessed January 28, 2023).

Regulation (EU) 2021/241 of the European Parliament and of the Council, of February 12, 2021 establishing the Recovery and Resilience Facility, document available at: https://eur-lex.europa.eu/legal-content/EN/TXT/?uri=CELEX%3A32021R0241 (accessed January 28, 2023).

US

Department of Energy, DOE Releases Energy-Saving Rules for Federal Buildings and Proposes New Standards for Consumer Appliances, March 30, 2022, available at: https://www.energy.gov/articles/doe-releases-energy-saving-rules-federal-buildings-and-proposes-new-standards-consumer (accessed January 28, 2023).

Executive Order Executive Order 14008, Tackling the Climate Crisis at Home and Abroad, January 27, 2021 — Presidential Actions, document available at: https://www.whitehouse.gov/briefing-room/presidential-actions/2021/01/27/executive-order-on-tackling-the-climate-crisis-at-home-and-abroad/ (accessed January 28, 2023).

Executive Order 14027, Establishment of the Climate Change Support Office, May 7, 2021, document available at: https://www.govinfo.gov/content/pkg/DCPD-202100388/pdf/DCPD-202100388.pdf (accessed January 28, 2023).

Executive Order 14030, Climate-Related Financial Risk, May 20, 2021 — Presidential Actions, document available at: https://www.whitehouse.gov/briefing-room/presidential-actions/2021/05/20/executive-order-on-climate-related-financial-risk/, (accessed January 28, 2023).

Executive Order 14037, *Strengthening American Leadership in Clean Cars and Trucks*, August 5, 2021 — Presidential Actions, document available at: https://www.whitehouse.gov/briefing-room/presidential-actions/2021/08/05/executive-order-on-strengthening-american-leadership-in-clean-cars-and-trucks/ (accessed January 28, 2023).

Fact Sheet: Biden Administration Advances Expansion & Modernization of the Electric Grid, April 27, 2021, available at: https://www.whitehouse.gov/briefing-room/statements-releases/2021/04/27/fact-sheet-biden-administration-advances-expansion-modernization-of-the-electric-grids (accessed January 28, 2023).

Fact Sheet: President Biden Announces steps to Drive American Leadership Forward on Clean Cars and Trucks, August 5, 2021, available at: https://www.whitehouse.gov/briefing-room/statements-releases/2021/08/05/fact-sheet-president-biden-announces-steps-to-drive-american-leadership-forward-on-clean-cars-and-trucks/ (accessed January 28, 2023).

Fact Sheet: Vice President Harris Announces Actions to Accelerate Clean Transit Buses, School Buses, and Trucks, March 7, 2022, available at: https://www.whitehouse.gov/briefing-room/statements-releases/2022/03/07/fact-sheet-vice-president-harris-announces-actions-to-accelerate-clean-transit-buses-school-buses-and-trucks/ (accessed January 28, 2023).

Fact Sheet: Biden Administration Advances the Future of Sustainable Fuels in America Aviation, September 9, 2021, available at: https://www.whitehouse.gov/briefing-room/statements-releases/2021/09/09/fact-sheet-biden-administration-advances-the-future-of-sustainable-fuels-in-american-aviation/ (accessed January 28, 2023).

Fact Sheet: The Biden-Harris Electric Vehicle Charging Action Plan, December 15, 2021, available at: https://www.whitehouse.gov/briefing-room/statements-releases/2021/12/13/fact-sheet-the-biden-harris-electric-vehicle-charging-action-plan/ (accessed January 28, 2023).

Fact Sheet: Developing a Bold Vision for Commercial Fusion Energy, March 15, 2022, available at: https://www.whitehouse.gov/ostp/news-updates/2022/03/15/fact-sheet-developing-a-bold-vision-for-commercial-fusion-energy/ (accessed January 28, 2023).

Fact Sheet: Biden-Harris Administration Ensuring Future Is Made in America, February 8, 2022, available at: https://www.whitehouse.gov/briefing-room/statements-releases/2022/02/08/fact-sheet-biden-harris-administration-ensuring-future-is-made-in-america/ (accessed January 28, 2023).

Fact Sheet: The Biden-Harris Action Plan for Building Better School Infrastructure, April 4, 2022, document available at https://www.whitehouse.gov/briefing-room/statements-releases/2022/04/04/fact-sheet-the-biden-harris-action-plan-for-building-better-school-infrastructure/ (accessed January 28, 2023).

Fact Sheet: Biden-Harris Administration Launches Coalition of States and Local Governments to Strengthen Building Performance Standards, January 21, 2022, document available at: https://www.whitehouse.gov/briefing-room/statements-releases/2022/01/21/fact-sheet-biden-harris-administration-launches-coalition-of-states-and-local-governments-to-strengthen-building-performance-standards/ (accessed January 28, 2023).

Fact Sheet: President Biden Sets 2030 Greenhouse Gas Pollution Reduction Target Aimed at Creating Good-Paying Union Jobs and Securing US Leadership on Clean Energy Technologies, document available at: https://www.whitehouse.gov/briefing-room/statements-releases/2021/04/22/fact-sheet-president-biden-sets-2030-greenhouse-gas-pollution-reduction-target-aimed-at-creating-good-paying-union-jobs-and-securing-u-s-leadership-on-clean-energy-technologies/ (accessed January 28, 2023).

Fact Sheet: Biden Administration Open Pacific Coast to New Jobs and Clean Energy Production with Offshore Wind Department, May 25, 2021, available at: https://www.whitehouse.gov/briefing-room/statements-releases/2021/05/25/fact-sheet-biden-administration-opens-pacific-coast-to-new-jobs-and-clean-energy-production-with-offshore-wind-development/ (accessed January 28, 2023).

Fact Sheet: Biden Administration Jumpstarts Offshore Wind Energy Projects to Create Jobs, March 29, 2021, available at: https://www.whitehouse.gov/briefing-room/statements-releases/2021/03/29/fact-sheet-biden-administration-jumpstarts-offshore-wind-energy-projects-to-create-jobs/ (accessed January 28, 2023).

Fact Sheet: Biden-Harris Administration Races to Deploy Energy that Creates Jobs and Lowers Costs, January 12, 2022, available at: https://www.whitehouse.gov/briefing-room/statements-releases/2022/01/12/fact-sheet-biden-harris-administration-races-to-deploy-clean-energy-that-creates-jobs-and-lowers-costs/ (accessed January 8, 2023).

GeoVision — *Harnessing the Heat Beneath Our Feet,* May 29, 2019, US Department of Energy, document available at: https://www.energy.gov/sites/default/files/2019/06/f63/GeoVision-full-report-opt.pdf (accessed January 28, 2023).

Inflation Reduction Act of 2022 (HR 5376) (The IRA or the Act), on August 16, 2022, act available at: https://www.congress.gov/bill/117th-congress/house-bill/5376?q=%7B%22search%22%3A%5B%22inflation+reduction+act%22%2C%22inflation%22%2C%22reduction%22%2C%22act%22%5D%7D&r=1&s=1.

Kilcher, Levi, Michelle Fogarty, and Michael Lawson. 2021. *Marine Energy in the United States: An Overview of Opportunities*. Golden, CO: National Renewable Energy Laboratory. NREL/TP-5700-78773, document available at: https://www.energy.gov/sites/default/files/2021/02/f82/78773_3.pdf (accessed January 28, 2023).

J. Larsen and others, "A Just Green Recovery," 2020, available at: https://rhg.com/research/a-just-green-recovery/ (accessed January 28, 2023).

K. Rosenberg and others, "Decline of the North American avifauna," Science, 2019, available at: https://science.sciencemag.org/content/366/6461/120 (accessed January 28, 2023).

B. Stein and others, *Reversing America's Wildlife Crisis: Securing the Future of Our Fish and Wildlife*, 2018, available at: https://www.nwf.org/-/media/Documents/PDFs/NWF-Reports/2018/Reversing-Americas-Wildlife-Crisis_2018.ash (accessed January 28, 2023).

The Long-Term Strategy of the United States Pathways to Net-Zero Greenhouse Gas Emissions by 2050, November 2021, available at: https://www.whitehouse.gov/wp-content/uploads/2021/10/US-Long-Term-Strategy.pdf (accessed January 28, 2023).

US Climate Change Policy, October 28, 2021. A document prepared by the Congressional Research Service which contains an explanation of the US policy on Climate Change is available at: https://crsreports.congress.gov/product/pdf/R/R46947 (accessed January 28, 2023).

U.S. Department of Agriculture, USDA Invest $464 Million in Renewable Energy Infrastructure to Help Rural Communities, Businesses and Ag Producers Build Back Better, September 9, 2021, available at: https://www.usda.gov/media/press-releases/2021/09/09/usda-invests-464-million-renewable-energy-infrastructure-help-rural (accessed January 28, 2023).

U.S. Department of Agriculture, USDA to Invest $1 Billion in Climate Smart Commodities, Expanding Markets, Strengthening Rural America, February 7, 2022, available at: https://www.usda.gov/media/press-releases/2022/02/07/usda-invest-1-billion-climate-smart-commodities-expanding-markets (accessed January 28, 2023).

U.S. Department of Agriculture, USDA Announces Steps to Restore Roadless Protections on Tongass National Forest, November 2021, available at: https://www.usda.gov/media/press-releases/2021/11/19/usda-announces-steps-restore-roadless-protections-tongass-national (accessed January 28, 2023).

U.S. Department of Energy — Offshore Wind Energy Strategies, January 2022, document available at: https://www.energy.gov/sites/default/files/2022-01/offshore-wind-energy-strategies-report-january-2022.pdf (accessed January 28, 2023).

U.S. Department of Energy — Growing America's Energy Future, document available at: https://www.nrel.gov/docs/fy11osti/51241.pdf (accessed January 28, 2023).

U.S. Department of Energy, DOE to Build a Consortium of Experts to Expand Geothermal Deployment by Leveraging Knowledge, Technologies, and Skills from the Oil and Gas Industry, article available at: https://www.energy.gov/articles/doe-invest-165-million-advance-domestic-geothermal-energy-deployment (accessed January 28, 2023).

U.S. Department of Energy, DOE Establishes New Office of Clean Energy Demonstrations under the Bipartisan Infrastructure Law, December 21, 2021, available at: https://www.energy.gov/articles/doe-establishes-new-office-clean-energy-demonstrations-under-bipartisan-infrastructure-law (accessed January 28, 2023).

U.S. Department of Energy Announces $25 Million for Cutting-Edge Wave Energy Research, January 2022, available at: https://www.energy.gov/articles/doe-announces-25-million-cutting-edge-wave-energy-research (accessed January 28, 2023).

U.S. Department of Energy, DOE Sets 2025 Community Solar Target to Power 5 Million Homes. October 8, 2021, available at: https://www.energy.gov/articles/doe-sets-2025-community-solar-target-power-5-million-homes (accessed January 28, 2023).

U.S. Department of Energy, Biden Administration, DOE Invest $3 Billion to Strengthen US Supply Chain for Advanced Batteries for Vehicles and Energy Storage, February 11, 2022, available at: https://www.energy.gov/articles/biden-administration-doe-invest-3-billion-strengthen-us-supply-chain-advanced-batteries#:~:text=President%20Biden's%20Bipartisan%20Infrastructure%20Law,sourcing%20materials%20for%20domestic%20manufacturing (accessed January 28, 2023).

U.S. Environmental Protection Agency, EPA and Army Take Action to Provide Certainty for the Definition of WOTUS, November 18, 2021, document available at: https://www.epa.gov/newsreleases/epa-and-army-take-action-provide-certainty-definition-wotus (accessed January 28, 2023).

U.S. Environmental Protection Agency, EPA Finalizes Greenhouse Gas Standards for Passenger Vehicles, Paving Way for a Zero Emissions Future, December 20, 2021, available at: https://www.epa.gov/newsreleases/epa-finalizes-greenhouse-gas-standards-passenger-vehicles-paving-way-zero-emissions (accessed January 28, 2023).

U.S. Environmental Protection Agency, Through Public-Private Partnerships, EPA Helps to Advance Efficiency and Reduce Emissions of American Homes and Buildings, May 17, 2021, document available at: https://www.epa.gov/newsreleases/through-public-private-partnerships-epa-helps-advance-efficiency-and-reduce-emissions (accessed January 28, 2023).

U.S. Environmental Protection Agency, President Biden, EPA Announce $1 Billion Investment from the Bipartisan Infrastructure Law Will Significantly Accelerate Cleanup and Restoration of Great Lakes, February 17, 2022, document available at: https://www.epa.gov/newsreleases/president-biden-epa-announce-1-billion-investment-bipartisan-infrastructure-law-will (accessed January 28, 2023).

U.S. Environmental Protection Agency, EPA Announces New Steps in Process to Protect Bristol Bay Watershed under Clean Water Act Authority, September 9, 2021, document available at: https://www.epa.gov/newsreleases/epa-announces-new-steps-process-protect-bristol-bay-watershed-under-clean-water-act (accessed January 28, 2023).

U.S. Department of the Interior, U.S. Department of Agriculture, U.S. Department of Commerce, Council on Environmental Quality, '*Conserving and Restoring America the Beautiful*,' document available at: https://www.doi.gov/sites/doi.gov/files/report-conserving-and-restoring-america-the-beautiful-2021.pdf (accessed January 28, 2023).

U.S. Department of the Interior, Interior Department Approves Second Major Offshore Wind Project in US Federal Waters, see Press releases 24/11/2021, available at: https://www.doi.gov/pressreleases/interior-department-approves-second-major-offshore-wind-project-us-federal-waters (accessed January 28, 2023).

U.S. Department of Interior, Interior Department Suspends Oil and Gas Leases in Arctic National Wildlife Refuge, January 6, 2021, available at: https://www.doi.gov/pressreleases/interior-department-suspends-oil-and-gas-leases-arctic-national-wildlife-refuge (accessed January 28, 2023).

U.S. Department of Interior, Interior Department Takes Action on Mineral Leases Improperly Renewed in the Watershed of the Boundary Waters Wilderness, January 26, 2022, available at: https://www.doi.gov/pressreleases/interior-department-takes-action-mineral-leases-improperly-renewed-watershed-boundary (accessed January 28, 2023).

U.S. Department of the Interior, Biden-Harris Administration Sets Offshore Energy Records with $4.37 Billion in Winning Bids for Wind Sale, see Press releases 24/11/2021, available at: https://www.doi.gov/pressreleases/biden-harris-administration-sets-offshore-energy-records-437-billion-winning-bids-wind (accessed January 28, 2023).

U.S. Department of Interior, Biden-Harris Administration Fundamental Principles for Domestic Mining Reform, February 22, 2022, document available at: https://www.doi.gov/sites/doi.gov/files/biden-harris-administration-fundamental-principles-for-domestic-mining-reform.pdf (accessed January 28, 2023).

U.S. Department of Transportation, USDOT Announces New Vehicle Fuel Economy Standards for Model Year 2024-2026, April 1, 2022, available at: https://www.transportation.gov/briefing-room/usdot-announces-new-vehicle-fuel-economy-standards-model-year-2024-2026 (accessed January 28, 2023).

U.S. Department of Energy — Growing America's Energy Future, document available at: https://www.nrel.gov/docs/fy11osti/51241.pdf (accessed January 28, 2023).

China

14th FYP is available at: https://cset.georgetown.edu/wp-content/uploads/t0284_14th_Five_Year_Plan_EN.pdf, although in this document Chapters are named as Articles! A bilingual version of the 14th FYP is available at: http://extwprlegs1.fao.org/docs/pdf/chn205796.pdf (accessed January 28, 2023).

Action Plan for Carbon Dioxide Peaking Before 2030, National Development and Reform Commission (NDRC), document available at: https://en.ndrc.

gov.cn/policies/202110/t20211027_1301020.html (accessed January 28, 2023).

Changes, Challenges and Choices: China Is Driven by the Path It Takes, Xinhua, August 28, 2019, article available at: http://www.xinhuanet.com/english/2019-08/28/c_138345879.htm (accessed January 28, 2023).

Chang Lei Ma, *Ocean energy management policy in China*, National Ocean Technology Center, Tianjin, 2019, available at: https://www.sciencedirect.com/science/article/pii/S1877050919308440 (accessed January 28, 2023).

China's 40 Years of Reform and Development 1978–2018, Edited by Ross Garnaut, Ligang Song, and Cai Fang, Published by ANU Press, The Australian National University, 2018.

China's Mid-Century Long-Term Low Greenhouse Gas Emission Development Strategy, document available at: https://unfccc.int/sites/default/files/resource/China%E2%80%99s%20Mid-Century%20Long-Term%20Low%20Greenhouse%20Gas%20Emission%20Development%20Strategy.pdf (accessed January 28, 2023).

China's National Plan on Implementation of the 2030 Agenda for Sustainable Development, document available at: https://www.fmprc.gov.cn/mfa_eng/zxxx_662805/W020161014332600482185.pdf (accessed January 28, 2023).

China's Progress Report on Implementation of the 2030 Agenda for Sustainable Development, this document recalls comprehensively the progress made by China to achieve the 17 SDGs, 2019, report available at: https://www.fmprc.gov.cn/mfa_eng/topics_665678/2030kcxfzyc/P020190924780823323749.pdf (accessed January 28, 2023).

China's Vision 2035: From Beijing's Forbidden City to Interconnected Eurasian Megacity, Bob Savic, March 24, 2021, article available at: https://www.china-briefing.com/news/chinas-vision-2035-from-beijings-forbidden-city-to-interconnected-eurasian-megacity/ (accessed January 28, 2023).

Chinese Perspective on International Relations in the Xi Jinping Era, The International Bureau of Asian Research, NBR Special Report #85, June 2020, by Ren Xiao and Liu Ming.

Department of Resource Conservation and Environmental Protection of the National Development and Reform Commission (NDRC) People's Republic of China, see the '*Working Guidance for Carbon Dioxide Peaking and Carbon Neutrality in Full and Faithful Implementation of the New Development Philosophy*,' October 24, 2021, document available at: https://en.ndrc.gov.cn/policies/202110/t20211024_1300725.html (accessed January 28, 2023).

Global China Daily, *China announces plans to boost biomass energy sector*, August 2021, article available at: https://global.chinadaily.com.cn/a/202108/19/WS611e296ba310efa1bd669e3d.html (accessed January 28, 2023).

Reform of China's Environmental Governance: The Creation of a Ministry of Ecology and Environment, Jinpeng Wang, Chinese Journal of Environment, CJEL, available at: https://brill.com/view/journals/cjel/2/1/article-p112_8.xml?language=en, (accessed January, 28, 2023).

Singularity Hub, *China is taking the worldwide lead in wind power*, Marc Prosser, April 4, 2019, article available at: https://singularityhub.com/2019/04/04/china-is-taking-the-worldwide-lead-in-wind-power/ (accessed January 28, 2023).

Su, Wei, *Enhanced Actions on Climate Change: China's Nationally Determined Contributions*, 2015, document available at: https://www4.unfccc.int/sites/ndcstaging/PublishedDocuments/China%20First/China%27s%20First%20NDC%20Submission.pdf (both in Chinese and English language) (accessed January 28, 2023).

The 14th Five-Years Plan in the New Era of China's Reform — Asian Integration, Belt and Road Initiative and Safeguarding Multilateralism, Michel Aglietta, Guo Bai and Camille Macaire, in Policy Brief, CEPII, No. 2020-36, May 2021.

Towards Carbon Neutrality and China's 14th Five Years Plan: Clean Energy Transition, Sustainable Urban Development, and Investment Priorities, in Environmental Science and Ecotechnology, Vol. 8, October 2021 multi authors, article available at: https://www.sciencedirect.com/science/article/pii/S2666498421000545 (accessed January 28, 2023).

Working Guidance for Carbon Dioxide Peaking and Carbon Neutrality in Full and Faithful Implementation of the new Development Philosophy, the full text of this document is available at the official website of the NDRC, available at: https://en.ndrc.gov.cn/policies/202110/t20211024_1300725.html (accessed January 28, 2023).

World Economic Forum, *Seizing Business Opportunities in China's Transition Towards a Nature-Positive Economy*, 2022, 57, available at: https://www3.weforum.org/docs/WEF_New_Nature_Economy_Report_China_2022.pdf (accessed January 28, 2023).

Xi Jinping, *Build a New Type of International Relations Featuring Win-Win Cooperation, Create a Community of Common Destiny for Mankind,* Xinhua, September 30, 2015, available at: http://www.china.org.cn/xivisitus2015/2015-09/30/content_36720941.htm (accessed January 28, 2023).

Xi Jinping, *Let the Torch of Multilateralism Light up Humanity's Way Forward,* Special Address by H.E. Xi Jinping, President of the People's Republic of China at the World Economic Forum Virtual Event of the Davos Agenda, 25 January 2021, text of the speech available at: https://www.fmprc.gov.cn/mfa_eng/zxxx_662805/t1848323.shtml (accessed January 28, 2023).

Xi Jinping, "*Work Together to Build a Community of Shared Future for Mankind*" (speech, Geneva, January 18, 2017), available at: https://america.cgtn.com/2017/01/18/full-text-of-xi-jinping-keynote-speech-at-the-united-nations-office-in-geneva (accessed January 28, 2023).

Zhao, X., Qi, Y. *Three Decades of Climate Policymaking in China: A View of Learning. Sustainability*, 2022, available at https://mdpi-res.com/d_attachment/sustainability/sustainability-14-02202/article_deploy/sustainability-14-02202-v2.pdf (accessed January 28, 2023).

Bilateral Cooperation

EU-China 2020 Strategic Agenda for Cooperation, available at: https://eeas.europa.eu/archives/docs/china/docs/eu-china_2020_strategic_agenda_en.pdf (accessed January 28, 2023).

EU-China Green Partnership for Better Global Governance, document available at: https://www.kas.de/en/web/mned-bruessel/european-green-deal/detail/-/content/eu-china-green-partnership-for-better-global-governance (accessed January 28, 2023).

"*EU-China Green Partnership for Better Global Governance*," Yanzhu Zhang — Foreign Environmental Cooperation Center, Ministry of Ecology and Environment, Beijing, China, document available at: https://www.kas.de/documents/272317/12679503/EU%E2%80%93China+Green+Partnership+for+Better+Global+Governance.pdf/27f58f22-0798-7b2a-d3ad-8b7263c43461?version=1.0&t=1623391813946 (accessed January 28, 2023).

EU-China Summit: Restoring Peace and Stability in Ukraine Is a Shared Responsibility, available at: https://ec.europa.eu/commission/presscorner/detail/en/IP_22_2214 (accessed January 28, 2023).

EU Commission Staff Working Document — *Impact Assessment Report on the EU-China Investment Relations*, COM (2013) 297 final, and SWD (2013) 184 final.

Next Steps in US-China Climate Contribution, by Shiran Victoria Shen, Jean C. Oi, Yi Cui and Liang Min, The Hill, document available at: https://thehill.com/opinion/energy-environment/3464062-next-steps-in-us-china-climate-cooperation/ (accessed January 28, 2023).

Strategic Analysis and Framework Design on International Cooperation for Energy Transition: A Perspective from China, Pingkuo Liu, Zhaohui Hei, in Energy Reports 8, 2022, 2601–2616, document available at: https://www.sciencedirect.com/science/article/pii/S2352484722001743#tbl1 (accessed January 28, 2023).

"*US-China Joint Glasgow Declaration on Enhancing Climate Action in the 2020s,*" available at: https://www.state.gov/u-s-china-joint-glasgow-declaration-on-enhancing-climate-action-in-the-2020s/ (accessed January 28, 2023).

Green (Sustainable and Climate) Finance

Amacker, J. (2021), Marathon or Sprint? The Race for Green Capital in Emerging Markets, The Centre for Climate Finance & Investment at Imperial College Business School, available at: https://imperialcollegelondon.app.box.com/s/ge9thj52rcehma4bwxyt0fchi3q2niv5 (accessed January 28, 2023).

Amundi (2020), *Facts and Fantasies about the Green Bond Premium*, available at: https://research-center.amundi.com/article/facts-and-fantasies-about-green-bond-premium (accessed January 28, 2023).

Amundi & IFC (2021), *Emerging Market Green Bonds* — Report 2020, available at: https://research-center.amundi.com/article/emerging-market-green-bonds-report-2020 (accessed January 28, 2023).

Amundi Asset Management Company, International Finance Corporation (IFC) (2021) *Emerging Market Green Bonds Report 2020: On the Road to Green Recovery,* available at: https://www.ifc.org/wps/wcm/connect/0fab2dcd-25c9-48cd-b9a8-d6cc4901066e/IFC+Amundi+Emerging+Market+Green+Bonds+Report+2020+%2816April21%29.pdf?MOD=AJPERES&CVID=nzGuFTM (accessed January 28, 2023).

Barton, M. (2021), *Green and Sustainable Bonds in Emerging Markets*, Funds Society, available at: https://www.fundssociety.com/en/news/markets/PICT21-green-and-sustainable-bonds-in-emerging-markets (accessed January 28, 2023).

Capital Market, *Luxembourg Exchange Opposes Mandatory Green Bond Standards*, article available at: https://capitalmonitor.ai/asset-class/fixed-income/luxembourg-exchange-opposes-mandatory-green-bond-standard/ (accessed January 28, 2023).

Climate Bonds Initiative (2017), *Green Securitisation: Unlocking Finance for Small-Scale Low Carbon Projects*, available at: https://www.climatebonds.net/files/files/March17_CBI_Briefing_Green_Securisation.pdf (accessed January 28, 2023).

Climate Bonds Initiative (2018), *Green Securitisation: Unlocking Finance for Small-Scale Low Carbon Projects*, available at: https://www.climatebonds.net/files/reports/green_securitisation_cbi_conference_final.pdf (accessed January 28, 2023).

Climate Bonds Initiative (2019), *Unlocking Green Bonds in Indonesia: A Guide for Issuers, Regulators and Investors*, available at: https://www.climatebonds.

net/files/reports/climate-bonds-indo-barriers-20191219.pdf (accessed January 28, 2023).

Climate Bonds Initiative (2020), ASEAN Sustainable Finance: State of the Market 2020, available at: https://www.climatebonds.net/files/reports/asean-sotm-2020.pdf (accessed January 28, 2023).

Climate Bonds Initiative (2020), *Green Bond Pricing in the Primary Market*, available at: https://www.climatebonds.net/resources/reports/green-bond-pricing-primary-market-h2-2020 (accessed January 28, 2023).

Climate Bonds Initiative (2020), *Sustainable Debt: Global State of the Market*, available at: https://www.climatebonds.net/files/reports/cbi_sd_sotm_2020_04d.pdf (accessed January 28, 2023).

Climate Bonds Initiative (2021), *Climate Bonds Releases Green Bond Pricing Report for H2 2020:* Greenium increasingly visible including German Sovereign Green Bund, available at: https://www.climatebonds.net/resources/press-releases/2021/03/climate-bonds-releases-green-bond-pricing-report-h2-2020-greenium (accessed January 28, 2023).

Climate Bonds Initiative (2021), *Post-Issuance Reporting in the Green Bond Market*, available at: https://www.climatebonds.net/files/reports/cbi_post_issuance_2021_02c.pdf (accessed January 28, 2023).

Climate Bonds Initiative (2021), *Sovereign Green, Social, and Sustainability Bond Survey: The Ultimate Power to Transform the Market*, available at: https://www.climatebonds.net/files/reports/cbi-sovereign-green-social-sustainability-bond-survey-jan2021.pdf (accessed January 28, 2023).

Environmental Finance (2020), *Green Bond Funds Take Varied Approach to Impact Reporting*, available at: https://www.environmental-finance.com/content/analysis/green-bond-funds-take-varied-approach-to-impact-reporting.html (accessed January 28, 2023).

Environmental Finance (2020), *Sustainable Bonds Insight* 2020, available at: https://www.environmental-finance.com/pages/sustainable-bonds-insight-2020.html (accessed January 28, 2023).

Environmental Finance (2021), Award for innovation — bond structure (green bond): Symbiotics, available at: https://www.environmental-finance.com/content/awards/winners/award-for-innovation-bond-structure-(green-bond)-symbiotics.html (accessed January 28, 2023).

Environmental Finance (2021), *Sustainable Bonds Insight 2021*, available at: https://www.environmental-finance.com/assets/files/research/sustainable-bonds-insight-2021.pdf (accessed January 28, 2023).

European Commission (2021), Press release: Commission puts forward new strategy to make the EU's financial system more sustainable and proposes new European Green Bond Standard, available at: https://ec.europa.eu/commission/presscorner/detail/en/ip_21_3405 (accessed January 28, 2023).

European Commission, Sustainability-related disclosure in the financial services sector, available at: https://ec.europa.eu/info/business-economy-euro/banking-and-finance/sustainable-finance/sustainability-related-disclosure-financial-services-sector_en (accessed January 28, 2023).

EU, *Common Ground Taxonomy — Climate Change Mitigation,* International Platform on Sustainable Finance, Taxonomy Working Group Co-chaired by the EU and China, document available at: https://ec.europa.eu/info/sites/default/files/business_economy_euro/banking_and_finance/documents/211104-ipsf-common-ground-taxonomy-instruction-report-2021_en.pdf (accessed January 28, 2023).

EU, Opinion of the European Central Bank of 5 November 2021 on a proposal for a regulation on European green bonds (CON/2021/30) , *Official Journal of the European Union*, 19.1.2022, document available at: https://eur-lex.europa.eu/legal-content/EN/TXT/?home=ecb&uri=CELEX:52021AB0030 (accessed January 28, 2023).

EU Technical Expert Group on Sustainable Finance (2020), Usability Guide: EU Green BondStandard, available at: https://ec.europa.eu/info/sites/default/files/business_economy_euro/banking_and_finance/documents/200309-sustainable-finance-teg-green-bond-standard-usability-guide_en.pdf (accessed January 28, 2023).

EU, *Technical Expert Group on Sustainable Finance, Report on EU Green Bond Standard, Proposal for an EU Green Bond Standard*, version June 2019, document available at: https://ec.europa.eu/info/sites/default/files/business_economy_euro/banking_and_finance/documents/190618-sustainable-finance-teg-report-green-bond-standard_en.pdf (accessed January 28, 2023).

EU, Usability Guide — *EU Green Bond Standard, EU Technical Expert Group on Sustainable Finance, Proposal for an EU Green Bond Standards*, March 2020, this document also contains (Annex 1) the Draft Model of the EU Green Bond Standard, document available at: https://ec.europa.eu/info/sites/default/files/business_economy_euro/banking_and_finance/documents/200309-sustainable-finance-teg-green-bond-standard-usability-guide_en.pdf (accessed January 28, 2023).

Finance and Sustainability-Linked Financial Instruments, PENN State, document available at: *https://majorsustainability.smeal.psu.edu/finance/concepts/sustainability-linked-financial-instruments/* (accessed January 28, 2023).

Feng Kong, *A Better Understanding of the Role of New Energy and Green Finance to Help Achieve Carbon Neutrality Goals, with Special Reference to China*, Science Progress 2022, 105(1):1–23, article available at: https://Journals.sagepub.com/doi/epub/10.1177/00368504221086361 (accessed January 28, 2023).

GCA (2021), Issuance in Emerging Market Green Bonds to Reach $100 Billion by 2023, Amundi and IFC Find, available at: https://pressroom.

credit-agricole.com/news/issuance-in-emerging-market-green-bonds-to-reach-100-billion-by-2023-amundi-and-ifc-find-0d7d-94727.html (accessed January 28, 2023).

Green Finance & Development Center — China's "Two Sessions" 2022 — What it Means for Economy, Climate, Biodiversity, Green Finance and the Belt and Road Initiative (BRI0), available at: https://greenfdc.org/chinas-two-sessions-2022-what-it-means-for-economy-climate-biodiversity-green-finance-and-the-belt-and-road-initiative-bri/ (accessed January 28, 2023).

Green Finance, *Green Finance for Energy Transition, Climate Action and Sustainable Development: Overview of Concepts, Applications, Implementation and Challenges*, 2022, 4(1), document available at: https://www.aimspress.com/article/doi/10.3934/GF.2022001 (accessed January 28, 2023).

Greening China's Financial System, DRC — Financial Research Institute and IISD International Institute for Sustainable Development, 2015, document available at: https://www.iisd.org/system/files/publications/greening-chinas-financial-system.pdf (accessed January 28, 2023).

Guidelines for Establishing the Green Financial System (Yinfa 2016 Doc No 228), with the approval of the State Council. The Guidelines — issued jointly by the People's Bank of China, the Ministry of Finance, the National Development and Reform Commission, the Ministry of Environmental Protection, China Banking Regulatory Commission, China Securities Regulatory Commission, and China Insurance Regulatory Commission — will provide an essential next step for implementing the overall strategy of promoting ecological civilization, formulated by the Central Party Committee and the State Council. They will also advance the development concepts of innovation, harmony, greenness, openness and sharing, and promote the establishment of China's green financial system, available at: http://www.pbc.gov.cn/english/130721/3131759/index.html (accessed January 28, 2023).

Guidelines for Establishing the Green Financial System, this is the full version published on April 2015, guidelines available at: https://www.cbd.int/financial/privatesector/china-Green%20Task%20Force%20Report.pdf (accessed January 28, 2023).

G20, *2021 Synthesis Report — G20 Sustainable Finance Working Group*, document available at: https://g20sfwg.org/wp-content/uploads/2021/11/Synth_G20_Final.pdf (accessed January 28, 2023).

Handbook on Sustainable Investments, document available at: https://www.sustainablefinance.ch/upload/cms/user/201712_Handbook_on_Sustainable_Investments_CFA.pdf The CFA Institute Research Foundation is a not-for-profit organization established to promote the development and dissemination of relevant research for investment practitioners worldwide.

Hesary-Taghizadeh F, Yoshino N, Phoumin H (2021) *Analyzing the Characteristics of Green Bond Markets to Facilitate Green Finance in the Post-COVID-19 World. Sustainability*, 13, 5719, available at: https://doi.org/10.3390/su13105719 doi: 10.3390/su13105719 (accessed January 28, 2023).

ICMA (2018), *The Green Bond Principles*, available at: https://www.icmagroup.org/sustainable-finance/the-principles-guidelines-and-handbooks/green-bond-principles-gbp (accessed January 28, 2023).

ICMA (2020), *The Sustainability-Linked Bond Principles*, available at: https://www.icmagroup.org/assets/documents/Regulatory/Green-Bonds/June2020/Sustainability-Linked-Bond-Principles-June-2020-171120.pdf (accessed January 28, 2023).

ICMA, International Capital Market Association, *Overview and Recommendations for Sustainable Finance Taxonomies*, May 2021, document available at: https://www.icmagroup.org/assets/documents/Sustainable-finance/ICMA-Overview-and-Recommendations-for-Sustainable-Finance-Taxonomies-May-2021-180521.pdf?utm_source=ICMA%20Total%20Subscribes&utm_campaign=fa800ab3d8-EMAIL_CAMPAIGN_5_18_2021_12_18&utm_medium=email&utm_term=0_74a993020a-fa800ab3d8-75741622 (accessed January 28, 2023).

ICMA (2021), *The Social Bond Principles*, available at: https://www.icmagroup.org/sustainable-finance/the-principles-guidelines-and-handbooks/social-bond-principles-sbp/ (accessed January 28, 2023).

ICMA (n.d.), *The Principles, Guidelines and Handbooks*, available at: https://www.icmagroup.org/sustainable-finance/the-principles-guidelines-and-handbooks (accessed January 28, 2023).

International Finance Corporation (IFC), *Guidelines for Blue Finance Guidance for Financing the Blue Economy, Building on the Green Bond Principles and the Green Loan Principles* January 2022, available at: https://www.ifc.org/wps/wcm/connect/cdbfb6c5-2726-47a6-9374-6a6f86032dd4/IFC-guidelines-for-blue-finance.pdf?MOD=AJPERES&CVID=nWxsyxN (accessed January 28, 2023).

IFC, *Guidance for Financing the Blue Economy, Building on the Green Bond Principles and the Green Loan Principles, International Finance Corporation — Guidelines for Blue Finance*, document available at: https://www.ifc.org/wps/wcm/connect/industry_ext_content/ifc_external_corporate_site/financial+institutions/resources/guidelines-for-blue-finance (accessed January 28, 2023).

IIFG, *China Green Finance Task Force Report: Establishing China's Green Financial System,* document available at: https://www.unepfi.org/psi/wp-content/uploads/2015/07/Establishing-Chinas-Green-Financial-System_PBoC_UNEP_Inquiry.pdf. This is the April 2015 version which is the complete version. See also: Green Finance Info, International Institute of

Green Finance, article available at: https://iigf-china.com/green-finance-info-2 (accessed January 28, 2023).

International Platform on Sustainable Finance — *Common Ground Taxonomy — Climate Change Mitigation*, document available at: https://ec.europa.eu/info/sites/default/files/business_economy_euro/banking_and_finance/documents/211104-ipsf-common-ground-taxonomy-instruction-report-2021_en.pdf (accessed January 28, 2023).

KPMG, *Green Financing: A Necessary Step towards a Greener Future — Climate Change has become the Defining Political and Economic Issue and is Likely to Remain so for Many Years*, document available at: https://home.kpmg/th/en/home/media/press-releases/2022/04/green-financing.html (accessed January 28, 2023).

LSE and Grantham Research Institute on Climate Change and the Environment *Out of the Window? Green Monetary Policy in China: Window Guidance and the Promotion of Sustainable Lending Investment*, Working paper, May 14, 2021, document available at: https://www.lse.ac.uk/granthaminstitute/publication/out-of-the-window-green-monetary-policy-in-china-window-guidance-and-the-promotion-of-sustainable-lending-and-investment/ (accessed January 28, 2023).

Morgan Stanley Institute for Sustainable Investing (2019), Blue Bonds: The Next Wave of Sustainable Bonds, available at: https://www.morganstanley.com/content/dam/msdotcom/ideas/blue-bonds/2583076-FINAL-MS_GSF_Blue_Bonds.pdf.

OECD (2020), Global Outlook on Financing for Sustainable Development 2021: A New Way to Invest for People and Planet, OECD Publishing, Paris, available at: https://dx.doi.org/10.1787/e3c30a9a-en (accessed January 28, 2023).

OECD (2020), "How Islamic finance contributes to achieving the Sustainable Development Goals," OECD Development Policy Papers, No. 30, OECD Publishing, Paris, available at: https://dx.doi.org/10.1787/ac1480ca-en (accessed January 28, 2023).

Stockholm International Peace Research Institute, Promoting China-European Union Cooperation on Green and Sustainable Finance, document available at: https://www.sipri.org/publications/2021/sipri-policy-briefs/promoting-china-european-union-cooperation-green-and-sustainable-finance, accessed January 28, 2023).

Sustainable Debt — Global State of the Market, 2021, document available at: https://www.climatebonds.net/files/reports/cbi_global_sotm_2021_02h_0.pdf (accessed January 28, 2023).

The Global Treasurer, *Green Bond Issuance Soars as Sustainable Debt Tops $1trn in 2021*, by Kam Patel, May 6, 2022, article available at: https://www.theglobaltreasurer.com/2022/05/06/green-bond-issuance-soars-as-sustainable-debt-tops-1trn-in-2021/ (accessed January 28, 2023).

Tsinghua University National Institute of Financial Research, *Green Finance in China: Overview, Experience and Outlook*, January 20, 2021, document available at: http://eng.pbcsf.tsinghua.edu.cn/upload/default/20210120/a9d979c5405c2e5b461afa03f7925b36.pdf (accessed January 28, 2023).

Tolliver, C., H. Fujii, A.R. Keeley, *et al.* (2021) Green innovation and finance in Asia. *Asian Econ Policy Rev*, 16, 67–87, available at: https://doi.org/10.1111/aepr.12320 doi: 10.1111/aepr.12320 (accessed January 28, 2023).

UNEP-The People's Bank of China, *Establishing China's Green Financial System* (构建中国绿色金融体系), this is the preliminary version published in March 2015, document available at: https://www.unepfi.org/fileadmin/communications/EstablishingChinasGreenFinancialSystem.pdf (accessed January 28, 2023).

UNEP Definitions and Concepts — Background Note, Inquiry Working Paper 16/13, September 2016, document available at: https://wedocs.unep.org/bitstream/handle/20.500.11822/10603/definitions_concept.pdf?sequence=1&isAllowed=y (accessed January 28, 2023).

Xinhua, *China's Green Credit Balance Tops 15 Trillion Yuan*, article available at: https://english.news.cn/20220327/e747f4f597ed4caf8dbcf443d67521b2/c.html (accessed January 28, 2023).

Yi Wu, *China's Green Financial Market: Policies, Incentives, Investment Opportunities*, China Briefing, article available at: https://www.china-briefing.com/news/chinas-green-finance-market-policies-incentives-investment-opportunities/ (accessed January 28, 2023).

Internet Sources

Belt and Road Portal. https://eng.yidaiyilu.gov.cn/info

China Council for the Promotion of International Trade (CCPIT). www.ccpit.org/

China Securities Regulatory Commission (CSRC). www.csrc.gov.cn/pub/csrc_en/

China Foreign Investment Registration. www.wzj.gov.cn

China Internet Information Center. www.china.org.cn

Department of Agriculture (USA). https://www.usda.gov/

Department of Energy (USA). https://www.energy.gov

Department of Interior (USA). https://www.doi.gov/

Department of Transportation (USA). https://www.transportation.gov/

DG Trade of the European Commission. http://europa.eu.int/comm/trade/index_en.htm

Environmental Protection Agency (USA). https://www.epa.gov/

EU-China Energy Cooperation Platform (ECECP). http://www.ececp.eu/en/about-eu-china-energy-cooperation-platform-ececp/
EU Delegation in China. www.delchn.cec.eu.int/
European Chamber of Commerce in China (EUCCC). www.euccc.com.cn/
European Commission: Trade policies. http://ec.europa.eu/trade/policy/countries-and-regions/countries/china/
Intergovernmental Panel on Climate Change (IPCC). https://www.ipcc.ch/about/
International Air Transportation Association — IATA. https://www.iata.org/
International Capital Market Association (ICMA). https://www.icmagroup.org
International Civil Aviation Organization — ICAO. https://www.icao.int/
International Centre of the Legislative Office of the State Council. https://www.chinalaw.gov.cn
International Energy Agency (IEA). https://www/iea/org
International Institute for Sustainable Development (IISD). https://www.iisd.org
International Monetary Fund. http://www.imf.org/en/About
International Platform on Sustainable Finance (IPSF). https://finance.ec.europa.eu/sustainable-finance/international-platform-sustainable-finance_en
Luxembourg Stock Exchange. https://www.bourse.lu/home
Ministry of Commerce. www.mofcom.gov.cn
Ministry of Labor and Social Security. www.molss.gov.cn
National Development and Reform Commission People's Republic of China (NDRC). http://en.ndrc.gov.cn//mfndrc/default.htm
People's Bank of China. www.pbc.gov.cn
State Administration for Industry and Commerce. www.saic.gov.cn
State Administration of Taxation. www.chinatax.gov.cn
State Council Information Office of the People Republic of China. www.english.scio.gov.cn
United Nations — UNDP. https://www.undp.org/
United Nations — Sustainable Development Goals — United Nations. https://www.un.org/ and https://www.un.org/sustainabledevelopment/development-agenda/
White House (For Executive Orders and Other Policy Documents). https://www.whitehouse.gov/
World Economic Forum. https://weforum.org
World Trade Organization (WTO). http://wto.org

Index

C

D

E

F

G

T

www.ingramcontent.com/pod-product-compliance
Lightning Source LLC
LaVergne TN
LVHW011629150926
848129LV00005B/377